Insurance Operations
Volume 1

Insurance Operations
Volume 1

Bernard L. Webb, CPCU, FCAS, MAAA
Consultant

Connor M. Harrison, CPCU, AU
Director of Underwriting Education
American Institute

James J. Markham, J.D., CPCU, AIC, AIAF
Senior Vice President and General Counsel
American Institute

Second Edition • 1997

American Institute for Chartered Property Casualty Underwriters
720 Providence Road, Malvern, Pennsylvania 19355-0770

Dedication

The American Institute for Chartered Property Casualty Underwriters dedicates this edition of *Insurance Operations* to the memory of Ronald M. Hubbs, past Chairman of the Institute's Board of Trustees. In addition to his many other accomplishments, Mr. Hubbs wrote the first chapter of this textbook, entitled "Overview of Insurance Operations."

During his thirty-year tenure with the St. Paul Insurance Companies, Mr. Hubbs served as Chief Executive Officer and was largely responsible for their innovative strategies. Mr. Hubbs's commitment to continuous learning and personal growth was reflected in the naming of the prestigious "center for tomorrow" in St. Paul, Minnesota, as the Ronald M. Hubbs Center for Lifelong Learning. His sense of social responsibility was evident by his participation and leadership in many educational, civic, cultural, philanthropic, and historical organizations.

Ron Hubbs's career and accomplishments exemplify the traits of insurance professionals that the American Institute for CPCU was designed to develop and serve.

It is with deep respect that the Institute dedicates this edition of *Insurance Operations* to Ronald M. Hubbs, renowned insurance statesman, leading insurance innovator, lifelong learning advocate, preeminent community leader, and dedicated humanitarian.

Foreword

The American Institute for Chartered Property Casualty Underwriters, the Insurance Institute of America, and the Insurance Institute for Applied Ethics are independent, nonprofit, educational organizations serving the needs of the property and liability insurance business. The Institutes develop a wide range of programs—curricula, study materials, and examinations—in response to the educational requirements of various elements of the business.

The American Institute confers the Chartered Property Casualty Underwriter (CPCU®) professional designation on those who meet the Institute's experience, ethics, and examination requirements.

The Insurance Institute of America offers associate designations and certificate programs in the following technical and managerial disciplines:

Accredited Adviser in Insurance (AAI®)
Associate in Claims (AIC)
Associate in Underwriting (AU)
Associate in Risk Management (ARM)
Associate in Loss Control Management (ALCM®)
Associate in Premium Auditing (APA®)
Associate in Management (AIM)
Associate in Research and Planning (ARP®)
Associate in Insurance Accounting and Finance (AIAF)
Associate in Automation Management (AAM®)
Associate in Marine Insurance Management (AMIM®)
Associate in Reinsurance (ARe)
Associate in Fidelity and Surety Bonding (AFSB)
Associate in Insurance Services (AIS)
Associate in Surplus Lines Insurance (ASLI)
Associate in Personal Insurance (API)
Certificate in General Insurance

Certificate in Insurance Regulation
Certificate in Supervisory Management
Certificate in Introduction to Underwriting
Certificate in Introduction to Claims
Certificate in Introduction to Property and Liability Insurance
Certificate in Business Writing

The Insurance Institute for Applied Ethics was established in 1995 to heighten awareness of the pervasiveness of ethical decision making in insurance and to explore ways to raise the level of ethical behavior among parties to the insurance contract. The Ethics Institute sponsors seminars and workshops on the role of ethics in the insurance transaction. It also identifies and funds practical research projects on ethics-related topics and publishes the findings. In addition, it produces booklets, newsletters, and videotapes on ethics issues.

The Institutes began publishing textbooks in 1976 to help students meet the national examination standards. Since that time, we have produced more than ninety individual textbook volumes. Despite the vast differences in the subjects and purposes of these volumes, they all have much in common. First, each book is specifically designed to increase knowledge and develop skills that can improve job performance and help students achieve the educational objectives of the course for which it is assigned. Second, all of the manuscripts of our texts are widely reviewed before publication, by both insurance business practitioners and members of the academic community. In addition, all of our texts and course guides also reflect the work of Institute staff members. These writing or editing duties are seen as an integral part of their professional responsibilities, and no one earns a royalty based on the sale of our texts. We have proceeded in this way to avoid even the appearance of any conflict of interests. Finally, the revisions of our texts often incorporate improvements suggested by students and course leaders.

We welcome criticisms of and suggestions for improving our publications. It is only with such constructive comments that we can hope to improve the quality of our study materials. Please direct any comments you may have on this text to the Curriculum Department of the Institutes.

Lawrence G. Brandon, CPCU, AIM, ARM
President and Chief Operating Officer

Preface

Without the insurance product, families and businesses would have to live with the uncertainty that their financial well-being could be destroyed. Additionally, few lenders or investors would be willing to lend money without some guarantee that their money would be secure. Those who offer insurance-related services to the public make a valuable contribution to our society. Nevertheless, the public has become suspicious of the objectives and operations of the insurance business because of instability in the insurance marketplace, the politicization of insurance, and misunderstandings about the nature of the insurance mechanism. One solution to many of the problems faced by the insurance industry today is increased knowledge about how our business works. It is to that end that *Insurance Operations*, the textbook for CPCU 5, was written.

The predecessor to *Insurance Operations* was entitled *Insurance Company Operations*. We changed the title of this text to reflect the inclusion of entities other than insurance companies that offer consumers insurance products and services. The new title and the extent of the revision warranted the creation of a new edition.

Despite the changes in this text, it continues to reflect the work of its original authors. Their organization of the material and approach to many topics have been retained. Those original authors are:

J. J. Launie, Ph.D., CPCU
Professor of Finance and Insurance
California State University, Northridge

Willis Park Rokes, J.D., Ph.D., CPCU, CLU
Peter Kiewit Distinguished Professor of Law and Insurance
University of Nebraska at Omaha

Norman A. Baglini, Ph.D., CPCU, CLU, AU
Chairman & Chief Operating Officer
The Institutes

In order to prepare this new edition, we solicited ideas for improvement from course leaders and students. Their comments served as a starting point for this revision. Authors and reviewers urged us to completely revise some sections, eliminate others, and preserve those that required little change. The assistance they provided was indispensable in validating the content of *Insurance Operations*. The authors are deeply appreciative of the critical reviews submitted by the following persons:

Michael J. Apanowitch, CPCU, APA
Product Development Consultant
The Hartford

Ronald E. Arthur, CPCU, ARM
Chapter Services Manager
CPCU Society

Robert Bambino, CPCU
Assistant Vice President—Risk Management
Wright Risk Management Company, Inc.

Michael M. Barth, Ph.D., CPCU
Senior Research Associate
National Association of Insurance Commissioners

Walter G. Barth, P.E.
Senior Account Engineer
Allendale Insurance

Rick Becker, CPCU, CLU, ChFC
Underwriting Manager
Nationwide Insurance

Mark Berry, CPCU
Vice President
Mid-Ocean Reinsurance

Paula L. Bortel, CPCU, CLU, ChFC
Service Supervisor
State Farm Insurance Companies

Boyd Bruce, CPCU, AIM
President
Bruce & Company

Walter G. Butterworth, CPCU
Cohen-Seltzer (Retired)

Stephen W. Campbell, CSP, CIH
Assistant Manager—Technical Services
The Hartford

Michael J. Cascio, FCAS, MAAA
Director and Vice President
Stockton Reinsurance Limited

Patricia M. Coleman, CPCU
Director—Marketing, International Development
The Hartford

Deborah Conley, CPCU, AU
Research Analyst
PMA Reinsurance Corporation

James M. Cunningham, CPCU
Managing Underwriting Director
The Hartford

Paul O. Dudey, CPCU
Editor
Malecki on Insurance

Linda K. Edgell, CPCU, ARM, AU, ARe
Consultant
Interisk Limited

Jon L. Elsea, CPCU, CLU, LUTCF, AIM, AAI, AAM
Sales Director
Allstate Insurance Company

Kevin Flannery, CPCU, AAM, AIS
Lead Systems Designer
CIGNA

Edward W. Frye, Jr., CPCU, ARe
Consultant
Underwriting Consultant Services

William R. Gawne, CPCU
Claims Manager
CIGNA

Sandra Gingras, CPCU, AIM, ARP, ARM
CM Senior Business Consultant
The Hartford

George N. Gould, CPCU
Regional Claims Manager
Commercial Union Insurance

Joseph L. Grauwiler, CPCU
Vice President—Corporate Underwriting
National Grange Mutual Insurance Company

Jerome M. Hermsen, CPCU, CIC, ARM, AU, AIM
Product Management Specialist
The Hartford

Kathleen Hinds, FCAS
Director of Commercial Casualty Pricing
The Hartford

Don Hurley, J.D., CPCU, CLU, AU, ARM
Executive Director
Maryland Insurance Group

Anne M. Iezzi, CPCU, AIC
Division Consultant—Property/Marine Claims
The Hartford

Marcia S. Kulak, CPCU, AIC, ARM, CIC, ARe, CPIW
Director of Pollution Claims
The Hartford

Kevin G. Kupec, CPCU
Assistant Vice President—Personal Lines Insurance Center
    Product Department
The Hartford

Christian J. Lachance, CPCU, CLU, AIC, SCLA
Special Investigative Unit
State Farm Insurance Companies

Thomas E. Lyman, CPCU, AIM, ARM
CIGNA (Retired)

C. Alan Mauch, CPCU
Senior Vice President
Employers Reinsurance Corporation

Robert M. McFarland, CPCU, ARP, AAM, AMIM
Secretary—Casualty Product Management
The Hartford

Kathleen McMonigle, FCAS, CPCU
Director Commercial Lines—Actuarial
The Hartford

Thomas R. Michaels, CPCU, SCLA, AIC
Account Director—Hartford Environmental Facility
The Hartford

Andrew Mulligan
Training Director—Premium Audit
The Hartford

J. Brian Murphy, CPCU, ARM, ARe, AMIM
Vice President—Catastrophe Management
CNA Insurance Companies

Jeffrey G. Olmstead, CPCU
Property Team Leader—Product Management
The Hartford

Philip E. Olmstead, ARM
Senior Technical Consultant—Construction Services Loss Control
The Hartford

John M. Parker, CPCU
Vice President—Counsel
International Insurance Company

Leigh N. Polhill, CPCU, CPIW, AU
Commercial Underwriting Supervisor
Seibels Bruce Insurance Company

Laureen Regan, Ph.D.
Assistant Professor
Department of Risk Management and Insurance
School of Business and Management
Temple University

Jon A. Rhodes, CPCU, ARM
Vice President, Underwriting
The Central Companies

John F. Russo
Manager—Premium Audit
The Hartford

Charles F. Slagle, CPCU, AIM
Compliance Specialist
Environmental Data Center

Andrew W. Snorton, CPCU, AIC, SCLA
Agent
State Farm Insurance Companies

Philip N. Spinelli, CPCU, ARM
CIGNA (Retired)

David C. Sterling, CPCU, CLU, ChFC, CIC
Secretary and Corporate Risk Manager
The Hartford

Rodney K. Stoffels, CPCU, ARe, AIS
Senior Commercial Lines Underwriter
Minnesota Fire and Casualty

A. Larraine Stroman, CPCU, ALCM
Umbrella Manager
Crum & Forster Insurance

David J. Swanson, CPCU, CIC, AIAF
Director—Business Development and Administration
The Hartford

William M. Tarbell, CPCU, AU, ARM, AFSB
Vice President—Commerical Underwriting
Providence Washington Insurance Company

Rudolph F. Trosin, CPCU, AIC
Vice President of Claims
Old American Insurance Group

Jerome Trupin, CPCU, CLU, ChFC
Trupin Insurance Services

Jerome E. Tuttle, FCAS, CPCU, ARM, ARe, AIM
Senior Vice President
Mercantile & General Reinsurance Company

Sam Waters, J.D., CPCU, AU
Claims Attorney
Continental Western Insurance Co.

John S. Wemyss, CSP, ARM
Assistant Director—Operations Management
The Hartford

Paul Wollmann, CPCU, ARe, ARM
Senior Insurance Analyst
Oil Insurance Limited

James Wright III, CPCU, AIAF, ARe
Accountant—State Rating Bureau
Commonwealth of Massachusetts

This revision of CPCU 5 has been a cooperative effort of many Institute staff members. Michael W. Elliott, CPCU, AIAF, Assistant Vice President and Senior Director of Curriculum Design and Director of the Associate in Reinsurance program, extensively reviewed the reinsurance chapters. Albert C. Wagner III, ASP, Director of Loss Control Education, did the same for the loss control chapters. James R. Jones, CPCU, ARM, AIC, ARP, Director of Claims Education, updated the claims chapters. Everett Randall, CPCU, CLU, AU, APA, AIM, ARe, ARM, AIS, FLMI, Director of Examination Development and Director of the Associate in Premium Auditing program, synchronized our discussion of premium auditing with the latest developments in this field. Kenneth N. Scoles Jr., Ph.D., AIAF, Director of Curriculum and Director of the Associate in Insurance Accounting and Finance program, reviewed and revised the text's discussion of risk-based capital. Karen K. Porter, J.D., CPCU, ARP, Assistant Director of Curriculum and

Permissions Editor, reworked sections of the text regarding legal aspects of insurance. Lowell S. Young, CPCU, CLU, Director of Curriculum, performed a comprehensive review of the exhibits and numerical calculations contained in the text. Audrey R. Rhodes, CPCU, Curriculum Projects Coordinator, assisted with the revision of the course guide that accompanies this text.

The Institute's publications department is charged with editing and typesetting our texts. Both Yvette Stavropoulos and Michael Betz, AIM, edited manuscript chapters for this edition. Although others assisted, Esther Underhill patiently and accurately typeset the text. Jackie Limongelli served as editor for this edition. Most of the improvements in clarity, conciseness, and readability are due to the diligent efforts of Mrs. Limongelli. Her persistence in questioning the sense of what the text was trying to convey has made for a textbook that will benefit everyone attempting to master this material.

Thank you all.

Bernard L. Webb
Connor M. Harrison
James J. Markham

Contributing Authors

The American Institute for CPCU and the authors acknowledge, with deep appreciation, the work of the following contributing authors:

Joseph M. Boslet, PE, CPCU, ARM, ALCM, APA
Manager—Loss Control and Premium Auditing
Pennsylvania National Insurance Companies

Kenneth J. Brownlee, CPCU, ARM, ALCM, AIC
Corporate Risk and Claims Manager
Crawford & Company

Arthur L. Flitner, CPCU, ARM, AIC
Assistant Vice President and Senior Director of
  Curriculum Design
American Institute for CPCU

Larry Gaunt, Ph.D., CPCU, CLU
Professor of Risk Management and Insurance
Georgia State University

Joseph F. Mangan, CPCU
Insurance Consultant

Barnard P. McMacking, Jr.
President (Retired)
The National Underwriter Company

Larry M. Robinson, Ph.D., CPCU, CLU
Vice President—Marketing
Nationwide Insurance

Contents

Chapter 1

Overview of Insurance Operations

Insurance is a system in which the payments of participants (individuals, businesses, and other entities) are made in exchange for the commitment to reimburse for specific types of losses under certain circumstances. The organization or entity that facilitates the pooling of funds and the payment of benefits is called an **insurer**. Participants in this mechanism benefit through reimbursement of losses that occur, reduction of uncertainty, and additional services provided by insurers to reduce the possibility of a loss and the resulting consequences.

The principal function of an insurer is the acceptance of risks transferred to it by others. This task is divided into insurer functional areas consisting of marketing, loss control, underwriting, premium auditing, and claims. To reduce uncertainty even further, insurers use reinsurance as a mechanism to spread the consequences of financial loss. Underlying the operation of an insurer is the **law of large numbers** (also known as the law of averages). The operation of the law of large numbers permits insurers to predict their ultimate losses more accurately, thereby enabling them to charge an adequate premium. Adequate product pricing is fundamental to an insurer's continued solvency.

Because of their complexity and the degree of specialized knowledge required, insurer functions are segmented into specialty departments. These departments must work together if the enterprise as a whole is to be successful in performing the task of risk transfer.

To understand the operations of an insurer, one must understand its reason for being, such as to make a profit for its owners, to fulfill a social need, or to satisfy a legislative mandate. How success is achieved or measured directly relates to the nature of the insurer's objectives.

Types of Insurers[1]

The property-liability insurance business in the United States can be classified by (1) legal form of ownership, (2) place of incorporation, (3) licensing status, and (4) marketing or distribution system used.

Legal Form of Ownership

The first insurers in the United States were individuals rather than insurance companies. However, most states in the United States do not now permit individuals or partnerships to act as insurers, although they may act as agents for insurers. Consequently, most U.S. insurers are corporations. Reciprocal exchanges, which are discussed below, constitute the major exception.

Proprietary Insurers

Proprietary insurers are formed to earn a profit for their owners. Proprietary insurers include stock insurance companies, Lloyds, and insurance exchanges.

Stock Insurance Companies

The principal class of proprietary insurers in the United States comprises **stock insurance companies**. Such companies are owned by their stockholders, who elect a board of directors to oversee the operations of the company. In turn, the board of directors appoints officers and employees to conduct the day-to-day operations.

Lloyds

The second category of proprietary insurers consists of Lloyd's of London and American Lloyds organizations (the apostrophe is usually omitted in references to American Lloyds organizations). **Lloyd's of London** is not an insurance company. It is a marketplace, similar to a stock exchange. All of the insurance written at Lloyd's is written by or on behalf of individual or corporate members. The insurance written by each individual member is backed by his or her entire personal fortune. However, each individual member is liable only for the insurance he or she agrees to write, and not for the obligations assumed by any other member. Lloyd's had 9,959 individual members in 1997.[2] Each member belongs to one or more syndicates and delegates the day-to-day management of the insurance process to the syndicate manager. Lloyd's is a major insurer in the United States. Its exact share of the U.S. market is not known, but it probably accounts for 4 to 5 percent of direct U.S. premiums. If its direct insurance and reinsurance operations are combined, U.S. business accounts for approximately 31 percent of Lloyd's total business.[3] Lloyd's now admits corporations as members. Unlike the individual members, the corporate members do not have unlimited liability. The first corporate members were admitted to Lloyd's in 1994. In that year, corporate members accounted for about 15 percent of Lloyd's premium capacity. Their share increased to 30 percent in 1996, with the individual members providing the balance.[4]

American Lloyds are much smaller, accounting for approximately one-tenth of 1 percent of U.S. premiums. Most American Lloyds are domiciled in Texas, although a few are domiciled in other states. Most of the Texas Lloyds have been acquired or were formed by insurance companies because of the favorable regulatory climate under Texas law. They are usually reinsured 100 percent by their parent companies.

Texas laws require that each Lloyds organization have at least ten members (underwriters), and most have slightly more than the minimum. They operate as a single syndicate, under the management of an attorney-in-fact. The attorney-in-fact need not be a lawyer and can be a corporation. The liability of underwriters is limited to their investment in the Lloyds. Unlike the individual members of Lloyd's of London, underwriters for American Lloyds do not have unlimited liability.

Insurance Exchanges

Three **insurance exchanges** were organized in the early 1980s: the New York Insurance Exchange, the Illinois Insurance Exchange, and the Insurance Exchange of the Americas, headquartered in Miami. These exchanges, like Lloyd's, are marketplaces. Any insurance or reinsurance purchased on the exchanges is underwritten by the members. A member can be an individual, a partnership, or a corporation. The members have limited liability. Members belong to syndicates and delegate day-to-day operations to the syndicate manager.

The New York Insurance Exchange and the Insurance Exchange of the Americas have discontinued operations because of financial problems. They wrote both primary insurance and reinsurance. The Illinois Insurance Exchange continues to operate but has discontinued its reinsurance operations.

Cooperative Insurers

Unlike proprietary insurers, **cooperative insurers** are not necessarily formed for profit. They are owned by their policyholders and are usually formed to provide insurance protection to their members at minimum cost. The types of cooperative insurers include mutual insurance companies, reciprocal exchanges, fraternal organizations, and what will here be called other cooperative insurers.

Mutual Insurance Companies

Mutual insurance companies constitute the largest category of cooperative insurers. **Mutual insurance companies** are corporations owned by their policyholders. The policyholders elect a board of directors to oversee operations. The directors, in turn, appoint officers and employees to carry out the day-to-day operations of the company. Some profits are retained to increase surplus. Profits in excess of those added to surplus are usually returned to policyholders as dividends.

Early mutuals were assessment companies. They collected a small advance premium to cover expenses and levied an additional assessment on members whenever a loss occurred. Very few assessment mutuals remain in operation, and those which do are small and operate in a limited geographic area.

Some mutual insurance companies in the United States avoid the problem of collecting assessments, or even future premiums, by writing perpetual policies. Their members pay a rather large premium deposit initially so that the investment earnings cover the premiums for subsequent years. Only a handful of perpetual mutuals remain in operation.

Most mutuals, and all of the large ones, are advance premium mutuals. Their policyholders pay a premium at the inception and at each renewal of the policy. This premium is intended to cover all expenses and losses during the policy period. Some mutuals retain the right to levy an assessment for additional premiums if they encounter financial difficulties. The larger mutuals issue nonassessable policies, so their policyholders are not subject to such assessments.

Reciprocal Exchanges

Reciprocal exchanges (also called interinsurance exchanges), like mutuals, are usually formed to provide insurance at minimum cost to members and are owned by their members. However, mutuals and reciprocals have significant differences. When insurance is purchased from a mutual, the risk is transferred to the corporation. In a reciprocal exchange, the risk is transferred to the other members. Also, a reciprocal exchange is managed by an attorney-in-fact. A reciprocal is a nonprofit organization, but the attorney-in-fact can be formed for profit.

Fraternal Organizations

Fraternal organizations resemble mutual companies, but they combine a lodge or social function with their insurance function. They primarily write life and health insurance.

Other Cooperative Insurers

A number of new types of insurers have been formed for specific reasons, usually to make insurance available to a certain organization or group of entities and to make the insurance available at affordable rates. These insurance organizations include captive insurers, risk retention groups, and purchasing groups.

Captive insurers can take several forms, but the essence of the captive concept is to insure the exposures of the owners of the captive. The ultimate purpose of the captive is to fund the losses of its owners. This approach has sometimes been referred to as "formalized self-insurance." Several states have enacted special captive legislation designed to ease the formation and operation of captive insurance organizations within their jurisdictions.

Special legislation has also allowed the formation of risk retention groups and purchasing groups. These are cooperative insurers. They can be stock companies, mutuals, or reciprocal exchanges, but they are usually organized so that a limited group or type of insured is eligible to purchase insurance from them. These types of insurance organizations are growing in importance in the insurance marketplace.

Other Insurers

Some insurers do not fit neatly into any one of the above categories. For example, a **health maintenance organization (HMO)** can be either nonprofit or for profit. In either case, an HMO provides an agreed schedule of medical services in return for a preset periodic payment by the member. The membership fee is usually payable monthly and does not depend on the health status of the member or the amount of medical services used. A co-payment is usually required for services. For example, one HMO requires members to pay $5 for each office visit in addition to the regular monthly fee.

The Blues (Blue Cross and Blue Shield) are also difficult to classify. Both are nonprofit. **Blue Cross organizations** were formed by hospital associations to ensure payment of hospital bills. Although they still perform that function, they are not now controlled by the hospital associations.

Blue Shield covers surgical fees. The Blue Shield organizations were formed by medical associations but are not now controlled by them. Consequently, both Blue Cross and Blue Shield organizations are considered here to be cooperative insurers. Most Blue Cross and Blue Shield organizations were incorporated under special enabling statutes permitting the formation of hospital service plans (Blue Cross) or medical service plans (Blue Shield). A few were incorporated under insurance laws, and, more recently, some have been reincorporated as insurance companies. Over sixty Blue Cross and Blue Shield organizations cover various geographic sections of the country. Collectively, they are the largest insurers of hospital and surgical expenses in the United States.

Other financial institutions have either entered the insurance business or competed with insurers in recent years. Mutual savings banks have engaged in the life insurance business in some states for many years. They act as insurers and not as agents or brokers.

Federal laws and some state laws generally prohibit banks and bank holding companies from acting as insurers, although they may act as insurance agents or brokers under some circumstances. A few holding companies own banks or savings and loan companies along with insurance companies. Some of them started as holding companies for banks or savings and loan organizations and later acquired insurers. Others started as insurance holding companies and later acquired banks or savings and loan companies. Banks are now regularly challenging the prohibitions that have kept them out of the insurance business.

Some banks compete with insurance companies by using traditional banking instruments to serve functions traditionally served by insurers. For example, some banks are promoting letters of credit as substitutes for surety bonds. Letters of credit have also been used as a substitute for municipal bond insurance to protect investors against the failure of a municipality to pay the principal or interest due under its bonds. However, this kind of competition is not yet a major factor in the insurance business.

Pools and Associations

Insurers sometimes encounter exposures that they are unwilling to insure individually because the losses either occur too frequently or are potentially too large. Pools or associations can be formed to handle such exposures, either voluntarily or to meet statutory requirements.

A **pool** or an **association** consists of several insurers, not otherwise related, that have joined together to insure risks that the individual members are not willing to cover alone. For example, the losses from an accident at a large nuclear power plant might reach several billions of dollars for liability and property damage combined. Since no single insurer is willing to assume such tremendous liability, nuclear energy pools were formed with many member insurers to absorb the losses when they occur. In addition, the pools buy reinsurance from nonmembers to increase their capacity.

Pools operate either as a syndicate or through reinsurance. A **syndicate pool** issues a joint (or syndicate) policy to the insured, listing all pool members and specifying the part of the insurance for which each member is responsible. Under such policies, the insured has a contractual relationship with each member of the pool and may sue any or all of them directly if a disagreement arises.

Under a **reinsurance pool,** one member of the pool issues the policy to the insured, and the other pool members reinsure an agreed proportion of each risk insured. In this kind of arrangement, the insured only has a direct contractual relationship with the company that issued the policy. The policyholder has no direct legal rights against the other members of the pool and may not even know that they exist.

Many pools and associations are required by law. Virtually all states require some kind of pooling arrangement to provide automobile liability insurance for drivers who are unable to obtain such insurance from an insurer directly. Similar pools are required for workers compensation insurance in most states. **Fair Access to Insurance Requirements (FAIR) plans** are required by law in twenty-eight states. They provide property insurance to qualified property owners who are otherwise unable to obtain coverage from an insurer. At least two states have joint underwriting associations (JUAs) to provide liquor liability insurance for sellers of alcoholic beverages that are unable to obtain coverage otherwise. Other similar statutory pools or associations for other lines of insurance are required by the laws of some states. Although these pools and associations are required by state law, the protection provided through them is underwritten by private insurers and not by the state governments, although state and federal governments do act as insurers in some situations.

Government Insurers

A number of states have government insurance operations. A third of the states have state insurance funds that provide workers compensation insurance for some or all employers in the state. Most of the funds compete with private insurers, but several are, by law, the only source of workers compensation insurance in their respective states.

Two states (Pennsylvania and Illinois) have state insurance funds that insure property owners against property damage resulting from collapse of old underground coal mines. Several states provide income-loss disability insurance for workers or medical expense insurance for some segments of their respective populations.

The U.S. federal government has many insurance operations. The largest federal insurance program is the Social Security System, which provides life insurance, annuities, disability income coverage, and medical expense coverage for millions of Americans. A complete discussion of federal insurance programs is beyond the scope of this course, but some of the major programs are as follows:

- Deposit insurance for banks, savings and loan associations, and credit unions
- Export credit insurance
- "All-risks" crop insurance
- Flood insurance
- Crime insurance
- Insurance against expropriation of foreign investments
- Mortgage insurance
- Life insurance for some veterans of the armed forces

At one time, the federal government provided reinsurance to protect private insurers against excessive riot losses, but that program no longer exists.

Place of Incorporation

Classification by place of incorporation categorizes insurers as domestic, foreign, and alien. A **domestic insurer** within any given state is an insurer that is incorporated within that state, or, if it is not incorporated, was formed under the laws of that state. Reciprocal exchanges are the only unincorporated insurers permitted in most states. Insurance exchanges and Lloyds organizations are permitted in a few states.

A **foreign insurer** is one that is incorporated or formed in another state of the United States. **Alien insurers** are incorporated or formed in another country.

Licensing Status

A **licensed** (or **admitted**) **insurer** with regard to any particular state is an insurer that has been granted a license to operate in that state. An **unlicensed** (or **nonadmitted**) **insurer** is one that has not been granted a license. Agents and brokers for primary insurance (except surplus lines brokers) are licensed to place business only with admitted companies. Surplus lines brokers are licensed to place business with nonadmitted insurers, but only if licensed insurers will not write it. Licensing status is also important for purposes of reinsurance.

Marketing Distribution System Used

Insurers can be categorized based on the distribution system used to deliver insurance products to the marketplace. These approaches to the market, discussed extensively in Chapter 3, are the independent agency system, exclusive agency system, direct writer system, and direct response system.

The Risk Transfer Process

Many kinds of entities transfer risks to insurers. Among them are individuals, families, business firms, charitable and educational institutions, and government agencies. Even insurers sometimes transfer risks to other insurers.

The risk transfer process is a part of a larger process called **risk management**, whereby loss exposures are identified and addressed to reduce potential adverse effects on the organization. The risk management process is described in detail in other CPCU texts, so only an outline of it is provided here in the interest of continuity.

The principal steps in the **risk management process** are the following:

1. Identify and analyze the loss exposures to which the entity is subject.
2. Select the technique or techniques to be used to handle the loss exposures.
3. Implement the chosen techniques.
4. Monitor the results of the decisions, and implement necessary changes.

Risk transfer is one of the alternatives in steps (2) and (3) of the process outlined above. The other alternatives are risk avoidance, risk retention, and loss control. The other steps in the outline are essential to the satisfactory implementation of the risk transfer process.

Many persons or firms play a role in the risk transfer process. For a large corporation, these can include a risk manager, consultants, insurance agents or brokers, and one or more insurers. If the risk involves potentially large losses, the insurer that originally accepts it might transfer all or a part of it to other insurers through reinsurance. The role of each of these entities is discussed below.

Risk Manager

The term **risk manager** is used here in its broadest sense, meaning the person responsible for identifying and treating risks. Large companies are likely to employ a person with the title of risk manager who devotes full time to the management of risks. In smaller firms, the risk management function might be a part-time duty of a person who has other responsibilities. In either case, the risk manager initiates the risk transfer process by identifying the risks that are present and deciding which ones should be transferred. The risk manager might want or need to seek assistance from consultants or insurance agents or brokers.

Consultants

Many consultants are willing to assist and advise the risk manager in the performance of the risk management process. Many small or medium-sized businesses rely almost entirely on consultants for risk management services. Larger firms, including those with one or more risk management employees, might turn to consultants for advice in unusual or complex situations. Consultants are usually compensated for their services by fees, based on the time required and expenses incurred in providing agreed services. Many insurers have formed subsidiary operations to offer consulting services. These insurers are then able to address the needs of those entities that have the financial resources to self-insure their loss exposures but not the loss control expertise afforded by a commercial insurer.

Insurance Agents and Brokers

Insurance agents and brokers perform a dual role in the risk transfer process. They provide risk management advice to potential insurance buyers, helping them to identify the risks to which they are subject and assisting them in deciding which form of treatment is most appropriate for each of the identified risks. In this role, they compete with consultants.

If a risk is to be transferred to an insurer, the agent or broker assists in (1) finding an insurer that is willing and able to assume the risk and (2) negotiating the terms of the transfer. They might also provide assistance with loss adjustment and loss control. Agents and brokers are usually compensated for their services by commissions on the insurance they sell. Compensation by fees based on the effort expended has become increasingly common in recent years. The fees can replace commissions entirely, or the compensation might consist partly of fees and partly of commissions.

Insurers

Insurers are specialists in the risk transfer process. Consequently, they naturally bear the heaviest responsibility for the smooth functioning of the risk transfer process. Among the insurer functions that are necessary to the risk transfer process or that facilitate the process are the following:

- Policy contract development
- Pricing
- Marketing
- Underwriting
- Claims adjustment
- Loss control
- Reinsurance
- Investments

Policy Contract Development

The transfer of a risk to an insurer is a contractual matter. Although the laws of most states do not require that insurance contracts be in writing, a written contract helps to facilitate the transaction and reduces the chance of disputes. An agent, a broker, a consultant, or even a prospective policyholder might sometimes draft an insurance contract, but insurers usually perform this task. Insurers may delegate the drafting to an advisory organization, such as the Insurance Services Office, the American Association of Insurance Services, the National Council on Compensation Insurance, or the Surety Association of America. Many insurers develop their own policy forms when addressing the needs of a specific market niche, such as florists or churches, or when an enterprise has insurance needs not exactly suited for standard policy forms.

Pricing

An integral part of the insurance contract is the premium charged. The determination of rates and premiums is therefore an essential function of an insurer. A **rate** is the price per unit of insurance. A **premium** is the total cost for all units of insurance under a policy. For example, in private passenger auto liability insurance, the rate is the price of insurance for a single car, and the premium is the cost for all cars covered under the policy.

Rates for some lines of insurance are determined on the basis of judgment and intuition, with little or no statistical basis. This approach is especially true for lines of insurance that involve wide variations in risks. Ocean marine insurance is an example of such a line. Each ship is different from any other, and the risk also varies with the skill of the officers and crew, the area of operation, and the cargo carried. These wide variations in risk, combined with a limited body of statistical information, require a substantial reliance on judgment in ratemaking.

At the opposite end of the ratemaking spectrum is private passenger automobile insurance. A great mass of statistical information is available, and the risk variation is much smaller. These factors, plus the great public interest in automobile insurance, lead to a much more refined ratemaking system for private passenger auto insurance than for ocean marine insurance.

Custom and tradition might also be important determinants of the ratemaking method to be used. The ratemaking process, like the policy drafting process, might be delegated to an advisory organization.

Marketing

No matter how well the policy is drafted or the rating plan designed, the risk transfer does not take place until the risk manager knows about the exposures and chooses to treat them through insurance. The objective of the marketing function is to inform the risk manager about the policies, rating plans, and services available from the insurer that will address specific needs.

Underwriting

The underwriting function is also essential to the successful operation of the risk transfer process. The purpose of the underwriting function is to determine what risks the insurer will assume and avoid, the premium to be charged for the risks assumed, and the policy terms and conditions under which the risks will be assumed. For most lines of insurance, the underwriter determines the premium to be charged by applying the manual rates and rating plans approved by management. However, for some lines of insurance the rates and premiums are determined by the underwriter and are based on the underwriter's experience and judgment without the benefit of predetermined manual rates and rating plans.

Claims Adjustment

The claims adjustment function is a crucial element in the risk transfer process. A contract of insurance is merely a promise to perform in the future. The purpose of this function is to see that the insured or claimant receives proper payment for covered losses.

Loss Control

The loss control function assists policyholders in the prevention of accidents and the minimization of the losses from accidents that occur. It is an important element in the risk transfer process because it helps to minimize the transfer cost. It also makes some risks acceptable to the insurer that would not be acceptable in the absence of loss control. Loss control personnel also assist the underwriter by providing reliable information for the underwriting process.

Reinsurance

The risk that the risk manager wants to transfer might involve potential losses larger than the insurer is willing to assume. If so, the insurer can pass a part of the risk on to another insurer. This process is known as reinsurance. Reinsurance facilitates the risk transfer process by spreading loss exposures among many insurers.

Investments

The insurer's investment operations might seem at first glance to have only a remote relationship to the risk transfer process. In fact, however, they are an important element in the process. Investment income helps to keep the cost of risk transfer low and makes some risks acceptable to insurers that would not be acceptable on the basis of premiums alone.

All of these insurer functions will be explained in greater detail in a later section of this chapter and in other chapters of this text.

Objectives of Insurers

An insurer's management must strive to meet several objectives established by the owners of the company. The major objectives (not necessarily in order of importance) are (1) to earn a profit, (2) to meet customer needs, (3) to comply with legal requirements, and (4) to fulfill the humanitarian and societal duties established for all institutions.

These objectives conflict to a substantial degree. The objective of earning a profit conflicts with all of the other objectives listed. Management must resolve the conflicts in such a way as to provide the most good for the largest number of people.

Profit Objective

The profit objective is most readily associated with proprietary insurers (stock companies and Lloyd's organizations). However, cooperative insurers (mutuals and reciprocal exchanges) must also earn a profit.

Proprietary insurers must earn a profit in order to compensate the people and institutions that provide their capital. Capital markets allocate funds to those companies, insurers or otherwise, that provide the greatest return consistent with the investment risk involved. Consequently, insurers can attract capital only as long as their profits are comparable to the profits of other companies that are subject to the same level of risk.

Cooperative insurers normally do not compete directly in the capital markets. Their policyholders are the source of their capital. These insurers obtain their capital from the profits they earn on the insurance they provide to their customers. In some infrequent instances, mutuals and reciprocals can obtain capital by borrowing funds under subordinated notes, called **surplus notes**. These notes can usually be repaid only out of profits, so funds from that source are also likely to depend on the anticipated profitability of the company.

Customer Needs Objective

An insurer's customers need insurance to handle their risks at a cost they can afford to pay. Most of them also need ancillary services, such as loss adjustment, loss control, and risk management advice. Any insurer that wants to achieve long-term success must strive to meet those needs.

Of course, this objective and the profit objective might conflict significantly. Quality insurance at a price that customers can afford might not permit the profit that the insurer needs to attract and retain capital. Conflicts of this nature sometimes result in substantial dislocations in the marketplace. Proposition 103, adopted in California in 1988, is a prominent example of consumer perception that insurers are not providing insurance at a cost consumers can afford.

Subject only to some regulatory constraints, insurers have almost complete control of the quality of the insurance products they offer. Their control of insurance costs is much more limited. The cost of insurance is determined primarily by losses, and losses are largely beyond the control of insurers, especially in the personal lines. Underwriting selection might provide some control of losses for an insurer, but it does so at the cost of denying insurance to some who need it. Savings realized through strict underwriting can be offset, at least in part, by the insurer's increased obligations under JUAs or other residual market mechanisms. Loss control measures and vigorous resistance to fraudulent claims might reduce losses, but the effect of such measures is limited.

The second major determinant of insurance costs is insurer expenses. Insurers have greater control of expenses than of losses, but major expense reductions usually involve a reduction in services provided to customers, perhaps with some failure in meeting customer needs.

The third determinant of insurance cost is the insurer's profit. The insurer has more control over this element of cost than it has over losses, but it might have difficulty attracting capital if the profit margin is cut too low. It might also have difficulty attracting and retaining policyholders if it sets the profit margin too high.

Legal Requirement Objective

Insurers, like other legitimate business firms, want to meet all of the obligations imposed on them by law. This desire to comply with the law stems largely from an urge to be good and responsible corporate citizens. However, insurers might also fear that failure to comply with the law might brand them as irresponsible in the eyes of the public and public officials. It might also be expensive in terms of fines and other penalties.

The cost of complying with regulatory requirements imposed on insurers is, however, substantial. These costs include the expense incurred directly in regulatory compliance, such as accounting and legal costs. They also include the cost of participating in assigned risk plans, FAIR plans, insolvency funds, and similar facilities. To the extent that these expenses increase the cost of insurance, they create a conflict with both the profit objective and the customer needs objective.

Humanitarian and Societal Objectives

Managers of insurance companies, like other responsible members of society, want to avoid human suffering and promote the well-being of society. These societal concerns are expressed in many ways, such as contributions to medical, educational, and other public service organizations and benefits plans established for employees. Although such programs are socially desirable and beneficial, they do involve costs. Consequently, they create conflicts with some of the other objectives discussed above.

Constraints on Achieving Objectives

The conflicts among objectives are not the only reasons that insurers do not always achieve them. There are several other constraints, both within the insurer and in its environment.

Internal Constraints

Several conditions within an insurer might prevent it from meeting all of its objectives. Fortunately, all of these constraints do not apply to all insurers.

Efficiency

For various reasons, all insurers are not equally efficient. The lack of efficiency might stem from inadequate management, insufficient capital, failure to automate processes, inability to adapt to change, or other causes. Less efficient insurers are at a disadvantage in competing with more efficient ones in the marketplace. This competitive weakness might prevent them from meeting their profit objectives and, consequently, their humanitarian and societal objectives. In more serious cases, it can even prevent them from meeting their customer needs objectives. Extreme cases of inefficiency can result in insolvency and consequent failure to meet legal and regulatory objectives.

Expertise

The insurance business is very complex. A considerable amount of expertise is required for the successful operation of an insurance company. Expertise permits an underwriter to select insurance applicants that have fewer losses than the insureds contemplated in the insurance rate. Expertise is evident when a claim is settled for what the claim is worth. A lack of expertise might prevent an insurer from achieving some of its objectives. An extreme lack of expertise might prevent the achievement of any of the objectives. Lack of expertise has resulted in a number of insurer insolvencies in recent years.

Size

The size of an insurer can sometimes make the achievement of its objectives more difficult. Small insurers cannot afford all of the resources available to larger insurers. For example, large insurers can afford to purchase comprehensive information systems for increased efficiency. Such systems are beyond the reach of smaller insurers.

Larger insurers can also afford the personnel and other facilities for greater research efforts to determine customer needs and to develop products to meet those needs. Smaller insurers must operate in more of a seat-of-the-pants mode. Smaller insurers can sometimes compensate for their more limited resources by greater flexibility, but their limited resources remain a handicap.

Financial Resources

Small insurers are usually constrained by limited financial resources, but even the largest insurers sometimes find that their financial resources limit their ability to achieve their goals. In recent years, several large insurers have had their financial resources reduced by underwriting losses, investment losses, or both. These financial reverses have reduced their ability to achieve their profit objectives and their societal objectives.

Miscellaneous Internal Constraints

Other internal constraints can also interfere with the achievement of goals. For example, a newly established insurer might lack the market recognition necessary to achieve its profit goals even if it has the expertise and financial resources to do so. A company that has established an unfavorable reputation in the past might have difficulty overcoming that reputation, even if it currently operates flawlessly.

External Constraints

Factors in a company's environment can also limit its ability to achieve its objectives. These constraints include regulation, public opinion, competition, economic conditions, distribution systems, and others.

Regulation

The insurance industry is one of the most closely regulated businesses in the nation. The regulation extends from incorporation to liquidation and encompasses almost anything an insurer does between those extremes.

Insurance regulators monitor the solvency of insurers to protect the company's policyholders and members of the public that benefit from the existence of insurance. A primary tool to monitor solvency is the **National Association of Insurance Commissioners (NAIC) Annual Statement** prescribed by regulators in all states. The Annual Statement displays insurer finances based on conservative statutory accounting principles.

The necessity for having rates and policy forms approved by regulatory authorities might hamper an insurer in achieving its profit and customer needs objectives. Regulation might also constrain an insurer from meeting some of its societal objectives if the regulations limit the use of company funds for charitable purposes. The mere complexity of regulation by the fifty states, the District of Columbia, and, to a lesser degree, the federal government might hamper an insurer in achieving its goal to comply with laws and regulations.

Public Opinion

Public opinion sometimes acts as a constraint on achieving objectives. Perhaps the most serious effect of public opinion is achieved through the regulatory process. If the public becomes convinced that insurers are not adequately meeting the needs of their customers, the public outcry pressures legislators and regulatory bodies to take corrective action. In recent years, public dissatisfaction with automobile insurance has resulted in numerous legislative and regulatory measures to stabilize or reduce automobile insurance rates.

To the extent that these measures are effective, they will reduce the ability of insurers to meet their profit and societal objectives. Even if the measures are not effective, the costs incurred in opposing them might interfere with the achievement of objectives.

Competition

The property-liability insurance industry in the United States consists of about 3,300 companies, of which about 900 operate nationally or over most of the country and write most of the business.[5] This large number of insurers, coupled with a product that is essentially standardized and cannot be effectively protected by patents or copyrights, leads to periods of intense price competition.

These periods of price competition make it very difficult for insurers to achieve their profit objectives. The shortage of profits, in turn, makes it difficult for them to meet their societal objectives. Excessive competitive zeal might also tempt insurers to neglect their objective of compliance with legal and regulatory requirements.

Economic Conditions

The demand for insurance is relatively inelastic, so the premium income of insurers is not drastically affected by most downturns in economic activity. An extreme economic depression, such as the Great Depression of the 1930s, might affect premium income severely, however.

Also, economic change might affect insurers in other ways. For example, losses for some kinds of insurance, most notably surety bonds, might be severely affected by changes in economic activity, especially changes in the demand for construction work.

Inflation affects insurance losses. Inflation also affects insurance premiums, but the effect on losses is felt more quickly than the effect on premiums. This difference in timing makes it difficult for insurers to achieve their profit objectives during periods of rapid inflation.

Insurers' investment operations can also be severely affected by economic changes. In recent years, a slump in the real estate market has caused financial strains for some insurers, though life insurers have been affected more severely than property-liability insurers.

Distribution Systems

An insurer's distribution system might impose some limits on its ability to meet its objectives. Each of the various distribution systems now in use can meet the needs of some insurer customers, but each fails to adequately meet the needs of others. For example, the independent agency system seems to be very successful in meeting the needs of commercial insurance customers, but it has failed to meet the needs of personal lines customers as well. The other distribution systems now dominate the personal lines markets.

On the other hand, some insurers using the exclusive agency system or the direct writer system have experienced difficulty in reaching personal lines customers in rural areas. Some have resorted to dealing through independent agents in those areas.

The direct response distribution system is tailored to the needs of those customers who are concerned primarily with price and are willing to settle for less personal service to obtain a lower price.

The limitations of these distribution systems might restrict an insurer's ability to achieve goals in growth and profits. Some insurers have tried to overcome these limitations by using more than one of the distribution systems, but very few have been successful. Resistance from elements within the distribution systems, especially independent agents and brokers, is one reason for the failure of mixed marketing systems.

Miscellaneous External Constraints

Other external factors can reduce an insurer's ability to achieve its goals. Some of these factors are natural or manmade catastrophe losses, the breakdown of law and order, changes in the legal system that affect liability claims, technological developments, and other similar factors.

Measurement of Insurer Performance

An insurer's performance is measured by its success in meeting its goals. The measure of performance for some goals is subjective in some cases. Financial performance is measured by statistical evidence and is generally considered objective, yet some measurements include an element of subjectivity.

Profit Measurement

Several financial figures might be considered in measuring the profitability of an insurer. These include premium volume, expense ratios, loss ratios, combined ratios, investment income, and operating profit and loss.

Problems in Measuring Profitability

Several problems are inherent in the measurement of insurer profit over short periods of time. For example, the occurrence of a major catastrophe, such as a hurricane, might cause the profitability for a single year to be very unsatisfactory even though the company's business might be profitable over the long term.

An even greater problem arises from the indefinite nature of loss reserves. An insurer must establish reserves for losses that have already happened but have not yet been paid. These reserves include an amount for losses that have already happened but have not yet been reported to the insurer, called **incurred but not reported (IBNR)** losses. Since the amount that will eventually be paid for such losses cannot be known exactly, the reserves are simply estimates of ultimate loss payments. Errors in these estimates are common, and insurers must adjust these loss reserves as more concrete information about them becomes known.

These errors in estimating outstanding losses cause distortions in reported profits of insurers, both in the year that improper estimates are originally made and in the years that the improper estimates are corrected. When loss reserves are underestimated, the insurer's profits for that year are overstated. When the inadequate reserves are corrected in a later year, the profit for the year of correction is understated. The opposite effects apply to overestimates. Since reserve corrections of up to a billion dollars or more have been made in a single year by some large insurers, the effects can be substantial. Available methods to adjust for these effects are complex and not completely satisfactory.

Premiums

An insurer's profits heavily depend on the premium income it receives. Even much of an insurer's investment profit depends on premium income, since premium income creates funds for investment. Consequently, a review of an insurer's success in meeting its profit objectives must consider the volume of premium it writes. Companies that do not grow tend to stagnate. Some growth in premiums is desirable. Ideally, the growth should be real, resulting from writing new business, and not merely growth resulting from rate increases and inflation.

Some growth is desirable, but too much growth might be a warning sign. It might indicate that the company has relaxed its underwriting standards or is charging rates that are inadequate for the risks assumed. In either case, the premium growth might result in lower profits or no profits at a later date.

Of course, premium growth, or the lack thereof, must be evaluated in light of current market conditions. During periods of intense competition, significant premium growth is difficult to achieve.

Exhibit 1-1 shows the total net written premiums for the property-liability insurance industry for 1986 through 1995. Growth, in current dollars, varied from

Exhibit 1-1

Property-Liability Insurance Net Written Premiums in the United States From 1986 to 1995 (billions)

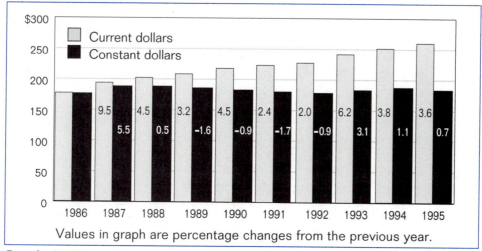

Values in graph are percentage changes from the previous year.

Data for Net Written Premiums in current dollars are from *Best's Aggregates & Averages—Property-Casualty,* 1996 Edition, p. 191. The U.S. Bureau of Labor Statistics Consumer Price Index for all urban consumers was used in the calculation of the real rate of premium growth.

2.0 percent in 1992 to 9.5 percent in 1987, reflecting competitive conditions in the market. When measured in constant 1986 dollars, the industry's total net written premium actually declined in four years during the period studied.

Establishing reasonable rules to measure the adequacy, inadequacy, or excessiveness of premium growth is difficult. Growth slower than the industry average probably indicates a problem. Likewise, a growth rate substantially higher than the industry average might indicate some changes that might be unfavorable in the long term. Did growth result from some real competitive advantage, or from relaxed underwriting, inadequate rates, or both?

Expenses

Insurance company expenses are most conveniently measured by the **expense ratio,** the ratio of expenses to premiums. Exhibit 1-2 shows the expense ratios for all lines combined for the years 1986 through 1995. The loss adjustment expense ratio shown is the ratio of loss adjustment expenses to earned premiums. The other ratios are to net written premiums. The loss adjustment expense ratio is frequently combined with the loss ratio rather than with the other expenses (sometimes referred to as the underwriting expenses). It is shown in Exhibit 1-2 with other expenses. The expense ratio varies rather widely among the various lines of insurance.

Exhibit 1-2

Property-Liability Insurance Expense Ratios—All Lines Combined in the United States From 1986 to 1995

Year	Loss Adjustment Expense (LAE)	Commission Expense	Other Expense	Total Underwriting Expense (excluding LAE)
1986	11.3	11.9	13.2	25.1
1987	11.4	11.9	13.4	25.3
1988	12.0	11.7	13.9	25.7
1989	12.7	11.5	14.4	25.9
1990	12.9	11.3	14.8	26.0
1991	12.6	11.1	15.2	26.3
1992	13.3	11.1	15.2	26.3
1993	12.8	10.6	15.5	26.1
1994	13.0	10.8	15.2	26.0
1995	13.2	10.8	15.4	26.1

Note: Rounding of underlying data prevents the commission expense and the other underwriting expense from summing to the total underwriting expense in years 1988, 1990, and 1995.

Best's Aggregates & Averages—Property-Casualty, 1991 Edition, p. 51; 1996 Edition, p. 66.

As shown in Exhibit 1-2, the expense ratio also varies over time. When rates are rising rapidly, the expense ratio tends to decline because expenses do not rise as rapidly as losses. When competition or regulation holds rates down, the expense ratio tends to increase because expenses, in dollar terms, continue to rise with inflation. This relationship is apparent in a comparison of the total underwriting expense ratio from Exhibit 1-2 with the change in net written premiums from Exhibit 1-1.

In general, a company expense ratio higher than the average expense ratio of the industry might indicate inefficiency. Conversely, a company expense ratio lower than the industry average might indicate superior efficiency. However, such comparisons must be made on a line-by-line basis, since the expense ratio varies substantially by line. For example, the total underwriting expense ratio for fire insurance was 34.5 percent in 1995, and the ratio for medical malpractice liability insurance was 17.5 percent.[6] Additionally, expense ratios differ by the distribution systems used by insurers. Comparisons should be made between insurers operating similarly to best gauge their relative efficiency.

Losses

An insurer's success in controlling insured losses is most conveniently measured by the **loss ratio**, the ratio of incurred losses to earned premiums. The loss ratio can be calculated with or without loss adjustment expenses. It is important to know whether loss adjustment expenses have been included, since they can constitute a significant percentage of losses. For example, in 1995, losses alone were 47.3 percent of earned premiums for medical malpractice insurance, and loss adjustment expenses were 31.6 percent.[7]

A company's loss ratio must be evaluated in light of its expense ratio. A company with an expense ratio lower than the industry average can afford a loss ratio higher than the industry average while still earning an acceptable profit. Exhibit 1-3 shows industry loss ratios for all lines combined for the years 1986 through 1995.

Exhibit 1-3

Property-Liability Insurance Loss Ratios—All Lines Combined in the United States From 1986 to 1995

Year	Pure Loss Ratio	Loss Adjustment Expense (LAE) Ratio	Loss and LAE Ratio
1986	70.4	11.3	**81.7**
1987	66.7	11.4	**78.1**
1988	66.5	12.0	**78.5**
1989	69.2	12.7	**81.9**
1990	69.4	12.9	**82.3**
1991	68.4	12.6	**81.0**
1992	74.7	13.3	**88.0**
1993	66.6	12.8	**79.5**
1994	68.1	13.0	**81.0**
1995	65.7	13.2	**78.9**

Note: Rounding of underlying data prevents the pure loss ratio and the loss adjustment expense ratio from summing to the loss and LAE ratio in years 1993 and 1994.

Best's Aggregates & Averages—Property-Casualty, 1991 Edition, p. 51; 1996 Edition, p. 66.

Combined Ratios

Since the loss ratio and the expense ratio each must be interpreted in light of the other, combining them is convenient. The sum of the loss ratio and the expense ratio is known as the **combined ratio**. A combined ratio of less than 100 percent indicates that the company earned a profit on its insurance operations (often referred to as an underwriting profit), not including any investment profit or loss. A combined ratio in excess of 100 percent indicates a loss on insurance operations.

Two combined ratios are used in the insurance industry: the statutory combined ratio and the trade basis combined ratio. The **statutory basis combined ratio** is calculated in the manner specified in the Annual Statement. It is calculated by dividing the sum of incurred losses and incurred expenses by earned premiums. For a growing company, earned premiums lag behind net written premiums. Since most underwriting expenses are closely related to net written premiums, the statutory combined ratio tends to understate the profitability of a growing company. On the other hand, it tends to overstate profit for a company with a shrinking premium volume.

The **trade basis combined ratio** was developed in an effort to avoid the weaknesses of the statutory combined ratio. In calculating the trade combined ratio, the incurred losses and loss adjustment expenses are divided by earned premiums, and the incurred underwriting expenses are divided by net written premiums.

An example will clarify the difference. Insurance Company reported the financial data for last year as shown in Exhibit 1-4.

Exhibit 1-4
Combined Ratio Calculation—Insurance Company

Incurred underwriting expenses	$ 5,000,000
Incurred losses and loss adjustment expenses	14,000,000
Written premiums	25,000,000
Earned premiums	20,000,000

Insurance Company's *statutory basis* combined ratio would be:

$$= \frac{\text{Incurred losses and loss adjustment expenses}}{\text{Earned premiums}} + \frac{\text{Incurred underwriting expenses}}{\text{Earned premiums}}$$

$$= \frac{14,000,000 + 5,000,000}{20,000,000}$$

$$= .95 \text{ or } 95\%$$

Insurance Company's *trade basis* combined ratio would be:

$$= \frac{\text{Incurred losses and loss adjustment expenses}}{\text{Earned premiums}} + \frac{\text{Incurred underwriting expenses}}{\text{Written premiums}}$$

$$= \frac{14,000,000}{20,000,000} + \frac{5,000,000}{25,000,000}$$

$$= .70 + .20 = .90 \text{ or } 90\%$$

Insurance Company's premium volume was growing rapidly last year, as shown by net written premiums 25 percent greater than earned premiums. Consequently, its trade basis combined ratio was less than its statutory combined ratio.

Exhibit 1-5 shows the trade combined ratio for all lines combined for the years 1986 through 1995. The industry sustained an underwriting loss in all years of the period, with the combined ratio reaching its peak of 115.6 percent in 1992.

Like the expense ratio and loss ratio, a company's combined ratio must be evaluated with due consideration to competitive conditions within the industry. Also, the combined ratio for a single year might be adversely affected by catastrophic events. Such was the case in 1992, which is the worst year on record for catastrophic losses. In that year, the United States endured Hurricanes Andrew and Iniki and the Los Angeles riots.

Exhibit 1-5

Property-Liability Insurance Trade Basis Combined Ratio—All Lines Combined in the United States From 1986 to 1995

Year	Combined Ratio Before Policyholder Dividends	Policyholder Dividends	Combined Ratio After Policyholder Dividends
1986	106.8	1.3	**108.1**
1987	103.4	1.3	**104.7**
1988	104.1	1.4	**105.5**
1989	107.9	1.3	**109.2**
1990	108.3	1.2	**109.6**
1991	107.3	1.3	**108.6**
1992	114.4	1.2	**115.6**
1993	105.6	1.2	**106.8**
1994	107.0	1.3	**108.3**
1995	105.0	1.4	**106.4**

Note: Rounding of underlying data prevents the combined ratio before policyholder dividends and the policyholder dividends from summing in year 1990.

Best's Aggregates & Averages—Property-Casualty, 1991 Edition, p. 51; 1996 Edition, p. 66.

Investment Income

Up to this point, the discussion of insurer profitability has dealt only with underwriting profit or loss, without any consideration of the insurer's investment operations.

Insurance operations generate large amounts of investable funds, primarily from loss reserves, loss adjustment expense reserves, and unearned premium reserves. Loss and loss expense reserves are especially significant for liability insurance. The long delay inherent in the liability loss adjustment process generates very large loss reserves. The gradual change from a predominantly property insurance industry to a predominantly liability insurance industry, coupled with rising interest rates, placed greater emphasis on investment earnings. Although interest rates have declined in more recent years, investment income is still the sole source of profit for most insurers. Exhibit 1-6 shows the industry's combined ratio after policyholder dividends, net investment ratio, and operating ratio.

Exhibit 1-6

Property-Liability Insurance Operating—Profit or Loss—All Lines Combined in the United States from 1986 to 1995

Year	Combined Ratio*	Net Investment Ratio	Operating Ratio
1986	108.1	13.2	94.9
1987	104.7	12.8	91.9
1988	105.5	13.9	91.6
1989	109.2	15.1	94.1
1990	109.6	15.2	94.3
1991	108.6	15.4	93.2
1992	115.6	14.8	100.8
1993	106.8	13.9	93.0
1994	108.3	13.8	94.6
1995	106.4	14.5	91.9

*After policyholder dividends   100%

Note: Rounding of underlying data prevents the combined ratio after policyholder dividends less the net investment ratio from equaling operating ratio in years 1990, 1993, and 1994.

Best's Aggregates & Averages—Property-Casualty, 1991 Edition, p. 51; 1996 Edition, p. 66.

Operating Profit or Loss

Operating profit or loss is the sum of underwriting profit or loss and investment profit or loss. Insurers realize investment earnings from three sources. The first and most stable is investment income, consisting of interest, dividends, and rents derived from bonds, stocks, real estate, and other assets held for investment purposes. The second source is **realized capital gains or losses,** which result when an investment asset is sold for more or less than its cost. The final source is **unrealized capital gains or losses,** resulting when the market value of an asset rises above or falls below its cost, but the asset is not sold. The investment profit figures in Exhibit 1-6 do not include unrealized capital gains or losses.

Meeting Customers' Needs

How well insurers meet customer needs is difficult to determine. Insurers are more likely to hear from those customers who do not believe they have been treated fairly. All insurers receive complaints, and each one should be evaluated. In some instances, there is a real problem the insurer should address. In many more instances, the customer holds expectations that the insurer had not intended to fulfill.

Several state insurance departments tabulate complaints they receive and publish lists showing the number of complaints received for each company. The number of complaints might indicate one company's success or failure relative to other companies in the industry.

Consumers Union periodically surveys its membership to determine their level of satisfaction with the performance of auto and homeowners insurance. The results are infrequently published in that organization's magazine, *Consumer Reports*. It includes a list of the most satisfactory and least satisfactory insurers as indicated by the survey responses. Only a few of the largest insurers are included in the list because smaller insurers are not mentioned in the responses with sufficient frequency to evaluate their performance fairly.

Insurance agents and brokers can also be a source of information for evaluating an insurer's success in this area. They are in frequent contact with consumers and hear their complaints and praise of insurers. Collectively, agents and brokers seldom make formal tabulations of such consumer reactions, so their evaluations are likely to be subjective.

Many insurers emphasize a customer focus to maintain and raise levels of customer satisfaction with the insurer's products and services. Insurers use response cards and phone surveys to determine whether customers feel properly treated by the insurer after a transaction, particularly following a claim.

Insurers marketing insurance through independent agents and brokers usually view this network of producers as their customers in addition to the ultimate insurance consumer. These insurers recognize that producers have many insurance companies available to them and that a competitive marketplace exists within their offices. Being responsive to producer requests and permitting access to insurer policy data and information systems are examples of how insurers maintain and strengthen the company-producer relationship.

Meeting Legal Requirements

An insurer's success or failure in meeting legal requirements is indicated by the number of criminal, civil, and regulatory actions taken against it. These actions are automatically brought to the attention of management and should be evaluated carefully to see whether they result from a consistent pattern of disregard of legal requirements.

State insurance departments monitor the treatment of insureds, applicants for insurance, and claimants, as well as providing oversight to four insurer operational areas: sales and advertising, underwriting, ratemaking, and claims settlement. This regulatory activity, market conduct regulation, is in addition to the state insurance regulation's role in solvency surveillance.

Most states publish a listing of regulatory actions against insurers. This information can be useful in showing how one insurer's performance in this area compares to the performance of its competitors.

Meeting Social Responsibilities

Meeting social responsibilities is the most difficult of all of the major objectives to evaluate. There are no standards for judging an insurer's performance in this area, and very little information on an individual insurer's performance is publicly available. Of course, an insurer can get information from its own records to show its own performance, but comparisons with competing insurers are difficult to make because of the lack of available information.

One possible indicator of social responsibility is the benefits that an insurer provides for its employees. Comparative information for employee benefits is available from the United States Chamber of Commerce and from various insurance company trade associations. Although generous employee benefit plans can be construed as merely another method of competing for good employees, they might also indicate a company's concern for the welfare of its employees.

Another indicator of an insurer's humanitarian concern is its expenditures on loss control activities. Some insurers go beyond the typical efforts in loss control to improve the safety conditions for their policyholders. Many insurers contribute to associations that do research and raise public concern for safety.

Contributions to medical, welfare, and educational institutions and programs are another indication of humanitarian concerns and social responsibility.

Functions Required To Meet Needs

An insurance company consists of many departments, all of which must function properly if the insurer is to survive and succeed. The principal functions or departments of an insurer are the following:

- Marketing
- Underwriting
- Claims
- Loss control
- Premium auditing
- Reinsurance
- Actuarial
- Investments

Marketing

No matter how well the policy contract is drafted and regardless of the accuracy of the rating plan, an insurer cannot succeed without an adequate marketing program. Potential buyers of insurance must be adequately informed of the company's products, including its policies, rating plans, loss adjustment services, loss control capabilities, and other services that make a complete insurance product. Communicating this information to potential customers and producers is the function primarily of the insurer's marketing personnel.

There are several methods for marketing insurance and many variations of each of the principal marketing methods. Many insurers sell through independent agents and brokers, who are independent business people representing several otherwise unrelated insurers. Some market through exclusive agents, who represent only one insurer or a group of insurers under common ownership and management. Others rely on the sales efforts of their own employees. Several very successful insurers advertise through the mail, on television, or in newspapers and magazines to market their services, with no direct face-to-face contact with their customers. All of these and perhaps other methods have been used successfully to reach certain groups of insurance buyers. Some insurers use more than one of the methods mentioned in an effort to reach the widest possible audience.

The objectives of the marketing department must be balanced with other insurer goals. Too much emphasis on marketing might result in compromised underwriting guidelines. Premium growth that sacrifices profitability is not a successful market strategy.

Of course, marketing is more than merely making sales calls. A successful marketing program is likely to include (1) market research to determine the needs of potential buyers, (2) advertising and public relations programs to inform potential buyers about the company's products, (3) training programs to equip the company's employees and agents to meet the public's needs, (4) setting production goals and strategies for achieving them, and (5) effective motivation and management of the producer network.

Underwriting

The functions of the underwriting department are to decide the price and the terms and conditions under which the insurer will provide coverage and to decide which applicants will be insured. Underwriting is, in some regards, a counterbalance to the marketing department. In other respects, it is an aid to the marketing department.

The underwriting department acts as a counterbalance to the marketing department in the development of underwriting guides and the selection of applicants to insure. The primary purpose of these functions is to ensure that the insurer writes a book of business that is profitable and reasonably stable.

Tighter restraints on underwriting policy can lead to fewer applicants being accepted. Over time, an unduly restrictive underwriting policy and an aggressive marketing department will drive up the expenses of the insurer. An increased expense ratio results because the cost of investigating and rejecting applicants is almost the same as processing acceptable business. Additionally, the restricted premium volume produces a lower denominator in the insurer's loss ratio.

The underwriting department aids the marketing department by developing policy forms and rating plans that are marketable and by trying to find ways to insure marginal risks by modifying the policy contract, the rating plan, or the risk.

Claims

An insurance contract is a promise to make a payment to or on behalf of the policyholder if some fortuitous event occurs. The department that has primary responsibility for the loss adjustment function is frequently called the claims department and is staffed by employees who are trained in the skills necessary to negotiate or, if necessary, litigate the settlement of claims by or against policyholders.

Some think the purpose of the loss adjustment process is to minimize losses. Its real purpose is to achieve a fair settlement, neither too high nor too low. Loss settlements that are too high increase the cost of insurance for everybody. Settlements that are too low deprive the policyholder of some of the benefits of the insurance contract. Consistently inadequate loss settlements can hamper the insurer's marketing efforts and can lead to litigation and regulatory actions against the company.

Loss Control

The primary function of an insurer's loss control department is to prevent those losses which can be prevented and to minimize those which cannot be prevented. Loss control has been an important insurer function almost since the beginning of insurance, and it receives even greater emphasis now than in the past.

From an economic standpoint, loss control is preferable to risk transfer because it reduces the waste of valuable resources, both human and material. As a practical matter, both risk transfer and loss control are likely to be used jointly for most large risks because preventing all losses is seldom possible.

The loss control department provides information to the underwriting department to assist in the selection and rating of risks. It might also assist the marketing department in the solicitation of commercial and industrial accounts.

Premium Auditing

When insurers introduced workers compensation and employers liability with a variable policy premium, producers were given the responsibility of obtaining the insured's statement of actual wages paid during the policy period, calculating the premium according to the rate stipulated in the policy, and collecting the additional premium due or returning the excess premium previously paid. This process proved to be unreliable and was replaced by premium auditors to ensure equitable treatment of insureds.

The role of premium auditors has expanded as the number of insurance products subject to variable rating has increased. Compounding the difficulty of this task is the numerous rating bases used in insurance pricing and the size of the commercial accounts subject to audit.

Reinsurance

To the uninitiated, large corporations transferring risk to much smaller insurance companies might seem illogical. For example, all of the nation's 500 largest business corporations are larger than the vast majority of insurance companies, but all of them buy insurance. Reinsurance is the tool that makes such transfers practical. When a primary insurer accepts a risk that is larger than it is willing or able to bear, it can transfer all or a part of that risk to other insurers around the world through reinsurance transactions. For example, the explosion of the Piper Alpha oil rig in the North Sea in 1988 caused total losses of about $1 billion. Many insurers in many parts of the world shared that loss through reinsurance.

Reinsurance also helps cushion the effects of natural disasters on individual insurers and the insurance industries of individual nations. For example, Hurricane Andrew caused over $15 billion of losses in the United States. It would have been a severe blow if borne by the U.S. insurance industry alone. However, the reinsurance process spread the cost of that catastrophe throughout the worldwide insurance industry, softening its effects substantially.

A well-designed reinsurance program enables a primary insurer to provide insurance for risks that would otherwise be too large. Reinsurance also enables insurance buyers to obtain all of the coverage they need in one or a few policies, rather than buying many smaller policies from many insurers. Reinsurance also protects the financial solvency of primary insurers by enabling them to meet their obligations to policyholders and claimants.

Actuarial

The actuarial department performs the mathematical functions of an insurer. These include the calculation of rates, the development of rating plans, and the estimation of loss reserves. Actuaries might assist in corporate planning. Actuaries are often involved in establishing corporate goals and assessing the company's success in meeting those goals.

Advisory organizations, formally called rating bureaus, once served the insurance industry as a source for final rates. Now, advisory organizations are providing loss costs in lieu of final rates. Insurance company actuaries or actuarial consultants are involved in developing factors (reflecting expenses and anticipated profits) that will convert loss costs to final rates for use with their distribution system.

Investments

At first glance, the relationship between an insurer's investment operations and risk transfer would seem to be remote. Actually, the relationship is quite close for two reasons. First, an insurer's investment operations enable it to earn investment income on the funds generated by its risk transfer activities. The investment income, in turn, reduces the premium that the insurer must charge in exchange for the risks it assumes.

The relationship works in both directions, however. The kinds of insurance risks that an insurer assumes is one of the factors that determine the kinds of investments it acquires. An insurer that assumes only moderate insurance risks might be able to assume greater investment risks, with their higher investment yield. An insurer that assumes very high insurance risks must be more conservative in its investment strategy.

Property insurance losses vary substantially from year to year, in part because of catastrophes such as hurricanes and earthquakes. Also, property insurance losses are paid quickly. Consequently, an insurer that writes mostly property insurance must hold very stable and liquid investments that can be converted quickly to cash to pay losses. Liability insurance is not subject to catastrophic losses and is therefore more stable than property insurance. Liability claim payments are subject to a longer delay between the time of occurrence and the time of payment. Consequently, an insurer that writes mostly liability insurance might be able to hold investments that are slightly less liquid than those held by property insurers. The positive effect of interest rates and investment returns was illustrated in Exhibit 1-6.

Other Functions

Insurers also involve a number of other functions that need not be discussed in detail here. These include accounting, information systems, personnel, legal services, and training.

Though insurers serve society in many ways, their principal purpose is to facilitate the transfer of risk. Their other functions in the economy, such as the preservation of human and material assets and the accumulation of investment capital, are incidental to that principal purpose. All of the foregoing departments of an insurer must work together to serve its principal function and to meet company objectives.

Interdependence Among Functions

Although each function within an insurer must have some autonomy to perform its work, those functions are far from being completely independent. They must interact constantly if the insurer is to function smoothly and efficiently.

Marketing and Underwriting

Although the underwriting department functions in part as a counterbalance to the marketing department, the two departments must cooperate in many phases of insurer operations. For example, the underwriting department has primary responsibility for deciding what products the insurer will sell and the circumstances under which it will sell them. However, in making those decisions, the underwriting department must give full consideration to the marketing department's opinion about the salability of those products.

In addition, the underwriting department must cooperate with the marketing department in finding ways to make marginal risks acceptable. This can be done (1) by modifying a policy with large deductibles, special exclusions, or other modifications, (2) by modifying the rating plan to produce more premium, (3) by modifying the risk through loss control, or (4) by a combination of all three. In some cases, the underwriting department might be able to use special reinsurance arrangements to make a marginal risk acceptable.

In turn, sometimes the marketing department can assist the underwriting department. Marketing personnel are more likely than underwriting personnel to be in direct contact with policyholders and prospective policyholders. In the course of these contacts, marketing personnel might acquire information that is important in the underwriting process. Such information should be passed on to underwriting.

Underwriting and Loss Control

The loss control department is sometimes called the eyes and ears of the underwriting department. An underwriter who is considering an application for insurance might ask the loss control department to visit the applicant and survey the risks involved in the submission. In providing normal loss control services for existing policyholders, the loss control department might also obtain information that is important to the underwriting process.

Loss Control and Marketing

The loss control department might also be able to assist in marketing. Some insurers feature their loss control activities as a selling point in their advertising and sales presentations. A loss control engineer might accompany a marketing person on sales calls to prospective policyholders who are especially concerned about loss control assistance. Finally, loss control personnel might be able to offer suggestions to improve a marginal risk to make it acceptable to the underwriting department.

Claims and Other Departments

The claims department must also interact with the underwriting, marketing, and loss control departments. It can assist the underwriting department by passing on important underwriting information that arises in the loss adjustment process. In turn, it might ask the underwriting department to interpret the underwriting department's intent when a marginal claim arises.

The claims department can help the marketing effort by providing good claims service to policyholders, thus helping the marketing department to retain existing business and write new business. The claims department can also notify the marketing department before it refuses to pay claims because they are not covered under existing policies.

In the loss adjustment process, the claims department might learn of aspects of the policyholder's operations that need loss control attention. Such information should be passed on to the loss control department. In turn, the loss control department might be able to provide information about a policyholder's operations to assist the claims department in the settlement of a claim.

Actuarial and Other Departments

The actuarial department interacts primarily with underwriting and marketing. Its interactions with claims and loss control, especially the latter, are more limited.

The actuarial department devises most of the rates and rating plans used by the underwriting department. It also prepares the statistical information used to evaluate the performance of the underwriting department. In determining the applicable rates and rating plans, the actuarial department must also consider the views of the marketing department concerning the acceptability of the rates in the marketplace.

The actuarial department has responsibility for the development of loss reserves for Annual Statement purposes. For this function, it must maintain contact with the claims department, since the case claims reserves established by the claims department are an important element in establishing statement reserves.

Summary

Insurance is a system under which risk of loss is transferred to another party (the insurer) for a premium payment. The insurer promises to reimburse the policyholder for covered losses and shares the cost of these losses among all participants in the system. The financial suffering relieved by property-liability insurers is significant.

Insurers can be classified in many different ways. Typical categories are the legal form of ownership, place of incorporation, and licensing status.

The fact that an insurer is a stock insurer (operating for a profit) or a reciprocal exchange (operating for the benefit of the exchange membership) directly relates to the overall set of objectives that guide the insurer in day-to-day operations. The insurer's objectives and the obstacles to those objectives need to be understood by its management and staff so that company strengths can be exploited and weaknesses improved.

The principal function of an insurance company is to accept risks transferred to it by others. Although insurers perform many other functions, all of them are incidental to this risk transfer function.

Many entities might be involved in the risk transfer process. These include risk managers, consultants, and insurance agents and brokers. However, insurers are the principal players in most risk transfers, and without them, most transfers could not be made. Among the insurer functions that are necessary to the risk transfer process are policy contract development, pricing, marketing, underwriting, loss adjustment, loss control, reinsurance, and investments.

Insurers' major objectives include earning a profit, meeting customer needs, complying with legal requirements, and fulfilling the social and humanitarian duties society imposes on its institutions. Insurers must recognize and develop strategies to deal with internal and external constraints that restrain insurers from meeting these objectives.

An insurance company pursues its objectives by segmenting them into functional areas or departments. Those departments must function properly if the company is to be successful and grow. The principal functions are marketing, underwriting, claims, loss control, premium auditing, reinsurance, actuarial, and investments. Each department must have some autonomy to perform its assigned functions, but the departments are far from independent. Each department must interact constantly with other departments if the company is to achieve its objectives.

Chapter Notes

1. Michael W. Elliott, Bernard L. Webb, Howard N. Anderson, and Peter R. Kensicki, *Principles of Reinsurance*, 2d ed. (Malvern, PA: Insurance Institute of America, 1995), pp. 39-47.

2. Homepage of Lloyd's of London, copyright 1997, http://www.lloydsoflondon.co.uk/info/keyfacts.htm (accessed March 28, 1997).

3. Homepage of Lloyd's of London, copyright 1997, http://www.lloydsoflondon.co.uk/info/keyfacts.htm (accessed March 28, 1997).

4. Homepage of Lloyd's of London, copyright 1997, http://www.lloydsoflondon.co.uk/info/fact.htm (accessed March 28, 1997).

5. *The Fact Book, 1997: Property Casualty Insurance Facts* (New York, NY: Insurance Information Institute, 1997), p. 5.

6. *Best's Aggregates and Averages—Property-Casualty*, 1996 Edition, pp. 2, 3.

7. *Best's Aggregates and Averages—Property-Casualty*, 1996 Edition, p. 176.

Chapter 2

Principles of Marketing

Peter Drucker, noted author on management, economics, politics, and society, observed that the fundamental purpose of a business is to "create a customer."[1] To do that, management must build an enduring relationship with a growing group of consumers whose needs are served by the company. The marketing department is the function charged with the task of developing strategies and plans to get and keep customers.

Marketing is not only a department or function; it is also a *management philosophy.* It is the total organization's responsibility to implement the strategies and plans that lead to profitable growth. Many departments and functions must interact effectively for the company to meet its growth and profit objectives. This chapter examines how property-liability insurers get and keep customers. The focus of the chapter is on the marketing activities that occur in the insurer's home office. Insurance marketing is different from the marketing done by other types of businesses. Insurers generally do not have a particular department charged with responsibility to market the company's products. Rather, marketing is the primary responsibility of the underwriting department. It is underwriting that generally identifies market opportunities, develops new products, and measures success in delivering those products to targeted markets. For insurers using independent insurance agents, these targeted markets are the agents who represent several insurers and can put their clients' insurance with any of them. Other departments generally collaborate on the insurer's marketing activities. The fact that insurers do not relegate this activity to their own department does not lessen the value of understanding general marketing concepts. Insurance marketing activities conducted outside the home office—principally the functioning of marketing distribution systems—will be described in Chapter 3.

The Market for Property-Liability Insurance

A market consists of buyers and sellers engaged in voluntary exchanges for their mutual benefit. Thus, the market for property-liability insurance consists of insurers (sellers) and individuals or organizations with assets subject to loss from fortuitous events (buyers). The industry commonly uses the term "market" in a wide variety of senses: the select risk market, the surplus lines market, the London market, the private passenger auto market in Massachusetts, the market for contractors equipment floaters in Chester County, Pennsylvania, and so on. In each of these examples, a group of people with a need (buyers) interacts with a group of insurers (sellers) for their mutual benefit.

The market for property-liability insurance in the United States is large: over 98 million households and roughly 5 million businesses spent $259.7 billion in 1995 to insure assets and provide coverage against liabilities arising from fortuitous events. Three thousand forty property-liability insurers serve the property-liability insurance needs of the American public. These insurers employ approximately 598,000 people. An additional 697,000 people work in insurance agencies or brokerages.[2] Agency and brokerage employment data do not distinguish between those people employed in the property-liability business and those who work in the sales force of the life and health business.

The world insurance market and the United States' role in it are significant. The world's premium income was $1.968 trillion in 1994.[3] The United States accounts for just over 30 percent of the world market, as shown in Exhibit 2-1.

Measuring the Market

The property-liability insurance market in the United States can be measured in several ways, including net written premiums, number of insurable units, and number of insurers participating in the market. Exhibit 2-2 shows growth in net direct written premium in the property-liability industry. Of the $259.7 billion of net written premiums in 1995, approximately 49 percent were in personal lines, and 51 percent were in commercial lines.[4]

Exhibit 2-1
The World's Leading Insurance Countries in 1994 ($ millions)

Rank	Country	Non-life premiums	Life premiums	Total premiums	Percentage of total world premiums
1	Japan[1]	$ 128,999	$477,016	$606,015	30.80%
2	United States[2]	342,776*	251,419	594,195	30.20
3	Germany[3]	77,058	51,400	128,459	6.53
4	United Kingdom	42,144	74,786	116,930	5.94
5	France	40,724	69,741	110,465	5.61
6	South Korea	10,415	34,766	45,181	2.30
7	Italy	22,819	11,551	34,370	1.75
8	Canada	17,461	16,687	34,148	1.74
9	The Netherlands	14,329	15,092	29,421	1.50
10	Switzerland	9,651	15,419	25,070	1.27

* Includes health insurance premiums written by commercial insurers.
(1) March 31, 1994, to March 31, 1995.
(2) Net premiums written.
(3) Includes new federal states; gross premiums earned.

Swiss Reinsurance Company, *sigma*, No. 4/96.

Total property-liability insurance net written premiums grew by 6.1 percent per year in the ten-year period ending in 1995, with personal lines growing about 7.1 percent and the commercial lines growing by 5.2 percent. During this same period, the consumer price index grew by 3.5 percent per year. Total insurance premiums after the effects of inflation were removed grew in this period at an average annual rate of 2.5 percent per year.

Another way to measure the market for property-liability insurance is by number of households, automobiles, businesses, or other units in need of insurance. Exhibits 2-3 and 2-4 indicate the magnitude of the market for property-liability insurance. For example, the personal insurance market, as measured by a the number of households, has grown 6 percent from 1990 to 1995. New housing starts, perhaps an indication of growth opportunities for homeowners insurers, has grown 5 percent in that period. Housing and auto data are available by state and could be used to identify geographic areas that may be underserved for insurance. Similarly, the type of data presented in Exhibit 2-4 might guide an insurer to develop insurance products for a particular industry grouping.

Exhibit 2-2
U.S. Property-Liability Insurance Market
Net Written Premium ($ billions)

Year	Personal Lines^	Annual Percentage Change	Commercial Lines^	Annual Percentage Change	All Lines*	Annual Percentage Change
1986	72.4	14.0	104.2	29.1	176.6	22.4
1987	80.9	11.7	112.3	7.8	193.2	9.4
1988	86.6	7.0	115.4	2.8	202.0	4.6
1989	91.2	5.3	117.2	1.6	208.4	3.2
1990	97.0	6.4	120.9	3.2	217.8	4.5
1991	102.1	5.3	120.9	0.0	223.0	2.4
1992	108.8	6.6	118.7	−1.8	227.5	2.0
1993	114.9	5.6	126.6	6.7	241.6	6.2
1994	119.4	3.9	131.3	3.7	250.6	3.7
1995	126.0	5.5	133.7	1.8	259.7	3.6

^ The personal lines data cover private passenger auto and homeowners multiple peril. Commercial lines data include all other lines, including earthquake.

* Rounding in years 1990, 1993, and 1994 prevent totals from exactly matching personal and commercial net written premium combined.

Best's Aggregates & Averages—Property-Casualty, 1996 Edition, p. 178.

A third way of measuring the property-liability insurance market is by number of insurers. The $259.7 billion of property-liability insurance premiums in 1995 were written by 3,340 insurers. Many of those insurers associate together as subsidiary or parent companies called "groups." Some of these insurers operated on a national basis, but most were either single-state or regional in scope.

Measuring Market Share

The premiums earned by property-liability insurers can be subdivided by line of insurance within each state in the United States. Thus, a company can track its growth and profitability by line over time and in comparison with other companies. For example, if an insurer knows that last year industry net written premiums for homeowners insurance in a particular state were $500 million and its own homeowners premiums for that state were $20 million, it can compute its market share for that line and state as 4 percent (or $20 million divided by $500 million). Market share figures help an insurer's management to determine the success or failure of current strategies and serve as input into planning.

Exhibit 2-3
Measure of the U.S. Personal Lines Insurance Market—Number of Risks

	1990	1995
Number of households (millions)	93.3	99.0
Number of single-family homes (millions)	66.1	69.5
Number of housing starts and building permits (millions)	1.2	1.4
	1990	1994
Number of cars in use (millions)	123.3	122.0
	1990	1995
Number of new retail sales of cars (millions)	9.5	8.6

Statistical Abstract of the U.S. 1996, Table No. 66—Households, Families, Subfamilies, Married Couples, and Unrelated Individuals: 1960 to 1995, p. 58, and Table No. 1002—Motor Vehicles in Use: 1980 to 1994, p. 623.

Exhibit 2-4
Measure of the U.S. Commercial Lines Insurance Market—Number of Risks

Number of Business Establishments (thousands)			
Industry	1985	1990	1993
Agricultural services	64	85	100
Mining	37	30	29
Construction	476	578	598
Manufacturing	358	378	387
Transportation	203	235	267
Wholesale trade	438	476	509
Retail trade	1,407	1,530	1,552
Finance and insurance	488	545	609
Services	1,712	2,059	2,289
All industries	5,701	6,176	6,403

Statistical Abstract of the U.S. 1996, Table No. 839—Establishments, Employees, and Payroll, by Industry: 1980 to 1993, p. 540.

The information needed by insurers to compute market share is widely available because insurers are required to report premiums, losses, expenses, and other financial data to state insurance departments under a standard format known as the NAIC Annual Statement, promulgated by the National Association of Insurance Commissioners. The financial statements filed by insurers are public information, which means that anyone can review them. In most cases, insurers obtain this information from commercial publishers, such as A.M. Best Company, that collect the NAIC Annual Statement information from all jurisdictions and combine and analyze the information to make it more useful to insurers and others.

Measuring Competitiveness Within the Market

The market for insurance products is extremely competitive. One indication of this is the number of insurers in the marketplace. Although economies of scale in the insurance business can be exploited to give an insurer a competitive edge, no insurer has been able to capitalize on such an advantage to prevent smaller, less efficient insurers from thriving. As shown in Exhibit 2-5, some insurers are clearly the market leaders, yet the market share of the leaders is still relatively small.

Market share of individual lines of insurance can be further analyzed using A.M. Best data. Exhibit 2-6 shows the leading writers of homeowners and auto insurance. Most insurers evaluate market opportunities on a state-by-state basis. Again, A.M. Best data can provide a ranking of leading insurers by line within each state.

An analysis of insurance industry data on a nationwide basis, by line of insurance, or by state shows that no one insurer has enough market share to dominate the market.

Exhibit 2-5
Leading Writers of Property-Liability Insurance

Company/Group	1995 Direct Premiums ($1,000)	Percentage Market Share		
		1993	1994	1995
State Farm Group	$32,966,532	12.1	12.4	12.5
Allstate Ins. Group	17,607,955	6.4	6.4	6.7
CNA Ins. Group	10,134,602	4.1	4.1	3.9
Amer. Intern. Group	9,598,261	3.6	3.7	3.6
Farmers Ins. Group	9,175,949	3.6	3.4	3.5
Nationwide Insurance Enterprise	8,344,383	3.2	3.2	3.2
ITT Hartford Ins. Group	5,564,313	2.3	2.2	2.1
Liberty Mutual Group	5,513,606	2.6	2.3	2.1
Zurich Ins. Group-US	5,077,673	1.4	1.5	1.9
Aetna Life & Cas. Group	5,033,523	2.2	2.1	1.9

A.M. Best Company, Inc., *Best's Review*, August 1996.

Exhibit 2-6
Leading Writers of Homeowners and Auto Insurance

Homeowners Insurance				
Company/Group	1995 Direct Premiums ($1,000)	Percentage Market Share		
		1993	1994	1995
State Farm Group	$6,056,327	23.3	23.6	23.5
Allstate Ins. Group	3,039,452	11.8	11.9	11.8
Farmers Ins. Group	1,518,643	5.6	5.7	5.9
USAA Group	857,854	3.1	3.2	3.3
Nationwide Insurance Enterprise	759,074	2.8	2.9	3.1
Chubb Group of Ins. Cos.	519,852	2.1	2.0	2.0
Aetna Life & Cas. Group	512,987	1.9	1.9	2.0
Prudential of Am. Group	474,714	2.1	1.9	1.8
Safeco Ins. Cos.	440,521	1.6	1.7	1.7
CNA Ins. Companies	420,174	0.9	0.9	1.6

A.M. Best Company, Inc., Best's Executive Data Service.

Auto Insurance				
Company/Group	1995 Direct Premiums ($1,000)	Percentage Market Share		
		1993	1994	1995
State Farm Group	$23,151,980	18.9	19.2	19.0
Allstate Ins. Group	13,148,856	10.6	10.4	10.6
Farmers Ins. Group	6,293,928	5.6	5.2	5.2
Nationwide Insurance Enterprise	4,416,221	3.5	3.6	3.6
USAA Group	3,375,224	2.8	2.8	2.8
Progressive Group	2,959,026	1.7	2.2	2.4
Berkshire Hathaway	2,685,808	1.7	2.1	2.2
Liberty Mutual Group	2,147,874	1.9	1.8	1.8
CNA Insurance Group	2,028,105	1.8	1.8	1.7
ITT Hartford Ins. Group	1,780,790	1.5	1.5	1.5

A.M. Best Company, Inc., *Best Week*, September 3, 1996.

The Property-Liability Insurance Product

A product may be defined as anything that can be offered to someone to satisfy a need or want. All products have elements of tangibility and intangibility. A **tangible product** is one that can be seen and touched. In insurance, the tangible product is a legal contract represented by words on paper and known as an insurance policy. Other dimensions of tangibility may include a product name (for example, the Executive Yacht Policy), endorsements, and packaging. Packaging of an insurance policy includes its graphic design and any container, such as a folder or binder, which can be used to present the policy to the insured.

Insurance products also have elements of intangibility. The **intangible product**, according to Theodore Levitt, marketing professor at Harvard, is that which "prospective customers can't taste, test, feel, smell, or watch in operation in advance; they are asked to buy simply promises of satisfaction."[5] Although promises are intangible, they can be described tangibly. This explains why an insurer might offer a "blanket of protection" under an "umbrella."

An insurer must develop the tangible products (policies) and intangible products (services to fulfill the promises) that uniquely satisfy the needs of its customers. An insurer may differentiate its products from competitors' by (1) changing the coverage provided by the policy, (2) charging a different price, or (3) providing a different level of service.

Contract Differentiation

Many of the policies and endorsements now considered standard started as efforts by insurers to differentiate their products from the competition. For example, the homeowners policy was developed for that purpose in the 1950s. It became a standard product, and insurers have continued to differentiate their homeowners policies by offering new or expanded coverage features.

Contract differentiation is restricted somewhat by state laws requiring some types of policies to contain prescribed language. For instance, an automobile no-fault statute, an uninsured motorists statute, or a financial responsibility law may specify certain language or provisions that insurers must include in their auto policies. Similarly, some states have their own rating bureaus that promulgate forms to be used by all insurers when writing certain lines.

Contract differentiation may also be hampered by state laws requiring regulatory approval of new policy forms. Some insurers feel that policy differentiation is not worth the time and effort necessary to gain regulatory approval. Consequently, they prefer to use the standard policy forms filed on their behalf by an advisory organization. In some cases, an insurer may not be able to gain approval for a new form even if it is willing to make the required filings. For example, some states have been unwilling to approve claims-made wording for general liability policies.

Price Differentiation

In the marketing of tangible products, management may use price differentiation as a strategy to get customers. An insurer that wants to charge a lower price than its competitors must reduce its costs, its profits, or both, below those of the competition. It must comply with the statutory requirement that rates be adequate and also with the economic necessity of having enough income to remain in business over the long term.

An insurance rate consists of allowances for losses, expenses, and profit. An insurer might justify a reduction in rate by reducing any one of these three elements. The allowance for losses might be reduced through more careful underwriting selection or less generous claims settlement practices. The allowance for expenses may be reduced through expense control measures. Acquisition expenses may be reduced by lowering commissions. Price differentiation may also result from refining rating classes. For example, one rating class might be divided into two classes, with a lower rate for some members of the old class and higher rates for others. Experience, retrospective, and schedule rating plans may also be used as means of price differentiation. These plans closely tailor the rate to the policyholders' hazard characteristics or loss experience.

Service Differentiation

Many insurers use service differentiation in their marketing programs. For example, several large workers compensation insurers emphasize their loss control services, ability to assist employers in complying with government health and safety regulations, and capabilities for rehabilitation of injured workers. These services are usually provided at no additional cost, thus precluding the need to purchase such services from an outside vendor. Of course, these services may also be promoted as price differentiation, since they can reduce insurance costs.

Service differentiation in personal lines property-liability insurance may focus on prompt and fair claim settlement. Several large personal lines insurers emphasize the convenience of their drive-in claims centers, and some insurers guarantee repair work, provided repairs are made by a recommended repair shop. Also, many insurers use slogans and trademarks to create the impression that their services are superior to those of their competitors.

Contract, price, and service differentiation efforts are intended to add value to the tangible product. The insurer may add value to the basic product in many ways beyond those cited above, including conveniently located agents, financing terms, policy delivery, agent participation in the claims process, account billing, annual insurance reviews, computer quotes, long-term policyholder recognition, and agent newsletters.

The Role of Marketing in Property-Liability Insurance

Many definitions of marketing exist. One of the simplest yet clearest is the following: "Marketing is human activity directed at satisfying needs and wants through exchange processes."[6]

Marketing helps an insurer focus on satisfying the asset protection needs of selected groups of customers so that the insurer's profitability and growth objectives are met. By understanding the wants and preference of targeted markets, marketing activities help the insurer use its resources and capabilities to influence sufficient numbers of consumers to become long-term customers of the insurer.

Needs of Insurance Buyers

Property-liability insurance buyers have several needs that insurance can satisfy. Insurance consumers own property that they could not afford to replace without insurance. Insurance coverage is often required by lenders; for example, a bank lending money for the purchase of a house or a car will require the purchaser to buy and maintain property or physical damage insurance. Insurance consumers also need insurance protection to pay for the consequences of injuries to others. Many states have laws requiring that liability insurance be maintained in case others are injured by the policyholder's activities.

Businessowners also need protection against property-liability losses. Business property such as buildings, equipment, fixtures, and inventory might be damaged, stolen, or destroyed. Such losses could interrupt business operations, with many expenses continuing during repair or replacement of property. The businessowner needs to protect against costs of injury or sickness to employees. Finally, businessowners need protection against liabilities to others caused by business operations, ranging from injuries suffered by a customer on the premises to injuries arising from the use of defective or unsafe products.

Insurance marketers do not create the need for insurance; instead, they point out how a particular policy would satisfy an existing need. For instance, apartment dwellers may have a need for property-liability insurance. However, only those who recognize their exposure to liability or property losses actually want such coverage. Marketers also try to influence intentions to buy by making the product fit perceived needs at an affordable rate.

Insurance buyers want and expect their insurance to provide certain benefits. Research has consistently shown that personal lines insurance buyers want "price/value"; that is, they seek the lowest price for the best available coverage. When they have a loss, they want superior claim service delivered in a timely, friendly, and fair manner. Many consumers want the coverage and professional service to be from an insurer that is large, local, and familiar. Many others rely on their agent to "shop around" for them to get the best policy to fit their needs. Most of all, insurance buyers want and expect their agent and insurer to deliver on the "promise to pay" at the time of a loss covered by their policy.

The insurance wants and expectations of businessowners are similar to those of personal lines buyers in most respects. The principal differences between businessowners and personal lines insurance buyers are the complexity of the risk management problems and the alternative means of treatment.

Every business has a unique set of exposures to loss, and the exposures can change very rapidly as the business competes in its marketplace. The complexities produce a desire for professional assistance not only in design of the insurance policy but also for loss prevention and loss control services. For instance, even a small business can implement safety and anti-theft measures to control or prevent losses and thus keep insurance premiums down. Businessowners want and expect their insurance agent or broker to understand their business well enough to provide competent counsel in designing and implementing a risk management program uniquely tailored to that business.

Philosophies of Marketing Management

An insurer's marketing function must perform a variety of activities in order to fulfill its objective of getting and keeping customers. The activities, which will be described later in this chapter, can be managed according to various philosophies of management. Four common philosophies are the production concept, the product concept, the sales concept, and the marketing concept.

The Production Concept

The basic assumption of the **production concept** is that the consumer does not distinguish among the products offered by the various insurers in the industry and thus is only interested in the one that costs the least. Insurers that manage according to the production concept provide little, if any, service beyond the basic product. The production concept emphasizes efficiency; it is often applied in mass production environments. The Model-T Ford is a classic example of a business built around the production concept. Insurers that sell standard policies with few, if any, services other than claim settlement are following the production concept.

The Product Concept

The **product concept** focuses strategy almost exclusively on achieving the highest possible quality of products and services. Insurers who adhere to the product concept assume that customers will seek out the insurer providing the highest quality available in the marketplace and will pay more to be assured they are receiving it. Hospitals traditionally have managed relationships with patients and doctors assuming that everyone wants and is willing to pay for the best quality. Insurers that provide customized policies or state-of-the-art loss control services embody the product concept.

The Sales Concept

The **sales concept** assumes that products are sold, not bought. This approach to management is common in businesses where customers only buy the product one time, such as encyclopedia sales or pre-planned funeral services. Management assumes that potential customers will initially resist buying but can be induced to buy by sales effort. It is further assumed that there are many potential customers.

The Marketing Concept

Insurers that practice the **marketing concept** recognize that consumers can be grouped into segments according to differences in their wants and needs. Management assumes that consumers will favor the products and services that come closest to satisfying their particular needs and wants. The task of management is to research and choose target markets and to develop effective offers and marketing programs to attract and keep customers.

Relatively few companies practice the marketing concept. Examples include McDonald's, Procter and Gamble, and Coca-Cola. Such companies are known for their passionate attention to consumer wants, preferences, expectations, and satisfaction levels. Insurers that practice the marketing concept recognize the need to balance the needs and wants of agents and policyholders with the insurer's objectives to achieve favorable results for all three parties.

Key Marketing Decisions

The key decisions that any marketer must make are suggested by the following definition of marketing:

> . . . getting the right goods and services to the right people at the right place at the right time at the right price with the right communication and promotion with the right customer service.[7]

In an insurer, thousands of decisions are made each day at all levels of the organization to do the "right thing right" in satisfying the wants and needs of the insurance-buying public. The key marketing questions faced by management in a property-liability insurer can be summarized as follows: (1) Whom to serve? (2) What products and services? (3) With what distribution? (4) At what price? (5) With what communications? and (6) At what levels of customer service?

Whom To Serve?

An insurer must decide whom to serve. Markets must be measured and segmented, and targets must be selected for marketing attention. Attractive market opportunities occur because current competitors are unable to satisfy the needs of customers. Any market is filled with more customer groups with specific needs than any one insurer can possibly serve in a superior way. Management must define logical market segments that are *measurable* in that geographic and demographic characteristics can be identified, *accessible* in that they can be effectively reached and served, *substantial* in that size and purchasing power suggest potential profitability, and *responsive* in that actions the insurer might take should produce satisfactory levels of profitable sales.

Exhibit 2-7 shows five strategies a property-liability insurer might follow in providing products to target markets. One option for the insurer is to concentrate on one product for one target market. As an example of **product market specialization**, Exhibit 2-7 shows the insurer targeting automobile insurance to auto club members as the only product and market to be served. Other examples of product market specialization are an association captive that sells only professional liability insurance to physicians and an assessment mutual "P&I club" that sells only protection and indemnity insurance to shipowners.

An insurer can pursue a **product specialization** strategy by providing one line of insurance to multiple target markets. Exhibit 2-7 shows an example of the homeowners product line targeted to farmers, teachers, and retired persons. Each of these markets would feature different key competitors. The segments would have different needs suggesting different products, sales strategies, and

Exhibit 2-7

Strategies for Market Coverage

Strategy	Market Coverage
	The insurer sells:
Product Market Specialization	Only *one* type of insurance to *one* type of customer Example: auto insurance to auto club members
Product Specialization	Only *one* type of insurance to *various* types of customers Example: homeowners insurance to farmers, teachers, and retired persons
Market Specialization	Various types of property-liability insurance to only *one* type of customer Example: commercial package policies to automobile dealers
Selective Specialization	Various types of property-liability insurance to specific, selected markets Example: commercial package policies to schools, places of worship, and funeral homes
Multi-Product/ Multi-Market	A wide variety of property-liability coverages to a large part of the total marketplace Example: all lines to habitational, mercantile, service, and manufacturing segments

so on. As additional markets are added, the homeowners product line would become broader with more product variation to meet the special needs of each segment.

An insurer could follow a **market specialization** strategy by selling various coverages to one type of customer. For instance, an insurer could serve the multiple-lines needs of automobile dealers. The insurer would grow by identifying additional insurance and financial services needs of the target market and developing products to meet those needs.

A fourth approach is **selective specialization**, a niche strategy allowing the insurer to grow in markets and/or products that show future profitability potential. For example, the insurer could decide to specialize in property-liability coverages for schools, places of worship, and funeral homes.

The fifth option is to be a **full-service multi-product/multi-market insurer** that offers many segments a wide array of products. For example, the insurer might sell all lines of insurance to habitational, mercantile, service, and manufacturing segments. The insurer might do this in recognition that each segment has needs for a wide variety of insurance coverages.

What Products and Services?

Management must decide which insurance products and services will be sold to selected markets. There are many product decisions, ranging from what product lines to offer to the detailed evaluation of various coverages, limits, and deductibles included in the policy.

Product Life Cycle

The answers to product-related questions largely depend on where the product is in its "life cycle." Exhibit 2-8 depicts the product life cycle, including four recognizable stages of sales volume over time. The four stages—introduction, growth, maturity, and decline—may take months or decades, depending on the characteristics of a given market. Exhibit 2-8 shows predictable characteristics, including sales, cost, profits, customers, and competitors.

In the **market development stage**, an insurer offers a product not previously available in a given market. The marketing objective in such an instance is to create product awareness and trial. The product strategy would be to offer a basic product. For instance, management might decide to offer a basic earthquake policy in an area previously thought to be relatively unlikely to experience earthquakes.

In the **growth stage** of the product life cycle, management might augment the basic product to add value, which might increase market share at the expense of competitors who have also entered the growth market. The insurer with an earthquake policy might broaden coverage or otherwise modify the basic policy to make it more attractive to a larger number of potential customers.

Insurers operating in the **maturity stage** of the product life cycle attempt to get the widest possible market coverage by having available a wide variety of product alternatives. Such insurers attempt to maximize profit while defending market share. Thus, a major homeowners writer might create a "market value" policy to expand the total homeowners market to include lower value dwellings.

A product enters the **decline stage** of the product life cycle when total sales become smaller as time goes by. The marketing objective pursued by many insurers in this stage is to treat the product as a "cash cow," "milking" profits by reducing expenses as sales decline. In this stage of the life cycle, product

Exhibit 2-8
Product Life Cycle

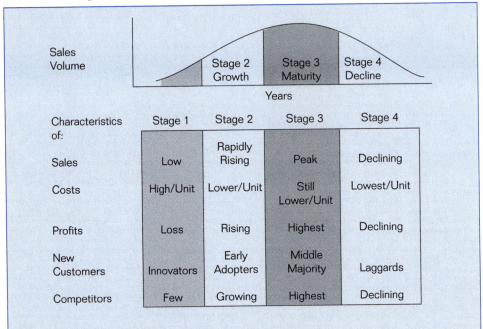

Adapted with permission from Theodore Levitt, "Exploit the Product Life Cycle," *Harvard Business Review*, November/December 1965, pp. 81-94.

decisions typically focus on reducing the number and variety of product choices offered to the market. Thus, an insurer might decide to eliminate or restrict one of its policy forms based on declining sales and inability to control or reduce expenses.

Product Development Process

Insurers introduce new products at all stages of the product development life cycle. Exhibit 2-9 shows the steps in the product development process for property-liability products.

Opportunity Assessment

The first step, **opportunity assessment**, consists of monitoring the marketplace to identify potential opportunities.

Monitoring the market consists of several activities. Producers may alert the insurer when they learn of innovative products offered by competitors. Some insurers use agent advisory councils to advise on market threats and ways to counter them. New product ideas are often developed based on these sugges-

Exhibit 2-9
Product Development Process

Major Steps

I.   Opportunity Assessment
   - Monitor market
   - Identify opportunity
   - Relate opportunities to business strategy
   - Develop specifications
   - Secure approval to proceed

II. Development of Contract, Underwriting, and Pricing
   - Develop coverage/policy forms
   - Develop guidelines for underwriting/claims
   - Develop classifications
   - Develop pricing structure
   - Secure approval

III. Business Forecast
   - Review with profit center management
   - Identify requirements for statistics
   - Develop business forecast
   - Secure approval

IV. Regulatory Requirements
   - File with regulators
   - Develop statistical information systems
   - Communicate regulatory approval

V.   Distribution Requirements
   - Develop sales promotional information
   - Develop advertising
   - Develop sales training
   - Plan roll-out strategy

VI. Introduction
   - Implement sales training and promotion
   - Measure/compare results to plan

tions. Producer associations provide their members with information on insurer product development on a state-by-state basis. A. M. Best publishes a monthly report describing the filings made by insurers in each state. In addition to describing the features of new products, the newsletter gives information on modifications to existing programs. Programs are typically described in terms of what type of policyholder is eligible for the program, the rate deviation from bureau filed rate levels, and the policy endorsements that either expand or restrict coverage.

An insurer may rely on **focus groups** to analyze the opportunities suggested. Representatives from several insurer areas combine their talents and perspectives to determine the feasibility of the new product idea. In many instances, the new product suggestion can be modified to revitalize an existing product.

After the insurer marketing personnel have identified the opportunities, they evaluate them against the insurer objectives and competing opportunities to determine whether management is willing to continue the process. Management may determine that the long-term objectives of the insurer would be well served if it were to offer a product rather than waiting until the market was further developed and the major participants in that market had emerged.

Development of Contract, Underwriting, and Prices

Once approval is secured to continue the process, the next phase is to develop the policy forms, underwriting guidelines, and price. Cooperation among various insurer functions—including underwriting, actuarial, claims, reinsurance, premium audit, and loss control—are essential to the process. These departments often contribute personnel to create a task force to investigate the implications the product will have on the insurer's operations. Each representative not only contributes to enhancing the product but also assists in identifying operational changes required to make the implementation feasible. For instance, the underwriting representative would want to create new applications to capture the factors essential in underwriting and pricing the new product.

An important consideration in product development is the ability of the insurer's information system to accommodate the new product. Data processing personnel usually require extensive lead time to determine the effect of the new product on automated system resources. Some relatively simple product innovations may require substantial programming to accomplish. For instance, many insurers discovered that offering a combination personal automobile and homeowners policy was an expensive proposition when the computer programming costs were considered. Although these insurers had existing systems in place, they were not engineered to interchange information. As a result, the efficiency of the combination personal lines policies was not realized until both systems were rewritten. The second phase concludes with the tangible product, which is then submitted to a rigorous assessment of sales potential.

The focus group that initially determined the qualities the new product should contain may evaluate the product's sales potential. The focus group often includes producers who are shown the proposed product to obtain their reaction. With the input of the sales force, the product can be modified and promoted more easily.

Business Forecast

The business forecast phase establishes benchmarks for evaluating the success of the program. Such measures include the number of policies expected to be issued, the premium volume expected to be generated, the number of producers who will be expected to participate, and the loss ratio expected to develop.

Regulatory Requirements

After the business forecast is approved, the development process enters the regulatory arena. State regulators require, at a minimum, notification of new policy forms, rating plans, and policy writing rules. In most states, the state regulatory officials must approve changes in existing programs and the introduction of new ones to safeguard policyholder interests. Inherent in the design of a new product are methods to gather data that can be used to further analyze its success or failure. Coded policy information permits subsequent evaluation to ensure that the product is priced effectively. Regulators also require this information to monitor the market and individual insurers. Regulatory approval is handled on a state-by-state basis, and often the product must be modified to obtain approval in each jurisdiction.

Distribution Requirements

Following regulatory approval, the insurer completes the distribution requirements, including training and promotional materials for the sales force.

Introduction

The product is introduced in one or more states with advertising and sales promotion. Management must also make tough decisions about eliminating weak products. Many insurers carry products that do not contribute to profitability objectives. Management must be able to identify such products; determine whether the continued existence of the product line is appropriate; and take action to improve the product performance, to phase it out, or to eliminate it altogether.

With What Distribution?

The distribution system is the marketing variable that gets the right products to the right target markets efficiently and effectively. A distribution system is efficient when it produces sales results at a competitive expense level for the functions performed. The system is effective when it gets and keeps sufficient numbers of customers.

The distribution system or systems used by an insurer produce the sales needed to meet premium objectives. Hence, the sales force in property-liability insurance is often referred to as "producers." Sales management meets premium objectives by recruiting, selecting, training, motivating, and rewarding producers. Chapter 3 covers the types of distribution systems and the functions performed by producers and sales management.

The major marketing decisions concerning distribution are how many producers to have, where they should be located, and the degree of control to be exercised over the distribution system. In addition, the marketing department may be charged with developing a profile of the ideal producer so that support services can focus on building an efficient and effective distribution system.

The marketing function might be asked to study the potential of additional distribution systems. Such an assignment would include a review of critical success factors in developing and maintaining other sources of production. The study might also consider possible conflict between additional distribution systems and the existing system.

At What Price?

Ideally, the distribution system sells the right products to the right customers at the right price. In many industries the price variable is a major tool available to the marketing department. In fact, pricing strategies are often used to achieve sales and market share objectives. Many insurers use sophisticated computer models to determine when to raise and lower prices and by how much. Insurance regulators restrict how much and how often insurance rates can change in personal lines and some commercial lines.

An insurer must manage the pricing variable with caution. Even a small increase or decrease in price compared to its principal competitors may lead to significant change in sales results. The insurer's actuarial department is charged with determining the adequate rate, the price dictated by loss-cost and expense trends experienced by the insurer. Smaller insurers depend heavily on advisory organizations to provide loss cost data to assist them in determining adequate rates. Chapters 10 and 11 describe the ratemaking function performed by the actuarial department of a property-liability insurer.

The primary role of the marketing department in pricing is to work with the sales and actuarial departments to resolve the conflicts between the need for competitive prices for target markets and the need for adequate rates to achieve the insurer's financial objectives.

With What Communications?

An insurer must decide how best to communicate with the markets to be served. There are four basic ways to communicate with target markets: advertising, personal selling, sales promotion, and publicity. Exhibit 2-10 shows examples of tools for each of the four basic modes of communication. The insurance marketer must decide on communication objectives, expenditure levels, messages, media, and measures of effectiveness. All communications must be managed consistently in support of marketing and business objectives.

Exhibit 2-10
Communication Tools in Property-Liability Insurance

Advertising	Sales Promotion	Publicity	Personal Selling
Print and broadcast ads	Giveaway items	Press kits	Sales presentations
Mailings	Fairs and trade shows	Speeches	Sales meetings
Brochures and booklets	Exhibits	Seminars	Telemarketing
Posters and leaflets	Premium financing	Annual reports	
Directories	Entertainment	Charitable donations	
Billboards	Inserts in premium renewal notices	Public relations	
Display signs			
Point-of-purchase displays			
Symbols and logos			

Adapted with permission from Philip Kotler, *Marketing Management: Analysis, Planning and Control* (Englewood Cliffs, NJ: Prentice-Hall, Inc., 1984), p. 603.

Communication objectives depend on what response management seeks from consumers. The marketer may want to build consumer awareness of the insurer or product, change consumer attitudes, or persuade consumers to take specific actions.

After the intended consumer response is defined, a marketer can develop messages that draw attention, hold interest, arouse desire, and cause action. The marketing department must decide what to say, how to say it, and by whom it should be said. The message, theme, and content of property-liability insurance marketing communications are often intended to personalize the insurance product and represent it tangibly. For instance, the message might be that the insurer is "your partner" with a "blanket of protection."

Both personal and nonpersonal communication channels are used to communicate with prospective and existing clients. Personal channels involve two or more people communicating directly with each other. In insurance the agent and the agent's staff communicate regularly with current and prospective policyholders. Nonpersonal communication channels include newspapers, magazines, radio, television, and billboards.

Expenditure levels may be determined by one of four methods: percentage of sales, competitive-parity, objective and task, or the balanced budget approach. The **percentage of sales method** keeps communication expenses closely related to the movement of sales volume over the business cycle. This method assumes that a certain amount of advertising creates a certain amount of sales. The **competitive parity method** is used when management wants to maintain a level of spending relative to that spent by certain competitors. The **objective and task method** is used to develop communication budgets by defining specific objectives, determining the tasks to be performed, and estimating the costs of performing those tasks. Although this method is the most detailed, its use relies on knowledge of consumer behavior and the amount of advertising required to trigger that behavior. The sum of these costs is the proposed communication budget. Finally, the **balanced budget approach** is used when the insurer is particularly cost-conscious or when senior management is not convinced that advertising is a good investment. This method limits the permissible expenditure on advertising to pre-set amounts.

Many insurers participate in trade associations that produce broad-based insurance advertising for a large segment of the industry. The best known of these emphasizes the advantage to the consumer of dealing with a producer representing several insurers.

Communications expenses for property-liability insurers include the amounts spent for sales promotion, publicity, and personal selling. Exhibit 2-11 shows the results of a marketing communications study. In the period between 1987 and 1992, the companies responding increased their use of spot radio, spot television, network radio, network television, and cable television.

The effectiveness of marketing communications can be measured in several ways. Pre-testing can be used to help design effective messages. Post-testing helps to determine whether the target-audience members recognize or recall the message, how many times they saw it, how they felt about the message, and their previous and current attitudes toward the product and insurer. Sales and customer retention measures may also be useful, especially when the communication objectives are to persuade or remind the consumer.

At What Levels of Customer Service?

The last and most important marketing question concerns the level of customer service. The insurer can have the right products sold through the right

Exhibit 2-11

Percentage of Companies Using Specific Corporate Advertising Media

	1987	1992
Trade Print	87%	81%
Yellow Pages	73	69
Consumer Newspaper	48	49
Consumer Magazines	45	41
Spot Radio	27	37
Other Corporate Media	22	27
Spot Television	18	22
Outdoor	17	20
Network Radio	13	22
Network Television	13	16
Cable Television	12	20

Insurance Marketing Communications Association, Budgeting for Marketing Communications, October 1993, p. 15. Copyrighted by Insurance Marketing Communications Association; reproduction without permission is prohibited.

distribution system at the right price and with the right communications to the right customers and yet fail in the marketing mission to get and keep customers. The insurer must provide the value-added service that justifies the consumer's decision to buy from and stay with that insurer.

The marketing department represents the customer perspective in the management decision-making process. The marketing department *knows* the customer by monitoring satisfaction levels, wants, needs, attitudes, perceptions, preferences, and expectations. This information is intended to answer the question: "What is value to the customer?" Customers value fair, friendly, accurate, and timely service during those "moments of truth" when they come in contact with the insurer or its representatives. The marketing department works with all of the insurer's other functions to develop and deliver quality service to customers.

The quest for excellence in customer service should motivate a company to do the following:

1. Senior management must be committed to superior service as the primary value in the company.

2. The corporate culture must be passionate, even obsessive, about serving customers.

3. Customer satisfaction must be measured frequently for each type of moment of truth and actions taken based on the measurements.

4. Customer service excellence must be recognized and rewarded whenever and wherever it occurs.

In the best companies, customer service legends become part of the corporate culture in each department, defining the standard of excellence for service to customers.

Marketing Objectives, Strategies, and Plans

The key marketing decisions based on the corporate mission and business strategies are adopted by senior management. Management must develop a strategic plan for the insurer to provide a framework for planning done at the market and product levels. After management has answered the question, "What business are we in?" it must develop marketing objectives, marketing strategies, and market plans.

Marketing Objectives

Marketing objectives state the results that management desires to achieve in providing products and services to selected markets. The most common marketing objectives focus on sales growth, profitability, innovation, diversification, and customer satisfaction. The objectives should be arranged in priority order and should be quantified, realistic, and consistent. As it grows, the insurer must identify priority products and markets. The insurer must also quantify premium, underwriting gain, return on surplus, and market share targets. The targets guide the development of strategies and plans to achieve the objectives.

Exhibit 2-12 shows examples of marketing objectives for a property-liability insurer in five areas. All of these objectives have time frames for accomplishment, and some of the objectives are stated in terms of progress compared to past periods or the performance of key competitors.

Growth objectives provide measures of progress in achieving increased sales. The examples of growth objectives in Exhibit 2-12 show various ways to increase sales: by selling to new customers, by increasing sales to existing customers, and by keeping more of the existing customers than in the past.

Profitability objectives recognize the imperative that markets must provide revenue that will more than cover losses and expenses. A basic measure of

Exhibit 2-12
Examples of Marketing Objectives

Growth	Increase market share in a line of business in a territory from X percent in one year to Y percent in the next year.
	Sell X auto policies in current year.
	Increase multiple-line account base from current percentage to X percent in three years.
	Improve retention to the level of a certain key competitor in two years.
	Grow premium in product line X or Y percent in next five years.
Profitability	Increase underwriting gain by X percent in product line Y in the current year.
	Add X dollars to policyholders' surplus in current year.
	Increase return on equity by X percent in current year.
Innovation	Achieve X percent of total premium from new products in next five years.
	Achieve parity with industry leaders on critical success factors (loss cost trends, expenses, computer technology, agent growth) by year Y.
Diversification	Change product mix by X percent by year Y.
	Achieve X percent of company premium from new territories by year Y.
	Increase percentage of premium coming from most profitable states by X percent by year Y.
Satisfaction	Increase satisfaction levels of policyholders or claimants to be equal or better than satisfaction levels of policyholders or claimants of two key competitors by year X.
	Reduce complaints to state insurance departments by a level that ranks our company as one of best three companies in each state we operate in by year Y.

profit is underwriting gain, which is defined as earned premiums less incurred losses and expenses. Other measures of profitability shown in Exhibit 2-12 include additions to policyholders' surplus from current-year operations.

Innovation objectives remind management of the reality that markets and the strategies of key competitors change. Innovation can take the form of new or revised products. It can also refer to improved competitiveness for success factors crucial to the business, such as loss cost trends.

Diversification objectives refer to the product and geographic sources of premium and profitability. Management may want to reduce the risk of adverse results from a major line of insurance by increasing the percentage of premium volume generated by other lines. New or underdeveloped territories may be targeted for substantial growth, or more profitable territories might become the focus for additional support and growth.

Satisfaction objectives focus attention on how well the insurer is meeting the expectations of its existing customers. Claims satisfaction measurements are one way to determine results of the insurer's efforts to satisfy the needs of its policyholders. Reducing complaints to regulatory authorities is another measure of how well an insurer is delivering on its promises to customers.

Marketing objectives may conflict with sales objectives. Sales management and the sales force are often focused on achieving short-term objectives. Their principal objective is to achieve current sales objectives. They may also be motivated by the compensation system to be profitable, have high persistency (renewal of policies), and cross-sell to existing clients. The marketing department, on the other hand, typically looks at objectives from the multi-year perspective of building enduring relationships and consistent patterns of profitable growth.

The marketing and sales perspectives can come into conflict when the pressure for short-term results causes sales behavior inconsistent with long-term direction. For instance, the core lines of business may be uncompetitively priced, so producers sell other lines of business, thus affecting the product mix objectives.

Marketing objectives may also conflict with the objectives of other functions. For instance, growth objectives may be in direct conflict with the underwriting objectives of the insurer. The underwriting department is charged with ensuring that new and renewal business fit a quality profile desired by management. Competitive forces may make it a challenge to achieve growth objectives consistent with the quality portfolio required by the underwriting function.

Marketing objectives may also differ from actuarial objectives. The actuarial department is charged with setting rates that are adequate to cover loss costs and allow for profits and contingencies. There is a constant tension between rate adequacy and rate competitiveness. The marketing function must interact with underwriting, actuarial, and sales personnel to ensure teamwork toward meeting the objectives of the insurer.

Marketing Strategies

Marketing objectives become operational when included in strategies and plans. The objectives in Exhibit 2-12 refer to insurer sales and profitability results to be expected in a competitive environment. The insurer also needs to develop strategies for competitive positioning and growth.

Competitive Positioning

A **competitive positioning strategy** expresses how aggressively management intends to compete. A company can decide on one of four basic competitive marketing strategies: market leader, market challenger, market follower, or market nicher.

The **market leader** strategy is only available to the insurer with the highest market share in the targeted market. The market leader exploits the relationship that often exists between market share and profitability. The leader has more financial resources to focus on developing customer loyalty, which often translates into operational efficiencies. For instance, the market leader in a property-liability insurance market can provide the most agent and claims service locations. With competitive rates and higher levels of advertising, the leader may gain high levels of persistency and a high level of multi-line policyholders. High persistency and multiple policy accounts spread acquisition costs over more customers to reduce expense ratios. Since long-term policyholders typically average fewer claims, loss ratios may be affected as well.

A **market challenger** pursues an offensive strategy in an attempt to become the market leader. This approach focuses on knowing the strengths and weaknesses of the market leader so well that the challenger can attack at points of weakness. The number two or three insurer in automobile or homeowners insurance in a state might aggressively attempt to displace the number-one company, focusing financial and human resources at the point at which the market leader is most vulnerable. For instance, the challenger might outspend the leader on advertising or in compensation for agents or might develop a different type of distribution system from the one used by the leader.

The **market follower** strategy avoids direct comparison with market challengers or market leaders on either a product or a price basis. For an insurer this approach could mean offering only standard insurance contracts at noncompetitive rates.

A **market nicher**, like a market follower, also avoids confrontation with market leaders. A nicher specializes in meeting the needs of a market too small or specialized for market leaders to consider. Insurers that have sponsor or endorser relationships with farm organizations or employers or associations are examples of market nichers.

Growth Strategies

Once management has decided on a competitive positioning strategy, the question becomes how best to meet market growth objectives. The **growth strategy** provides direction for moving the insurer from where it is to where management wants it to be. Growth strategy concentrates on a multi-year time period as opposed to tactical activities, which focus on the current year. Exhibit 2-13 shows four approaches to growth opportunities: market penetration, market development, product development, and diversification.

Exhibit 2-13
Growth Strategies

		Markets	
		Current	**New**
Products	**Current**	**Market Penetration** Increase sales of current products to current markets	**Market Development** Increase sales by taking current products to new markets
	New	**Product Development** Increase sales of current markets by developing new or improved products	**Diversification** Develop new products correlated to current products that could appeal to new markets

Market penetration growth strategy is intended to increase sales of current products to current markets. A national property-liability insurer with a full range of personal lines products might use a market penetration strategy to develop more multi-line customers or to increase the coverage levels and average premium for policies currently in force. The concept is to increase the revenue per customer to amortize fixed overhead over a larger base. The market penetration strategy also applies to the practice of prospecting competitors' policyholders.

A **market development** approach to growth focuses on increasing sales by taking current products into new markets. For example, an automobile club insurance company operating in one major city might increase its personal automobile portfolio through penetration of suburban markets or by opening an operation in another state.

A **product development** approach to growth focuses on increasing sales to current markets by developing related or improved products. This approach can be used to introduce new product features that can be added to existing policies by endorsement. The insurer might also develop different versions of a product, such as a homeowners product for high market-value homes. Or the insurer could develop entirely new products that meet other needs of current markets. For instance, a homeowners and auto insurer might introduce a policy to cover boats owned by policyholders.

Still another way for a company to grow is through **diversification**. This approach to growth should be followed when the existing business is mature and foresees limited future growth. As one example of diversification, an insurer might develop a line of mutual funds or deferred compensation variable annuities, which its distribution system could market and its investment office could manage. Also, a property-liability insurer might develop unbundled services, such as third-party administration or administrative services for self-insurers. Or an insurer might market to other insurers expert system software of other computer systems that were developed internally.

Marketing Plans

The marketing objectives, along with competitive and growth strategies, form the basis for the development of marketing plans. The marketing plan summarizes the objectives, strategies, and tactics to be used in gaining and maintaining the competitive position and results sought by management in that market. The overall plan can be subdivided by product line, specific product, operating territory, or even by key customer type. An effective marketing plan contains a situation analysis, objectives, a strategy statement, action programs, budgets, and controls.[8] The objectives and strategy statements for each market are intended to support insurer objectives and strategy while responding to specific market conditions.

Situation Analysis

A **situation analysis** begins with a background section summarizing recent operating results for the product or product line. Such a summary is followed by a review of the facts and trends relative to customers, distribution channels, and competitors. The background section may also include results of buyer behavior studies.

The background is followed by the normal forecast. The forecast shows expected premium levels assuming no major changes in the external environment or in the insurer's marketing efforts. Some insurers forecast premium levels based on rates of change experienced by the insurer in the past. Other insurers develop alternative scenarios using a combination of their results and economic forecasts.

The situation analysis also includes statements of opportunities and threats. This exercise requires management to list and explain the major external forces affecting the insurers. Management can review these assumptions after the plan has been implemented to determine which opportunities and threats came to pass and what responses were taken.

A final component of the situation analysis is a list of strengths and weaknesses. The weaknesses should be harshly realistic, and the strengths should be confirmed by industry experts. Strategies should be developed based on strengths. Weaknesses may be subject to action programs to make the insurer more competitive in selected markets.

Objectives

The marketing objectives defined for the coming period must be included in the marketing plan. As an example, the marketing plan of a regional property-liability insurer might include objectives such as the following:

- Expand premium volume at a rate of 20 percent greater than the growth rate of the total insurance premiums in the region for relevant product lines.

- Reduce concentration of portfolio of one line from 60 percent to 55 percent by emphasizing another line, which will grow from 10 percent of premium to 15 percent.

- Reduce expense ratio from present level to average expense ratio of three key competitors within three years.

- Provide agency office automation capability to 50 percent of the producer force within three years.

These objectives would be referenced in the strategy statement and action programs for the company.

Strategy Statement

The four objectives in the example above could be reached in various ways, including acquisition, internal investment in computer software, development of new markets, increased emphasis on cross-selling, and so on. The strategy is a result of careful study of alternative approaches to achieving the objectives. The strategy statement should be both clear and brief. For example, the four objectives might lead to a strategy statement like this one:

> Our basic strategy for achieving our objectives will include expansion of our agency force in our existing operating territory and the opening of a new regional operation in the western zone. We will introduce a new homeowners product to increase our penetration in the upscale homeowners market. We will increase our premium volume from agents in the Quality Agents Program through increased incentives and full support of agency office automation for these agents. Our expense management programs will keep

home office expenses at a level equal to last year. We will convert personal lines auto underwriting to a fully automated system effective mid-year.

This strategic statement is an example of a "word picture" that conveys how the objectives will be reached. The statement should be evaluated and refined by a process intended to build full commitment on the part of management at all levels.

Action Programs

Action programs answer the question, "How do we get there?" The **action programs** show the steps by which strategies will be implemented to reach the objectives. The typical action program includes such specifics as "how to," "by whom," "by when," "with what help," "at what cost," and "with what priority." For the sample strategic statement there would be an action program or programs for each objective. For instance, the introduction of a new homeowners policy for the upscale market would have an action program detailing the steps involved, the accountable staff, timing, and cost.

Budgets

The activities spelled out in the action programs must be budgeted. Depending on how an insurer is organized and how it develops its marketing and sales budgets, any or all of the following expense categories may be budgeted under marketing:

- Consumer research
- Advertising and promotional expenses
- Marketing information gathering and analysis
- Agent recruitment selection and training
- Sales management recruitment, selection, and training
- Agent awards and recognition conferences
- Product development
- Sales results reports

These expense categories are only examples. An insurer may, for instance, place all product development functions and tasks within the underwriting department. Alternatively, sales administration expenses may be budgeted within the operating territories.

Marketing Plan Control Systems

Marketing plan control systems serve as a base against which to compare actual results with planned results. Control systems are developed at four levels: annual plan control, profitability control, efficiency control, and strategic control.

Annual plan control focuses on sales analysis, market share analysis, sales expense ratio, and so on, to determine whether sales activity is producing desired results. Such information is needed to guide sales management efforts to achieve sales objectives.

Profitability control shows the contribution to overhead made by product, territory, customer type, distribution channel, and so on. The purpose is to determine where the insurer is making and losing money.

Efficiency control measures the cost benefit of changes in expenses for marketing so that spending decisions can be made. Efficiency controls consider the results of advertising, promotion, agent recruitment, and development efforts. This type of information serves as input into the next cycle of planning.

Strategic control evaluates the fit between the insurer and its marketing environment. The **marketing audit** is a systematic, comprehensive, independent, and periodic examination of the marketing environment, objectives, strategies, and activities.[9] It is a tool used for strategic control and determines problem areas and opportunities so that action can be taken to improve marketing performance.

In preparing a marketing audit, the auditor asks about fifty to seventy-five questions relating to the insurer's products, organization, marketing environment, customers, distribution system, competitors, marketing strategies, plans, information, and control. The questions are administered to senior management, key customers, producers, and industry experts to determine how well the insurer is doing in executing its marketing program. Typical questions include "What are the major market segments?" "What are the projected rates of growth?", and "Does the advertising program have clear objectives and sufficient resources to accomplish the objectives?"

Answers to the marketing audit questions help management review the effectiveness of the marketing function. Recommendations help management to fine-tune the market plan to keep it focused on supporting the company mission, marketing objectives, and market strategy.

Marketing Functions

Many different departments usually conduct the marketing functions in an insurance company. Perhaps because of tradition or a concern over unbounded product marketing, insurer underwriting departments have exercised control over marketing efforts. Even when separate marketing departments exist, many of the marketing functions are handled by underwriting, actuarial, or other departmental units. Because of the diversity in which insurers are organized to conduct this activity, this section describes marketing as though it were conducted in a single departmental area within the insurer. Exhibit 2-14 shows the marketing functions in which an insurer might be engaged.

Marketing Research

The **marketing research** function performs research to develop information and recommendations on marketing issues. The research may consist of qualitative studies (focus groups, mystery shopper studies, and the like) and quantitative studies using survey research techniques and statistical analysis of data included in corporate databases. The research function might also test concepts such as agent and customer survey panels, telemarketing, prospecting sources, and so on, to determine whether the concept is worthy of prototype development and pilot testing on a larger scale.

Marketing research is typically done on a project basis with a stated objective, research design, data collection, analysis, and formal report. Effective marketing research includes conclusions and implications or recommendations. Ideally, cost-benefit measures are used to track the value of information developed from the various studies. For instance, management may want to know why policies lapse or are terminated by policyholders as an input into conservation programming. Decisions based in part on the research input are then implemented and evaluated on a cost-benefit basis.

The research staff conducts consumer research studies and thus must understand insurance purchase and ownership behavior and must keep informed of how and why insurance consumers make the choices they do. An example of consumer research studies is shown in Exhibit 2-15, which depicts a model of the factors that influence consumer behavior and the steps consumers go through in making decisions. The first column in Exhibit 2-15 shows the outside factors influencing consumer behavior, including the actions taken by insurers in making policies available and affordable and making consumers aware of the company and its services. The model also shows the personal factors influencing behavior: the personal and psychological makeup of the person making the purchase decision. The model includes the predictable steps in the problem-solving process, beginning with problem recognition and ending with post-purchase behavior to evaluate the purchase decision. The fourth column in Exhibit 2-15 shows the possible results of the consumer purchase process.

Exhibit 2-14

Functions of the Home Office Marketing Department in a Property-Liability Insurance Company

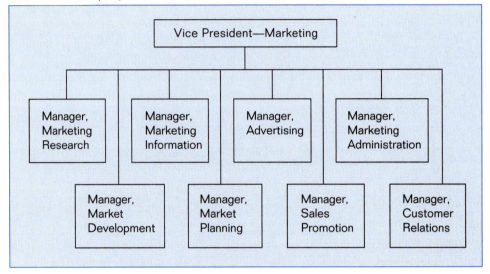

Some commercial insurers use comprehensive databases to identify potential markets. The databases employ data obtained from various bureaus and state agencies that are then cross-referenced to the U.S. Government's Standard Industrial Classification (SIC) coding system. By combining this information with census data, premium and loss data can be organized by ZIP Code. This information can be used to segment the market into geographic areas.

U.S. Government data identify large urban areas as Metropolitan Statistical Areas (MSAs), which can be stratified from large to small and dissected by industry category. With this information, an insurer can identify those areas with a significant market size for the insurer's products and profit potential.

Market Development

The **market development function** provides leadership when management wants to enter a new market. The new market may be a new territory, a new customer type, or a new product. Other examples of major projects managed might include new approaches to (1) selling the insurer's products, (2) delivering superior service in the claims adjustment process, (3) billing premium renewals, or (4) delivering electronic applications for insurance policies.

The market development staff consists of project management specialists. A market development project manager is an expert in creativity exercises to generate and screen ideas. The project manager is also skilled in developing

Exhibit 2-15
Model of Consumer Behavior

External Influences		Buyer Characteristics	Buyer Decision Process	Buyer's Decisions
Marketers	**Others**			
• Product	• Economic	• Personal	• Problem recognition	• Product choice
• Price	• Technological	Age		
• Distribution sales force	• Political	Life cycle stage	• Information services	• Brand choice
• Promotion	• Cultural Sub-cultural Social class	Occupation Economic circum- stances	• Evaluation of alternatives	• Dealer choice
• Advertising				• When to buy
• Public relations	• Social reference groups Family Roles Statuses	Lifestyle Personality Self-concept	• Purchase decision	• Where to buy
• Sales promotion		• Psychological Motivation Perception Learning Beliefs Attitudes Values	• Post-purchas- ing behavior	• How much to buy

project scope documents, decision grids, task outlines, progress reports, and project reports. The project manager usually handles only one or two projects at a time because of the high level of effort and responsibility involved in each project.

Marketing Information

The **marketing information function** develops and maintains information needed in market planning to support management at all levels in answering specific questions concerning markets, customers, producers, and competitors. The marketing information function serves the company best when it can deliver in a timely and cost-effective manner information essential to decision making.

The marketing information function is ordinarily responsible for maintaining two major types of marketing information systems: internal accounting and market monitor. The internal accounting system provides report and analysis capability based on transactions associated with sales activity. Much of the essential information on production, retention, and policies in force is available as a byproduct of the systems that keep track of commissions and billings.

The **market monitor system** provides intelligence about the external environment to keep in touch with important developments and changing conditions. The market monitor should provide current, unfiltered, and unbiased information to senior management about customers, producers, and competitors. Customers are monitored to determine their satisfaction levels with the service they receive from the insurer. The customer monitor should include samples of new customers, those who have left, those who renew their policies, and those who have had a claim. Such studies are done in a systematic, periodic way. They provide senior management with key information that helps shape decisions related to growth and profitability objectives.

The market monitor also provides information about producer satisfaction with services provided by the insurer. The monitor helps determine which producers are placing business with the insurer, how, how much, and why.

The market monitor maintains up-to-date competitive intelligence about the strategies and actions of key competitors. Competitor monitoring also includes benchmark studies of competitors who excel on success factors crucial to a property-liability insurer. Benchmark information helps management to develop strategies for closing the gap between company performance and that of key competition. For instance, competitor monitoring may show that a key competitor has lower-than-average loss cost trends for automobile injury claims. The insurer might discover why and then take action to lessen the gap.

Marketing Planning

The **market planning function** provides the planning tools and facilitation skills to assist operating management in developing fact-based marketing plans. This functional area also assists senior management for the company and for each strategic business unit in developing and updating strategic plans for the company. The market planning function may also be charged with maintaining progress reports on the implementation of marketing objectives, strategies, and market plans.

Advertising

The **advertising function** is responsible for managing the company's communications through mass media with its chosen target markets. The advertising program is developed to be consistent with strategic direction and marketing plans and supportive of distribution system efforts. Advertising is intended to build and reinforce the company's image as an acceptable choice in the minds of target customers. The advertising function may also develop programs to share the cost of advertising done by the company's distribution system. Many insurers, for instance, pay the cost of the yellow-page advertisements that promote their local producers.

Sales Promotion

The **sales promotion function** supports the efforts of the distribution system to get and keep customers. Sales promotion is intended to reinforce the image and positioning created by the insurer's advertising efforts when carried down to the agency level. Sales promotion includes brochures used in the sales process, giveaway items promoting the insurer and the agent, awards merchandise, and the like. Regular communications with producers and sales management, such as newsletters, may be part of the sales promotion function.

Marketing Administration

The **marketing administration function** manages budgets and reports on activities included in the scope of the marketing department. This department serves the controllership role for the marketing units to help control costs and to assess the costs and benefits of various marketing activities.

Customer Relations

The **customer relations function** manages communications with individual customers from the home office. This functional area ensures that all written communications seen by customers are understandable and consistent in quality and tone. The customer relations function also provides a forum for communications to the insurer initiated by customers, including complaints, suggestions, and questions. Insurers are often asked to respond to state insurance departments, which themselves are responding to consumer complaints about the insurer. Typically, the complaint is addressed to the insurer's CEO and must be addressed within a specified period, often ten working days. The customer relations function provides management with low-cost, high-value information about the evolving wants and needs of policyholders.

Staffing the Marketing Functions

The marketing function is most typically staffed by company employees who were hired into the company in operations or sales. As the marketing function evolves, the tendency is to hire specialists with education and work experience relevant to the marketing function.

Functional Interdependencies

Insurers following the market concept focus all of their resources on meeting the needs of policyholders. To complete this mission, all of the functional departments must act in harmony to ensure the consumer's satisfaction.

Customer satisfaction depends on several factors, and if one function fails, if policies are processed slowly or premium billing is mishandled, then the marketing effort spent securing that policyholder is wasted.

Other than the marketing department, the four functional areas most likely to have direct contact with the insured are underwriting, loss control, premium audit, and claims.

Marketing and Underwriting

Much of an insurer's success can be linked to the degree of cooperation between the marketing and underwriting departments. Unfortunately, these two departments have a natural tendency to work at cross-purposes. Marketing typically uses a measure such as growth in premium volume to determine success. Underwriting, on the other hand, concentrates on the loss ratio to evaluate effectiveness. Neither an ultraconservative underwriting policy nor a marketing strategy of being the lowest-cost provider of broadly written policies will be effective for the insurer in the long term. Marketing and underwriting must adopt a common strategy in order to avoid sending conflicting messages to producers.

Experienced marketing personnel develop an appreciation of the factors that affect the local insurance marketplace. New products and pricing programs and commission changes are frequently presented to marketing personnel to gauge the reaction of producers. Marketing personnel are often the first to be alerted when there are problems with a product, such as an ambiguity in eligibility. Changes in competitors' products or new competitors are usually discovered by the marketing personnel in conversations with producers. In these instances, the marketing department serves as a communications link between the sales force and the underwriting department.

The communication process may benefit the marketing department as well. Underwriters may receive a number of new applications that do not meet the insurer's underwriting requirements. The underwriting department may call on the marketing department to initiate visits with these producers or have them revise the promotional materials to reflect underwriting eligibility more accurately.

Marketing and Loss Control

Insurance programs tailored to a particular market segment, such as convenience stores, churches, or morticians, require in-depth knowledge of the hazards involved. Trade and industry associations can assist the marketing department in determining the specific features that would attract a particular type of business, and loss control personnel can provide information to help ensure adequate pricing and to determine what underwriting restrictions should apply.

Loss control personnel can alert marketing to fundamental changes in the class of business that may affect the overall profitability of the program. New exposures or exposures not anticipated by the program's original design may create adverse results. Identifying these exposures can alert the marketing department to coverage features that should be included in its redesign.

Marketing and Premium Audit

Like loss control personnel, premium audit personnel can provide valuable information to the marketing department on current business. Premium auditors' direct contact with policyholders affords them a knowledge of individual policyholders and an appreciation of the characteristics of the typical policyholder in that class. Abnormalities are typically communicated to the underwriting department, but in some instances information about an individual policyholder or class of policyholders is appropriate for the marketing department. The marketing department of one insurer uses a company-agency newsletter to remind producers of the problem of uncollectible premium audits and how to avoid them.

Marketing and Claims

Claims personnel play a key role in new product design by helping to anticipate the type of losses that will be paid under the proposed coverage. After a new product has been introduced, the claims department can provide the marketing department with information on the types of losses being presented. Additionally, the claims department can make the marketing department aware of any adverse trends or opportunities to broaden coverage.

Special Constraints on Property-Liability Insurance Marketing

Every market has unique characteristics that require serious attention in meeting marketing objectives. Generally the property-liability insurance market features a mature product that is intangible but service-intensive. Moreover, most consumers have low involvement in the purchase and use decisions related to the insurance product. Finally, insurance is regulated at the state level, which places constraints on the flexibility of the insurer's marketing strategies and plans.

The intangible nature of the insurance product means that to customers, the service rendered is inseparable from the person who delivered it. Thus, satisfaction ratings for an agency depend heavily on the quality of service provided by the staff within the agency. Customers evaluate service quality based on the professionalism, friendliness, and efficiency of the staff member providing the service.

As an example of the challenges imposed by service intensity, consider the owner of an automobile. The owner may, over one year, change cars, drivers, driving usages, coverages, limits, deductibles, and the like. Each change is a "moment of truth" for the agency and insurer providing the insurance coverage to that owner. In addition, should the insured have a claim, additional services are required to document, adjust, and close the claim. The insured has every reason to expect timely, accurate, friendly, and fair treatment in each moment of truth.

Property-liability insurance is an example of a "low-involvement" product. Such products are characterized by a limited amount of time and effort devoted to shopping behavior. Research by the Insurance Research Council on patterns of shopping behavior for automobile insurance, for instance, shows that less than 30 percent of car owners actively shop for auto insurance in a given year. Of those who do shop, less than 27 percent spend more than two hours in the search process.[10] The fact that insurance is, for many people, a low-involvement product makes it difficult for an insurer to get the attention of the insurance decision maker in a cost-effective manner.

Property-liability insurance is regulated at the state level. This means that insurers operating in more than one state must recognize the legislative, regulatory, and judicial differences in each state. Each state has a distinct set of competitors as well. Changes in the regulatory environment directly affect the results and strategies of all competitors within the state. The fact that insurance is regulated somewhat differently in each state requires insurers to develop separate market strategies for each state in which the insurer operates.

Marketing strategies must reflect the unique characteristics of each state created by individual state regulatory agencies. One state promulgates "standard contracts" for insurer use. Any product innovation must be as liberal as the state-approved contract. Some states mandate personal auto insurers to offer coverage to all who want it. Many states severely limit the number of rate level changes; some states even limit insurers to one rate level adjustment per line of business a year. A realistic marketing strategy recognizes the individual state limitations and prepares for them. A new product or pricing plan would be best introduced in a jurisdiction that permits flexibility so that its features can be fine-tuned.

Each state has its own unique mix of regulations and legal precedents. Additionally, the political environment in the state may affect market strategies. State regulators serve as public watch dogs of the insurance industry. In some jurisdictions, the scrutiny under which insurers are held impedes the operation of a competitive market.

Summary

Marketing is the function charged with the task of developing strategies and plans to get and keep customers. This chapter has described the property-liability insurance market and the products and services offered by insurers to meet the insurance needs of individuals, families, and businesses.

The role of marketing is to research the insurance wants and needs of consumers and business owners; to plan to identify attractive markets; and then to develop distribution, communications, pricing, and service programs to serve the chosen markets. The chapter reviewed the key decisions faced by management in a property-liability insurer in fulfilling marketing's role. Those decisions are represented by the following questions: "Whom to serve?" "What products and services?" "With what distribution?" "At what price?" "With what communications?" "At what levels of customer service?"

Marketing objectives include profitability, growth, diversification, innovation, and customer satisfaction. These objectives may be in conflict with the objectives of other departments.

The marketing objectives become operational when developed into strategies and plans. The insurer needs to decide whether it wishes to be a market leader, market challenger, market follower, or market nicher. Then it needs to adopt a strategy for growth, using either market penetration, market development, product development, or market/product diversification approaches.

Marketing plans translate the objectives and strategies into actions for each market. A marketing plan includes a situation analysis, objectives, a strategy statement, action plans, budgets, and controls.

To be effective in the marketplace, all of the insurer's functional departments must coordinate their efforts. Because of the significant amount of interaction, the marketing department must communicate and cooperate with underwriting, loss control, premium audit, and claims personnel.

The marketing function is constrained in property-liability insurance because the product is mature, intangible, and service-intensive. The product is one about which most buyers have little knowledge or interest. And the industry is regulated at the state level, which requires different market plans for each state and for each product offered in the state. Each plan must recognize each state's unique characteristics, which are created by the existing regulatory and social environment.

Chapter Notes

1. Peter F. Drucker, *The Practice of Management* (New York, NY: Harper and Row, 1954), p. 37.

2. *The Fact Book 1997: Property Casualty Insurance Facts* (New York, NY: Insurance Information Institute, 1997), p. 10.

3. *The Fact Book 1997: Property Casualty Insurance Facts* (New York, NY: Insurance Information Institute, 1997), p. 11.

4. *The Fact Book 1997: Property Casualty Insurance Facts* (New York, NY: Insurance Information Institute, 1997), pp. 14-15.

5. Theodore Levitt, *The Marketing Imagination* (New York, NY: The Free Press, 1983), p. 96.

6. Philip Kotler, *Marketing Management: Analysis, Planning and Control*, 5th ed. (Englewood Cliffs, NJ: Prentice Hall, Inc., 1984), p. 4.

7. Philip Kotler, p. 4.

8. David S. Hopkins, *The Marketing Plan* (New York, NY: The Conference Board, Inc., 1981), pp. 16-27. Also see *The Market Plan in the 1990s, Conference Board Report 951* (New York, NY: The Conference Board, Inc., 1990), pp. 7-21.

9. Philip Kotler and Richard S. Lopata, "The Marketing Audit" in Steuart Henderson Britt and Normal F. Guess, eds., *Marketing Manager's Handbook*, 2d rev. ed. (Chicago, IL: Dartwell Corporation, 1983), pp. 1239-1250.

10. *Patterns of Shopping Behavior in Auto Insurance* (Oakbrook, IL: All-Industry Research Advisory Council), January 1985, pp. 11, 24.

Chapter 3

Distribution Systems

Any firm that sells a product must have a distribution system to carry out some of the marketing functions outlined in Chapter 2. The functions of the distribution system depend on the nature of the product sold and the buyers to whom it is sold. The system might be very complex or very simple, again based on the nature of the product and the needs of the buyers and prospective buyers.

This chapter focuses on the insurance market intermediaries that deliver the insurance product to insurance consumers through various distribution systems. The phrase *insurance consumers* is used here in its broadest sense to encompass all buyers of insurance, including individuals, families, businesses, government bodies, and others. There are, in fact, several insurance distribution systems, each designed to meet the needs of a select group of insurers and insurance consumers.

Insurance Market Intermediaries

A **distribution system** consists of the necessary people and physical facilities to (1) communicate information between the seller of the product and buyers or potential buyers and (2) move the product between the seller and the buyers. For tangible products, such as automobiles or refrigerators, the distribution system might include extensive and expensive physical facilities, such as trucks, terminals, warehouses, and showrooms. Distribution systems for intangible products, such as the insurance product, are more flexible and adaptable because they are not constrained by large investments in physical facilities.

Since insurance is a business that offers an intangible product, it gives the insurance market special qualities. Understanding these qualities requires a knowledge of the market intermediaries' activities. Representing others in the insurance relationship requires an understanding of the principles of agency.

Unique Characteristics of Insurance Marketing

The marketing of insurance differs substantially from the marketing of other products, especially the distribution of tangible products. The distribution of tangible products usually involves several levels of distribution between the manufacturer and the ultimate consumer. For example, a distributor might buy the product from the manufacturer and sell it to a wholesaler. The wholesaler sells it to a retailer, who in turn sells it to consumers.

Insurance is less involved. In most cases, only one intermediary is between the insurer and the consumer. In some cases there are two, but seldom more than two. Often there are none, with the insurer selling directly to the consumer. The levels of intermediaries are discussed in more detail later in this chapter.

Intermediaries in insurance marketing perform several functions. Their principal function is selling. Some kinds of insurance are compulsory, required either by law or by various contractual relationships. For example, workers compensation and auto liability insurance are required by law in most states. Auto physical damage is required by lenders if the car is financed, and homeowners or dwelling insurance is required by mortgage agreements. For these types of required insurance, the principal role of the intermediary is to assist consumers in selecting an insurer and to explain specific details of policies.

Many kinds of insurance are purchased solely at the option of the consumer. For these lines, the intermediary must assist the consumer in determining the coverages needed as well as in selecting an insurer.

Some of the intermediaries might issue policies and collect premiums, though insurers often perform these functions. Many intermediaries adjust claims, most often relatively small property insurance claims.

Legal Status of Agents

Most insurers are corporations. As such, they can operate only through agents. An **agent** can be defined as a person or firm authorized to represent another person or firm in the performance of some function. The person or firm represented by an agent is called the **principal**. At law, an agent may be either an employee of the principal or an independent contractor. Within the insurance industry, the term agent is sometimes reserved for independent contractors who represent insurers. The term **broker** is applied to independent contractors who represent policyholders and prospective policyholders in their dealings with insurers.

Another term frequently used in insurance marketing is **producer**, which refers to a person who sells insurance to consumers. It includes brokers, agents of the insurer, employees of insurance companies or of intermediaries, and independent contractors.

Powers and Duties of Agents

An agent has only the powers conferred by the principal. When an insurer appoints an agent, a written contract is usually executed. The contract usually specifies the powers and duties of the agent. The powers granted usually include the lines of insurance to be written, the agent's authority to bind coverages, claims adjustment authority of the agent, and similar matters. The duties deal with accounting for policies and other supplies furnished by the insurer, accounting for insurer funds in the hands of the agent, adherence to rules adopted by the insurer, and so forth.

The law recognizes certain **apparent authority** of an insurance agent. This apparent authority is a concern only when the agent is dealing with a buyer or prospective insurance buyer who has no knowledge of the agent's **actual authority**, authority conferred by the principal under the agency contract. For example, a property-liability insurance agent has apparent authority to bind coverage in most states. Thus, an agent can bind coverage even if the agency contract does not specifically mention such action.

Although insurance agents primarily represent insurers, the law imposes on them certain duties to insurance consumers as well. The extent of these duties depends on the relationship established between the agent and the insurance consumer. If the agent merely agrees to provide one or more specific insurance policies to the policyholder, he or she has only two duties to the client: (1) to provide the agreed policies and (2) to place the agreed policies with a solvent insurer. If the policies are placed with an insurer licensed in the state where the insured exposures are located, it is usually sufficient if the agent has no knowledge of any information to indicate that it is financially impaired. If insurance is placed with an insurer not licensed in the state, the agent might have a duty to exercise greater care regarding the insurer's financial status.

The liability outlined above is the minimum liability imposed on agents. An agent's liability can be expanded substantially through his or her actions or by specific contract. For example, if an agent undertakes to provide risk management advice to a policyholder, the agent might be held liable for overlooking loss exposures. For example, one agent was held liable for failing to advise a client of the need for fire legal liability insurance for a leased building.

Attributes of Insurance Intermediaries

All property-liability insurance agents, whether company employees or independent contractors, share certain powers and duties. Beyond these shared powers and duties, agents differ greatly in their relationships with insurers and consumers. The principal differences are in (1) their relationship to the insurers with which they do business, (2) how they are compensated for their services, and (3) the degree of control they have over contacts between the insurers they represent and the clients for whom they write coverages, usually referred to as "ownership of expirations."

Relationship With Insurers

The agent's contractual ties to insurers determine the amount of control the insurers can exercise over the agent. Viewed from the opposite perspective, the agency contract determines the extent of the agent's independence from the insurer or insurers represented. Generally, an insurer does exercise greater control over agents who are company employees than it can over independent contractors. In fact, this greater control is one of the characteristics that distinguish employees from independent contractors when a legal distinction must be made. As a general rule, if an agent is an independent contractor, the insurer cannot control the methods the agent uses to accomplish the purposes of the agency. The agent is free to use any legal and ethical methods to accomplish the purposes set forth in the agency contract. For an employee, on the other hand, the employer can control the method, and not merely the goals and objectives of the agency arrangement.

Some insurers specify in their agency contracts that their agents cannot represent other insurers. Thus, those agents are restricted to representing only one insurer or a group of insurers under common ownership and management, even though the agents are independent contractors. Other agents are not subject to such contractual restrictions and may represent as many insurers as they wish, or at least as many insurers as are willing to enter into agency contracts with them.

Some insurers take an intermediate stance between these extremes. For example, an insurance company might permit its agents to represent other insurers provided the other insurers are used only to write business that the company does not want to write.

The level of independence of the agent is an important consideration in distinguishing among the several distribution systems used in marketing property-liability insurance.

Compensation Methods

The way an agent is compensated is another characteristic of insurance distribution systems. The method of compensation tends to vary with the closeness of the agent's relationships to the insurers represented. Agents who represent several unrelated insurers are usually compensated by a commission on the premiums they write.

Agents who are employees of the insurer might be compensated by salary or by a combination of salary and commissions. Agents who are independent contractors but who are restricted to representing one insurer are usually compensated by commissions. However, some insurers might provide a guaranteed minimum income to such agents during a training period.

Agents who are compensated by commissions might receive two kinds of commissions. A flat commission, stated as a fixed percentage of premiums, constitutes the principal source of compensation for such agents. The commission percentage can vary by line of insurance. The commission rate might differ for new business and renewal business. When the rates are different, a lower commission is usually paid for renewal business, reflecting the lesser effort required of the agent for renewal business.

In addition to the flat commission, agents may receive a variable commission, sometimes called a **contingent commission, bonus commission,** or **profit-sharing commission**. The amount of the variable commission usually depends on the loss ratio of the business written by the agent. Sometimes, the variable commission also depends on the increase in the agent's premium volume with the insurer. Thus, variable commissions can be used to motivate agents to write preferred risks, to write more business, or to do both.

Sometimes insurers authorize agents to appoint and supervise subagents. The supervising agent then receives a commission on all business written by the subagents. This commission, called an **override** (sometimes overwrite) commission, is usually smaller than the commission paid to the subagents who originate the business. The various commission arrangements are discussed in greater detail later in this chapter.

Ownership of Expirations

Historically, insurers and agents have disagreed as to which of them owns the expirations for policies sold by the agent. Ownership of expirations means ownership of all records showing when existing policies expire, but it also means much more. If the agent owns the expirations, the insurer cannot try to renew the policies, either directly or through another agent. Moreover, ownership of expirations means that the insurer cannot take those policies away or transfer them to another agent.

To illustrate the significance of the ownership of expirations, assume that an agency has been an agent of an insurer for many years. The agency contract specifies that the agency owns the expirations. The agency terminates its agency contract with the company and, on renewal, rewrites all of its policies with another insurer. The original insurance company is powerless to prevent the transfer of the business to another insurer. Since the agency owns the expirations, the insurer is prohibited from soliciting the business either directly or through another of its agents.

Ownership of the expirations is important to both agents and insurers. Ownership of expirations provides agents with an important asset with a substantial market value. Ownership of expirations gives insurers greater control over their business, since their agents cannot move the business to another insurer either on termination of the agency contract or while the agency contract continues in force.

Of course, ownership of expirations controls only the conduct of the specific insurer and its agents. Ultimate ownership of expirations rests with the policyholders. They can move their business among insurers and agents as they see fit.

The ownership of expirations is usually specified in agency contracts, though some classes of agents may have ownership of expirations as a matter of law in the absence of a contractual provision to the contrary. Practices regarding ownership of expirations vary widely among the various insurance marketing systems. These practices are discussed in greater detail later in this chapter.

Types of Insurance Distribution Systems

Four main distribution systems are employed by property-liability insurers in the United States: (1) the independent agency system, (2) the exclusive agency system, (3) the direct writer system, and (4) the direct response system. The principal characteristics that distinguish one distribution system from another include (1) the extent to which the agent is tied to the insurers represented, (2) the methods of compensating the agents, and (3) the ownership of expirations.

Independent Agency System

The **independent agency system** uses agents that are independent contractors. They are usually free to represent as many insurers as they want. Independent agents own the expirations and can switch business among the insurers they represent, subject only to the policyholder's approval.

Insurance brokers represent policyholders rather than insurers, but they are included within the independent agency system. One reason for including them in the independent agency system is that the same person can act as an agent on one transaction and as a broker on another. A person must act as an agent when placing business with an insurer for which he or she is licensed as an agent but may act as a broker when placing business with other insurers. Generally, insurance brokers are legally agents for the insured; they are not granted binding authority. The client base for the large broker is very different from that served by most independent agents in terms of sophistication and services required. Finally, compensation schemes may be different for independent agents and brokers. Brokers perform some or all of their services on a fee basis, while independent agents are compensated almost exclusively by commission.

Managing general agents (MGAs) are also included within the independent agency system. MGAs serve as intermediaries between insurers and agents who sell insurance directly to the consumer, in much the same position as wholesalers in the distribution system for tangible goods. The exact duties and responsibilities of an MGA depend on its contracts with the insurers it represents. Some MGAs are strictly sales operations, appointing and supervising subagents or dealing with brokers within their contractual jurisdiction. That jurisdiction can be specified in terms of geographic boundaries, lines of insurance, or both.

Excess and surplus lines brokers resemble MGAs in that they usually do business primarily with other brokers and agents and not directly with consumers. In fact, some firms operate as both managing general agents and surplus lines brokers.

Excess and surplus lines brokers place business with insurers not licensed in the state in which the transaction occurs. Other brokers and agents are usually limited to placing business with licensed (or admitted) insurers. The circumstances under which business can be placed with an unlicensed (or nonadmitted) insurer through a surplus lines broker vary by state. A reasonable effort to place the coverage with licensed insurers is frequently required. The agent or broker may be required to certify that a specified number (often two or three) of licensed insurers have refused to provide the coverage or to provide letters from the insurers rejecting the coverage. Some state insurance departments maintain lists of coverages eligible for surplus lines treatment without first being rejected by licensed insurers. Some states also maintain lists of eligible surplus lines insurers.

The variety of participants operating within the independent agency system makes it a very flexible distribution system, able to cope with the requirements of a wide variety of insurance consumers. Its flexibility is a great advantage in competing for complex commercial lines business, for which substantial expertise and flexibility are needed. The independent agency system is typically more expensive to operate than other systems. Its cost is a handicap in competing for personal lines business, for which price is often more important than expertise or flexibility from the perspective of the consumer.

The agents and brokers that operate within the independent agency system are compensated by commissions on the business they write. Many of them receive two types of commissions: (1) a flat percentage commission on all business submitted and (2) a contingent or profit-sharing commission earned through volume or by meeting profit goals.

Exhibit 3-1 shows the average percentage commissions rates received by independent agencies of various sizes as reported in one survey. The commission scales shown are the average for all reporting agencies in each size group. These averages mask significant variations in rates from one agency to another. Commission rates also vary by line of insurance.

Exhibit 3-1
Commission Rates by Size of Agency, 1995

Average Agency Property-Liability Premium Volume	Percentage Personal Lines	Commission Rates Commercial Lines
$ 400,000	14.0%	13.8%
850,000	13.8	14.3
1,250,000	14.9	13.3
1,750,000	13.1	12.8
2,500,000	13.9	13.4
3,500,000	14.6	13.0
5,500,000	14.5	12.0
14,000,000	14.4	10.9

Adapted from Thomas A. McCoy, ed., *What It Costs*, 1996 edition (Carmel, IN: The Rough Notes Company, Inc., 1996), pp. 8-22.

Exhibit 3-2 shows an illustrative contingent commission scale. The contingent commissions shown in Exhibit 3-2 vary only with the agency's loss ratio. Some companies use scales that vary with the amount of business the agency writes with the company as well as the agency's loss ratio. Exhibit 3-3 shows such a commission scale.

Managing general agencies are usually compensated by an override commission on business sold by their subagents. They might also receive a contingent commission based on the profitability, and possibly the volume, of business they write.

Exhibit 3-2
Profit-Sharing Commission Based on Loss Ratio

Loss Ratio	Profit Sharing Commission as Percentage of Earned Premiums
0.00	14.00%
0.05	12.05
0.10	10.35
0.15	8.65
0.20	7.15
0.25	5.65
0.30	4.50
0.35	3.30
0.40	2.25
0.45	1.30
0.50	0.60
0.55	0.00

Independent agents and brokers own the expirations for the business they write. This ownership is usually clearly stated in the agency contract. However, the ownership exists as a matter of custom and law even in the absence of a contractual provision. The expirations usually constitute the largest and most marketable asset of an insurance agency.

Although independent agents are primarily the sales force of the insurers they represent, they might offer several other services to their clients. Many independent agents adjust some losses under the policies they write. This service might be limited to small property losses, but some agents also adjust small liability claims. Empowering the agent to provide loss adjustment services is advanta-

Exhibit 3-3

Percentage Increase in Profit-Sharing Commission Based on Premium Volume and Growth Rate

| Earned Premiums | Percentage Growth in Premium Volume | | | | | |
	10%	15%	20%	30%	40%	60%
$ 50,000	3.50%	7.00%	10.50%	17.50%	24.50%	38.50%
75,000	4.69	8.50	12.31	19.94	27.56	42.81
100,000	5.87	10.00	14.12	22.38	30.62	47.12
150,000	8.25	13.00	17.75	27.25	36.75	55.75
200,000	10.62	16.00	21.37	28.37	42.87	64.38
250,000	13.00	19.00	25.00	37.00	49.00	73.00
400,000	20.12	28.00	35.87	51.62	67.37	98.87
500,000	24.87	34.00	43.12	61.37	79.62	100.00

geous to both policyholders and the insurance company. The principal advantage to policyholders is rapid service; the insurance company benefits from lower adjustment expenses and possibly greater customer goodwill.

Independent agents and brokers might also provide risk management advice to their clients, helping them to select the insurance coverages needed and assisting them in obtaining the needed coverage on the most advantageous terms. Many agents and brokers also assist their clients in the establishment and management of self-insurance programs, loss control measures, and other alternatives or supplements to insurance.

Exclusive Agency System

The **exclusive agency system** uses independent contractors called exclusive agents (or captive agents) who are not employees of the insurance company. Unlike independent agents, exclusive agents are usually restricted by contract to representing a single insurance company. Consequently, the insurance company principal can exercise greater control over exclusive agents than over independent agents.

Exclusive agents are usually compensated by commissions. Some of them receive a salary, guaranteed minimum income, or drawing account during an initial training program. Paying one commission rate for new business and another, lower rate for renewal business is common in the exclusive agency system. Independent agents, on the other hand, usually receive the same commission rate for both new and renewal business. Lower renewal commissions might tempt an independent agent to switch business to a different insurer on renewal to get the higher new business commission. This option is not available to exclusive agents because of their exclusive representation agreement.

Exclusive agents do not have ownership of expirations as a matter of custom or law, as independent agents do. Some insurers that market through the exclusive agency system do grant limited ownership of expirations to their agents by contract. Usually, such contracts grant ownership of expirations only while the agency contract is in force. When the agency contract is terminated, the ownership of expirations reverts to the insurance company. The insurer might be obligated to pay the agent for the expirations upon termination of the agency contract, but the agent does not have the option of selling the expirations to anyone other than the insurer.

Exclusive agents might offer loss adjustment services similar to those offered by independent agents. However, their exclusive representation agreements might restrict their ability to offer some risk management services to their clients.

Direct Writer System

The **direct writer marketing system** uses sales agents who are employees of the insurance companies they represent. They are not independent contractors like independent agents and exclusive agents. The agents in the direct writer system might be compensated by salary, commission, or a combination of the two. They usually do not have any ownership of expirations and, like exclusive agents, are usually restricted to representing a single insurer or a group of insurers under common ownership and management.

Direct Response System

In the **direct response marketing system** (sometimes called the mail order system), the insurer does not employ sales agents to make direct, face-to-face contact with policyholders or prospective policyholders. Instead, the insurer offers its services to prospective insureds by direct mail, by telephone, or by advertising through the mass media such as radio, television, newspapers, and magazines.

This marketing system has been used primarily for marketing personal lines of insurance. It has not been widely effective in marketing commercial lines because of the more complex nature of the commercial coverages and rating plans.

Combination Systems

Of the four marketing systems outlined above, no one is most advantageous to all insurance companies or all classes of insurance consumers. The independent agency system is likely to be most satisfactory for buyers who have very complex insurance needs or who consider service more important than cost. Independent agents are also very effective in reaching insurance consumers in rural areas and small towns.

The exclusive agency and direct writer systems have been most successful in dealing with insurance buyers who have relatively simple needs, primarily individuals, families, and small, main-street type businesses. Only a few companies in these systems have been successful in marketing to larger businesses.

Exclusive agency and direct writer systems have also been most successful in reaching urban consumers, though some have specialized in farm and rural consumers. Generally, exclusive agents and direct writers have appealed most successfully to consumers who are more concerned with price than personal service, but many agents among both groups are well qualified to provide the services needed in their markets.

Historically, insurance companies participated in only one of the marketing systems, and most of them marketed through the independent agency system. The other systems have expanded dramatically during the past four or five decades.

Some insurers began to diversify into more than one of the marketing systems as a means of reaching buyers whom their traditional marketing systems had not reached successfully. The first attempts at using mixed marketing systems were probably made by a few direct writers that specialized in commercial lines coverage. They experimented with selling through independent brokers in order to reach larger commercial lines buyers who were not being served successfully by their direct writer agents.

Later, some direct writers began using independent agents to sell personal lines and small commercial lines. Their initial objective was to reach the rural and small-town markets not adequately served by direct writer agents and exclusive agents.

Direct writers and exclusive agency companies incur substantial start-up costs and fixed costs in establishing an agent in a new territory. These heavy costs make it difficult for them to market through their traditional methods in rural areas and small towns, where the amount of business available is very limited. Independent agents usually succeed in rural areas because they represent more insurers, offer more products, and, consequently, have a larger market.

Companies that traditionally marketed through the independent agency system have also adopted mixed marketing systems. One large insurer that had participated in the independent agency system for over a century has experimented (with limited success) with all three of the other systems. It purchased a direct writing subsidiary, which it sold about a decade later. It tried direct response marketing but discontinued the program after only a few months. It also entered into contracts with some of its agents providing that the agents would give it first refusal of all business they wrote and would place business elsewhere only if the insurer refused to write it.

Another recent development that seems likely to expand is the movement toward vertical integration in property-liability insurance marketing. Vertical integration occurs when an organization owns several stages in the process of providing a product to the consumer. For example, an agent or a broker might own an insurance company, or an insurance company might own an agency or a brokerage firm.

Vertical integration seems to have been initiated by the acquisition of insurance companies by the large brokerage firms. Regulatory authorities have discouraged such acquisitions in recent years because of the insolvency of some broker-owned insurers and because of the apparent conflict between the brokers' duties as representatives of the policyholders and their interest in the profits of the insurers they own. Several large brokerage firms have sold off their subsidiary insurance companies.

More recently, several large insurance agency and brokerage firms have been acquired, in whole or in part, by insurance companies or by holding companies that also own insurance companies. The acquired agencies or brokerage firms are units of the independent agency system. Company ownership of agencies and brokerage firms would seem to be a close approximation of the exclusive agency system. The relationship differs from the exclusive agency system in that the subsidiary agency or brokerage firm is still permitted to deal with other unrelated insurance companies. However, some observers question whether the subsidiary agencies and brokerage firms can deal with unrelated insurers on an equal footing with their parent companies.

Several insurers have been very successful in using mixed marketing systems. The use of mixed marketing systems will probably continue to grow in the foreseeable future.

Alternative Marketing Mechanisms

Despite the variety of marketing systems that insurers have traditionally used, they have not always been able to satisfy the requirements of all insurance consumers. Various alternative markets have been created to fill the gaps left unmet by traditional insurers.

One of the largest of these gaps consists of consumers who do not meet the underwriting standards of insurers operating in the voluntary market. These alternative market mechanisms can also be called **shared-market mechanisms** because all licensed insurers are required to share in the risks insured through them.

The market mechanisms discussed in the following section do not conform to the traditional meaning of insurance distribution. This section takes a broader approach to describing insurance markets while recognizing that most of these alternative market mechanisms use the same distribution systems as conventional private insurers.

Involuntary Market Mechanisms

Insurers that use one of the marketing systems discussed in the previous section and seek to write insurance exposures they view as desirable are sometimes referred to as the **voluntary market** because they voluntarily provide coverage to entities that meet their underwriting requirements. Several **involuntary market mechanisms** have been developed to provide coverage for entities that do not qualify for coverage in the voluntary market. These mechanisms are *involuntary* in that the insurers have been required to establish them by statute, regulation, or regulatory pressure. The involuntary market mechanisms are sometimes called **residual market mechanisms** because they insure the entities that remain uninsured after the insurers have accepted all insureds who meet the underwriting requirements for the voluntary market.

Involuntary Auto Insurance Market

Perhaps the largest and oldest of the involuntary market mechanisms are those that provide automobile insurance for persons who cannot qualify for coverage in the voluntary market. All states, including the District of Columbia, have an involuntary market mechanism to ensure automobile insurance availability. In 1994, 5.90 million cars were insured in the involuntary market, compared to 140.31 million in the voluntary market. Thus, the involuntary market mechanisms had a 4.0 percent share of the market nationally. The market share varied widely by state, from less than 0.1 percent in several states to 41.0 percent in South Carolina.[1] Other states with high market shares included North Carolina, 25 percent; New York, 16 percent; Massachusetts, 12 percent; and the District of Columbia, 10 percent.[2]

There are four kinds of auto insurance residual market mechanisms: (1) assigned risk plans, (2) joint underwriting associations, (3) auto reinsurance plans, and (4) state funds.

Assigned Risk Plans

Assigned risk plans are often called *auto insurance plans* in an effort to avoid the perceived stigma attached to the inability to obtain coverage in the voluntary market. The term *assigned risk plan* will be used here because it more clearly distinguishes this type of plan from the other three types.

All states have some kind of involuntary market mechanism for automobile insurance, and most of them are assigned risk plans. Under an **assigned risk plan**, any licensed driver who cannot obtain insurance in the voluntary market is assigned to a specific insurance company. That insurer must then provide coverage for the assigned driver for a specific period of time (usually three years) unless the driver later obtains voluntary coverage. Coverage for the assigned drivers is handled in essentially the same manner as for the insurer's voluntarily insured drivers.

The number of drivers assigned to each licensed insurer is determined by the insurer's share of the voluntary auto insurance market. For example, an insurer that writes coverage for 10 percent of the cars in the voluntary market would be assigned 10 percent of the cars insured under the assigned risk plan.

In the past, all states had assigned risk plans. The other types of auto insurance residual market mechanisms were developed to avoid or reduce the perceived stigma attached to the assigned risk plans.

Joint Underwriting Associations

Several states now have **joint underwriting associations (JUAs)** to provide auto insurance to those who cannot qualify for coverage in the voluntary market. A JUA resembles an assigned risk plan in that all licensed auto insurers are required to participate in the plan and to share the burden of providing coverage for those who cannot meet the underwriting requirements of the voluntary market.

A JUA differs from an assigned risk plan in that drivers insured under the JUA are not assigned to specific insurers. The JUA provides all coverage, retains all premiums, and pays all losses and expenses. Participating insurers share the profits or (more likely) losses of the JUA in proportion to their shares of the voluntary market.

The JUA appoints several insurers as servicing companies. A driver who is insured by the JUA receives a policy issued by a servicing company, and that company adjusts all losses incurred under the policy. The servicing company receives a fee from the JUA to reimburse it for the cost of providing services. The insured driver might not even know that the coverage is being provided by the JUA.

Auto Reinsurance Plans

A small number of states have **auto reinsurance plans** instead of assigned risk plans or JUAs. In those states, an insurer that regularly sells automobile insurance cannot refuse to provide coverage for any licensed driver. However, it can transfer to the reinsurance plan all or a part of the risk for any driver who does not meet its normal underwriting standards.

The insurer must issue its own policy to cover the driver. It keeps a part of the premium to cover its expenses and pays the balance of the premium to the reinsurance plan. The originating insurer pays all losses under the policy but is reimbursed by the reinsurance plan. All profits or losses of the reinsurance plan are shared by all licensed auto insurers in the state in proportion to their shares in the voluntary market.

The principal difference between a JUA and a reinsurance plan is the number of *servicing insurers*, although that term is not used in connection with reinsurance plans. Under a JUA, a relatively small number of insurers are designated as servicing companies, and every application for coverage through the JUA must be submitted to one of the servicing companies. Under a reinsurance plan, any insurer licensed to write auto insurance in the state can submit an application for coverage through the plan. Consequently, all licensed auto insurers could be considered to be servicing companies.

State Funds

Maryland has taken a different approach to the involuntary automobile insurance market. It established a state fund, the **Maryland Automobile Insurance Fund (MAIF)**, to provide coverage for drivers who cannot obtain insurance through the voluntary market. The fund, which is operated by the state, collects premiums from the drivers it insures and pays losses on their behalf. It operates essentially as an insurance company with one major exception. If the premiums it collects are inadequate to pay the losses and expenses it incurs, it can assess all auto insurers licensed in Maryland an amount sufficient to cover its deficit.

Involuntary Property Insurance Market Mechanisms

Involuntary market mechanisms for property insurance have also been established in some states. Two kinds of such mechanisms now exist. **Fair Access to Insurance Requirements (FAIR) plans** now operate in twenty-seven states and the District of Columbia. Beach and windstorm plans operate in seven states.

FAIR plans were established to make property insurance available to persons who cannot obtain it through the voluntary market. The plans provide at least fire and extended coverage insurance. Homeowners coverage is provided in some states. FAIR plans also provide crime coverage in a few states and earthquake coverage in at least one state. FAIR plans operate in a manner very similar to that outlined for auto JUAs above. The FAIR plans provided $96.5 billion of property insurance in 1994.[3]

Beach and windstorm plans exist in the coastal states in the hurricane belt of the Gulf and South Atlantic coasts. Each coastal state from Texas to North Carolina (except Georgia) has a beach and windstorm pool to provide windstorm coverage in the coastal areas. These plans also operate in a manner similar to the auto JUAs. They had a total of $53.5 billion of insurance in force in 1995.

Workers Compensation Involuntary Market Mechanisms

Workers compensation insurance market mechanisms consist of a national pool, state pools, or workers compensation state funds. The national pool covers thirty-two jurisdictions and includes the high-risk employees in five states with competitive state funds. Eight jurisdictions have state pools, and twelve other jurisdictions operate a state fund.[4]

The workers compensation involuntary market mechanisms function in a manner similar to the auto JUAs discussed above. In addition, a **National Reinsurance Pool**, administered by the National Council on Compensation Insurance, provides reinsurance for the state pools. These pools, collectively, are the largest writer of workers compensation, with about 20 percent of the market nationally.

Other Involuntary Market Mechanisms

A number of other involuntary market mechanisms exist. Several states have JUAs for medical malpractice liability insurance. At least two states have JUAs for liquor law liability insurance. Some states have standby JUAs for other lines. These JUAs are not active, but enabling legislation has been adopted so that the insurance commissioner can activate them quickly if they are needed.

Government Insurance

Private insurers provide most property-liability insurance in the United States. However, a number of government insurers exist at both the state and federal levels.

Supporters justify government insurance programs on several grounds. The first and most convincing argument is the inability or unwillingness of private insurers to provide a form of protection that is necessary for the public welfare. Flood insurance and war risk coverage are examples.

Lower cost to consumers also seems to be a consideration in the establishment of some government insurance plans. Lower cost was probably the major factor in the establishment of the state life insurance fund in Wisconsin and possibly in the establishment of state funds for crop hail insurance.

In some cases, proponents justify government insurance plans on the grounds that it is unfair to enrich private insurers by permitting them to profit on insurance that is required by law. This seems to have been a major consideration in the establishment of state workers compensation insurance funds.

Some government insurance programs seem to have been started to promote social, economic, or scientific developments. For example, mortgage guaranty insurance was established at least in part to encourage home ownership and to provide financial support to the construction industry. A federal agency provides export credit insurance in order to promote exports and thus to foster a healthy national economy.

Whatever the reasons, a number of government insurance programs have been established over the past few decades, and more are under consideration.

State Insurance Funds

State insurance funds exist in many states to provide insurance that would otherwise be written by property-liability insurers. Twenty-five states have state funds to provide workers compensation insurance. In six of those states,[5] employers are required to purchase their workers compensation insurance from the state fund. Private insurers are not permitted to write workers compensation insurance in those states.

In the remaining states,[6] workers compensation state funds compete with private insurers for business. In 1993, the market shares of the competitive state funds ranged from less than .05 percent of the market in Oklahoma and Utah to 53 percent in New Mexico.[7] In most of the states, the state fund is the largest single insurer. In 1994, all of the state funds combined had premiums of over $9 billion, compared to insurance industry workers compensation premiums of $31.2 billion nationally.[8]

States also have insurance funds for other lines of coverage. The Maryland Automobile Insurance Fund was mentioned previously in this chapter. Several states have funds for crop hail insurance. At least two states have funds to compensate property owners for damage to property on the surface resulting from the collapse of underground coal mines. Several states have patient compensation funds, which provide compensation for patients injured as a result of medical malpractice incidents. These funds usually provide coverage for losses in excess of some substantial amount, such as $100,000, with private insurers providing the basic coverage.

Federal Insurance Programs

The federal government has numerous insurance programs. Those most closely related to property-liability insurance are discussed below.

Flood Insurance

Private insurers debated the insurability of the flood exposure for many years. It was the prevailing belief within the industry that the flood exposure was not commercially insurable. The principal reasons given for uninsurability were the following:

- The catastrophic nature of losses
- The repetition of claims
- Adverse selection (the tendency of only those people in flood-prone areas to buy flood insurance)

Consequently, flood insurance was not generally available in the private insurance market. Some commercial and industrial firms could purchase flood coverage under a difference in conditions policy (DIC), but even that was not usually available to firms located in flood-prone areas.

The National Flood Insurance Act of 1968 established the National Flood Insurance Program (NFIP), which provided a federal subsidy for flood insurance. The program has been subsequently broadened and modified. The NFIP is administered by the Federal Insurance Administration (FIA), which is part of the Federal Emergency Management Agency. The original legislation required state and local governments to adopt land-use control measures to minimize flood damage before they could qualify to participate in the flood insurance program. The program was originally available only to one- to four-family dwellings and small business firms. Now the program has expanded eligibility to include many types of residences and businesses. Coverage limits of $250,000 can be written on residential structures and $100,000 on their contents. Nonresidential structures can be provided coverage limits up to $500,000 on buildings and $500,000 on contents.

Federal flood insurance is marketed through normal insurance marketing channels. Beginning in 1983, under the new cooperative venture called Write Your Own (WYO), participating private insurers began to write flood insurance under their own names and through their normal distribution systems.

NFIP's goal in cooperating with private insurers was to accomplish the following:

- Increase the flood insurance policy base as well as the geographic distribution of policyholders.

- Improve service to policyholders and insurance agents through the infusion of insurance industry knowledge and through access to existing insurance company communication capabilities that have been designed to meet their needs.

- Provide insurance companies with operating experience under the NFIP particularly in ways that greatly increase the program's ability to settle claims promptly in post-catastrophe situations.[9]

Under this arrangement, the insurers keep part of the premiums for expenses, premium taxes, and commissions, with the balance being deposited in a separate account to pay for losses. Participating insurers have no risk-bearing role in the WYO program.

Federal Crime Insurance

Urban unrest and the sometimes violent disturbances in the 1960s made crime insurance very difficult to obtain in many metropolitan areas of the country. As a part of the Housing and Urban Development Act of 1970, Congress authorized the Department of Housing and Urban Development to underwrite crime insurance in those areas in which it was not available.

Crime insurance in the federal program is underwritten by the federal government and sold either directly by the government or through insurance agents and brokers. The program is authorized to insure against robbery, burglary, larceny, and similar crimes for personal and commercial insureds. Coverage in force has dropped from $669 million in 1981 to $158.4 million in 1995. Part of this decline in coverage is due to availability in the voluntary insurance market and the creation of state-sponsored residual markets.

The Federal Insurance Administration appoints a private organization to serve as servicing company. Any licensed producer can sell the coverage and be compensated by commission for the services rendered.

FAIR Plans

FAIR plans, like federal crime insurance, resulted primarily from the general deterioration of cities that began in the 1960s. Many city residents found themselves unable to obtain property insurance for their homes and businesses. A federal study commission suggested, as one method of providing such protection, the establishment of FAIR plans and federal reinsurance for riot losses.[10] The riot reinsurance program was terminated in 1983.

The FAIR plans were authorized by the Urban Property Protection and

Reinsurance Act of 1968. FAIR plans are associations of insurers formed under state law but required to meet certain minimum requirements established by the U.S. Department of Housing and Urban Development. Persons who cannot obtain property insurance in the voluntary market can apply to the FAIR plan. Some state FAIR plans also provide crime insurance. The FAIR plan cannot refuse coverage solely because of the location of property but *can* refuse coverage if the property is in such poor condition as to be uninsurable and if the insured refuses to restore it to insurable condition. However, these options are unenforceable in some states. The premiums, losses, and expenses of FAIR plans are allocated to participating insurers in proportion to their property insurance premiums in the state.

Insurance Exchanges

The early 1980s saw the formation of three insurance institutions that had the potential to bring significant changes to insurance marketing in the United States: the New York Insurance Exchange, the Illinois Insurance Exchange, and the Insurance Exchange of the Americas, based in Miami. Only the Illinois Insurance Exchange survived the 1980s.

Insurance exchanges operated in a manner similar to Lloyd's of London, except that their members could be partnerships or corporations as well as individuals. Also, their members did not have unlimited liability as is a characteristic of Lloyd's members.

The exchanges were expected to write much of the U.S. premium volume that is exported to Lloyd's each year. It seemed, in their early years, that this goal might be achieved. By the end of 1983, over forty syndicates were on the New York exchange, eight at the Illinois exchange, and nine at the Insurance Exchange of the Americas. By 1986, the New York exchange had risen to number thirteen on the listing of the world's top fifteen reinsurance firms. But by the end of the 1980s, many syndicates on the New York Insurance Exchange and the Insurance Exchange of the Americas had become insolvent, and those exchanges had ceased operations.

The Illinois Insurance Exchange continues to operate. It no longer writes reinsurance, but functions as a surplus lines insurer. In 1995, ten syndicates were active on the Illinois Insurance Exchange, and their gross written premiums were $294 million, up 10 percent over 1993.[11]

The Illinois exchange has survived the demise of the other two exchanges and appears to be operating successfully as a surplus lines insurer. However, it poses little threat to the U.S. business of Lloyd's in the foreseeable future.

Risk Retention Groups

During the tight insurance market of the mid-1970s, many business firms experienced difficulty in obtaining product liability insurance. In 1981, Congress passed the Product Liability Risk Retention Act, which permitted businesses to join together to form risk retention groups to provide product liability coverage. The act was amended in 1986 to permit risk retention groups to write all kinds of commercial liability coverage except workers compensation.[12]

A **risk retention group** is an insurance company chartered under the laws of a state or other U.S. jurisdiction. Once chartered and authorized by its home state, a risk retention group can operate in all other states without obtaining licenses or meeting the state admission requirements that other insurers must meet. They are, however, required to inform state regulators of their intention to do business in the state. They must also furnish state regulatory authorities with a plan of operation and a feasibility study. The latter must include details of the coverages, rates, and rating plans to be offered in the state.

If the insurance commissioner determines that a risk retention group is in hazardous financial condition, he or she can seek a court order barring the group from doing business in the state. Also, the risk retention groups are required to comply with state unfair claims practices acts. They must also participate in JUAs or similar plans. Risk retention groups are exempted under federal law from virtually all other state regulation.

A risk retention group must be composed of members whose business activities are similar, and it must be controlled by its members. It can be organized as a stock insurer, mutual, or reciprocal exchange.[13]

At the beginning of 1996, there were sixty-nine risk retention groups. Their gross written premium was $585.5 million.[14]

Purchasing Groups

The Risk Retention Act also enabled businesses to form purchasing groups. A **purchasing group** is any group of persons that purchases liability insurance on a group basis, presumably to save premium. The act allows groups to avoid the "fictitious group" laws enacted by various states that prohibit groups from forming solely for the purchase of insurance and also permits purchase groups to avoid state regulation.

As with risk retention groups, purchasing groups can buy all types of commercial liability coverage except workers compensation. In addition, a purchasing group must be composed of members whose business activities are similar, and only members can purchase insurance through the group. A purchasing group can purchase insurance from an insurer that is licensed or admitted in the state where the purchasing group is located. The term "located" has been interpreted to mean every state in which the purchasing group has members. Thus, the underwriter of the purchasing group must be admitted in every state where the group has members. One of the key advantages to a purchasing group is that state insurance commissioners cannot deny rate reductions for a group based on its loss and expense experience.

At the beginning of 1996, there were 531 purchasing groups. Combined, these groups wrote $2 billion in gross written premiums.[15]

Mass Merchandising

The term mass merchandising encompasses a wide variety of marketing methods, but they are all characterized by efforts to sell insurance, either personal lines or commercial lines, to individual purchasers whose only relationship is membership in a common organization. Although mass merchandising is the generally accepted term for this marketing method, quasi-group marketing would seem to be more descriptive because of the strong resemblance to group marketing techniques used in connection with life and health insurance.

There are no generally accepted definitions for mass merchandising or quasi-group marketing. Because of inherent differences in personal lines and commercial lines, slightly different definitions are used. *Personal lines* programs are categorized according to the following criteria:

- The method of premium collection
- The restrictions, if any, on the insurer's underwriting prerogatives
- The effect of the plan on the cost of insurance to participants

Franchise merchandising is a plan for insuring a number of employees of an employer under a single plan of insurance. Employee premium payments are made by payroll deduction. Franchise merchandising does not provide participants a discount but rather the convenience of small, regular payments. Insurers offering this type of plan retain the right to decline individual participants.

Mass merchandising is a plan for insuring a number of otherwise independent purchasers of insurance under a single program of insurance at a discounted premium. As with franchise merchandising plans, the insurer retains the right of individual underwriting selection.

A **group marketing** plan offers guaranteed issue and discounted premiums to participants. Under this type of plan, no individual underwriting or proof of insurability is required.

Franchise merchandising programs, which were once common, have now become rare. They have been replaced by mass merchandising programs and, in a few instances, by group marketing programs. In general, such programs have been provided most often for employees of a single employer or for members of a labor union. However, some plans have been written for members of social organizations or for customers of a specified business firm, such as a credit-card issuer, a public utility, or a credit union.

The foregoing definitions do not apply to commercial lines marketing. Franchise marketing, as defined, would be meaningless for commercial lines programs; at the time of this writing, the authors are not aware of any commercial lines programs that have been written on a guaranteed issue basis. Consequently, all known programs in the commercial lines area fall into the mass merchandising category. Unfortunately, within the industry, a mass merchandising program is variously referred to as "a commercial group," "an association/franchise," or "commercial mass marketing."

Commercial lines programs can be categorized as trade association plans and safety group plans. Under a **trade association plan**, any member firm of the trade association would be eligible to participate if it meets the insurer's underwriting requirements. **Safety group plans** usually are not restricted to the members of a trade association but are available to any firm in the selected industry, provided the firm meets the insurer's underwriting requirements and agrees to undertake a loss control program specified by the insurer. For example, a trade association plan written for a state restaurant association would be available only to members of that association and only to those members that meet the underwriting standards of the insurer. On the other hand, a safety group plan for restaurants would be available to any restaurant in the state that (1) meets the insurer's underwriting standards and (2) agrees to adopt the loss control program specified by the insurer. Membership in the trade association would not be a requirement for participation in the safety group program. However, adoption of a loss control program might also be required as a condition of participation in a trade association program.

No reliable data are available to indicate the current status of mass merchandising. Less than 1 percent of personal lines insurance seems to be sold through mass merchandising plans. The market share for commercial lines is probably higher, but still well under 5 percent. The development of risk retention groups and group self-insurance has probably siphoned off some commercial lines business that would otherwise have been written through mass merchandising programs.

Market Distribution System Management

An insurer must provide some means of supervising its producers in order to accomplish the following:

- Motivate them to sell the kinds and amounts of business it wants

- Assist them in handling unusual or difficult insurance situations

- Continually reappraise their performance so that corrective action can be taken promptly

- Recruit additional or replacement producers when necessary

Small insurers operating in restricted geographic areas might be able to provide supervision through the home office. However, larger insurers with more widespread operations usually provide supervision in or near the locality in which each producer operates. In general, two systems are in use in the United States for providing producer supervision: (1) the branch office or regional system and (2) the managing general agency system.

Branch Office System

Under the **branch office system**, the insurer maintains offices in strategically located cities and towns in its operating territory. A small branch office, sometimes called a service office, might consist of only a sales manager, special agent, or field representative (the title varies by company) whose principal duty is maintaining contact with and supervision of producers. Larger branch offices might also include company officers, management personnel, underwriters, claims people, loss control engineers, premium auditors, and other service personnel.

Some insurers have two or more levels of branch offices. For example, a large branch office, sometimes called a regional office, might supervise smaller branches scattered throughout one or more states. Regional offices of some insurers are largely autonomous and perform most of the insurance functions, though not the investment functions, usually associated with home office operations. Others function primarily as communications facilities, gathering information from producers, sending it to the home office, and returning home office decisions to the producer.

A great deal of expense is involved in maintaining a widespread system of branch offices. An insurer can afford to maintain such offices only in those territories in which it has or expects to obtain a substantial volume of business.

Managing General Agency System

A managing general agency is an independent business firm that performs for one or more separate insurers some or all of the functions usually performed by company branch offices. A managing general agent might perform such services for a single insurer, though they more commonly represent several insurers. The general agency usually does not sell directly to insurance consumers but appoints and supervises producers throughout the territory. Its territory might consist of an entire state or several states. A few managing general agencies cover very large territories, though frequently for specialty lines of insurance.

The advantage to an insurer of operating through a managing general agent is the low fixed cost. The general agency is compensated by an overriding commission on the business sold by the producers it appoints. Consequently, the insurer does not have the large fixed cost of maintaining a branch office. The general agency, by writing relatively small amounts of business for each of several insurers, earns enough commissions to cover its expenses and earn a profit.

The managing general agency system was a major marketing system for property-liability insurers in the nineteenth century when most insurers were small and much of the nation was sparsely populated. As the population and insurers grew larger, many insurers accumulated sufficient premium volume to operate through branch offices in many areas. In some cases, the insurers merely terminated their relationships with managing general agencies and established their own branch offices staffed with their own personnel. In other cases, insurers purchased the general agencies and converted them to branch offices.

As a result of additional insurers moving to the branch office system, the total number of managing general agencies has been declining. Those that remain have had their underwriting authority restricted as insurers increased their producer supervision activities at the home office level. As a result, most managing general agencies were forced into the excess and surplus lines and into specialty markets such as mobile homes, snowmobiles, nonstandard automobile, and other lines not normally sought by the majority of insurers.

Functions Performed by Agents

The functions to be performed by insurance agents are generally specified in the agency contract. They vary rather widely from one distribution system to another and also from one agent to another within a given distribution system. Several of the functions sometimes performed by agents are discussed below.

Some agents perform all of the functions discussed; others perform fewer functions.

Prospecting

Virtually all agents prospect. This function consists of locating persons, business firms, and other entities that might be interested in purchasing the insurance services offered by the agent's principals. Prospects can be located by several methods:

- Referrals by present clients
- Advertising of various kinds, including media advertising and direct mail
- Telephone solicitations
- Cold canvass

Large agencies might have employees who specialize in locating prospective clients. However, in most agencies, the individual agent is responsible for his or her own prospecting operations. Insurance companies might also assist in the prospecting function, especially in the exclusive agent and direct writer systems.

Sales

Selling is the principal function of an insurance agent. Commission on business sold is the principal source of income for agents, and the ownership of expirations on business sold is the principal asset of an insurance agency. The steps in selling include contacting the prospective client, determining the prospect's needs, preparing a proposal, and closing the sale.

Risk Analysis

As noted above, determining the prospect's needs is usually an important step in the sales process. Risk analysis is the principal method of determining the prospect's insurance needs. For an individual or family, the process of risk analysis might be relatively simple. A brief questionnaire might provide the information needed for the analysis, and only an hour or two might be needed to perform the analysis. The risk analysis process for business firms is likely to be much more complex. Much time is required to develop and analyze risk information for a large firm with diversified operations.

Policy Issuance

Historically, most agents assembled policies using printed forms provided by the insurers. A copy of the policy, called the declarations "daily report" or simply the "daily," was sent to the insurer. In recent years, the trend has been for insurers to assemble the policies and either mail them directly to policyholders or send them to the agent for delivery.

The change to company issuance was undertaken primarily as a cost-cutting device. Insurers believed they could issue the policies at less cost, especially with the advent of computerized policy management systems.

Collection

Agents who issue policies might also prepare the bills and collect the premiums. After deducting their commissions, they send the premiums to the insurers. If the insurer issues the policy, the insured is usually directed to send premium payments to the company, bypassing the agent. In **direct billing**, the insurer sends the premium bill to the policyholder, collects the premium, and sends the commission to the agent.

For business that is **agency-billed**, the three widely used bases for transmitting the premiums to the insurer are (1) the item basis, (2) the statement basis, and (3) the account current basis.

Under the **item basis** method, the premium (less commission) is forwarded to the insurer when it is collected by the agent or becomes due. It is the least complex of the three bases.

Under the **statement method**, the insurer sends a statement to the agent showing the premiums that are due. The agent is obligated to pay the premiums indicated as due or to show that the statement is in error.

Under the **account current method**, the agent prepares a statement periodically, showing the premiums due to the insurer, after deducting appropriate commissions, and transmits that amount to the insurer. The agency contract indicates how often the agent must submit the account current statement. Monthly is most common.

Under the item basis, the agent is usually not required to pay the insurer until the premium is actually collected. Under the other two methods, the agent is required to pay the insurer when the premium is due, even if the policyholder has not paid the agent. To provide the agent some protection against the credit risk, premiums are usually not due to the insurer until thirty or forty-five days after the effective date of the policy. This delay also permits the agent to invest the premiums collected until they are due to the insurer. The resulting investment income might be a significant part of the agent's remuneration. This investment income is not available to the agent under direct billing or under the item basis of agency billing.

Claims Handling

All agents are likely to be involved to some degree in the handling of claims under the insurance they sell. Since the agent is the policyholder's principal contact with the insurer, the insured naturally contacts the agent first when a claim occurs.

In some cases, the agent might simply give the policyholder the telephone number of the claims department and possibly the name of a person to call. Alternatively, the agent might obtain some basic information about the claim from the policyholder, relay it to the insurer, and arrange for a claims person to contact the insured.

Finally, many agents are authorized by their principals to adjust some kinds of claims. Most often, the authorization is limited to small property claims, for example, property losses under $5,000. Some agents are also authorized to settle small liability claims, especially auto property damage liability claims. A few large agencies that employ skilled claims people might be authorized to settle larger, more complex claims. The limitations on the agent's claims-handling authority should be specified in the agency contract.

Claims handling by qualified agents offers two major advantages: quicker service to policyholders and lower loss adjustment expenses to the insurer. Of course, if the agent is not qualified to handle claims, overpayment of claims might offset the expense savings.

Consulting

Many insurance agents offer consulting services for which they are paid on a fee basis. Such services are usually performed on the agent's own behalf. Such services might be provided for a fee only, or the agent might set a maximum fee, to be reduced by any commissions received on insurance written because of the consulting contract. Laws in some states prohibit agents from receiving both commissions and a fee from the same client.

Other Services

Agents also provide other services to current and prospective policyholders. As policyholders' circumstances change, the agent must be able to advise them regarding desirable policy changes and process those changes selected.

The agent must also be able to answer questions regarding policyholders' existing coverage and additional coverage requirements. Also, questions frequently arise regarding premium billings and other accounting issues.

Finally, agents are expected to facilitate contacts between policyholders and insurer personnel, including premium auditors and loss control representatives.

Distribution System Decisions

An insurer usually selects a distribution system before it begins writing business. Changing distribution systems for existing business is very difficult and possibly expensive because of the existing agency contracts and possible ownership of expirations. However, an insurer that has previously elected one of the distribution systems might decide to use a different one when entering a new territory or launching a new insurance product. Several factors, discussed below, should be considered in selecting a distribution system.

Geographic Location

The geographic location of prospective policyholders must be considered in selecting a distribution system. The principal concern with regard to geographic territory is the population density. An insurer's fixed costs for establishing an exclusive agent or direct-writer agent in a territory are very substantial. Consequently, those marketing systems can be employed satisfactorily only when a sufficient number of prospects exist within a relatively small geographic area. The fixed cost of appointing an independent agent or using the direct response system is much lower, so those systems can be used in sparsely populated areas. Several insurers that traditionally used either the exclusive agency system or the direct-writer system have elected to use the independent agency system in rural areas and small towns because of the lower fixed costs.

Expertise and Reputation of Producers

The level of expertise required of a producer depends on the lines of insurance written. Generally, commercial lines require greater producer expertise. Some exclusive agency and direct writer producers have been successful in selling commercial lines, especially to small, main-street-type businesses. However, the medium- to large-size commercial lines business is still dominated by the independent agency system. This domination is especially notable in specialized lines, such as surety bonds and ocean marine insurance. Commercial lines require a level of service that cannot be handled satisfactorily by the direct response marketing system. Consequently, an insurer that wants to market medium- to large-size commercial accounts should probably use the independent agency system. An insurer that wants to sell personal lines could use any of the systems. Of course, it would need to consider the resources required and the high fixed costs associated with the exclusive agent and direct writer systems during the start-up period. An insurer that expects to sell to small business firms could use any of the systems, assuming there are adequate resources to meet the fixed costs of the system selected.

Nature of Existing Business

The characteristics of an insurer's book of business must be considered in any change in distribution system. As noted above, the independent agency system seems to have an advantage in marketing medium- to large-size commercial lines. The other systems are very successful in marketing personal lines and small commercial lines, except for the direct response system. Another factor that should be considered is the ownership of expirations. If the producers own the expirations, the insurer must either give up the business and start over or purchase the expirations from producers. Either option might be expensive, depending on the quality of the existing business.

Ability To Service Products

The amount of service required varies among lines of insurance. Personal lines generally require the least service, while commercial lines require greater direct involvement by the producer and insurer representatives. The producers available in the distribution system selected by an insurer must have the expertise required for the lines of insurance offered and the clients to whom insurance is offered. Although many producers within the other systems possess substantial expertise in handling complex insurance products, the independent agents, as a group, have an edge, both actual and perceived, in the expertise needed for such lines.

Markets To Be Targeted

The nature of the markets to be targeted might be a very important factor in choosing a distribution system. The personal-commercial dichotomy and geographic spread of prospects were mentioned above. The level of price consciousness is also important. Some insurance consumers are more interested in price than service, and others emphasize service more. The direct response system is likely to enjoy a significant advantage in cost in comparison with all of the other systems. It is likely, however, to offer less service than the other systems. Consequently, it is most effective in reaching buyers whose paramount concern is price.

At the other extreme, the independent agency system probably offers better service than any of the other systems, but it does so at a higher cost. Consequently, it is most effective in reaching buyers whose paramount consideration is service.

The direct writer and exclusive agent systems are approximately equal in both cost and service. They reach a wide middle audience for whom price and service are equally important.

Insurer Characteristics

The three characteristics of the insurer that should influence the selection of a distribution system are the following:

- The existence and nature of the current business, as discussed above
- The buyers it wants to reach, also discussed above
- Its financial resources

The initial fixed cost of entering the market through the exclusive agency system or direct writer system is greater than doing so through the independent agency system. The insurer must hire, train, and financially support the direct writer and exclusive agency producers at substantial cost before they become productive. The cost of appointing independent agents or conducting a direct response campaign is much lower. Consequently, insurers that enter the market through the exclusive agency or direct writer system require greater initial financial resources to reach a given level of production.

Degree of Control Required or Desired

The extent of control that the insurer wants to exercise over its marketing operations might influence its choice of a distribution system. An insurer can exercise the greatest control over producers in the direct writer system. Under that system, the producer is an employee of the company, and the company can exercise control over both the results achieved and the methods used to achieve them.

Under both the independent agency system and the exclusive agency system, the producers are independent contractors. As such, the insurer can control only the results they produce, not the means by which they produce them. In addition, independent agents can represent several insurers and can switch business among them. Ownership of expirations by the producer, more common in the independent agency system, also reduces the amount of control available to the insurer.

There are no producers involved in the direct response system. Consequently, the insurer has complete control of its distribution system.

Market Shares

One way of evaluating insurer distribution systems is by measuring the relative market shares of each system. A. M. Best data do not distinguish among the types of distribution systems in the same way this chapter does. A. M. Best categorizes insurers as either "agency writers" or "direct writers." The first category includes companies using the independent agency system. The latter category encompasses what this chapter has described as the direct writers, exclusive agents, and direct response systems. For continuity with previous discussions, the exhibits used in this section simply distinguish between "independent agency" and "other."

A historical analysis of this century shows the dramatic rise of the direct writer, exclusive agency, and direct response distribution systems. Throughout the period of those systems' growth, many industry analysts have questioned the viability of the independent agency system. Despite predictions to the contrary, the independent agency system persists. Actually, the rate of erosion in the independent agency system market share has slowed. In many lines of insurance, the independent agency system remains the dominant distribution system.

Exhibit 3-4 shows the market share for all lines combined. From 1991 to 1995, the independent agency system's market share declined 2.1 percent. Although the overall trend has been down for the independent agency system, additional insight into these trends is revealed when market share is segmented between personal and commercial lines as shown in Exhibit 3-5. The direct writer, exclusive agency, and direct response systems have a dominant market share in personal lines insurance. Although the independent agency system has seen its role in the personal lines insurance market decline substantially since the other distribution systems entered the marketplace, the rate of that decline has decreased significantly. In commercial lines, the independent agency system continues to lose market share, yet it remains the market leader.

Exhibit 3-4
Market Shares by Marketing System
All Property-Liability Lines Combined

Market Share as a Percentage of Industry Net Written Premium					
System	**1991**	**1992**	**1993**	**1994**	**1995**
Independent	53.1	51.3	51.0	51.3	51.0
Other	46.9	48.7	49.0	48.7	49.0

A. M. Best Aggregates and Averages, 1996 Edition, p. 237.

Exhibit 3-6 shows the relative market share for selected personal and commercial lines. The direct writers, exclusive agents, and direct response systems dominate the private passenger automobile market. They have also recently grown in the homeowners market. Commercial lines have remained the

Exhibit 3-5
Market Shares by Marketing System
Personal Lines vs. Commercial Lines of Property-Liability Lines

Market Share as a Percentage of Industry Net Written Premium					
Personal Lines					
System	**1991**	**1992**	**1993**	**1994**	**1995**
Independent	33.0	32.1	31.9	32.0	32.3
Other	67.0	67.9	68.1	68.0	67.7
Commercial Lines					
System	**1991**	**1992**	**1993**	**1994**	**1995**
Independent	72.1	70.9	70.4	70.9	70.7
Other	27.9	29.1	29.6	29.1	29.3

A. M. Best Aggregates and Averages, 1996 Edition, pp. 234-235.

domain of the independent agency system. The direct writers, exclusive agents, and direct response systems, however, have been successful in making inroads into the insurance market for small business owners. This fact is not disclosed in the combined data collected from the Annual Statement.

The direct writers, exclusive agents, and direct response systems have emphasized personal lines insurance for several reasons. First, private passenger auto insurance, to which they first turned their attention, is the major property-liability insurance line, accounting for about 39 percent of the industry's total premium volume. Direct writers, exclusive agents, and direct response systems have experienced exceptional growth. These insurers were able to address the needs of automobile owners when private passenger auto insurance rates were increasing significantly. They were later able to cross-sell homeowners insurance to their cost-sensitive policyholders. Second, because of its relative simplicity when compared with commercial lines, personal lines insurance can be sold successfully without the extensive involvement by insurance company personnel that is needed for most commercial insurance lines. The combination of a large market and relative simplicity permitted these distribution systems to build large sales forces with minimum training delays and expenses. One reason the independent agency system was less competitive on price than other distribution systems was the lower or no commission paid to other agency systems. Lastly, these insurers were early users of policy issuance automation, thereby reducing their underwriting expenses and creating efficiencies that independent agency insurers have had difficulty matching.

Exhibit 3-6
Market Shares by Marketing System
Selected Personal and Commercial Property-Liability Lines

Market Share as a Percentage of Industry Net Written Premium				
Private Passenger Automobile Liability Insurance				
System	**1991**	**1992**	**1993**	**1994**	**1995**
Independent	31.0	31.0	30.8	31.0	31.5
Other	69.0	69.0	69.2	69.0	68.5
Homeowners Multiple Peril				
System	**1991**	**1992**	**1993**	**1994**	**1995**
Independent	41.8	38.2	36.7	36.4	36.0
Other	58.2	61.8	63.3	63.6	64.0
Commercial Automobile Liability Insurance				
System	**1991**	**1992**	**1993**	**1994**	**1995**
Independent	77.0	76.7	77.2	78.1	78.6
Other	23.0	23.3	22.8	21.9	21.4
General Liability Insurance (including Products Liability)				
System	**1991**	**1992**	**1993**	**1994**	**1995**
Independent	86.6	83.0	83.4	84.0	84.5
Other	13.4	17.0	16.6	16.0	15.5
Workers Compensation				
System	**1991**	**1992**	**1993**	**1994**	**1995**
Independent	78.5	77.7	78.3	79.3	79.4
Other	21.5	22.3	21.7	20.7	20.6
Ocean Marine				
System	**1991**	**1992**	**1993**	**1994**	**1995**
Independent	90.1	86.9	86.3	84.9	86.5
Other	9.9	13.1	13.7	15.1	13.5

A.M. Best Aggregates and Averages, 1996 Edition, pp. 209, 211, 214, 215, 218.

The long-term future of the independent agency system continues to remain in doubt. A study conducted by Conning & Company predicts that the number of independent agencies will fall about 19 percent over the next decade.[16] This study echoes the evidence presented in the exhibits in this section; the independent agency system is better positioned to compete in the commercial lines market than in the personal lines market. The study suggests that those independent agencies that try to defy this trend will lose. This view of the future of the independent agency system market share is not universal. Independent Insurance Agents of America suggests that declines in the number of agencies reflect agency consolidations and that the number of independent producers overall has not declined.[17]

Summary

Distribution systems provide a means through which products are delivered to the ultimate consumer. In the case of insurance and other financial products, the marketing intermediary usually adds value to the nature of the product in terms of additional services. That is also a good way to view the insurance product—as a bundle of goods and services.

Distribution systems are typically categorized by the existence or degree of independence of the insurance agent, how agents are compensated, and the control that producers can exercise over client listings.

The independent agency system played a significant role in the development of the U.S. insurance industry. Because of independent agents' entrenchment as an institution, the newer forms of distribution are frequently compared to those of independent agents. Exclusive agents, direct writers, and direct response marketing systems have made substantial inroads in the market once dominated by independent agents.

The traditional markets do not meet all needs. Insurers have created new market mechanisms when they have had little opportunity for profit or where governments have determined that an unmet need exists. Those mechanisms include the following:

- Involuntary market mechanisms providing auto, property, workers compensation, and other kinds of insurance
- Government insurers at both the state and federal levels
- Insurance exchanges
- Risk retention groups
- Various mass merchandising systems

In general, the two systems in use in the United States for providing producer supervision are (1) the branch office or regional system and (2) the managing general agency system.

The functions to be performed by insurance agents are generally specified in the agency contract. These include prospecting, sales, risk analysis, policy issuance, collection, claims handling, consulting, and other services.

An insurer's selection of a distribution system is based on the following factors: geographic location, expertise and reputation of producers, nature of existing business, ability to service products, the nature of the buyers to be reached, insurer characteristics, and the degree of control required or desired.

An analysis of the independent agency system with the combination of exclusive agency, direct writer, and direct response systems indicates that the independent agency system has been displaced as the leading writer of private passenger auto and homeowners insurance. However, it is too early to judge the success of the other systems in penetrating the commercial lines markets.

Chapter Notes

1. *The Fact Book 1997* (New York, NY: Insurance Information Institute, 1996), pp. 42-43.
2. *The Fact Book*, pp. 42, 43.
3. *The Fact Book*, p. 44.
4. Roger K. Kenney, *Residual Markets Workers Compensation 1993 Experience* (Schaumburg, IL: Alliance of American Insurers, 1995), p. 1.
5. Nevada, North Dakota, Ohio, Washington, West Virginia, and Wyoming. Puerto Rico and the Virgin Islands operate mandatory territorial funds.
6. Arizona, California, Colorado, Idaho, Kentucky, Louisiana, Maine, Maryland, Minnesota, Missouri, Montana, New Mexico, New York, Oklahoma, Oregon, Pennsylvania, Rhode Island, Texas, and Utah.
7. *Workers Compensation Insurance: Profiles of the State Systems* (Schaumburg, IL: Alliance of American Insurers, 1995), various pages.
8. Adapted from *Best's Insurance Reports, Property-Casualty*, 1995 Edition, various pages.
9. WYO Operational Overview, Write Your Own National Flood Insurance Program, Federal Insurance Administration, Federal Emergency Management Agency, October 1993, pp. 1-1–1-2.
10. National Advisory Panel on Insurance in Riot-Affected Areas, *Meeting the Insurance Crisis in Our Cities* (Washington, DC: GPA, 1968). See also Richard F. Syron, *An Analysis of the Collapse of the Normal Market for Fire Insurance in Substandard Urban Core Areas* (Boston, MA: Federal Reserve Bank of Boston, 1972).

11. Homepage of Illinois Insurance Exchange, updated December 5, 1996, http://www.ilinex.com (accessed March 19, 1997).

12. For an explanation of the amendments, see David Daar, "Risk Retention Groups: The Law Has Changed," *CPCU Journal*, March 1987, p. 54.

13. For more details on regulation, see Robert H. Myers, Jr., "Regulatory Authority Under the Risk Retention Act," *Journal of Insurance Regulation*, September 1987, p. 72; and Richard M. Shaw, "Not a Simple Matter," *Best's Review* (Property/Casualty Insurance Edition), June 1988, p. 32.

14. Karen Cutts, ed., "Risk Retention Reporter," homepage of Risk Retention Reporter, copyright 1996, http://www.rrr.com (accessed March 20, 1997).

15. Cutts, "Risk Retention Reporter."

16. Victoria Sonsine Pasher, "Agency Ranks To Fall 19% By 2006," *National Underwriter—Property & Casualty/Risk & Benefits Management*, February 3, 1997, p. 1.

17. Jeffrey M. Yates, "Independent Agent Renaissance Defies Critics," *National Underwriter—Property & Casualty/Risk & Benefits Management*, March 17, 1997, p. 29.

Chapter 4

Underwriting

Underwriting is the process of selecting policyholders by recognizing and evaluating hazards, establishing prices, and determining policy terms and conditions. Yet, underwriting includes more than merely selecting policyholders. It also includes determining the insurer's selection criteria and the markets for the insurer's products. Underwriting is crucial to the success of any insurance company. Favorable underwriting results are necessary for the profitable growth and even the survival of the insurer. Although many insurance activities, such as marketing, loss control, ratemaking, and claims, are occasionally subcontracted to outside companies or individuals, underwriting is not likely to be delegated to others because of the importance of its success to the insurer.

Before the corporate form of insurance emerged, the underwriter was the insurer. This personal "risk-bearing" persists to this day at Lloyd's of London, where each individual participant or "name" at Lloyd's bears whatever portion of a risk the "name" has accepted. Although underwriting in modern insurance corporations has been delegated to specialized underwriting departments, the ultimate underwriters remain the top corporate officers of the insurance company.

The Purpose of Underwriting

The purpose of underwriting is to develop and maintain a profitable book of business. A **book of business** is all of the policies that an insurer has in force or some subgroup of those policies. For example, a book of business can refer to all the general liability policies or all commercial lines policies. A book of business can also refer to business produced in a specific geographic area or produced by a particular branch office or agency.

For underwriting to achieve its purpose, insurers must avoid adverse selection. **Adverse selection** occurs when the applicants for insurance present a higher-than-average probability of loss than is expected from a truly random sample of all applicants. In flood insurance, for example, those persons and businesses that expect flooding, rather than all persons and businesses, are more likely to purchase flood insurance. The term "adverse selection" is often used incorrectly to refer to the effects of competition in the selection process. If one insurer practices selective screening, accepting the best risks and declining the others, then the other insurers must practice selective screening or be prepared to suffer poor loss experience. Insurers have taken the stance that they must actively select applicants or, in effect, be selected against by those applicants. To appreciate the role of the modern underwriter in achieving the goal of underwriting, understanding how this discipline has evolved and the resources available to underwriters today is helpful.

Evolution of Underwriting

Before the 1950s, when states began enacting multiple-line rating laws, separate **monoline policies** provided particular types of insurance, such as fire, general liability, crime, or inland marine. Underwriting departments were compartmentalized and operated on a monoline basis. An underwriter was trained as a fire underwriter, a marine underwriter, or a casualty underwriter, for example.

The typical career path of the underwriter of forty or fifty years ago was different from an underwriter's career path today. Fire underwriters often began as "map clerks" who worked with the large, leather-bound volumes of the Sanborn Maps then in general use. Those maps, which contained scale drawings of all buildings, streets, and fire mains, showed the concentration of insured property in a single geographic area. After serving as a map clerk, the future underwriter served a type of apprenticeship as a junior underwriter or an assistant underwriter, working with and learning from an experienced underwriter.

Describing how the training process typically worked, a publication noted the following:

> [An underwriter] knew his craft. He had worked at this desk for 35 years—apprenticed there for 20 of those years at the elbow of a senior underwriter. When his senior retired, he slipped into that slot and, like his former boss, he, too, would retire there. But he wasn't worried about a replacement. For the past eight years a young assistant had worked at his side, learning everything there was to know about his particular line of underwriting. In another 10 years or so—maybe more—this lad would be ready to step into his shoes.[1]

This system produced underwriting specialists who could quote rates from memory and knew all of the intricacies of the contract provisions and coverage for their particular line. The system was disadvantageous for assistant underwriters because senior underwriters often blocked promotion for many years. Moving to another line of coverage would mean beginning the entire "apprentice" process again.

Multiple-Line Underwriting

Regulation of insurance has always been the responsibility of the states. A multiple-line insurance policy is one that insures more than one line of insurance, such as property and liability. For nearly a century, states believed that multiple-lines underwriting was too great a danger to insurer solvency and therefore limited the lines of insurance that one insurer could write. State regulation of insurance was affirmed in 1869, when the Supreme Court decided that insurance was not commerce.[2] This decision remained the law for 75 years, until the Court reversed its position and held that insurance was indeed commerce and subject to federal antitrust laws.[3] After that decision, Congress adopted Public Law 15 of 1945, known as the McCarran-Ferguson Act. That law states that regulation of insurance by the states is in the public interest. The law exempts the business of insurance from key federal antitrust laws to the extent that it is regulated by the states. With the passage of the McCarran-Ferguson Act in 1945, the regulatory environment began to change. Multiple-line laws appeared in several states, and in the 1950s, insurers began offering package policies that included more than one line of coverage. As package policies became more popular, underwriters who specialized in one line soon proved to be ill-prepared to underwrite package policies.

Many insurers changed both the structure of their underwriting departments and the training of their underwriters to deal with the multiple-lines innovations. Those changes, together with an increasing mobility in the insurance labor force, created more flexibility in underwriting organizations. Long apprenticeship programs gave way to intensive training programs. Today, underwriters must often learn the nuances of several lines of insurance in a relatively short period of time. An underwriter's training is further complicated because coverages, hazards, and exposures have changed rapidly in recent years. Technological advances have introduced both new materials and new industrial processes that have drastically altered the hazards in such lines as commercial fire, commercial liability, and workers compensation. Changes in the legal environment have profoundly affected products liability and professional liability coverage exposures. Regulation can also restrict the underwriter's ability to price the exposure properly. Those factors, combined with inflation, have placed heavy demands on today's underwriters. Rather than having the benefit of a lengthy apprenticeship to learn a single line of insurance in a stable technological, legal, and cultural environment, the modern underwriter must master several lines of insurance in a continually changing environment in a relatively short period of time. Underwriters, if they are to remain viable in the profession, must regularly educate themselves on matters that affect the business of insurance and factors that affect their book of business.

Underwriting Developments

Insurers have developed a variety of responses to the challenges of modern underwriting. Many insurers have developed intensive, ongoing training programs to provide underwriters with the necessary techniques and knowledge in the shortest possible time.

Advancements in computer hardware and software systems along with their widespread availability have revolutionized the daily work flow of underwriters. To a great extent, the use of paper files has been reduced in servicing policyholders and processing both new and renewal business. Computer terminals are connected to on-line databases that provide immediate access to policyholder information and to massive amounts of company and agency data. Underwriting decision support systems are emerging as tools to assist underwriters in making better informed decisions. These systems hold promise for streamlining and enhancing the process of treating every underwriting decision comprehensively. The tremendous advances in technology have increased productivity and efficiency in service. Additional advances in service quality can be expected as new technologies continue to emerge; among them is image processing, which involves transforming paper documents to digital images that can be stored electronically and recalled easily.

Despite the technological advances and increases in information availability, the key to successful underwriting remains sound, informed judgment. "Underwriting intuition," a trait often attributed to good underwriters, should be recognized for what it truly is—the ability to apply a rational (although internalized) decision-making process to a group of diverse policyholders.

Underwriting Activities

There are no hard and fast rules about how underwriting activities should be performed. Nor are there constraints on how underwriters or underwriting departments should be organized to conduct those activities. However, there is usually a relationship between how underwriting activities are segmented and how the underwriting group is physically organized.

An insurer organizes itself to make the best use of its strengths. Factors influencing this organization include the size of the insurer and the scope of the insurer's operation. A large national insurer, for example, might make major underwriting policy decisions at the home-office level. A regional insurer, on the other hand, might grant individual branch offices significant leeway in determining underwriting policy in their territories. In both cases, the authority granted affects where specific underwriting activities are performed in an insurance company.

A commonly used dichotomy distinguishes between activities performed by individual line underwriters and staff underwriters. **Line** (or desk) **underwriters** are responsible for evaluating individual applicants and policies subject to renewal. Line underwriters are generally located in branch or regional offices of insurers where day-to-day underwriting tasks are performed. **Staff underwriters** assist underwriting management in making and implementing underwriting policy.

Line Underwriting Activities

Line underwriters are responsible for the following activities:

- Selecting insureds
- Classifying risks
- Determining proper coverage
- Determining the appropriate rate or price
- Providing service to producers and policyholders

Certain hazardous classes of business or unusually large amounts of insurance often require review by a higher underwriting authority. That higher authority might be an underwriting manager or other senior staff underwriter in the branch office, regional office, or home office.

In addition to the above activities, some line underwriters also analyze insurance needs, design insurance coverages, set rates, and market products, including making visits with producers to present or prospective clients.

Selecting Insureds

The insurer must select those applicants it desires to insure. If an insurer does not select insureds carefully, some insureds will be able to purchase the insurer's products at prices that do not adequately reflect their exposures to loss. The **selection process** enables the insurers to ration available capacity to obtain the optimum spread of loss exposures by geographic distribution, class, size of risk, and line of business.

Selection is an ongoing process. Once an account has been placed on the books, the account must be monitored to determine that it *continues* to be acceptable. Corrective action might be necessary for those accounts with excessive losses or for accounts subject to adverse selection. Many consider the selection of insureds as a negative process, that is, the declining of unacceptable business. However, the selection process has positive aspects: the creation of risk management and insurance programs that enable insurers to attract desirable applicants for their products.

Classifying Risks

Correct classification is necessary to properly rate policies and to determine the risk. Accurate classification ensures a pooling of insureds whose expected loss frequency and loss severity are similar. Such a pooling of insureds enables the insurer to develop an adequate rate to pay the incurred losses and operating expenses and to produce a profit. Misclassification can have several adverse results, including insufficient premium to cover losses and expenses, the inability to sell policies because prices are higher than competitors' prices, and charges of unfair trade practices by regulatory authorities.

Determining Proper Coverage

Responsibility for determining the appropriate coverage that best meets the insured's needs rests with the risk manager and the agent or broker, but the underwriter can frequently offer invaluable assistance. The underwriter's role in this process can range from simply ascertaining that the policy is issued with the appropriate forms and endorsements to drafting manuscript policies and endorsements for complex or unique risks. The peculiar characteristics of each submission must be evaluated and related to policy provisions that deal with the potential loss characteristics.

In addition, producers and insureds might depend on the underwriter to determine whether the policy requested is appropriate for the applicant. For example, suppose an applicant has requested a building and personal property coverage form with the causes of loss broad form to insure a manufacturing location. While reviewing the applicant's operations as described in the inspection report, the underwriter discovers that the applicant also has an acceptable transportation exposure. The underwriter discusses this exposure with the producer and offers to provide the coverage. In this situation, the underwriter's actions exemplify a *positive* approach to underwriting.

An underwriter's knowledge of insurance contracts and ability to relate contract provisions to individual policyholders or applicants benefit producers and applicants. Producers often request broader coverage for a particular applicant than the underwriter is willing to provide. Rather than decline the application altogether, the underwriter might offer a more limited but adequate form of coverage through higher deductibles or limiting covered causes of loss. As a result, the producer has an opportunity to provide an adequate level of protection to the client.

Determining the Appropriate Rate or Price

The appropriate rate must be not only adequate to permit the insurer to continue to write profitable business, but also competitive with other insurers. In most personal lines, workers compensation, and some other commercial lines, proper classification automatically determines the appropriate rate. For major commercial lines, such as general liability, in which competitive pressures on individual accounts are often more focused, the underwriter might have the option to adjust the rate based on the individual characteristics of the insured. Many insurers operate through a number of subsidiary insurers. Each subsidiary has rates filed at different levels to reflect different groups of insureds in the marketplace. Personal lines insurers frequently have "good," "better," and "best" companies, and their underwriters can place an applicant with the company considered most appropriate. The underwriter must be assured that the characteristics justify the adjustment and must document that the adjustment was in accordance with the insurer's rating plan when filed with the regulatory authorities.

Providing Service to Producers and Policyholders

The extent of the line underwriter's responsibility for producer and policyholder service varies considerably. Many insurers using the independent agency marketing system allow their agents to issue certain types of policies and endorsements. Usually, an insurer's policyholder service department issues policies and necessary endorsements. The underwriter's responsibility in policy issuance often includes preparing the file for the policy typist or for data entry.

All underwriters prepare quotations and assist with proposals for agents and brokers. Underwriters are often a major source of technical expertise for the producers. The skill and efficiency with which the line underwriters perform this task help determine the insurer's success in the marketplace.

Staff Underwriting Activities

Although staff underwriting activities are usually performed at the home office, some regional underwriting managers have staff assistants. The major staff underwriting activities are as follows:

- Formulating underwriting policy
- Evaluating experience
- Researching and developing coverages and policy forms
- Reviewing and revising rating plans
- Preparing underwriting guides and bulletins
- Conducting underwriting audits
- Participating in industry associations and advisory organizations
- Conducting education and training

Formulating Underwriting Policy

Underwriters must continually research such fundamental issues as which markets the insurer should attempt to reach. This research includes evaluating the following:

- Adding or deleting entire lines of business
- Expanding into additional states or retiring from states presently serviced
- Determining the optimal product mix (the makeup of the book of business, such as general liability or workers compensation)
- Determining potential premium volume goals

For most insurers, the responsibility for those research activities is shared with actuarial and marketing departments. Determining present and prospective capacity to write business helps insurers achieve premium volume goals. Capacity is the volume of premium an insurer can safely write in a given year based on its policyholders' surplus (retained earnings). The overall underwriting policy is ultimately communicated to line underwriters and others through changes in underwriting guides, bulletins to producers, and home office directives.

The formulation of underwriting policy is influenced by how an insurer's underwriting management views the insurance marketplace and its desired position in it. Most insurers see their role as "standard lines" insurers. That is, they seek out better-than-average accounts. Some insurers, however, see an opportunity to offer coverage in areas of the market that are underserved by the standard market. The nonstandard or specialty insurers may use loss control, more restrictive coverage forms, or price to make "marginal" or "unacceptable" accounts in the standard market profitable. Either approach to the insurance marketplace can succeed or fail; neither approach is the "right" or "wrong" one. It is important to recognize this dichotomy in the insurance marketplace and that it reflects underwriting management's attitude toward risk bearing.

This chapter and the two that follow will focus on characteristics and conditions that distinguish the average risk from risks that are better or worse than average.

Evaluating Experience

Staff underwriters also analyze the loss and premium data of their own books of business and of the industry by line, class, size of risk, and territory to discern trends. That analysis is then used to determine whether changes must be made in the company's marketing or underwriting strategies. The necessary changes are usually communicated through the underwriting guide, but sometimes underwriting bulletins or bulletins sent to the insurer's producers describe special situations.

Researching and Developing Coverages and Policy Forms

As in many other businesses, researching and developing new products are vital to continued growth and prosperity in insurance. New coverages are developed to meet changing legal, social, economic, and technological conditions. Development activities by staff underwriters also include modifications in coverage to meet changes in market conditions or changes in various state statutes. Staff underwriters might also serve on industry or association committees that study policy forms and recommend changes.

Reviewing and Revising Rating Plans

Rates and rating plans must be continually reviewed and updated to respond to the effects of changes in expected loss experience, competition, and inflation. The review and update must occur whether the insurer files rates independently or belongs to an advisory organization. Until fairly recently, advisory organizations were known as "rating bureaus." An **advisory organization** is an organization of insurers formed to assist its members and subscribers in gathering the data necessary to calculate rates. The role of the advisory organization continues to evolve in response to regulatory and consumer group pressures. Most advisory organizations no longer publish final rates. Instead, they develop historical and prospective loss costs that they file with the appropriate regulatory authorities. The insurer must then examine its own operational costs and profit requirements and combine them with loss costs to create the final rates charged to policyholders. Production efficiencies or a superior risk-selection process can justify a lower rate that gives an insurer a competitive advantage in the marketplace.

For those coverages and lines of business for which advisory organizations do not develop loss costs, the insurer must develop its own rates completely. In such situations, the review and revision of rating plans become even more crucial.

Preparing Underwriting Guides and Bulletins

Underwriting guides and bulletins describe the underwriting practices necessary to implement underwriting policy. Staff underwriters periodically update the underwriting guides to reflect changes in underwriting policy. Underwriting guides, which distinguish between acceptable and unacceptable business, will be considered in detail later in this chapter.

Conducting Underwriting Audits

Staff underwriters are usually responsible for monitoring line underwriting activities to ensure compliance with the insurer's underwriting philosophy and practices. That monitoring is partially accomplished by analyzing underwriting results by line, class, size of risk, and territory and by conducting **field audits**. The typical field audit consists of a staff underwriter or a team of staff underwriters visiting a branch or regional office and checking individual underwriting files. The audit focuses on proper documentation, adherence to procedure, classification and rating practices, and conformity of selection decisions with the underwriting guide and bulletins.

Participating in Industry Associations and Advisory Organizations

Most insurers are members of national and state associations and advisory organizations that address industry concerns and issues. Staff underwriters are usually selected to participate in the activities of those organizations on behalf of their employers. In addition to advisory organizations, staff underwriters often work with trade associations that represent their members in legislative and other matters, automobile insurance (assigned risk) plans, and JUAs that deal with residual markets and pools for covering specialized risks.

Conducting Education and Training

Staff underwriters are usually responsible for determining the educational needs of line underwriters. The training department implements the resulting training program and continuing educational activities. If an educational need involves a technical insurance area, staff underwriters often develop the course and serve as instructors.

Centralized Versus Decentralized Underwriting Authority

A key element in any decision-making process is determining whether the decision-maker has the authority to make the decision. **Underwriting authority** is a degree of latitude granted individual underwriters or groups of underwriters (which might be organized in a department or branch). The authority granted varies by position, grade level, and experience.

Insurance companies vary considerably in the degree to which underwriting authority is decentralized. In the distant past, when most insurers operated out of a single office, underwriting authority was centralized in the home office. As insurers expanded their service areas geographically, some underwriting authority was moved out into regional and branch offices. Some insurers have even extended underwriting authority to specific producers.

The degree of decentralization of underwriting authority varies considerably by insurer and by line of business. Underwriters of specialty lines such as surety bonding, aviation, and livestock mortality operate with relatively centralized underwriting authority. On the other hand, some insurers delegate a substantial amount of underwriting authority to specific producers. Proponents of that type of decentralization believe that it eliminates duplication and capitalizes on the producers' familiarity with local conditions. When producers have underwriting authority, their compensation for the additional expense of underwriting, issuing policies, and handling claims is a high commission rate and a large percentage of profit sharing (contingent commission).

The amount of underwriting authority given to producers depends on the insurer's philosophy, the experience and profitability of the producer, the line of business involved, and other factors. Most insurers extend binding authority to the producer but reserve policy issuance for the company in order to preserve control over final underwriting and pricing. A notable exception is that most insurers provide their producers with a supply of homeowners and dwelling fire policies to be used for real estate closings when required by the mortgage company. A contingency commission agreement that provides the producer with an additional commission based on the loss ratio of the book of business and on the increase in premium volume can be further motivation for proper underwriting.

In certain lines of business, the producer might have no underwriting authority. High limits of insurance, specialized classes of business, and unusually hazardous classes represent instances when the producer is required to submit the account to the underwriter, who then makes the underwriting decision.

When granted underwriting authority, the producer uses an underwriting guide that shows those classes and lines of business that the insurer finds acceptable and unacceptable. The producer's experience and areas of expertise often determine the scope of the producer's underwriting authority. The insurer's underwriting policy governs cases that the producer must refer to higher underwriting authority.

Establishing Underwriting Policy

An effective underwriting policy translates the objectives of an insurer's owners and executive management into rules and procedures that will guide individual and aggregate underwriting decisions. Underwriting policy determines the composition of the book of business.

The composition of a book of business includes both the particular types of insurance products the insurer will offer as well as the amount of business to insure. Individual types of insurance or product lines are referred to as "lines of business." The Annual Statement, which is prescribed for financial reporting in all states, divides property-liability coverages into thirty-eight separate lines of business. Examples of those statutory lines of business are fire, allied lines, workers compensation, commercial multi-peril, and ocean marine. A complete listing appears in the Annual Statement. Insurers can group lines of business into related product lines or product mix. For example, an insurer that markets commercial auto insurance will have to offer the following Annual Statement lines of business: commercial auto no-fault (personal injury protection), other commercial auto liability, and commercial auto physical damage. Underwriters who use the term "line of business" are generally mentally combining the separate Annual Statement lines into a single reference such as "commercial auto."

Establishing an underwriting policy involves making compromises among underwriting objectives. Every insurer would like to expand premium writings, increase market share, and obtain profitable results. Conservative accounting rules prescribed by the NAIC prevent the immediate recognition of new insurance sales. Statutory accounting procedures (SAP) require that a liability be created on the balance sheet equal to the premiums written by the insurer. As the insurer earns premium over time, the liability is reduced, and cash is freed up for use by the insurer. The dilemma faced by the insurer is that acquisition expenses are required to be charged off immediately according to SAP rather than being amortized, as premium income is. That accounting requirement creates a cash flow problem that the insurer can alleviate only by drawing on its retained earnings or capital (policyholders' surplus). Unlike other businesses, an insurer's successful expansion of business can lead to a technical insolvency. For an insurer to be successful in the long term, it must maintain a balance of factors.

The principal dimensions of an insurer's underwriting policy, depicted in Exhibit 4-1, are (1) the lines of business and classes to be written, (2) territories to be developed, and (3) forms, rates, and rating plans. The major constraining factors of underwriting policy are (1) capacity, (2) regulation, (3) personnel, and (4) reinsurance. Those factors affect the various dimensions along which underwriting policy is structured.

Exhibit 4-1
Dimensions and Constraining Factors of Underwriting Policy

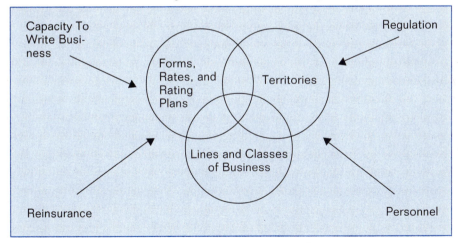

Any suggestion to change the current underwriting policy should be evaluated to determine its effect on the other dimensions and the constraining factors that might apply. For example, an insurer might decide to begin writing a new line of business. The insurer must determine the effect of that decision on other dimensions of underwriting policy. Which states and producers within those states will have the opportunity to sell the new line? Which combinations of forms and rates will be developed to create the product contemplated by management? Introducing a new product or expanding into a new jurisdiction will also necessitate changes in underwriting policy. Similarly, decisions to withdraw from lines of business, territories, and products should be evaluated using the framework. Underwriting policy will also change when decisions concerning the following are made:

- The emphasis placed on a particular territory
- Specific coverage options to offer
- Coverage limits to offer
- Policyholder acceptance guidelines
- Classes of business to write or avoid
- Pricing standards to employ
- Rating schedules to use
- Payment plan options
- Competitive need to offer new coverages and rating plans

All aspects of these topics should be described in detail in the insurer's underwriting guidelines.

Any change in underwriting policy must account for the effect of constraining factors on decisions in the insurance marketplace. The following discussion describes each constraining factor and illustrates some of the ways in which the factor constrains underwriting policy changes.

Capacity To Write Business

An insurer's **capacity to write business** refers to the relationship between premiums written and the size of policyholders' surplus. That relationship is critical in evaluating insurer solvency. The NAIC has created a series of eleven statistical ratios that are used in conjunction with analytical evaluations to identify insurers that should receive financial scrutiny by regulators. Premiums to surplus (net premiums written divided by surplus) is one of those key ratios and is considered too high when it exceeds 300 percent, or 3-to-1.

One way to exceed the premiums-to-surplus ratio is through rapid growth of premiums written. As mentioned, growth increases written premiums and reduces surplus to pay for immediate expenses. That constraint often precludes insurer expansion unless reinsurance is purchased.

Changes in surplus caused by underwriting gains and losses, and unrealized capital gains and losses, can also affect the premium-to-surplus ratio. Profitable growth permits additional expansion in subsequent years. Failure to underwrite successfully will produce losses that must be paid from surplus, thereby reducing the insurer's ability to write business in succeeding years. Generally accepted accounting principles (GAAP) do not recognize investment gains and losses until they are realized when the security or asset is sold. Statutory accounting procedures (SAP) require insurers to carry common stock on the balance sheet at market value (or association value) as of December 31.[4] Changes in the value of securities are immediately reflected in the insurer's surplus. An external method of increasing surplus and thereby improving the ratio is the infusion of new capital. That infusion could occur when the insurer sells additional stock or obtains a loan.

Insurers recognize that they have limited capacity to write business and must make prudent use of the capacity they have. Allocating that capacity is a matter of policy that insurers must evaluate on a regular basis. For example, an insurer might decide that commercial property insurance should be increased and that certain segments of the commercial general liability line should no longer be pursued. A particular class of general liability insureds might be experiencing a level of losses that exceeds the losses anticipated by the rate. Sometimes, the insurer might decide to stop writing a line of business or to add a line not previously written as a means of optimizing allocation of scarce capacity. Alternatively, the insurer might decide to limit its writing of a given line of insurance in a particular territory. In the past, for example, inadequate rate levels and rising benefit levels for claimants in many states have led some insurers to develop restrictive acceptance criteria for workers compensation insureds.

Regulation

States promulgate insurance regulations, which of some extent are coordinated under the auspices of the NAIC. State regulation takes the form of specific legislation enacted by the state legislatures and state insurance department regulations. Insurance regulation prescribes or affects virtually every major element of an insurer's operation. Regulation affects underwriting policy in several ways. Insurers must obtain licenses to write insurance by individual lines of insurance within each state. Rates, rules, and forms must be filed with state regulators. Some states, such as Florida, specifically require underwriting guidelines to be filed. In response to complaints by consumer groups, the federal government and the NAIC are considering the issue of insurance availability in geographic areas that consumer groups believe the insurance industry has not adequately served. In addition to financial audits, mentioned above, regulators perform market conduct examinations to determine whether insurers adhere to the classification and rating plans they have filed. When a market conduct examination discloses deviations from filed forms and rates or improper conduct, the insurer is subject to penalties.

The effect of regulation on underwriting policy varies by state. In some jurisdictions, insurers might be unable to get rate filings approved, or approval might be granted so slowly that rate levels are inadequate in relation to rising claim costs. Insurance, particularly personal auto and workers compensation insurance, has increasingly become a political issue. Some insurers have determined that regulation is too restrictive in some jurisdictions and have chosen to withdraw from those jurisdictions.

Personnel

Insurance requires the talents of specialists to market the product effectively, underwrite specific lines of insurance, service the account through loss control efforts, and adjust losses that occur. An insurer must have a sufficient number of properly trained underwriters to implement an insurer's underwriting policy. No insurer, for example, should pursue aviation, boiler and machinery, or ocean marine insurance without a sufficient number of experienced underwriting specialists in those lines of insurance.

In addition to having the skilled personnel to perform the job, the insurer must have the personnel *where* they are needed. All things being equal, insurance theory suggests that premiums should be obtained from a broad range of insureds to create the widest possible distribution of loss exposures. As a practical matter, policyholder service requirements and expenses related to regulatory requirements preclude small insurers from national operations in which efficiencies will be difficult to achieve with low volumes of business in each territory.

Reinsurance

The price and availability of reinsurance treaties can set limitations on what the insurer can write. Reinsurance involves a contractual relationship through which risks are shared with another insurer. Reinsurance is an essential tool in reducing the effect of expanded writings on an insurer's surplus. Through reinsurance, an insurer can shift the financial consequences of a loss and legal obligations for reserves, thereby increasing its own capacity.

The availability of adequate reinsurance and its cost are important considerations in implementing underwriting policy. Reinsurance treaties might exclude certain lines or classes of business, or the cost of reinsurance might be prohibitive. Reinsurers are also concerned with the underlying policy forms offered by the insurer. A reinsurer might have no reservations concerning an insurer's use of forms developed by advisory organizations but might expressly exclude reinsurance coverage for manuscript forms developed for a particular insured or forms developed independently.

Implementing Underwriting Policy

Once underwriting policy has been set, it must be communicated and implemented. The instruments used for this purpose in most cases are the underwriting guides and bulletins. After underwriting policy has been in place for a period of time, underwriting audits are conducted to determine whether underwriting policy is being followed. Underwriting results, properly measured, indicate the effectiveness of underwriting policy.

Underwriting Guides and Bulletins

Underwriting policy is reflected in a statement of objectives. Underwriting guides specify ways to achieve those objectives and are usually structured by major lines of business and class of business, and modified to meet changing conditions. Underwriting guides contain standards for eligibility and acceptability and establish underwriting authority requirements.

Some insurers have extensive underwriting guides with step-by-step instructions for handling particular classes of insureds. Such guides might identify specific hazards to evaluate, alternatives to consider, criteria to use in making the final decision, ways to implement the decision, and methods to monitor the decision. The guides might also provide pricing instructions and information pertinent to the reinsurance program. An excerpt from an underwriting guide with many of these characteristics is shown in Exhibit 4-2.

Some insurers take a less comprehensive approach to underwriting guides. For example, some underwriting guides might list all classes and indicate their acceptability by line of business. Codes are then assigned to indicate the desirability of the exposure and the level of authority required to write the class. An example of this type of underwriting guide appears in Exhibit 4-3.

Underwriting guides do the following:

- Provide for structured decisions
- Ensure uniformity and consistency
- Synthesize insights and experience
- Distinguish routine from nonroutine decisions
- Avoid duplication of effort

Exhibit 4-2
Commercial Property Underwriting Guide

RISK EVALUATION
UNDERWRITING EVALUATION EXHIBIT

This exhibit presents in schedule form the most important elements that might categorize a risk as "Below Average," "Average," or "Good." It is emphasized that there will be few risks that are totally "Below Average" or totally "Good" for all categories. Most risks will be subject to variations of one degree or another for each of the underwriting elements. The final classification by the underwriter will be determined by weighing the relative importance of each characteristic as applied to the risk.

IMPORTANT: IF THE RISK CLASSIFIES AS "BELOW AVERAGE" IN RESPECT TO "OWNERSHIP," IT IS UNACCEPTABLE IRRESPECTIVE OF ANY OTHER FAVORABLE RISK CHARACTERISTICS.

	BELOW AVERAGE	AVERAGE	GOOD
O W N E R S H I P	Abnormal loss history or unsatisfactory adjustment record	Loss record satisfactory	Little or no loss history
	Moral instability	Morally sound	Morally above reproach
	Criminal record	No criminal record	No criminal record
	Dishonest	Honest	Unquestionable integrity
	Illegal business	Legitimate business	Legitimate business
M A N A G E M E N T	Poor credit or bankruptcies	Good credit	Excellent credit
	Business unprofitable	Business profitable	Business highly profitable
	New venture and/or lack of experience	In business 3-5 years	In business 5 years
	Heating, wiring, plumbing over 20 years old	Heating, wiring, plumbing remodeled within last 20 years	Heating, wiring, plumbing less than 10 years old
	Poor control of common hazards	Minor common hazards	Common hazards well safeguarded
	Poor housekeeping–maintenance	Adequate house-keeping/maintenance	Good housekeeping/maintenance
	Usually careless	Reasonably careful	Exceptionally careful

	BELOW AVERAGE	AVERAGE	GOOD
C O N S T R U C T I O N	More than 25 years old	Less than 25 years old	Less than 10 years old
	No fire-stops where advisable	Minimum fire-stops	Effective fire-stops
	Poorly suited to occupancy	Basically suitable for occupancy	Especially suitable for occupancy
	Converted risks	Built for occupancy	Built for occupancy
	Large undivided area	Standard fire divisions	Important hazards cut off
	Poor design	Architecturally sound	Very well designed
	"Short-cut" construction	Good basic construction	Excellent construction and engineering
O C C U P A N C Y	Vacant, unoccupied	Occupied	Occupied
	Contents highly combustible (Cl. C4 & 5)	Contents moderately combustible (Cl. C3)	Contents low combustibility (Cl. C1 & 2)
	Contents highly susceptible (Cl. S4 & 5)	Contents moderately susceptible (Cl. S3)	Contents low susceptibility (Cl. S1 & 2)
	Extra-hazardous process for class	Normal processes for class	Processes well safeguarded
	Ordinary hazards not guarded	Ordinary hazards guarded	All hazards well guarded
	Obsolete merchandise or products	Merchandise and products saleable	Products or merchandise in demand
	Run-down equipment	Good equipment	Excellent equipment
	Undesirable tenancy	All occupants acceptable	Owner occupancy or all desirable tenants
	Susceptible to quick-spreading or flash fires	Quick-spreading fire unlikely	Quick-spreading fire unlikely

Continued on next page.

	BELOW AVERAGE	AVERAGE	GOOD
P R O T E C T I O N	No first aid Public protection at risk deficient No watch service Delayed alarm probable Inefficient public fire department	Minimum first aid Public protection equal to town protection Ordinary public police patrol Normal alarm expected Normal public fire department operations	Private protection good Public protection excellent Private watch service Early alarm probable Very effective public fire department
E X P O S U R E	Severe Large frame exposures Large concentrated values Unprotected wall openings or no parapets Neighborhood declining Poor location for type of business Outmoded business location Shore-front or hurricane exposure	Ordinary Frame exposure limited No large concentration of values Parapets and protection of exposed wall openings inadequate Neighborhood stable Acceptable location for type of business Stable or good business location No extraordinary storm exposure	Light or none No frame exposure Values well spread Exposed wall openings protected and exposed walls adequately parapeted Good environment Especially desirable location for type of business Prime business location economically prosperous No weather exposure
R A T E	Inadequate	Satisfactory	Satisfactory
INSURANCE TO VALUE	Less than 80%	At least 80%	At least 80%

UNDERWRITING ANALYSIS FORM 97-1564 GUIDELINES

Underwriting Analysis Form 97-1564 has been designed to set forth the underwriter's analysis of the risk elements that affect the quality of the risk. The purpose of the form is to document and record the underwriter's reasons for the risk grading so that the analysis will be available to managerial and supervisory staff and to other underwriters who may have occasion to handle or review the risk. The analysis form also provides a means to ensure that the necessary disciplines for risk selection will be observed.

Completion of this form is required for:

1. All risks written as "Exceptional Selection." (See section 15 of this Guide.)

2. All mono-line risks with limits of $100,000 or more.

3. (a)   All new commercial multi-peril risks with total property limits exceeding $150,000. *The analysis must be completed, however, for occupancies with combustibility gradings of 4 or 5 or occupancies listed on pages 12.1 and 12.2 of this Guide.*

   (b)   All renewal commercial multi-peril risks with total property limits exceeding $300,000. The analysis must be completed, however, for exposures under $300,000 if there has been a significant change in the character of the risk, such as change of location or change of occupancy.

4. All risks that require special surplus, facultative pro rata, or facultative excess of loss reinsurance.

5. All risks rated under individual risk premium modification, schedule rating, or similar plans.

6. All other risks not falling within the above criteria for which a completed Underwriting Analysis Form is required by your delegation of authority.

7. Any classes or limits of risks that may, from time to time, be required by national or branch underwriting managers.

It should be remembered that the Underwriting Analysis Form is the record of your evaluation of a risk. *The same mental process and discipline for risk evaluation must be followed even though completion of the form is not required.* A profitable experience can be attained only by a consistent assessment of each risk to determine quality. Careful consideration of the eight underwriting elements shown in the Underwriting Analysis Form is vital to such an evaluation.

Exhibit 4-3
Risk Selection Guide

A. GENERAL:

The Risk Selection Guide is a comprehensive alphabetical listing by class of business showing what The IIA Insurance Companies believe to be the desirability of insuring an average risk in the class. The Guide grades each class for Property, Commercial Automobile, Workers Compensation, Burglary and Robbery, Fidelity, Premises/Operations Liability, and Products/Completed Operations Liability. In addition, the final column titled "Form" indicates whether the General Liability coverage must be written on a Claims-Made Form (indicated by a "C"), or whether the Occurrence Form is available (indicated by an "O"). Please remember the risk selection guide is only a guide. The company retains final authority regarding the acceptance or rejection of any specific risk.

B. CLASSIFICATION ACCEPTABILITY RATINGS:

The Risk Selection Guide is being published as a section of this agent's manual to answer the question: "Are risks within a particular class likely to be accepted by The IIA Insurance Companies?" In light of this question, the risk grades as found in the Risk Selection Guide are defined as follows:

E — Excellent

This class of business is considered to have excellent profit potential. Unless a specific risk in this class has unusual hazards or exposures, it will rarely present any underwriting problems. Risk graded as "E" may be bound by the agent without prior underwriting consent.

G — Good

This class of business is considered to have good profit potential. Normally this risk may be written before obtaining an inspection or developing additional underwriting information other than that present on the application. The agent may bind risks graded as "G" without prior underwriting consent.

A — Average

Potential for profit is marginal due to high variability of risks within the class. It is understood that the underwriter might think it is necessary to inspect the risk before authorizing binding. In all instances, it is recommended that the agent call the underwriter and discuss the risk before binding.

S — Submit

The account presents little potential for profit. These risks will require a complete written submission before binding. The underwriter *must* obtain a complete inspection and evaluate any other underwriting information deemed necessary before authorizing the binding of this risk.

D — Decline

Due to the lack of potential for profit, this class of risk is prohibited and will not be considered. Under no circumstances may a risk classified as "D" be bound without the prior written approval of the Vice President of Commercial Underwriting.

C. FOOTNOTES:

Footnotes sometimes are indicated as applying to an individual classification for a specific line of insurance. These footnotes are displayed at the bottom of each page and are designed to make you aware of certain hazards or exposures that are unacceptable or need to be addressed in an acceptable manner.

We hope the Risk Selection Guide will be valuable in understanding the types of business our companies want to be writing. However, please do not hesitate to call your underwriter if you are unsure as to how to classify a particular risk, or if you feel the factors associated with a specific risk make it considerably better or worse than the grading assigned by this guide.

DESCRIPTION	PROP-ERTY	AUTO	WC	BURG. & ROB.	FIDEL-ITY	PREM & OPS	PROD & CO	FORM
Abrasive wheel manufacturing	S	A	D	A	G	S	D	C
Abrasives or abrasive products manufacturing	S	A	D	A	G	S	D	O
Abrasives or abrasive products manufacturing—Artificial	S	A	D	A	G	S	D	O
Adhesives manufacturing	S	A	S	A	G	A¹	S¹	O
Adhesive tape manufacturing	S	A	S	A	G	A¹	S¹	O
Advertising sign companies—outdoor	A²	G	S³	G	G	A³	G³	O
Aerosol container manufacturing	S	A	D	G	G	A	D	C
Aerosol containers—filling or charging for others	D	A	D	G	G	A	D	C
Agate or enamelware manufacturing Workers' Compensation only			D					
Air conditioning equipment manufacturers	A²	A	S	A	G	A¹	S¹	O
Air conditioning equipment—dealers or distributors only	G	G	A	G	G	G	G	O
Air conditioning systems or equipment—dealers or distributors and installation, servicing or repair	G	G	A	G	G	G	G	O
Air pressure or steam gauge manufacturing Workers' Compensation only			D					
Aircraft or aircraft parts manufacturing	A	G	S	A	G	D	D	O
Airport control towers—not operated exclusively by the Federal Aviation Administration	D	A	D	D	D	D	D	O
Airport—lessees of portions of airports engaged in the sale of aircraft or accessories, servicing or repairing of aircraft, or pilot instructions	D	A	D	D	D	D	D	O
Airports—commercial	D	A⁴,⁵	D	D	D	D	D	O
Airports—private	D	A⁴	D	D	D	D	D	O
Airport runway or warming apron—paving or repaving, surfacing, resurfacing or scraping	A	G	S	G	G	D	D	O
Alarm manufacturing—burglar	A²	A	A	A	G	A	D	C

1 Acceptability will depend upon specific nature of the operation and specific types and uses of the products.
2 The risk is unacceptable if any painting or finishing is done inside without an approved spray booth.
3 Work done above two stories in height is unacceptable.
4 No vans, mini-vans, or buses. Any automobile used in public or private livery is unacceptable.
5 Emergency use vehicles, such as ambulances and rescue vehicles, are unacceptable.

Provide for Structured Decisions

Underwriting guides provide structure for underwriting decisions by identifying the major elements that should be evaluated with each type of insurance written. For example, an underwriting guide for a contractors equipment floater coverage would indicate that the use of the equipment is of paramount importance in determining acceptability and would specify the premium to be charged. The underwriting guide would therefore indicate that two identical bulldozers are exposed to different hazards if one is used in road construction on flat terrain and the other is used to clear fire breaks in a mountainous region.

By identifying the principal hazards associated with a particular class of business, the underwriting guides ensure that underwriters consider the primary hazard traits of the exposures being evaluated. In addition to orienting underwriters who are unfamiliar with the class, underwriting guides also serve as a reminder for experienced underwriters.

Ensure Uniformity and Consistency

Underwriting guides help ensure that underwriting policy and thus selection decisions are made on a uniform and consistent basis throughout all geographic regions. Ideally, submissions that are identical in every respect should elicit the same underwriting response at each of the insurer's branch offices. Underwriting management cannot review every decision made by line underwriters. Underwriting guides instruct and inform individual underwriters of an acceptable approach to evaluating applicants and the overall desirability of a particular type of risk or class of risks. These guides also assist in maintaining anticipated exposures commensurate with underwriting policy to develop a book of business with exposures that the planned rate level can cover.

Synthesize Insights and Experience

Underwriting guides also synthesize the insights and experience of seasoned underwriters and assist those less familiar with particular lines and classes. Each industry and industrial process has its own unique set of hazards and exposures. Underwriting guides summarize the most pertinent observations that have been accumulated from the insurer's past experience.

In addition to insurer underwriting guides, a few commercial publications contain a wealth of underwriting information. One such publication is *Best's Underwriting Guide*, which concentrates on the significant hazard areas of each classification reviewed. Commercial publications usually supplement the insurer's underwriting guide. Although those publications contain useful underwriting information, they do not reflect any one insurer's underwriting philosophy.

Distinguish Routine From Nonroutine Decisions

Another purpose of the underwriting guides is to distinguish routine from nonroutine decisions. Line underwriters are given authority to make selection decisions on routine submissions. Generally, nonroutine submissions must be referred to higher underwriting authority (in some cases, the home office) for approval. Underwriting guides usually indicate that a particular class of business must either be declined or submitted to a higher level of authority for approval.

Avoid Duplication of Effort

Many underwriting situations recur. If the problems inherent in a particular situation have been identified and solved, the solution should apply to all similar situations recurring in the future. Underwriting guides contain the information necessary to avoid costly duplication of effort.

Other Uses of Underwriting Guides

Underwriting guides also provide information to assist underwriters in policy preparation. Rules and eligibility requirements for various rating plans are also included. Specialized information, such as eligibility for experience and retrospective rating together with appropriate rating formulas, also often appears in the underwriting guide. Many underwriting guides describe specialized procedures required by the insurer. Underwriting guidelines also support compliance with state regulatory requirements.

Underwriting Audits

The **underwriting audit** is a management control tool used to determine whether underwriters in branch and regional offices are properly implementing underwriting policy. The larger and more decentralized the insurer's operation is, the more difficult is the task of achieving uniformity and consistency in underwriting standards and adhering to a particular underwriting philosophy. Audits also disclose whether underwriting guidelines cause undesirable results. If they do, the underwriting guidelines should be reviewed and revised. The audit might reveal that existing underwriting guidelines are perceived as being unrealistic and are not being followed. The audit should also identify unused guidelines and multiple or standing exceptions. Audits should disclose those situations in which underwriters have exceeded the authority granted through the underwriting guidelines. Most large insurers can conduct personal lines audits through the insurer's computer system. Commercial lines audits are usually performed using paper files.

The typical underwriting audit in a branch or regional office is conducted by one underwriter or a team of staff underwriters from the home office who visit the branch office and review selected files. Evaluating the quality of under-writing decisions is difficult, but the underwriting audit can determine whether proper procedures and policies are being followed. The simpler the line of business being underwritten is, the easier the audit task becomes. In personal lines, because the attributes of desirable insureds can easily be enumerated, the auditing team can identify lack of compliance quickly. Some companies use a point system to grade underwriters, assessing a penalty point for each violation of underwriting standards or procedure uncovered.

If underwriting data have been computerized, computers can evaluate the composition of a book of business to determine whether underwriting policy is being properly implemented. The audit teams can then explore problems identified in this manner in the field.

Measuring Underwriting Results

The success of underwriting is measured by the results obtained. The insurer's combined loss and expense ratio indicates the effectiveness of its underwriting program. Of course, inflationary trends, catastrophic losses, and adverse politi-cal and economic trends can distort these ratios in the short run. Evaluating results by line of business, territory, and source of production (that is, by agency) will identify problem areas. The above factors also affect the interpre-tation of underwriting results. In addition, because the insurance industry has proved to be cyclical over the years, the underwriting results of a particular insurer can be measured against the average performances of the industry during a given phase of the cycle.

Insurance Industry Trends

Countrywide underwriting results have indicated the presence of a continuing underwriting cycle. Within the past several years, extreme periods of both good and poor underwriting results have occurred, although investment income has offset underwriting losses in many years.

The exact causal mechanism for this cycle has not been defined; however, certain forces appear to significantly affect the cycle. Those forces include inflation, investment results, competition, and the effect of regulation. Slow regulatory responses to rate increase requests in periods of inflation might have been an important determinant of the subsequent unsatisfactory underwriting results. Delayed, reduced, or denied rate increases in recent years have reduced written premiums by hundreds of millions of dollars. The major component of loss costs are increasing rapidly because of inflationary factors, so the poor underwriting results are not surprising. At the same time, rate increases might be lower than necessary to respond to rising loss costs because of regulatory decisions or competition among insurers.

Additional factors influencing underwriting experience include automobile insurance plans, JUAs, and similar residual market plans to solve social as well as insurance problems. Once limited to substandard private passenger auto, residual market plans have expanded to include FAIR Plans and a variety of state-sponsored mechanisms, such as assigned risk plans for workers compensation and medical malpractice JUAs.

Competitive forces can also increase the amplitude of underwriting cycles. During periods of seemingly favorable results, insurers try to increase their premium volume. In commercial lines, desirable business might be written at less than adequate rates. Contributing to this problem is the belief on the part of certain managers that they can write increased volumes of commercial lines at an underwriting loss, which they can make up with superior investment results. This practice is called **cash-flow underwriting**. Although those tactics can be effective in the short run, they have resulted in disastrous operating losses for some insurers long term.

Difficulties in Interpretation of Results

The evaluation of underwriting results based on an insurer's loss and expense ratio is made more difficult because several complicating factors reduce the ratio's efficiency as a measurement device. The most significant of those factors are premium volume considerations and loss development delay.

Premium Volume Considerations

Premium volume and underwriting policy are directly related. Adherence to stricter underwriting standards than those previously employed usually causes premium volume to decline. Conversely, loosening underwriting standards typically results in an increase in premium volume. The interpretation of an insurer's combined loss and expense ratio, both on an aggregate basis and by line, should take into account the extent to which the insurer's premium volume goals have or have not been met. The *extreme* example shown in Exhibit 4-4 shows the two approaches used to determine underwriting profitability and the effect that changes in premium volume can have on insurer underwriting results.

In statutory accounting, the loss ratio is calculated by dividing incurred losses by earned premiums. The expense ratio also relates underwriting expenses to earned premium. The sum of those ratios is the financial basis combined ratio. The combined ratio as calculated by A.M. Best Co., which is also referred to as the trade basis combined ratio, uses the same loss ratio but divides underwriting expenses by written premium.

Exhibit 4-4
Underwriting Results—Financial and Trade Bases

This exhibit shows a hypothetical example of an insurer experiencing a 25 percent drop in written premium as a result of following a much more restrictive underwriting policy. On a *financial basis,* the combined results have improved from 102 percent to 96 percent. On a trade basis, however, the insurer's experience deteriorated from 99.9 percent to 102.2 percent. Analysis of underwriting results should be done on both bases to evaluate the effect of changes in premium volume correctly.

	Year 1	Year 2
Written premium	$10,000,000	$7,500,000
Earned premium	9,500,000	9,000,000
Underwriting expenses	3,990,000	2,790,000
Incurred losses	5,700,000	5,850,000

Financial Basis

Loss ratio:

$$\frac{\text{Incurred losses}}{\text{Earned premium}} = \frac{\$5,700,000}{\$9,500,000} = 60\% \qquad \frac{\$5,850,000}{\$9,000,000} = 65\%$$

Expense ratio:

$$\frac{\text{Underwriting expenses}}{\text{Earned premium}} = \frac{\$3,990,000}{\$9,500,000} = 42\% \qquad \frac{\$2,790,000}{\$9,000,000} = 31\%$$

Financial basis combined ratio	102%	96%

Trade Basis

Loss ratio:

$$\frac{\text{Incurred losses}}{\text{Earned premium}} = \frac{\$5,700,000}{\$9,500,000} = 60\% \qquad \frac{\$5,850,000}{\$9,000,000} = 65\%$$

Expense ratio:

$$\frac{\text{Underwriting expenses}}{\text{Written premium}} = \frac{\$3,990,000}{\$10,000,000} = 39.9\% \qquad \frac{\$2,790,000}{\$7,500,000} = 37.2\%$$

Trade basis combined ratio	99.9%	102.2%

The rationale for relating underwriting expenses to written premium is that most expenses are related to placing business on the books rather than maintaining it. The effect of the trade basis combined ratio is to recognize the "equity" in the unearned premium reserve.

Analyzing on a trade basis has some limitations, however. First, the extent to which expenses are related to written premium rather than earned premium varies by line. Commissions and acquisition expenses also vary by line. Certain specialty lines such as boiler and machinery have significant continuing inspection expenses, which are actually related more to earned premium. This is also true to a lesser extent for workers compensation insurance. For this reason, comparisons between insurers with different mixes of business on a trade basis can be misleading.

Loss Development Delay

In certain lines of business, particularly the liability coverages, a considerable amount of time elapses between the occurrence of a loss and the settlement of the claim. Although reserves are established as soon as the loss is reported, significant inaccuracy exists in estimating ultimate loss costs. That inaccuracy is known as loss development delay, or as the "long tail," and it has two major components: changes in the reserves for reported losses and changes in the reserves for incurred but not reported (IBNR) losses.

In lines of business written on an occurrence basis, which can have an extended discovery period between the time of the occurrence of the insured event and the discovery and subsequent suit by the claimant, the IBNR greatly affects the accuracy of current reported loss results. The change on the part of many professional liability insurers to claims-made forms and the introduction of the claims-made commercial general liability policy were intended to alleviate this problem.

If a policy is written on an occurrence basis, the insurer provides coverage for injuries that occur during the policy period even if claims for such injuries are not actually brought against the insured until years after the coverage has expired. If a policy is written on a claims-made basis, the insurer provides coverage only for claims made against the insured during the policy period. Thus, in theory, a pure claims-made policy does not cover losses that have not been reported by the end of the policy period. In practice, however, claims-made policies often cover losses reported after the policy period by virtue of "extended reporting periods." Thus, IBNR losses can be a problem under either type of policy.

In all liability lines, where several years can elapse between the notification of a claim and the final settlement, changes in reserves occur frequently. Since the incurred losses used to compile loss ratios include both paid losses and outstanding loss reserves, the loss ratio as an indicator of underwriting performance relies heavily on the accuracy and realistic evaluation of the reserve estimations. The more time that elapses between notification and settlement, the less accurate the estimation is. Exhibit 4-5 shows an example of a loss development delay for a particular group of general liability policies on a calendar-accident-year basis.

Standards of Performance

One technique that can be used to evaluate the performance of an underwriting department is to set standards of performance regarding several crucial areas of underwriting. Those standards of performance include the following:

- Selection
- Product mix
- Pricing
- Accommodated risks
- Retention ratio
- Success ratio
- Service to producers

Although some of those standards clearly apply only to commercial lines underwriting departments, others can be used for both personal and commercial lines.

Selection

To implement this monitoring technique, establishing well-defined selection rules in the underwriting guide is necessary. Those selection rules should define highly desirable, average, and below-average types of insureds, and each underwriter, branch, or region should have a goal specifying the balance of the three types of insureds. During an underwriting audit or review, the business written by a particular underwriter, branch, or region can be segmented into the various categories, and the percentages of the book of business in each category can be evaluated.

Product Mix

This monitoring technique requires a statement within the underwriting guide of the desired product mix for new and renewal business. For example, if product liability losses are causing an adverse effect on the entire book of business, the product mix standard might require a reduction in manufacturing classes but a concerted effort to increase the writing in the contractor, service, and mercantile classes. The comparison of the actual book to the desired one provides a straightforward evaluation of performance.

Exhibit 4-5
Loss Development Delay—Calendar-Accident-Year Basis

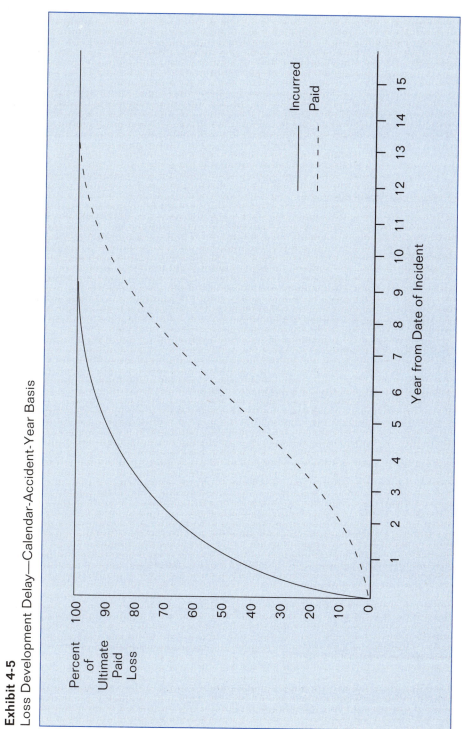

Pricing

Pricing standards are used to gauge the adequacy of the premiums being charged relative to some standard. In commercial insurance, insurance rates are typically modified to reflect features specific to the account being underwritten. Pricing standards provide guidance by indicating the extent to which these departures from the premium would be charged to the "normal" account. An underwriting audit might find that profitability in a line of insurance is being sacrificed for growth. Pricing standards are one way insurers communicate their pricing policy to line underwriters.

Accommodated Risks

This standard of performance requires a log in which all "accommodated risks" are entered along with the reasons for the accommodation. An **accommodation** is usually the acceptance of a substandard exposure in return for other, more profitable business. During regular underwriting audits and reviews, evaluation of the log can determine whether accommodations are being granted too often and can ensure that the producer has delivered increased volume or fulfilled some other promise.

Retention Ratio

The **retention ratio** is the percentage of business renewed. Since most, if not all, of the underwriting investigation work has been performed for existing policies, keeping those policies offers more profit potential than acquiring new business. An unfavorable percentage of renewals might indicate serious deficiencies, including poor service to producers, noncompetitive pricing, or unfavorable claims service. This standard requires careful monitoring of the renewal rate and evaluation of any trends discerned.

Success Ratio

The **success ratio**, sometimes called the "hit ratio," is the ratio of business written to business quoted. This standard is usually employed in commercial lines. Data must be gathered for a large number of quotations to determine the average range for this ratio. Ratios that are either inordinately high or low might require follow-up and further investigation. A high ratio might indicate any of the following:

- Easing of competition
- Rate inadequacy or rates lower than other insurers
- Broader coverage than other insurers
- Deterioration in selection criteria

Low success ratios might indicate one or more of the following:

- Increasing competition
- Rates that are too high
- Coverages or forms that are too restrictive
- Selection criteria that are too high
- Poor service

Service to Producers

Since producers usually rank insurers on the basis of service received, the insurer must be able to evaluate its own performance. This standard requires establishing a set of minimum acceptable standards for certain types of service to producers. The actual performance of each underwriter, branch, or region being evaluated is then compared with the targeted level of performance. An example of one such standard appears in Exhibit 4-6.

Exhibit 4-6
Example of "Service to Producers" Underwriting Standards

Category	Minimum Acceptable Standard
1. Quotations	3 working days
2. New policies	3 working days
3. Replies to correspondence	2 working days
4. Cancellations, endorsements, certificates	5 working days
5. Direct cancellation notices	Same-day service
6. Renewals	No later than 10 days before expiration

The Underwriting Process

Underwriting has been defined as the selection of policyholders through hazard recognition and the evaluation, pricing, and determination of terms and conditions. The **underwriting process** specifies the steps underwriters generally follow when evaluating a prospective policyholder.

Underwriters have traditionally resisted admitting that their underwriting intuition is actually the internalization of a decision-making process that can apply to a variety of loss exposures. They argue that it is difficult to identify one process that adequately addresses the many facets of underwriting decision making. Perhaps the skill described as "underwriting intuition" would be better described as the creative application of the underwriting process.

The underwriting decision-making process can be described as consisting of the following five steps:

1. Gathering information
2. Identifying, developing, and evaluating alternatives
3. Selecting an alternative
4. Implementing the decision
5. Monitoring the exposures

Gathering Information

Underwriters would like to have a comprehensive knowledge of the activities, operations, and character of applicants. That ideal objective cannot be achieved, however, because of the necessary tradeoffs required to minimize underwriting expenses. Concentrating too much time on a particular account is also impractical. Despite those limitations, underwriters try to balance the degree of hazard with how much information is needed and the cost to obtain it. For example, an underwriter would require an extensive investigation of a manufacturer. Conversely, the underwriter might require much less information for a low-hazard risk like a gift shop.

The underwriter draws together information from a number of sources to develop a profile of the applicant. The profile is a composite of information about the applicant that describes the nature of the operation, financial condition, and characteristics of the risk.

Sources of Information

The principal sources of information are the producer, the application, consumer investigation reports, government records, financial rating services, loss data, independent inspection reports, field marketing personnel, premium auditors, claim files, and production records.

The Producer

Typically, it is the producer who has personal contact with the applicant, has firsthand knowledge of the applicant's operations, and knows the applicant's reputation in the community. The producer usually performs the investigation required to determine the coverage needs of the applicant. The producer using this knowledge to provide the insurer with an acceptable applicant is serving to "pre-qualify" or **field underwrite** the applicant.

The degree to which an insurer depends heavily on the producer to evaluate thoroughly the acceptability of the applicant varies by producer and type or class of business and might differ based on the marketing system employed.

Direct writing and exclusive agency insurers are explicit about the characteristics of the ideal applicant. Producers for these insurers screen applicants with full knowledge of the parameters used by the underwriters in evaluating the applicants' hazard characteristics.

Producers for independent agency insurers have a number of markets available to them. Their task is more complex because they must understand the marketing goals and underwriting guidelines of the various insurers they represent. Additionally, independent agents must balance the placement of their business among their insurers to maintain preferential treatment and meet obligations under agency contracts. The ability to match applicants with an appropriate market (insurer) is an essential skill for independent producers.

The Application

Information about the applicant and information obtained by the producer to further entice the insurer to accept the prospective insured are combined in the application. Insurance applications gather general information required to process, rate, and underwrite the applicant. Usually, a different application exists for each line of business. Each insurer may develop its own application or use the ACORD standard applications. ACORD applications were developed by industry committees to reduce the amount of paperwork agents must handle when working with several insurers. In either case, the application attempts to target specific information necessary to properly evaluate the acceptability of the applicant. In the case of an ACORD application, individual insurers may take advantage of some free-form areas on the application to obtain unique information that the company believes is crucial to sound decision making.

Despite the completeness of the application, the underwriter usually finds it necessary to obtain additional information concerning the applicant. This information can be loosely categorized as internal or external, and objective or subjective. The underwriter needs to be aware of the insurer's internal sources of information because they can often be obtained quickly and economically. Likewise, external information might be expensive to obtain and delay processing of the application. Objective information consists of facts that have been recorded and can be verified. Subjective information consists of opinions or personal impressions. The underwriter needs to be able to distinguish between the two and be able to identify subjective influences that could exist in objective information.

Consumer Investigation Reports

Several independent reporting services provide background information on prospective policyholders. On personal lines coverages such as private passenger auto, these reports usually include a description of the neighborhood and environment of the applicant, and information for verification of proper classification assignment. Various types of reports are also available for most commercial lines coverages.

Government Records

Government records include motor vehicle reports; criminal court records; and civil court records, including records of suits filed, mortgages and liens, lists of business licenses, property tax records, and bankruptcy filings.

Motor vehicle records (MVRs) are a fundamental information source for auto underwriting. Some states require insurers to obtain MVRs each year so that driver violations can be incorporated into the rating scheme of each policy.

Most underwriters use independent services to obtain civil and criminal information even though they can obtain that information directly from court records. Civil and criminal reports will show any previous bankruptcies or judgments that are on record.

Financial Rating Services

Dun & Bradstreet (D&B), Standard & Poor's, and TRW are some of the major financial rating services. They provide data on the credit ratings of individual businesses, together with industry averages for purposes of comparison. Although the use of one or more of these financial rating services is almost universal in surety bond underwriting, the services are also used in many other commercial lines. They can be used to verify a financial statement provided by an applicant as well as to provide an overall picture of the applicant's financial stability and strength. A financially weak business might present an unacceptable hazard. Use of the data provided by the financial rating services is greatly enhanced if the underwriter is familiar with financial ratios used to evaluate a firm's liquidity, profitability, and debt structure. In addition, the 10-K form filed with the Security and Exchange Commission (SEC) contains a wealth of information on public companies.

Loss Data

Underwriters usually have loss experience on policyholders and producers and also on an aggregate basis by class, line of business, and territory, both for the insurer and the industry. In commercial lines, the loss experience of the policyholder might be extensive enough to have statistical significance on its own, while in personal lines it is the loss experience for the class or territory that has more significance.

Loss frequency, loss severity, and the type of loss are all important in analyzing loss data. The cause of loss and the date of loss provide further insights. There might be a possibility of either reducing the hazards through loss control measures or adding or increasing a deductible if these causes of loss can be identified. The date of loss provides information on possible seasonality or trends in loss experience. Results for a given line, class, or territory, as well as insurance industry results, might indicate rate inadequacy, causing a modification of underwriting policy pending approval of higher rate levels.

Inspection Reports

Inspection or loss control reports prepared by loss control personnel provide information on the physical condition of property, the safety of business operations, and the insured's management.

Most inspection reports in commercial lines contain lists of both mandatory and suggested recommendations. A follow-up on the degree of compliance provides the underwriter with insight into the attitude of management toward safety.

Field Marketing Personnel

In most companies, field marketing personnel (such as field representatives or special agents) can provide both specific and general information. Field marketing personnel can frequently obtain information that a producer omitted from an application or a submission. In territories that are sparsely populated or in other situations in which qualified loss control personnel are not available, many insurers use field marketing personnel to make simplified inspection reports. The field marketing person can also provide detailed background information on the producer and sometimes on the applicant. In some insurers, this function is fulfilled by sales managers, managing general agents, or the producer.

Premium Auditors

The premium auditor examines the policyholders' operations, records, and books of account to determine the actual insurance exposure for the coverages provided. The usual procedure is for the premium audit to be conducted after a provisional premium has been collected and the policy term has expired. It is increasingly common for the insurer to conduct a pre-audit so that policyholders will be aware that premium adjustments will be made after the term and that the information will be required to complete the audit. In either case, the premium auditor has the opportunity to gather information concerning the policyholders' operations that might have underwriting implications, including moral and morale hazards.

Claim Files

When underwriting renewals of existing policies, an underwriter can often obtain insights into the character of the policyholder by reviewing the policyholder's claim files. Claims adjusters frequently develop significant underwriting information during the course of their investigations. For example, an adjuster investigating a small fire loss at a machine shop might uncover evidence of poor housekeeping and a disregard for loss control on the part of the policyholder. Some insurers have an information system whereby claims adjusters notify the underwriter any time they obtain pertinent information on physical, moral, and morale hazards on any policyholder. In personal lines, the adjuster can often identify through an investigation an insured who is making many small claims that most people would attribute to normal wear and tear. In commercial lines, such as workers compensation, a review of claim files might indicate the presence of dangerous conditions requiring loss control engineering.

The claims adjuster is one of a few employees of the insurer who has an opportunity to make a firsthand appraisal of the locations insured. The value of his or her observation is so great that maximum effort is justified to ascertain that nothing inhibits full communication with underwriting. An example of a report that could facilitate communication is shown in Exhibit 4-7.

Production Records

Records are usually available on individual producers, indicating loss ratio, premium volume, mix of business, amount of supporting business, length of service, and industry experience. In the case of an independent agent, the number of insurers represented by the agency is also relevant. In auto underwriting, for example, the production records on the mix of business would indicate whether a particular producer is submitting an inordinately large percentage of young drivers or drivers with poor driving records. In commercial lines, the production records would indicate the producer's familiarity with complex or unusual classes of business. The background and experience of the producer might be of concern to the underwriter in the case of a large boiler and machinery application or a complex manufacturing submission. Such a submission from a producer whose book of business is 95 percent personal lines would raise questions in the underwriter's mind about the producer's familiarity with the coverage and his or her ability to service the account properly. In all marketing systems, producer results over a reasonably extended period of time (usually three to five years) are a good measure of his or her capability as an effective field underwriter.

Hazard Evaluation

A **hazard** is any condition that increases the expected frequency or severity of loss. Hazards can result from almost innumerable sources and can be classified in many ways. One such classification is to identify hazards as physical, moral, and morale. Much underwriting information is developed to enable the underwriter to identify and evaluate hazards. The underwriter is primarily concerned with whether the hazards in the applicant's operations or activities are greater than normal, unusual, or uncontrolled. The loss control representative can be directly involved in assessing those hazards for the underwriter.

Physical Hazards

Physical hazards are tangible characteristics of the property, persons, or operations to be insured that affect the probable frequency and severity of loss resulting from one or more causes of loss. Physical hazards can be attributes of the applicant, of the property to be insured, or of the environment in which the property is located. An untrained driver, damageability of cargo being shipped, and the quality of public fire protection are all examples of physical hazards.

Moral Hazards

Moral hazard is a condition that exists when a policyholder tries to cause a loss or exaggerates a loss that has occurred. Although most information on moral hazard is subjective, objective data might be available, such as a history of past financial difficulties or a criminal record. Potential indicators of moral hazard include weak financial condition, undesirable associates, and poor moral character.

Weak Financial Condition The owners of a financially weak commercial enterprise might intentionally cause a loss to obtain desperately needed cash. For example, the Persian Gulf War of 1991 and fear of domestic terrorism presented a backdrop for a failed insurance fraud attempt. The owners of two million gallons of sodium hydrosulfate stored near the Norfolk, Virginia, Naval Base planted pipe bombs after doubling their property insurance. Had the owners been successful, they would have been able to eliminate their back debts and make a $1 million profit.[5] Ocean marine underwriters are particularly aware that during periods of overcapacity, the owners of an idle or obsolete vessel might try to "sell it to the underwriters" by intentionally causing a loss.

Since the financial condition of a business can change quickly, detecting the hazard caused by weak financial condition requires constant monitoring. Changes in consumer tastes or innovation by competitors can leave a business with a sizable obsolete inventory. Economic downturns can postpone essential maintenance to vital services such as electrical, plumbing, and heating systems.

Exhibit 4-7
Claim Report to Underwriter

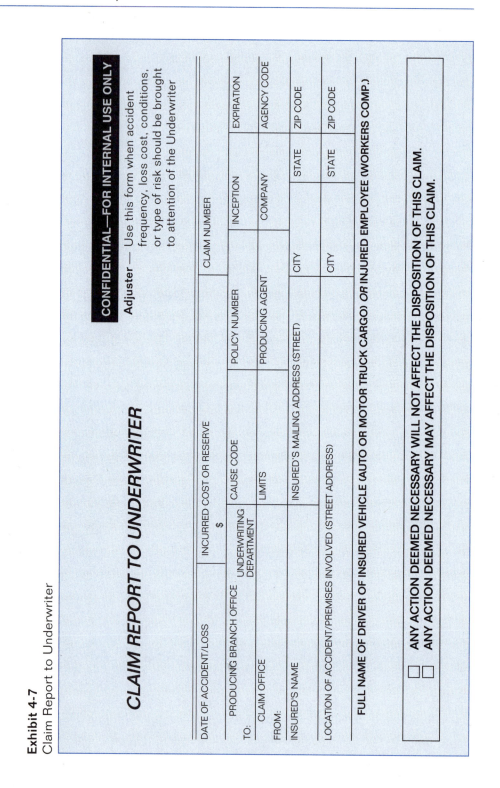

INSTRUCTIONS TO ADJUSTER: Check applicable blocks below and explain each item checked under REMARKS.

A. AUTOMOBILE

1. Physical disability
2. Vehicle in poor condition
3. Evidence of drinking
4. Reckless driving
5. Uncooperative
6. Loss frequency
7. Poor driving record
8. Driver under age 25*
9. Indiscriminate loan of vehicle
10. Driver fell asleep
11. Gross negligence
12. Total loss of insured vehicle
13. Late notice
14. Owned vehicle not on policy
15. Other

*Personal auto policy not so classified

B. WORKERS COMPENSATION OR GENERAL LIABILITY

1. Hazardous physical condition
2. Machinery
   a. Defectively manufactured
   b. Poorly designed
   c. Does not meet industry standards
   d. Inadequately labeled
3. Poor location
4. Uncooperative
5. Poor management or supervision
6. Inadequate records
7. Loss frequency
8. Late notice
9. Pollution loss
10. Other

C. FIDELITY OR, BURGLARY OR, PLATE GLASS OR, FIRE MARINE AND MULTI-LINE

1. Inadequate safeguards or training
2. Inadequate records
3. Loss frequency
4. Possible illegal activities
5. Questionable loss
6. Vacant premises
7. Underinsured
8. Questionable physical condition
9. Late notice
10. Poor housekeeping
11. Uncooperative
12. Possible financial problems
13. Exposure from adjoining risks
14. Fire protection/first aid system impeded
15. Carelessness
16. Other

REMARKS

ADJUSTER'S SIGNATURE

C.R.U. DATE

Undesirable Associates   A policyholder's association with criminals is another indicator of potential moral hazard. A business that is frequented by members of the underworld or other undesirables does not reflect well on the character of the proprietor.

Poor Moral Character   Moral hazard can arise from the poor moral character of the policyholder even when the financial condition is sound. Previous questionable losses, a criminal record, or evidence of moral turpitude can indicate a moral hazard. A reputation for unethical or illegal business practices would also indicate moral hazard.

Morale Hazards

Morale hazard is a condition that exists when people are less careful than they should be because of the existence of insurance. That hazard arises out of carelessness or indifference to loss and is usually more subtle and more difficult to detect than moral hazard. Morale hazard might better be termed "lack of motivation hazard" because it exists in policyholders that are poorly motivated to avoid and minimize losses. Morale hazards might be indicated by poor personality traits or poor management.

Poor Personality Traits   Personality traits such as carelessness and thoughtlessness indicate morale hazard. Careless persons might not intentionally cause a loss, but they can exhibit a cavalier attitude toward valuable possessions, increasing the likelihood of loss. Someone who thoughtlessly leaves his or her keys in the car exhibits this hazard. The absence of pride of ownership can indicate the existence of morale hazard.

Poor Management   Poor or inefficient management can also indicate morale hazard. Sloppy housekeeping and indifferent bookkeeping are overt manifestations of this condition. Indifference to loss can result in neglecting the maintenance of fire extinguishers and other safety devices. Poor or nonexistent internal control systems invite theft and embezzlement by employees. Failure to comply with recommendations or to cooperate with loss control personnel is a further indication of morale hazard.

Identifying, Developing, and Evaluating Alternatives

After all the essential information on a particular submission has been gathered and hazards have been evaluated, the underwriter is ready to make a decision. The underwriter must identify and develop the alternatives available regarding the submission and, after carefully evaluating each alternative, choose the optimal one under the circumstances.

Two alternatives are easily identified: the underwriter can accept the submission as is or reject it. In addition, the underwriter can accept the submission subject to certain modifications. Determining the appropriate modification to best meet the needs of the insurer, producer, and applicant can be a challenge.

The four major types of modifications that can be made are as follows:

- Adopt loss control programs or devices
- Change rates, rating plans, or policy limits
- Amend policy terms and conditions
- Use facultative reinsurance

Adopt Loss Control Programs or Devices

One alternative available to the underwriter for a submission that would otherwise be unacceptable is to reduce the hazards. Such loss control programs as the installation of sprinklers, addition of guard service, and improvements in housekeeping and maintenance are means of reducing physical hazards. Further examples are the requirement of clear space for insureds in brush or wooded locations or the installation of machinery guards to reduce employee injuries. Some of these programs are relatively inexpensive and simple to implement, while others, such as sprinklers, require considerable capital investment.

From the applicant's viewpoint, insurer recommendations to reduce hazards might have a very positive, long-term effect on the ultimate costs of doing business, or they might be viewed as wholly unnecessary expenses. A significant function of underwriting is the making of sound recommendations accompanied by well-reasoned and convincing explanations to the applicant.

Change Rates, Rating Plans, or Policy Limits

A submission that is not acceptable at the rate requested might be desirable business at a higher rate, on a different rating plan, or with a lower limit. In private passenger auto, for example, a submission may not be eligible for the "safe driver" program for which it is submitted but might qualify for inclusion in another program at standard rates.

The rate modification could be either positive or negative. A producer might submit an account that is particularly desirable, with the recommendation that a rate deviation would increase the producer's likelihood of obtaining the account. In commercial insurance, where more discretion in pricing is permitted, pricing of submissions is crucial to obtaining profitable accounts in a competitive market. For instance, "a" rated (estimated loss potential) general liability policies are those classes in which the underwriter is given a range of possible rates, or suggested rates due to the statistical uncertainty of these classes. Judgment is used to select a rate that will earn a reasonable profit and be competitive enough to obtain the account. Pricing modifications also play a key role in judgment-rated lines such as inland and ocean marine. A number of rating plans are available for commercial applicants. The principal ones come under the category of merit plans and include experience rating, schedule rating, and retrospective rating.

Experience Rating

Experience rating uses the policyholder's actual loss experience to develop a premium modification factor to adjust the manual rate that would normally be applied. These plans are sometimes referred to as *prospective experience rating plans* because the premium modification is calculated before the inception of the policy to which it is applied. Experience rating is available for general liability risks that develop a specific premium level (which varies by company) and have at least one year of experience. In application, the experience rating plan uses three years of past loss experience, when available, and a credibility factor based on the size of the policyholder's premium to determine the actual modification. In comparison to other individual rating plans, experience rating has a formal methodology and must be applied without discrimination to all risks that meet experience rating eligibility requirements.

Schedule Rating

Schedule rating provides for the awarding of debits and credits to a risk based on specific categories such as the care and condition of the premises and the training and selection of employees. The credits or debits vary by insurer and are limited by insurance statute (usually between 25 and 40 percent). When applied, they reflect the underwriter's estimate of the degree of potential risk an insured presents, and the underwriter uses debits and credits to appropriately adjust the manual rate upward or downward. Insurance statutes require that insurers apply these plans to all eligible risks without discrimination and that adequate documentation be kept on file to justify the pricing decision.

Retrospective Rating

Retrospective rating is an individual experience modification program that uses the current year as the experience period to develop the experience modification factor. Under this plan, a provisional premium is charged at the beginning of the policy period. At the end of the policy period, the actual loss experience for *that* period is determined, and a final premium is charged. The insured's premium is adjusted after the end of the policy period to cover the expenses and losses developed by the insured during the policy period subject to specified minimum and maximum premiums. These plans have several variations that protect the policyholder from fluctuations in the final premium.

Policy Limits

Underwriting policy usually specifies the maximum limits of liability that can be written. For property insurance, the underwriter must be alert to over-insurance situations that could lead to a fraudulent loss. Underinsurance might be a more common problem. Adequate insurance limits are essential to meet loss settlement and coinsurance requirements. The limits on liability coverage afforded usually reflect reinsurance limitations or reinsurance availability and a possible catastrophic loss from a single exposure.

Amend Policy Terms and Conditions

A problem submission might be made acceptable by modifying the policy form to exclude certain causes of loss or to add or increase a deductible. An insurer might not be willing to write replacement cost coverage on a run-down home but might be willing to provide the limited HO-8 or a dwelling form. In small commercial accounts in which a large number of small losses might have caused unsatisfactory experience in the past, increasing the deductible might greatly improve the viability of the coverage.

The degree of flexibility available to the underwriter varies considerably from one line of insurance to another. In those situations in which the coverage forms have been filed subject to approval by state regulatory bodies, coverage modifications are seldom possible. Even in those cases, it might be possible for the underwriter to suggest an alternative coverage form to the insurance applicant or producer when the requested form cannot be provided.

Use Facultative Reinsurance

If the applicant is in a class of business that is not covered by the underwriter's reinsurance treaty or if the amount of insurance needed exceeds net treaty capacity, the underwriter might be able to transfer the exposure that exceeds its capacity to a facultative reinsurer. Facultative reinsurance should not be used as a method to pass along a bad risk to a reinsurer. An alternative to purchasing facultative reinsurance is to suggest that the producer divide the insurance among several insurers.

Selecting an Alternative

The selection decision involves determining whether to accept the submission as offered, accept it with some modification, or reject it. Although rejection is sometimes unavoidable, underwriters should try to determine which modifications are necessary to make the submission acceptable, because one of the insurer's goals is to produce profitable business. Rejections produce neither premium nor commission, only expense.

Selecting an alternative involves weighing the positive and negative features of a submission. The underwriter must identify and evaluate the exposures, assess the degree of risk relative to the average exposure contemplated in the rate, review the controls and protection features in place, and assess management's commitment to loss prevention. Additional factors that need to be considered before a decision is made include the following:

- Amount of underwriting authority required
- Presence of supporting business
- Mix of business
- Producer relationships
- Regulatory constraints

Amount of Underwriting Authority Required

Before accepting an applicant, an underwriter must determine whether he or she has the necessary amount of underwriting authority. The underwriter's task differs when he or she has sufficient authority to decide and when the underwriter prepares the file for submission to higher underwriting authority. Thus, the underwriter should check the underwriting guide before promising a producer a quick answer on a submission because referral to higher underwriting authority is often time-consuming.

Presence of Supporting Business

An application that is marginal on its own might become acceptable on an account basis if the rest of the account is desirable. Premium volume alone might be unacceptable to an insurer, since the premiums from five separate marginal insureds are probably not comparable to one superior account. On the other hand, the prospect of obtaining some above-average business in other lines might make a marginal submission viable if the supporting business is profitable enough to subsidize the marginal business.

In account underwriting, all of the business from a particular applicant is evaluated as a unit that must stand or fall on its own merits. The account underwriting approach evaluates both the submission for a given type of insurance and its supporting business.

Mix of Business

The **mix of business** is the distribution of individual policies composing the book of business of a producer, territory, state, or region among the various lines and classifications. Underwriting policy, as determined by management and as specified in the underwriting guide, frequently indicates the insurer's goals regarding the mix of business. Particular classes, such as youthful drivers in private passenger auto insurance or restaurants in property fire coverage, might be overrepresented in the present book of business. Consequently, the insurer might decide to raise the criteria for acceptability or to prohibit new business.

Producer Relationships

Often an important producer pressures an underwriter to accept a marginal prospect as an accommodation. Usually, the producer assures the underwriter of the delivery of some outstanding business later. Underwriters should keep accommodation files to enable them to detect excessive requests for accommodations and to determine whether the promised business materializes.

The relationship between the insurer and the producer should be based on mutual trust and respect. Differences of opinion are common, particularly since some of the goals of producers and underwriters conflict. Nevertheless, the long-run goals of producers and insurers are growth and profit. Mutual accommodation and willingness to see the other's viewpoint are essential to building a satisfactory working relationship.

Regulatory Constraints

State regulatory authorities are increasingly constraining the freedom of underwriters to decline new business or refuse to renew applicants. Underwriters must know those constraints, usually codified within the state's unfair trade practices laws. If regulation limits reasons for cancellation or refusal to renew, the selection decision on new submissions should be very carefully evaluated. Many states also limit the time within which an underwriter can decline a submission or provide notice of refusal to renew. Therefore, a timely decision must be made to avoid a mandatory acceptance or renewal of an otherwise unacceptable risk.

The so-called privacy laws that several states have enacted also restrict underwriting. The effect of those laws is to restrict the type and the amount of information about an applicant that an underwriter can obtain.

Implementing the Decision

Implementing underwriting decisions generally involves three steps. The first step is communicating the decision to the producer, if necessary, and to other insurer personnel. If the decision is to accept with modifications, the reasons must be clearly communicated to the producer or applicant, and the applicant must agree with the modifications. The insurer must establish controls to verify that modifications requested are implemented, particularly loss control recommendations. If the underwriter decides to reject the application, the underwriter must communicate this decision to the producer in a positive manner to avoid damaging their long-term relationship. Underwriters must present clear and logical reasons stipulating why the particular applicant does not meet the insurer's underwriting requirements. Effective communication of both positive and negative decisions clarifies insurer standards as market conditions change.

The second step is developing appropriate documentation. The underwriter might need to issue a binder or send a policy work sheet to the policywriting department. In some lines of business, the underwriter might need to prepare certificates of insurance.

The third step involves recording information about the policy and the applicant for accounting, statistical, and monitoring purposes. Data entry personnel extract essential information so that the system contains the policy information details on each policy written. For example, the premium must be posted to bill the producer. Data about the policyholder include location, limits, coverages, price modifications, class, and risk features. Those data must be coded so that the insurer and the industry can accumulate information on all accounts for ratemaking, statutory reporting, financial accounting, and book of business evaluations. That information is also used to follow the progress of the account and to trigger renewals and situations requiring special attention. For example, expiring policies will be identified so that updated information can be obtained. One purpose of the policy information system is to alert underwriters to claims activity during the policy period, other problems, or substantial changes with the policyholder. A claims referral system can immediately refer the file to the underwriter if the frequency of losses exceeds a predetermined limit or if a severe loss occurs.

Monitoring the Exposures

After an underwriting decision has been made on a submission or renewal, the underwriter's task is not complete. He or she must monitor the activity on the policies to ensure that satisfactory results are achieved.

Underwriters must be alert to changes in the loss exposures of insureds. Changes in the nature of the policyholder's business operation, for example, could significantly raise or lower the loss potential of the policyholder. Underwriters do not have the resources necessary to constantly monitor all policies written and underwrite new submissions at the same time. Therefore, monitoring usually occurs when policy changes or losses are brought to the underwriter's attention.

Adding a new location for a property policy or a new driver to an auto policy can cause the underwriter to investigate further to determine whether the character of the risk will change significantly. A notice of loss provides the underwriter with another opportunity to review the policyholder and determine whether the nature of the loss that occurred is commensurate with the type of loss exposures the underwriter expected. Summary information about the claim or a review of the claim file will provide valuable information concerning the nature of the loss and the operations of the policyholder.

Other opportunities to review individual policies come from loss control and premium audit reports. The loss control and safety inspection could have made specific recommendations that were to be implemented as a condition of policy issuance. A follow-up investigation could reveal that only some of the requirements have been met. Premium audits usually lag behind the issuance of a renewal policy by several months. The audit report could disclose larger exposures than originally contemplated, unacceptable operations, new products, new operations, or financial problems.

Once a claim has occurred or a premium audit has been conducted, the underwriter has the opportunity to contact insurer personnel who have first-hand knowledge of the insured. They can often provide information on new exposures or uncover additional hazards or operations that will help the underwriter reevaluate the account and determine its continued acceptability.

A second aspect of monitoring requires evaluating an entire book of business. Underwriters use premium and loss statistics to determine where aggregate problems lie in a deteriorating book of business. The review of the book of business can determine whether underwriting policy is being complied with and can detect changes in the type, volume, and quality of policies that might require corrective action.

Relationship Between Decisions and Outcomes

Monitoring the quality of decisions affecting a book of business is complicated because underwriting decisions and results are not directly related. Since underwriting decisions are made under conditions of uncertainty, what appears to be a good decision might result in a poor outcome. An underwriter can accept a perfectly "clean" application, only to suffer a major loss. On the other hand, an underwriter might make a poor decision, such as accepting a substandard insured, and have no losses. Over the long run, however, the better the quality of the underwriting decisions are, the better the results are.

Monitoring a Book of Business

Monitoring a book of business means evaluating the quality and profitability of all business written during a specific period of time covering a certain territory for a specific type of insurance. To be effective, that evaluation should identify specific problems within a line of business. A line of business can be subdivided into class of business, size of account, territory, and producer for the purpose of evaluation. In each phase of the evaluation, the insurer is primarily concerned with the loss ratio that develops. The insurer is also concerned that sufficient premium volume be developed to cover fixed costs and overhead expenses.

Class of Business

A poor loss ratio in a particular class can indicate inadequate pricing or a disproportionate number of high-hazard policyholders relative to the average risk in the classification. Classes with poor or deteriorating experience can be identified and corrected through rate increases, coverage restrictions, or more stringent selection standards. Changes in technology, materials, and operations, as well as the social and legal environment in which they are employed, can have a significant effect on the desirability of a class.

Territory

A territory can be defined in various ways to reflect an insurer's operations. For example, territory could encompass the three-state area over which a branch office has domain, or a single state. Another definition of a territory is the rating territory used in pricing policies within a state. However defined, territories identify geographic areas where profits are or are not realized. Identifying areas can guide the insurer in future agency appointments for profitable regions or areas experiencing growth. If results are poor, the information could indicate areas where the insurer might withdraw if rate relief is not forthcoming.

The regulatory and legal climate for insurance varies by state. That climate alone can affect the desirability of conducting business in a state and the possibility of achieving a profit. Basic considerations in territorial analysis are physical differences in terrain, degree of urbanization, and the potential for natural disasters.

Producer

Ideally, each producer's book of business should be evaluated annually. The producer's premium volume, policy retention, type of business, and loss ratio are evaluated both on an overall basis and by line and class of business. That evaluation should include the balance desired between personal and commercial business and the projected growth factor. Key considerations are the goals the insurer and producer established and the progress made toward those goals. If the producer has a small premium volume with the insurer, a single large loss can distort the loss ratio. A similar situation can occur in a small line of business. For example, a producer might appear to have an unprofitable workers compensation experience based on loss ratio when he or she actually has only one policy with an unsatisfactory loss ratio.

Summary

Underwriting is selecting policyholders through hazard recognition and evaluation, pricing, and determination of policy terms and conditions. The practice of underwriting insurance policies began when insurance emerged as a commercial enterprise. In modern practice, underwriters strive to develop a larger market share of profitable business. Adverse selection, a natural opponent of this objective, occurs when the applicant for insurance presents a higher-than-average probability of loss than is expected from a truly random sample of all applicants. Underwriting activities are typically described with a distinction between day-to-day activities (line functions) and management activities (staff functions). Although that distinction is not universal, it helps differentiate between underwriters who make individual risk decisions and those who establish general policy guidelines for the insurer.

Establishing underwriting policy is a key objective of senior management. Effectively implementing underwriting policy is a criterion for the success of any insurer. An insurer's underwriting policy promotes the type and classes of insurance anticipated to produce a growing and profitable book of business. Although almost any restriction on acceptable business can be imposed, there are limitations on what an underwriting policy can contain and real-world limiting factors to that policy.

Implementing an underwriting policy means communicating the standards to line underwriters and following up periodically to ensure that standards are being met. Underwriting guides and bulletins are the primary tools for disseminating underwriting policy. Underwriting management conducts underwriting audits on a regular basis to determine how well individual underwriters, branch offices, and agents are adhering to standards.

As in most businesses, financial ratios are used to indicate the success of the underwriting effort. Key ratios are the loss ratio, expense ratio, and combined ratio. Combined ratios of less than 100 percent indicate profitable underwriting results, and unprofitable underwriting results are indicated by ratios over 100 percent. The combined ratio ignores investment income—an important component of an insurer's overall profitability.

An underwriter can make what appears to be a good underwriting decision but end up with poor results. The reverse of this is also true. The more common problems with evaluating individual underwriting results are the span of time between the decision and the results, and the occurrence of factors beyond the control of the underwriter. Several underwriting performance measures are more subjective and do not rely on account profitability.

The underwriting process can be viewed as comprising a five-step decision-making process:

1. Gathering information
2. Identifying, developing, and evaluating alternatives
3. Selecting an alternative
4. Implementing the decision
5. Monitoring the exposures

This chapter discussed each of those steps in a manner that can be applied to any specific line of business or insurance product.

Chapter Notes

1. "Is Underwriting a Lost Art?" *Producer*, Crum and Forster Insurance Companies, Winter 1976, p. 13.
2. Paul v. Virginia, 8 Wall 183 (1869).
3. United States v. South Eastern Underwriters Association et al., 322 U.S. 533 (1944).
4. Association values are set by the Securities Valuation Office (SVO), which is a unit of the NAIC. The SVO catalogs the values of all securities held by insurers and makes a determination of values in difficult situations. For example, the SVO would peg a value for a bond whose issuer had defaulted on repayment or on a security issue that is not publicly traded.
5. "Three Arrested in Fraud Scheme," *Business Insurance*, February 18, 1991, p. 11.

Chapter 5

Underwriting Property Insurance

Chapter 5 focuses on underwriting selected types of property insurance. Property underwriters have traditionally emphasized fire as a cause of loss. Analyzing the insured property's susceptibility to loss by fire is an appropriate approach to underwriting property insurance because fire is the covered cause of loss that has the greatest potential to inflict a *total* loss on the insured property. In addition to examining fire, this chapter analyzes the nature of and underwriting concerns associated with other causes of loss included in most property policies, as well as those insured by crime, inland marine, and ocean marine policies. This chapter also addresses underwriting other types of property-related loss, such as business income losses. Chapter 6 will similarly treat liability loss exposures.

Fire Insurance Underwriting

Whether written monoline or as part of a package, fire is generally the most important cause of loss to underwrite in property insurance. Fire insurance is one of the oldest types of property coverage, dating back to the seventeenth century. Fire insurance was an outgrowth of destructive conflagrations such as the fire of London in 1666. Early fire insurance contracts were written on property at a fixed location and provided little off-premises coverage and few, if any, additional causes of loss. Although loss frequency for a given insured is usually low and most losses that do occur are partial losses, fire always contains the potential for a total loss, which greatly influences underwriting practices.

Underwriting fire as a cause of loss focuses on the physical hazards presented by a particular loss exposure. To ensure a thorough review of these hazards, property underwriters use an approach that scrutinizes four specific areas, traditionally referred to as COPE: construction, occupancy, protection, and external exposures.

Construction

The construction of a building that is insured or contains insured property is a primary consideration when underwriting property insurance. The building's construction relates directly to its ability to withstand damage by fire and other perils and protect its contents against loss.

The policy application and a personal inspection by the producer or loss control representative can provide specific data on the construction of a particular building. For buildings subject to specific rating, advisory organizations publish information on building construction. If additional information is needed, independent inspection companies can perform a property survey.

Construction Classifications

Insurance Services Office (ISO) divides building construction into six classifications:[1]

1. Class #6—fire resistive
2. Class #5—modified fire resistive
3. Class #4—masonry noncombustible
4. Class #3—noncombustible
5. Class #2—joisted masonry
6. Class #1—frame

Those classifications are based on the following:

1. The materials used for the components of the structure that bear the weight of the building and its contents
2. The materials used in the roof and floors of the building, especially the supports for the roof and floors
3. The fire-resistance rating of the materials used in the building construction

Construction classifications are based on the ability of the materials used in constructing a building to resist damage by fire. Ratings consider the characteristics of (1) the vertical load-bearing members that ultimately support the weight of the building and (2) the materials used in the roof and floors, which spread the weight across the vertical load-bearing members.

Fire Resistive

The characteristic that defines **fire-resistive construction** is the ability of the load-bearing members of the structure to withstand damage by fire for at least two hours. This is a higher standard than simply requiring that the structure itself not burn. The load-bearing components of a fire-resistive building will not buckle or collapse as might the members of other construction types.

Fire-resistive construction is superior to other types of building construction but is not "fireproof." Fire-resistive ratings are assigned to construction material based on laboratory evaluations in test furnaces. Evaluations certify that materials will withstand damage by fire under certain weight loads regardless of whether materials can be repaired or reused. The performance of such materials may differ significantly under actual fire conditions.

From an underwriting standpoint, fire-resistive construction is the best type for most causes of loss. The strength of the structure gives it superior resistance to causes of loss such as windstorm, earthquake, and flood. The construction materials are either (1) noncombustible with a fire-resistance rating of at least two hours or (2) protected by a noncombustible covering such as concrete, masonry, plaster, or gypsum that provides at least a two-hour fire-resistance rating.

Modified Fire Resistive

A building of **modified fire-resistive construction** has bearing walls (walls supporting the weight of the upper floors and roof) and columns of masonry or reinforced concrete construction. It is similar to fire-resistive construction, except that the fire-resistance rating of the materials is one to two hours.

Masonry Noncombustible

In the **masonry noncombustible construction** class are buildings with exterior walls of fire-resistive construction with a rating of not less than one hour or buildings of masonry construction. The roof and floors must be of noncombustible or slow burning materials. The typical masonry noncombustible building has a masonry nonbearing wall surface, a concrete floor, a metal deck roof, and an unprotected metal frame. Low initial cost and low maintenance have made this type of construction extremely popular.

Noncombustible

A building of **noncombustible construction** has exterior walls, a roof, and a floor constructed of and supported by metal or other noncombustible materials. Although these buildings are noncombustible, they are not fire resistive. If this type of building is filled with combustible contents, structural failure is extremely likely in the event of a serious fire. The unprotected steel structural supports in this type of building will twist and bend when subjected to the heat of a typical fire. Even though these structures are constructed of noncombustible material and will not contribute fuel to a fire, their susceptibility to damage makes them only marginally safer from an underwriting perspective than joisted masonry or frame construction (described below).

Joisted Masonry

Joisted masonry construction has load-bearing exterior walls made of brick, adobe, concrete, gypsum, stone, tile, or similar materials, with floors and roofs of combustible materials. Joisted masonry construction is also referred to as "ordinary construction," "ordinary masonry," "brick," "wood joisted," and "brick joisted." Exterior walls may be of fire-resistive construction with a fire-resistance rating of at least one hour or of masonry construction. The walls are self-supporting, meaning that they stand without support from the building's frame. Because the exterior walls are load bearing, many underwriters regard them as part of the building's frame. Interior columns and floors are of combustible material, usually wood.

Joisted masonry buildings are found in most major metropolitan areas, especially in Northern states. The need for the exterior walls to support the weight of the structure places practical limits on the height to which these structures can be built. Joisted masonry construction is rarely used for buildings over five stories and is used in many areas only for buildings of three stories or less.

Mill construction is a type of joisted masonry construction that uses heavy timbers to internally support the floors and roof. In this construction type, there are no concealed areas under the roof and floors that might permit a fire to go undetected. The heavy wood floors serve as a firestop, thereby slowing the spread of fire.

The size of the wood members used in mill construction gives these buildings structural strength. Fires that would engulf the light joists used in typical joisted masonry might only char the heavy timber beams used in mill construction.

Frame

In **frame construction**, the load-bearing components of the building are wood or other combustible materials. In addition to the direct damage caused by a fire, frame construction can suffer structural damage because the weight-bearing supports are combustible. Many dwellings and small mercantile buildings are frame. Buildings of mixed construction, such as wood frame with brick veneer, stone veneer, aluminum siding, or stucco, are properly classified as frame buildings.

Construction Materials

The construction of the weight-bearing members of a building is a basic consideration in fire underwriting. Additionally, the construction materials used in partition walls and other components of the structure affect its combustibility and desirability from an underwriting standpoint.

Interior Finish

The interior finish of a structure affects its underwriting acceptability. A fire-resistive office building, for example, may have an interior finish that is highly combustible. Underwriters have to consider several characteristics of interior finishes, including their ability to spread fire, the fuel provided for a fire, and the smoke and noxious gases emitted while burning. Each of these characteristics affects the overall property loss potential of the structure and the safety of the occupants.

Relatively noncombustible interior finishes include wall coverings such as plaster, gypsum, and wallboard. Combustible interior finishes include wood or plywood, fiber ceiling tiles, and plastic wall coverings. Surface coatings such as certain paints, varnishes, and wallpapers when added to other combustible finishes could contribute significantly to the fuel load. The **fuel load** (also called the fire load) measures the expected amount and type of combustible material in a given fire area. Even the adhesives used in floor or ceiling tile can substantially affect a building's capacity to sustain or fuel a fire.

A fire that consumes combustible interior finish can generate highly toxic gases that can circulate quickly throughout a building. A fairly severe fire that started in the lobby of a hotel provides an example. As the highly combustible finishing materials on the wall and ceiling burned, they generated a large volume of hot smoke and gases. The smoke and gases seeped into a stairwell, quickly finding an open door twelve floors above the fire. People entering this twelfth-floor area perished even though the hotel suffered little damage to its structure overall. These deaths occurred not only because the interior-finish fumes were toxic but also because unprotected vertical openings allowed hot smoke and gases to travel upward.

Insulation

Just as the interior finish of a structure greatly affects its combustibility, insulation may also add problems. A common form of insulation is fiberglass, which is often installed with a paper backing. Insulation material may also include combustible substances such as finely chopped paper treated with fire-retardant chemicals. Insulation also serves as a sound barrier, and, therefore, combustible insulation can be found in the interior walls of otherwise highly fire-resistive buildings.

Whether the insulation is installed to conserve heat or to suppress sound, an attempt should be made to determine its flame spread, fuel contribution, and smoke contribution characteristics. This information should be available from the manufacturer of the insulation.

Rising energy costs in the 1970s led to renewed interest in conserving the energy consumed in heating and cooling buildings. As a result, insulation has been added to many existing structures. This insulation can contain the heat of a fire within a building, concentrating it on structural members. Such an insulated building may therefore weaken and collapse more quickly than anticipated.

Roofing

The exterior surface of a roof serves as a weather seal, but it also provides a barrier against exposure fires. Roofs are subject to attack from sparks and embers falling from fires outside the building. The combustibility of either side of the roof is important in retarding the spread of interior fires. Untreated wooden shingles invite the spread of exposure fires. Roof coverings vary in the fire resistance they provide. Underwriters Laboratories, Inc., evaluates and classifies roofing materials.

Asphalt shingles are probably the most common roof covering for residential buildings. Although they are somewhat combustible, they are excellent barriers to severe fire exposures when properly constructed and installed. Conversely, combustible materials such as wood shake shingles or tar paper afford almost no protection. In the presence of high winds, a wood shake roof may send firebrands downwind.

Other Construction Considerations

In addition to the fire resistance of a building's construction, underwriters have to consider other factors, including age, building height, fire divisions, building openings, and building codes.

Age

Property underwriters have to consider several factors that are directly related to the age of older buildings they insure or to buildings that contain covered property. Those factors concern the following:

1. A different building code was probably in effect at the time the building was constructed. As a result, the building may lack protective features and systems generally considered essential by today's standards.

2. The heating, cooling, electrical, and fire protection systems may have become obsolete.

3. The building may have been intended for a different occupancy and may not be suitable for its current use.

4. Conversion and remodeling may have created concealed spaces in which fire may burn undetected and spread rapidly.

5. Over the years, alterations and repairs may have left unprotected openings in vertical and horizontal firestops.

6. The need to comply with current building codes may increase the cost of making repairs following a loss.

7. The condition of the building may have deteriorated for numerous reasons, including normal wear and tear, hard use, or lack of maintenance.

8. The value of an older building is often difficult to determine, especially if the builder used construction techniques and materials that are no longer available.

Although proper maintenance mitigates the effects of age and deterioration, all buildings will eventually wear out. The degree of obsolescence or deterioration is directly related to the type of construction, occupancy, physical abuse of the building, and quality of the owner's maintenance.

A frame structure, for example, will normally show its age more quickly than a joisted masonry building. However, an office occupancy in a frame structure with good maintenance may be preferable to a fire-resistive building occupied by a foundry with minimal maintenance.

Construction methods and materials have changed over time. Building materials that were in use in the 1920s or 1930s have long been abandoned. Electrical systems of forty, fifty, and sixty years ago were designed primarily for lighting, while modern wiring systems are designed to accommodate space heating, air conditioning, computer systems, and heavy appliances.

A building that was designed for a dry-goods retailer fifty years ago might be inadequate for the laundry, printer, or beverage distributor that occupies the structure today. The weight of equipment, stock, and storage associated with the business may have increased since the building was designed and built. In addition to the increase in hazard that occurs because of the change in occupancy, the structural integrity of the building has probably deteriorated over time.

Building Height

The height of an insured structure is an important consideration. Buildings present unique problems when their height restricts the capability of the local fire service to fight a fire from outside. The National Fire Protection Association (NFPA) defines a high-rise building as one that is at least 75 feet tall. The tallest extension ladders in use today can reach 120 feet, but many municipal fire services are not capable of fighting a fire from the exterior of a building that is in excess of 100 feet (eight or nine floors).

In a high-rise building, the fire department has to fight the fire from inside. Firefighters must consider the fire-resistive characteristics of the structure and the presence or lack of approved horizontal and vertical barriers used to confine the fire to its area of origin. In one high-rise fire, the fire department could not approach the building because of flying glass caused by heat-shattered windows. Firefighters were forced to enter the building through a parking garage that permitted access to the basement.

Controlling combustible contents in high-rise buildings is crucial. The building should not contain occupancies that create a high fire hazard or a heavy fuel load. The most common uses of high-rise structures are as offices, apartments, and hotels. These occupancies present a light fire hazard. However, office occupancies often store highly combustible paper files, which create the potential of a severe fire.

High-rise structures sometimes have restaurants or bars on the upper floors. In that location, restaurants are a hazardous occupancy, and without adequate control or private protection, they constitute a significant hazard.

The effect of elevation on a fire is also an important consideration. When a fire starts, it becomes necessary to vent the smoke and toxic gases it produces and to introduce fresh air for firefighters and occupants who may be unable to escape. A state-of-the-art heating, ventilating, and air conditioning (HVAC) system can accomplish this. If mechanical ventilation fails, it may become necessary to open or break windows. This exposes the fire floor to winds that are much more intense at the height of upper floors than at ground level. In addition to the damage the wind causes directly, strong winds may assist in spreading the fire and hamper fire-fighting efforts.

More important than property damage in a high-rise building is the safety of human lives. A structure of 100 stories might have as many as 25,000 occupants. If a severe fire occurs on the fiftieth floor, over 12,000 people may be located above the fire and may therefore be subjected to potential injury from flame, smoke, and gas. The first priority of fire department personnel is the safety of a building's occupants. To the extent that lives are endangered, firefighters must concentrate on human safety before fighting the fire.

Fire Divisions

A different type of problem may be found in large horizontal buildings. Many structures have a total horizontal area approaching one million square feet. Vertical integrity is the solution to many fire problems in high-rise structures, and fire divisions are the corresponding solution for fires in large horizontal areas. A **fire division** is a section of a structure so well protected that fire cannot spread from that section to another.

A **fire wall** restricts the spread of fire by serving as a fire-resistive barrier. Interior walls may or may not be of sufficient fire resistance to qualify. Generally, fire walls must consist of at least eight inches of masonry material; however, fire wall adequacy also depends on the combustibility of building contents. A fire wall must also be free standing, which means that it has to support its own weight without assistance from other building components. A load-bearing wall, on the other hand, might not be a fire wall.

Fire walls cannot be effective if fire can easily spread over or around them. To prevent fire from spreading, fire walls have to extend above a combustible roof and through exterior walls. Vertical extensions of a fire wall above the roofline are called **parapets**. The Factory Mutual Research Corporation (FMRC) recommends that parapets extend at least thirty inches. Parapets may be higher or lower depending on local building codes.[2] Extensions of the fire wall through the outer walls are known as **fender walls**. They are common in frame construction that uses interior fire walls to create fire divisions. In many frame apartment structures, fender walls also provide privacy to terraces and patios.

A **definite firestop** is a special class of fire wall that is of substantial construction. At a minimum, such a wall must have a minimum fire-resistance rating of four hours with no openings, even if protected.

Some underwriters apply a similar concept to multiple-story buildings of fire-resistive construction. By doing so, they recognize the existence of vertical as well as horizontal firestops. They reason that a floor with a two-hour fire-resistance rating is effective in preventing the vertical spread of fire just as fire walls are effective in preventing the horizontal spread of fire. However, because fire spreads more readily upward than horizontally, very few underwriters will give the same weight to fire-resistive floors as they do to horizontal fire walls.

Building Openings

Building openings may increase the potential for loss by fire. Although the construction type may be appropriate for the intended occupancy, subcontractors, such as electricians and heating and air conditioning contractors, may have installed equipment that penetrates vertical and horizontal firestops. For example, a high-rise structure nearing completion in New York City had noncombustible structural members that were adequately protected and that afforded it at least a two-hour fire rating. Subcontractors subsequently diminished the protection by removing the insulation from the structural steel members resurfacing them with a protective coating. When a fire occurred, the steel members were weakened and required replacement. Although the damage to these members was minimal and their original cost was not inordinate, a multimillion-dollar loss resulted from replacing major building supports in a structure nearing completion.

Buildings contain many openings that without additional protection can violate the basic integrity of a fire division. These openings include doors between fire divisions, floor openings for stairs between floors, elevators, dumbwaiters, and conveyor belts. In most circumstances, fire doors can protect these openings. The most common causes of unprotected openings are oversight and poor loss control.

Openings in fire walls are sometimes needed if a building is to serve its intended purpose. If a fire wall is to perform its function, fire doors must protect those openings. Fire doors are classified based on their ability to resist fire. The classification scheme used by NFPA ranges from doors that withstand fire for three hours to those that withstand fire for one-third of an hour. Approved doors have a rating seal on the door's edge.

A fire door in a fire wall must be capable of withstanding the same fire as the wall itself. A one-hour fire door in a two-hour fire wall, for example, reduces the fire protection rating of the entire wall to one hour. A vertical opening such as an elevator or a stairwell is protected only when it is completely segregated into a separate fire division. A properly constructed elevator shaft or stairwell constitutes a building within a building.

A fire door cannot be effective if it is propped open. Each door must be automatically self-closing and unobstructed. Doors that must be left open to permit efficient industrial operations are fitted with fusible links that melt and release the door when the temperature reaches a predetermined level. This permits the doors to close automatically when exposed to the heat of a fire.

Fire can also travel up the side of a building by jumping from window to window. The Factory Mutual Research Corporation has done extensive studies of how fire spreads from one part of a building to another. It recommends that the distance between a floor and the bottom of a window on the next higher floor be at least 2.8 times the height of the window for closed windows or 3.8 times the height for windows that can open.[3]

Building Codes

Building codes are local ordinances or state statutes that regulate the construction of buildings within a municipality, county, or state. Studies have shown that well-designed and properly enforced building codes can reduce insured losses, especially from such causes of loss as windstorm and earthquake. In most areas of the country, however, underwriters must rely on their own resources to evaluate the effectiveness of building code enforcement. Assessing the effectiveness of building codes requires either extensive research or first-hand knowledge. Either alternative is time-consuming and expensive, but that is changing.

In 1995, ISO and the Insurance Institute for Property Loss Control (IIPLC) began rating communities on the quality of their building codes and the level of enforcement. The Building Code Effectiveness Grading Schedule (BCEGS) produces a classification, ranging from 1 to 10, that operates similarly to the community protection classification codes used in rating and underwriting fire coverage. ISO expects to publish BCEGS gradings for all communities in the United States by the year 2000.

Occupancy

The occupancy of a building affects the frequency and severity of losses. Factors affecting frequency and severity vary by occupancy and can be grouped under three headings: (1) sources of ignition or fire causes, (2) combustibility, and (3) damageability. In addition to these generic classifications of occupancy hazards are hazard concerns common to all occupancies. Specific occupancy classes such as restaurants have their own special hazards.

Ignition Sources

Ignition sources or causes provide the means for a fire to start. Underwriters must know the principal sources of ignition that an insured occupancy or the use of the covered building produces. Potential ignition sources include the following:

1. Friendly fires that escape containment. They can result from open flames and heaters, smoking, torches, lamps, furnaces, ovens and heaters, and welding and cutting torches.

2. Friction that generates enough heat to ignite nearby combustible material. Sources of friction include hot bearings, rubbing belts, grinding, shredding, picking, polishing, cutting, and drilling.

3. Electricity that produces either sparks or heat that can ignite exposed combustibles. Static electricity frequently causes sparks. Lighting fixtures,

overloaded circuits, and worn wiring can release potentially damaging amounts of heat.

4. Certain chemical reactions, called exothermic reactions, that produce heat sufficient to cause ignition.[4]

Although certain industrial occupancies present obvious hazards with respect to sources of ignition, some hazards are more subtle. The fire hazard presented by smoking and lit cigarettes, for instance, relates directly to the number of persons passing through the premises and the building's prevailing policy on smoking. Health concerns unrelated to fire potential have led many buildings to prohibit occupants from smoking indoors, but smoking materials remain a significant cause of fire losses.

Combustibility

A building's occupancy indicates to underwriters the type of property the building is likely to contain. The combustibility of contents depends on how quickly the material will ignite, the rate at which a fire will spread, and the intensity or amount of heat a fire will generate. Gasoline, for example, is easily ignited, spreads fire very quickly, and burns with explosive intensity.

The major classifications of materials that are highly combustible include the following:

1. Light combustible materials such as thin plywood, shingles, shavings, paper, cotton, and other fibers
2. Combustible dusts such as those produced when refinishing bowling alley lanes or refining flour
3. Flammable liquids
4. Combustible gases such as hydrogen
5. Materials subject to spontaneous combustion
6. Explosive materials, acids, and oxidizing agents[5]

The combustibility of a building's contents affects the underwriting desirability of that building. Management practices by the insured can make a significant difference in the acceptability of the insured regardless of the content's combustibility.

Damageability

The damageability of contents is a major underwriting consideration and is necessary for determining the probable maximum loss to contents should a fire occur. Even a small and quickly extinguishable fire can result in a severe loss to highly damageable contents, such as expensive clothing or furniture.

Hazards Associated With the Occupancy

The physical hazards that an occupancy presents can be classified into two categories: common hazards and special hazards.

Common Hazards

Certain hazards, called **common hazards**, exist in almost every occupancy. For convenience in analysis, underwriters generally recognize several broad (though not mutually exclusive) categories of common hazards.

Common hazards include the following:

1. Housekeeping
2. Heating equipment
3. Electrical equipment
4. Smoking materials

Housekeeping   Every occupancy generates waste and trash. Underwriters have to consider three aspects of the exposure this creates: uncollected litter, storage, and disposal.

Waste and trash in the form of uncollected litter can significantly contribute to the spread of fire. Paper, oily items, packing materials, and discarded smoking materials are common examples of this hazard.

Many industrial operations use lubricants in significant amounts, so the waste and litter they produce are often oily. Janitorial work frequently uses oily substances or is performed where oil and grease are present. An accumulation of greasy soot in vents and flues, particularly over cooking stoves, is a significant hazard.

Most commercial and institutional occupancies require that wastes be temporarily stored. Depending on the material and the nature of the storage, the concentration and confinement of the waste may increase or decrease the hazard. When neatly stacked and enclosed, paper and cardboard, for example, resist burning better than the same material piled haphazardly and loosely. In a confined space, oily materials are subject to spontaneous combustion.

Good housekeeping also requires the separation of materials that may react with one another. Trash and waste should be stored in noncombustible containers.

Disposing of waste by incineration on the insured premises requires special precautions. Incinerators constitute an additional source of heat and heat byproducts. Mixtures of wastes present special problems, since some explode when burned or give off toxic gases. A properly designed and operating incinerator can control these hazards.

Heating Equipment   Furnaces and other heating equipment provide a potential source of ignition. The hazard exists primarily in the burners or heating elements of the equipment; however, the equipment itself and the pipes, ducts, and flues leading from it also radiate heat. Some sources of heat present greater hazards than others. Wood-burning stoves and salamanders (portable heaters), for example, present a greater hazard than a gas furnace because fuel cannot be controlled or withdrawn once added to the fire. Sparks could also ignite combustible material in the vicinity of wood-burning stoves and portable heaters.

Electrical Equipment   NFPA reports that most of the fires started by electrical motors and appliances are due to careless use, improper installation, or poor maintenance. Management's interest in regular maintenance is a major factor in fire loss prevention.

Smoking Materials   Controlling fire caused by smoking and matches involves prohibiting smoking in certain areas and ensuring the safe handling of cigarettes, cigars, and matches where smoking is permitted. Management's smoking policy and its enforcement are important considerations in controlling this hazard.

Special Hazards

Each occupancy class creates its own special hazards. In addition, individual businesses sometimes contain hazards that are neither common to all occupancies nor usual for the class. In analyzing special hazards, underwriters usually identify two distinct types: special hazards of the class and special hazards of the risk.

Special Hazards of the Class   Potentially hazardous conditions that increase the likely frequency or severity of loss but which are typical for the type of occupancy are called **special hazards of the class**. Examples include cooking in a restaurant or using volatile chemicals in a manufacturing plant. Almost every occupancy has a hazardous activity that can reasonably be expected based on the nature of the occupancy. Underwriters must be familiar with the operations and hazards that are typical of the classes they entertain.

Special Hazards of the Risk   Some businesses engage in activities that are not typical of other businesses with which they would be classed. Those activities, termed **special hazards of the risk**, often create hazards neither contemplated by the underwriter nor charged for in the rates. A maintenance garage for a large fleet of trucks or taxicabs, for example, might contain a small body shop or welding equipment. The garage is a special hazard of the class, but the auto body work, typically performed by an auto body shop, would constitute a special hazard of the risk. Identifying special hazards of the risk usually requires a physical inspection of the insured's business.

Types of Occupancies

Underwriters have traditionally grouped occupancies into broad categories to aid in analyzing the hazards that might be present. The six categories that are frequently used are as follows:

1. Habitational
2. Office
3. Institutional
4. Mercantile
5. Service
6. Manufacturing

Habitational Occupancies

Habitational occupancies include apartments, hotels, motels, and nursing homes. Habitational occupancies are often in the control of someone other than the building owner, so detecting or controlling the presence of hazards can be difficult. Often, the hallmark of a superior habitational occupancy is the extent of building maintenance performed by the owner. Such activity demonstrates to the tenants that the owners care about the condition of the building. Also, regular maintenance permits the owner access to occupant-controlled areas that might have become substandard because of tenant neglect. Situations, once identified, can then be corrected.

Habitational occupancies are often affected by ups and downs in the economy. A proxy for the financial stability of the owner is the vacancy rate of the business. The vacancy rate of an account can be compared with the average vacancy rate of similar operations in the area.

Office Occupancies

The office occupancy is a relatively low-hazard classification. Materials found in offices are usually of limited combustibility and only slightly susceptible. Buildings used for office occupancies might have unusual features, such as restaurants or heliports. Office occupancies can be found in any type of structure and often share a building with other occupancies.

Institutional Occupancies

Institutional occupancies include schools, churches, hospitals, and property owned by governmental entities. Governmental entities often operate habitational properties such as public housing and nursing homes. Institutional occupancies also include special-purpose facilities such as prisons and police and fire stations.

During the liability insurance crises of the 1970s and 1980s, many institutional properties shifted to retention programs. Risk retention groups for public entities are commonplace in today's insurance market. The trend toward privatizing public functions has led many of these public facilities back to the insurance market.

Mercantile Occupancies

Mercantile occupancies include accounts whose primary business is buying and selling goods, wares, and merchandise, whether wholesale or retail. Department stores, clothing stores, hardware stores, specialty shops, and grocery stores are examples of mercantile occupancies.

The combustibility of a mercantile operation's contents varies with the type of merchandise sold. For example, a sporting goods store might stock ammunition and camping-stove fuel. Hardware stores and home centers normally have large quantities of flammables and combustibles, such as paints, varnishes, solvents, lumber, curtains, and wallpaper.

The stock of mercantile occupancies is usually a significant value and susceptible to fire, smoke, and water damage. For example, clothing is especially subject to severe loss from smoke and water damage, and the stock of a hardware store will rust from the water used in fighting a fire. Health authorities usually require food exposed to fire and smoke to be withdrawn from sale. In these classes, a small fire can produce a large loss.

Service Occupancies

Service occupancies include businesses that perform an activity for the customer rather than create or sell a product. This category includes dry cleaners and automobile service stations.

The hazards presented by a service occupancy are usually specific to the service being performed. Dry cleaners, for example, have several occupancy hazards. Lint accumulation presents a fire and an explosion hazard. Dry cleaners also have large boilers for the hot water used in cleaning, and irons and presses could serve as ignition sources. Many of the solvents used in dry cleaning are flammable and need to be handled and stored properly.

Manufacturing Occupancies

Manufacturers are in the business of converting raw stock into finished products. The special hazards of occupancies in this category vary with the nature of the product being manufactured. For example, a steel manufacturer has blast furnaces, rolling mills, and associated steel processing equipment, while a pasta manufacturer has an extensive drying process and a severe dust hazard.

Protection

Fire protection is of two types: (1) public or municipal protection provided by towns and cities or (2) private protection provided by the property owner or occupant. Public and private protection consist of three elements: prevention, detection, and suppression. The quantity and quality of fire protection available to individual properties vary widely. Although some exceptions exist, dwellings and small commercial buildings depend almost entirely on public protection, while larger commercial building owners are able to supplement public protection with private fire protection systems.

Public Protection

Public fire protection is defined as fire protection equipment and services made available through governmental authority to all properties within a defined area. The organization of public fire protection varies by community. Municipalities and sometimes counties often provide protection to all properties within their boundaries. In many areas of the country, however, the most effective use of available equipment and personnel dictates fire district boundaries.

ISO independently evaluates public fire protection and publishes its findings in the form of a public protection classification (PPC) for each community in the United States. The PPC is an integral part of the property insurance pricing process. Although most underwriters need only a basic understanding of the municipal grading system, a more extensive knowledge permits them to evaluate private protection efforts relative to available public protection.

The PPC system rates the quality of a public fire service on a scale of 1 to 10. The classification measures the adequacy of the equipment available to the public fire service, the water supply, and response time. Class 1 represents the ideal; it is not reasonable to expect any community to achieve this rating. Classes 1 through 8 define protected properties, while properties in classes 9 and 10 are unprotected. Properties that are located too far from a water supply adequate for fire suppression fall into Class 9. Public protection class 10 applies to properties that have no public fire protection service available.

A single public protection classification does not always apply to an entire municipality or fire district. Geographic features sometimes prevent prompt fire service response to some areas, and water mains and hydrants may not extend to all properties a fire service protects. These considerations produce a higher public protection classification (indicating lower-quality public protection).

A property may also take a public protection classification inferior to the community as a whole for two principal reasons. First, the property may present an exposure to more challenging fires than the fire service is equipped to handle, such as flammable metals or large quantities of flammable liquids. Second, the fire service may lack adequate year-round access to the property, especially when the property owner maintains private roads. The owners of some seasonal properties in colder climates, for example, maintain private roads but make no arrangements for snow plowing because they are closed for the winter. An accumulation of snow on the roads periodically makes such locations inaccessible to fire services. The PPC would take this into account and produce a classification of 9 or 10 for those locations.

Private Protection

The existence of private protection systems is a significant factor in underwriting. Although all three elements of prevention, detection, and suppression are important, this section focuses on detection and suppression. The loss control personnel of insurers often assist commercial policyholders with their prevention activities. Loss control will be discussed in Chapter 7.

Detection

Early detection is important to fire suppression because the size of a fire increases exponentially with time measured in seconds, and larger fires are more difficult to suppress. Because most fires start when the premises are unoccupied, mechanical detection systems are crucial for limiting the extent of fire damage. The major detection systems include (1) a guard service with a clock system, (2) a private patrol service, (3) smoke and heat detectors, (4) an automatic local alarm, and (5) a central station alarm or remote station system. In addition, certain sprinkler systems have an alarm that is triggered by the flow of water within the system.

The effectiveness of a **guard service** depends on the alertness of the guard. A **clock system** encourages the guard to make regular rounds. Each guard carries a device that time-marks the route through the premises. The disadvantage of a basic clock system is that the watchman's attention or lack thereof cannot be determined until the device is reviewed. Many businesses have connected certain locations to a central station. If these locations are not checked by the watchman, the personnel of the central station follow up.

Small merchants or businesses often employ **private patrol services** to check for break-ins. In many areas of the country, business and industry associations provide private patrol services as a benefit to their members. A guard visits each business several times during the night to ensure that all doors and windows are secure and that fire has not broken out. Although they provide some security, private patrols are unlikely to discover a fire on a timely basis. Some private patrol services employ a clock system to verify that guards complete their assigned rounds on schedule.

The use of **smoke detectors** in private residences and businesses has increased significantly with the development of inexpensive, battery-powered smoke detectors. NFPA standards now require that smoke detectors be wired directly to an AC power source in all newly constructed dwellings or buildings. NFPA 74 also recommends for residences that smoke detectors be located outside each sleeping area, on each floor serving as living quarters, and in the basement. Most smoke detectors perform independently, sounding an alarm only at the location of the detected smoke. More advanced systems interconnect the alarms so that all the units go off simultaneously. Often, these advanced systems also serve as burglar alarms by sounding a different alarm tone to indicate a break-in.

Heat detectors may be operated independently of suppression devices but are most frequently combined into devices like automatic sprinkler systems. Heat detectors are slow to activate, which makes them less desirable than smoke detectors in most areas. Heat detectors are used when other detection devices are not effective or are triggered too easily. Small storage rooms in which heat buildup would be rapid or kitchens in which some smoke is a usual byproduct may be better protected by heat detectors.

Heat detectors activate when heat causes a physical or an electrical change in a material or gas. They may be set to respond to a specific temperature or to a predetermined rate of rise in the ambient temperature. Automatic sprinkler systems commonly use a fusible material that melts rapidly at predetermined temperatures. Electric heat detectors are triggered similarly, but the melted link frees a spring-loaded mechanism, which completes an electrical circuit. Continuous line heat detectors activate the alarm when the heat-sensitive insulation surrounding paired steel wire is melted to complete an electrical circuit. Rate compression detectors respond when air temperature exceeds a specified level. Rate-of-rise detectors react to rapid changes in air temperature.

In order to perform their intended function, smoke and heat detectors must be connected to an alarm, which may be local, central station, remote station, or proprietary. A **local alarm** system, triggered by smoke or heat, sounds a siren or gong inside or outside the building. It relies on occupants or passersby to report the alarm to fire or police officials. For that reason, local alarms are not considered effective in reporting fires.

A **central station system** is a private service with personnel who monitor the systems of several commercial establishments and sometimes residences. Depending on the type of alarm received, the service either calls the appropriate authorities or dispatches its own personnel to investigate. A central station alarm, with or without sprinklers, greatly increases the likelihood of a rapid response to an outbreak of fire and should greatly reduce both insured and uninsured losses. Central station alarm systems eliminate the need for human intervention at the scene and offer a better solution to fire detection than a local alarm. The disadvantage of this method is its relative cost.

Remote station systems and **proprietary alarms** are similar to central station systems, except that they do not signal a commercially operated central station. A remote alarm directly signals the local police and fire stations. A proprietary system transmits an alarm to a receiving station located on the protected premises.

Suppression

Private fire suppression falls into four categories: (1) portable extinguishers, (2) standpipes and hoses, (3) automatic sprinkler systems, and (4) private fire brigades.

Every business and residence should have some type of **portable fire extinguishers** available. To be effective, extinguishers must receive regular maintenance, and users must be trained to operate them. Most fire extinguishers are classed as "ABC," meaning they can be used on all types of fires. Class "D" extinguishers are designed for fires involving flammable metals. NFPA publishes standards that indicate the number and type of portable fire extinguishers that the size and occupancy of a property require.

Standpipe and hose systems consist of water supply pipes located inside buildings and equipped with standard fire department connections at regular intervals. In a multistory structure, standpipes are commonly located in stairwells or fire towers with a hose connection at each floor landing. When the building covers a large horizontal area, standpipe outlets are typically spaced at regular intervals throughout the floor. Standpipe systems usually have fire hoses attached so that both the fire service and the occupants of the building can use them. A valve at the standpipe station controls the flow of water to the hoses. Even without attached hoses, standpipes are an invaluable aid in fighting a fire. They deliver water to the interior areas and upper floors of a building, eliminating the need for the fire service to drag charged hoses long distances to reach the fire.

Standpipe systems may draw their water from the building water supply, but they do not always contain water. All standpipe systems have a fire department connection, sometimes called a "siamese connection," on the outside of the building. This allows the fire service to introduce additional water into wet standpipe systems and to increase the operating pressure for more effective fire suppression.

Automatic sprinkler systems provide the most effective means of controlling damage caused by fire. They consist of a series of interconnected valves and pipes with sprinkler heads attached. In the most common type of system, each sprinkler head contains a heat-sensing element and responds individually to the heat generated by a fire. Automatic sprinkler systems respond more quickly than any other fire suppression system and deliver water where it is needed. Sprinkler systems always require their own water supply, but they also come equipped with an external fire department connection to supplement water and pressure.

Most automatic fire sprinkler systems are **wet pipe systems**, meaning that the pipes always contain water under pressure. The water is released immediately when a sprinkler head opens. In areas in which the sprinkler lines are exposed to temperatures below freezing, a dry pipe system may be appropriate. The pipes in a **dry pipe system** contain compressed air or a similar inert gas that holds a valve in the water line shut. The opening of a sprinkler head allows water into the previously dry piping. Dry pipe systems respond more slowly to fire than wet pipe systems because the gas must leave the system before water can flow through.

Many property owners have **Halon extinguishing systems**. Halon gas disrupts the chemical reaction in a fire, thereby eliminating the extensive damage to contents caused by water from sprinkler systems. However, because Halon is a chlorofluorocarbon (CFC) and depletes the ozone layer, the United States and other countries producing Halon agreed to phase out its production. Maintaining and replacing the extinguishant in Halon systems will therefore be expensive in the future.

Pre-action sprinkler systems consist of a sprinkler system equipped with an automatic valve controlled by a fire detection device, such as a smoke detector or heat detector. The valve remains closed until the smoke or heat detector opens it in response to fire conditions. Before the system will actually discharge water, the detection component has to detect a fire and heat has to actuate a sprinkler head. A dry pipe system is *not* advisable if water damage to sensitive property is a concern. When a fire can be expected to involve flammable liquids or live electrical equipment, extinguishants like dry powder and carbon dioxide are appropriate and effective. Well-protected restaurants, for instance, use dry chemical or CO_2 extinguishing systems, often called Ansul systems (the leading manufacturer of such systems), to protect hoods over cooking equipment and ducts that carry away the heated air and products of combustion. Water is not an appropriate extinguishant in these areas, where heavy accumulations of grease are commonplace.

Both sprinkler and standpipe systems can be connected to an alarm, called a water motor alarm, that will alert a monitoring station to the flow of water through the pipes. A sprinkler alarm may be connected directly to the fire department. Both sprinkler and standpipe alarms may be connected to a central station that will monitor them constantly and respond to any water flow. Sprinkler and standpipe alarms provide early notification of both fires and sprinkler leakage. Some alarms may still be connected only to a local gong on the outside of a building. Because they rely on passersby to notify the police or fire service, local gongs have never been effective as primary protection.

Private fire brigades are found only in the largest industrial businesses, such as petrochemical plants and rural areas in which municipal fire protection is unavailable or considered inadequate. Underwriters should evaluate private fire departments like they evaluate public fire departments. They should develop information on the number and training of personnel as well as on the amount and type of equipment and its location within the industrial complex. More than likely, ISO has already evaluated the characteristics of a private fire department.

External Exposures

External exposures are those outside the area owned or controlled by the insured. These exposures fall into two categories: (1) single-occupancy exposures and (2) multiple-occupancy exposures. Each of these categories presents different underwriting problems.

Single-Occupancy Exposures

When the property being underwritten consists of a single building, fire division, or group of buildings, all owned or controlled by the policyholder, a **single-occupancy exposure** exists. The external exposures in this case come from adjoining properties. Examples include buildings close enough to permit a fire in the exposing property to spread to the insured premises and fuel such as brush, woodlands, or trash left out in the open on adjoining properties. External exposure hazards differ in one significant characteristic from those previously considered. The policyholder's own loss control activities can correct deficiencies in construction, occupancy, and private protection on the insured premises. External exposures, on the other hand, are by definition outside the control of the policyholder. Little can often be done from an engineering standpoint to reduce or minimize external exposures.

Exposing Buildings

An exposing building may be considered present when another building significantly increases the possibility of a fire in the insured building. Factors that influence the severity of an exposure fire on a building, in addition to the intensity and duration of the exposure fire, include the following:

1. Type of construction of the exposing and exposed buildings
2. Height and width of the exposure fire
3. Openings in the exterior walls of the exposing and exposed buildings
4. Type of combustible contents in the exposure fire
5. Protection for openings in the wall of the exposed building
6. Interior finish of the exposing and exposed buildings
7. Distance between the exposing and exposed buildings
8. Shielding effects of noncombustible construction between the exposing and exposed buildings
9. Wind direction and velocity at the time of the fire
10. Public and private fire protection[6]

Fire walls, fire doors, special barriers, and parapets reduce the probability that an external fire will spread to the insured property. Clear space between buildings, good water supply, quick response from the fire department, and internal and external automatic sprinkler systems are additional methods of controlling external exposures. The methods by which the exposure hazard between two buildings can be reduced include the following:

1. Complete automatic sprinkler protection
2. Blank walls of noncombustible materials facing the exposure
3. Barrier walls (self-supporting) between the building and the exposure
4. Extension of exterior masonry walls to form parapets or fender walls
5. Automatic outside water curtains for combustible walls
6. Elimination of openings by filling them with construction equivalent to the wall
7. Glass block panels in openings
8. Wired glass in steel sash windows (fixed or automatic closing) in openings
9. Automatic or deluge sprinklers outside over openings
10. Automatic (rolling steel) fire shutters on openings
11. Automatic fire doors on door openings
12. Automatic fire dampers on wall openings[7]

Adequate clear space enables firefighters to respond properly to a fire in an adjoining building and to reduce the likelihood of sufficient heat being generated to ignite the exposed structure. Clear space should be free of fire fuel. An alley filled with trash, for example, would not provide adequate clear space.

Other Exposures

A variety of exposures other than structures can markedly increase the likelihood of a fire loss. Examples include lumberyards, gasoline storage tanks, brush, or woodlands. An underwriter might not recognize the exposure presented by an open area containing brush surrounding a structure, but significant brush fires have swept through developed areas with catastrophic results.

Multiple-Occupancy Exposures

In a multiple-occupancy building, persons other than the policyholder own or control portions of the fire division that contains the insured property. If the policyholder in question occupies part of a building that is divided from the rest of the building by an approved fire wall, that section is considered a single-occupancy. The rest of the building is then treated as an exposing fire division. If the policyholder, on the other hand, occupies part of a building with combustible walls separating the insured property from the other occupancies, a **multiple-occupancy exposure** exists. Shopping centers commonly have walls that can be moved to resize store areas to meet the needs of new occupants. Most office buildings occupied by more than one tenant are also multiple-occupancy structures.

A factor to consider in evaluating a multiple-occupancy commercial location is the occupancy class of the other occupants. In a typical commercial shopping center of ordinary construction, a craft store may be exposed by a restaurant or a paint store in adjacent portions of the same fire division.

Another factor to consider is the amount of protection available against fire originating in exposing occupancies. Although there is no approved fire wall between occupancies, there may be a noncombustible wall that does provide some protection. Alternatively, the walls separating occupancies could be no more than drywall partitions with continuous attics throughout the fire division.

Other Fire Underwriting Considerations

Construction, occupancy, protection, and exposure are the basic tools underwriters use to analyze the risk of loss by fire and related causes of loss. One of the most important applications of those tools is to craft the available information into an estimate of the most severe loss the insurer can expect the policyholder to sustain. Such judgments require underwriters to consider policy provisions that can affect the ultimate amount of loss that might be paid by the insurer. The two most commonly used measures of loss severity are amount subject and probable maximum loss (discussed below).

Policy Provisions Affecting the Amount of Loss

How much an insurer will have to pay when loss occurs is a significant consideration to property underwriters. The factors that determine that amount include the insurable interest of all persons insured, policy provisions for establishing the value of insured property, the relationship of the amount of insurance to that value, and the most severe loss the underwriter anticipates.

Property insurance forms limit recovery to the amount of the insured's insurable interest at the time of loss. The most common interest in property comes from its outright ownership. Other forms of ownership exist in which the insured may have something less than an insurable interest in the entire property or may have an insurable interest for only a period of time. For a given property, several persons or entities may have an insurable interest, and the insurable interests of all these parties may exceed the value of the property. Underwriters need to recognize that the amount of coverage provided may be less than insured or more than anticipated because of additional interests in the property and additional insureds added to the policy.

Policy valuation provisions determine, in part, the amount of loss that will be paid under a policy. Actual cash value (ACV) was once considered the best measure of a loss. Under that valuation approach, the insured received payment for the value of property replacement less depreciation. Underwriters liked this approach because the insured was essentially being restored to the same position it was in before the loss occurred. With an ACV valuation provision, there are few incentives for the insured to cause the loss and many incentives to maintain the property. Replacement cost valuation provisions do not deduct for depreciation. Under the ACV approach to valuation, depreciation was a real and uninsurable exposure that should have been budgeted for but more than likely was not. Replacement coverage is considered a necessity by insureds and is readily provided by insurers.

Another approach to property valuation is functional replacement cost. This approach measures the amount of loss by the cost of similar property that performs the same function. These alternative approaches to property valuation can serve to reduce the amount potentially paid on a loss.

Another policy provision affecting an insurer's ultimate payment under a property policy is the coinsurance provision. Coinsurance provisions reduce the amount an insurer pays on partial losses if the insured has failed to buy an amount of insurance close to the value of the property. Because of the coinsurance provision's punitive nature, underwriters have insisted on insureds' buying the proper amount of coverage so that this provision does not affect partial loss claim payments. Many underwriters simply decline accounts that do not buy adequate amounts of insurance to properly insure what is owned.

An insurer's ultimate loss exposure is affected when an insured uses blanket insurance, the alternative to specific insurance. With the specific insurance approach, an amount of insurance coverage is indicated for each location. The blanket insurance approach can insure several locations and types of property with one limit. There are several advantages to this approach to determining insurance coverage needs, and it works well for the policyholder if the properties insured are in separate locations. For the underwriter, blanket insurance means the limits overall must be kept within 90 percent of the total value to avoid penalizing the insured on partial losses.

Measures of Potential Loss Severity

The size of the largest loss an underwriter can anticipate is an important consideration in property underwriting. Most insurers use three related measures to estimate the largest loss a property is likely to produce:

1. Policy amount
2. Amount subject
3. Probable maximum loss (PML)

The policy amount is simply the coverage limits requested on the account. Amount subject and probable maximum loss are more valuable measures to underwriters but are, by their nature, subjective.

Amount subject measures the exposure to a single loss and varies by cause of loss. Amount subject represents a worst-case scenario—the total value exposed to loss at any one location from any one event. Amount subject can vary by cause of loss and may be different for the insurer and the insured. The insured might, for example, have two locations near one another. Although a single fire might not affect both locations, they both might be susceptible to total loss in the same tornado. Assuming that each location contains only a single fire division, the amount subject for fire insurance at each location would be the total value at risk at that site. The amount subject for a tornado, however, would be the sum of the values exposed at both locations. If the business insured each location with a different company or retained a substantial share of the property risk, the amounts subject would not be the same for the policyholder and the insurer.

After evaluating the individual risk characteristics of an account, an underwriter uses experience and judgment to determine the largest likely loss, or **probable maximum loss (PML)**. For example, an underwriter may decide that a total loss to a high-rise fire-resistive structure is conceivable but very unlikely. The underwriter would therefore set the PML at less than the full value of all insured property at that location.

Many underwriters regard PML as meaningful only for fire-resistive buildings and their contents. These underwriters assume that other types of construction will not effectively resist damage and will result in a total loss should a loss occur. Other underwriters take a more conservative approach by assuming that if a fire occurs it will breach at least one fire wall. Some underwriters apply this logic only when fire walls are breached by protected openings. This approach yields a PML that includes at least two fire divisions. Some underwriters develop a PML that is less than the full value of the exposed property in a single fire division. Those underwriters anticipate that detection and protection are adequate to limit the loss.

Determining the amount subject and probable maximum loss requires "best" guesses of what an insurer's exposure might be. Underwriters following similar logic in amount subject and PML calculations might develop different values because judgment plays a crucial role in their determination. Likewise, insurers calculate the values differently and place varying importance on them. Some insurers, for instance, view PML relative to the policy premium and ask, "How many years will it take for us to be repaid should the probable maximum loss occur?" For those insurers, PML is just another way of measuring loss severity. Some insurers integrate PML with their reinsurance program so that a PML above a specified amount indicates that reinsurance is required on an account. Underwriters must remember that probable maximum loss calculations, regardless of their apparent sophistication, are just subjective estimates. Actual losses commonly exceed the PML that an underwriter has determined for a location.

Underwriting Other Causes of Loss

In addition to fire, property underwriters have to consider other causes of loss that the policy forms cover. Not all covered causes of loss receive equal treatment. Some occur so infrequently or cause damage so slight that including them in the process would only waste time. Underwriters have to decide which causes of loss need investigation and focus their limited resources on those "key perils."

Lightning

Almost from its origin, insurance of fixed property on land has paired lightning with fire in coverage forms. Several reasons explain why. Lightning frequently causes fire, and the two causes of loss produce damage so similar that even trained observers cannot always determine which caused the loss. Early court decisions held that lighting was "fire from the sky" and, therefore, part of the peril of fire. Only within the past few years have commercial lines forms listed lightning as a separate cause of loss. Homeowners forms continue to cover "fire or lightning" as a single peril. This does not mean, however, that lightning cannot or does not cause insured damage independently of fire.

Underwriters usually pair fire and lightning together when evaluating an account. Lightning is a significant source of ignition for fires, but it can also be controlled by properly installed and maintained lightning arresters. When lightning is the source of ignition for fire, the analysis of the fire cause of loss is generally applicable.

Lighting can cause significant damage even when a fire does not ensue. For example, lightning can strike an electric transmission line and generate a power surge. The surge can then enter buildings the affected line serves and cause extensive damage. Such an event rarely causes fire, but damage by high voltage to an insured's electrical system can destroy it. Protection from electrical surges is usually done by grounding the electrical service The property owner can enhance surge protection by installing an external surge protector on power lines entering the building. Many types of electrical equipment, such as computers and electric motors, warrant interior surge protectors.

Explosion

Explosion is another cause of loss closely related to fire. Explosion is any violent expansion of gases into the atmosphere. The most common causes are the following:

- Ignition of flammable clouds (combustion explosions)
- Rupture of confined spaces (pressure explosions)

Combustion Explosions

Fire that develops so rapidly that the normal expansion of gases proceeds at a violent pace produces a **combustion explosion**. Events of this type occur when a flammable cloud of dust, vapor, mist, or gas reaches an ignition source. Combustion explosions are classified as either **deflagration** if they develop slowly or **detonation** if the rate of combustion exceeds the speed of sound. Gases, dust, mist, and low explosives (like black powder) generate deflagrations. Clouds of gas or dust and decomposition of unstable materials (including high explosives) produce detonations. Both types can be highly destructive. Detonations are much more severe than deflagrations, partly because they produce a shock wave that contributes to the overall damage.

Preventing the formation of combustible clouds is the surest protection against combustion explosions. Fire can occur only when the mixture of fuel and oxygen falls within its flammable range. The two most effective strategies for preventing combustion explosions are to limit the amount of fuel in the atmosphere and to restrict the oxygen supply that reaches the fuel. Controlling explosion losses also requires managing the sources of ignition. Electricity and friction are the most common sources of ignition for combustion explosions. They are easy to overlook and can be difficult to control. Limiting the potential of electricity to ignite a combustible cloud requires using explosion-proof electrical fixtures in hazardous environments and managing static electricity to prevent it from creating sparks. Techniques include grounding or bonding all electrical apparatus, using floor materials and coverings that do not conduct electricity, connecting ground wires on machinery with moving parts, and requiring nonconductive clothing.

Friction is inherent in the operation of machinery and presents few problems in an ordinary atmosphere. In potentially explosive environments, on the other hand, friction that would ordinarily pass unnoticed may generate enough heat to trigger an explosion. Techniques for containing friction to manageable levels include lubrication of moving parts, proper alignment of moving parts to minimize rubbing, and a comprehensive preventive maintenance program. Belts, pulleys, and rollers demand special care.

Because no amount of care can prevent all combustion explosions, making provision to minimize damage from those that inevitably occur is also important. Venting and isolation provide effective damage control. Venting incorporates design features to minimize explosion damage by relieving pressure on the structure itself and directing the force of the explosion away from property susceptible to damage. Isolation places space or barriers between the potential source of an explosion and property that it might damage.

Pressure Explosions

A second type of explosion, a **pressure explosion**, occurs when a confined space cannot contain internal pressure and bursts. Although any confined space may explode under sufficient pressure, explosion of pressure vessels is the principal concern. Pressure vessels common to most occupancies include water heaters, tanks, boilers, and process equipment. In commercial lines, boiler and machinery insurance covers explosions of steam boilers and piping, while commercial property forms insure explosions of other pressure vessels. Homeowners forms protect against both.

Pressure in fired vessels occurs when heat causes the contents of the vessels to expand. Fired vessels include water heaters, fired kettles, and hot water boilers. Steam boilers also provide pressure to unfired apparatus, such as steam jacketed kettles and other process equipment. Other unfired pressure vessels rely on mechanical means, such as compressors, to build and maintain internal pressure.

The leading cause of pressure vessel explosion is equipment failure in one of three areas: primary controls, safety devices, or the structure of the vessel. The main function of primary controls is to maintain optimal operating conditions. If primary controls perform as intended, the unsafe conditions that lead to a pressure explosion will not develop.

Safety devices may be secondary controls or pressure relief devices. Secondary controls shut equipment down as soon as an unsafe situation begins to develop. They are often identical to primary controls, except that they require manual reset. That feature demands operator intervention and calls attention to potential hazards. Pressure relief devices vent excessive pressure to prevent an explosion when all controls have failed and temperature or pressure builds to unsafe levels. Safety valves are the most common. They open when pressure reaches their rated capacity, closing again when it drops.

The structure of a pressure vessel may fail and cause an explosion for several reasons. Corrosion, erosion, or wear and tear can gradually thin the surface. Thermal expansion and contraction or excessive vibration may introduce cracks that weaken the shell and end sheets. Good maintenance and timely replacement of obsolete equipment offer the only protection against these types of failures.

Fire that reaches a pressure vessel can cause an explosion in two ways: (1) the vessel's contents, already under pressure, expand as fire drives the temperature up, and (2) the heat simultaneously causes even noncombustible materials to lose strength. Internal pressure increases while the vessel's ability to contain it diminishes. Although fire is the cause of loss in both instances, underwriters should evaluate this loss potential as part of the explosion exposure.

Windstorm

Underwriters have to give windstorm careful consideration because it is a major cause of loss and possesses the potential to generate a catastrophe. Virtually all personal and commercial property insurance policies include windstorm among the covered causes of loss. Although every part of the United States is subject to some form of severe wind, hurricanes and tornadoes are the two most significant sources of windstorm damage. Windstorm is a difficult cause of loss to underwrite. Short of identifying particular susceptible geographic areas and not writing property insurance or excluding windstorm as a cause of loss in those areas, underwriters can do little to limit the consequences of windstorm should one occur. Windstorm coverage is generally available in most parts of the United States because property owners with little exposure to windstorm damage purchase coverage. Additionally, reinsurance spread the catastrophic effects of windstorm losses to others.

Hurricanes

Hurricanes are tropical storms, and few natural phenomena can approach their destructive power. The Saffir/Simpson scale, shown in Exhibit 5-1, is the most familiar gauge of hurricane intensity. That scale, which has categories from 1 to 5, is useful in assessing potential hurricane damage for underwriting purposes.

Since 1989, the number of severe hurricanes making landfall in North America has increased. Such storms principally affect the southern Atlantic and Gulf Coasts of the United States, the Gulf Coast of Mexico, and islands in the Caribbean. Pacific Ocean hurricanes (called typhoons) also threaten Hawaii but rarely reach the continent. The most damaging hurricane on record is Hurricane Andrew. It struck South Florida and Louisiana in August 1992, causing more than $15.5 billion of insured losses. Hurricane Iniki, which struck the island of Kauai in Hawaii the same year, helped make 1992 the worst year of natural disasters the insurance industry has ever experienced.

Types of Hurricanes

Hurricanes that make landfall may be either penetrating storms or raking storms. A **penetrating storm** strikes the coastline at approximately a right angle and moves directly inland. These storms typically cause heavy wind damage over a relatively small area. Once the eye of the hurricane is over land, the storm quickly decreases in intensity. A **raking storm** parallels the coast. Because this type of storm can maintain its intensity for a long time if the eye remains over the ocean, it can inflict damage on a wider area. Storm surge damage is usually more serious in a raking storm.

Hurricane Damage

Hurricanes cause damage in several ways. Most hurricane damage results from the effect of high wind on exposed property. Wind-driven rain can also penetrate structures and cause significant damage. Most of that rain enters buildings through holes the wind creates in the roof or walls and is therefore insured as windstorm. When a hurricane comes ashore, it drives a wall of high

Exhibit 5-1
Saffir-Simpson Hurricane Disaster-Potential Scale

CATEGORY 1	Central Pressure	Winds	Storm Surge
	Greater than 980 millibars	74-95 MPH	4-5 feet

Winds of 74 to 95 miles per hour. Damage primarily to shrubbery, trees, foliage, and unanchored mobile homes. No real damage to other structures. Some damage to poorly constructed signs. Storm surge 4 to 5 feet above normal. Low-lying coastal roads inundated, minor pier damage, some small craft in exposed anchorages torn from moorings.

CATEGORY 2	Central Pressure	Winds	Storm Surge
	965-979 millibars	96-110 MPH	6-8 feet

Winds of 96 to 110 miles per hour. Considerable damage to shrubbery and tree foliage; some trees blown down. Major damage to exposed mobile homes. Extensive damage to poorly constructed signs. Some damage to roofing materials of buildings; some window and door damage. No major damage to buildings. Storm surge 6 to 8 feet above normal. Coastal roads and low-lying escape routes inland cut by rising water 2 to 4 hours before arrival of hurricane center. Considerable damage to piers. Marinas flooded. Small craft in unprotected anchorages torn from moorings. Evacuation of some shoreline residents and low-lying island areas required.

CATEGORY 3	Central Pressure	Winds	Storm Surge
	945-964 millibars	111-130 MPH	9-12 feet

Winds of 111 to 130 miles per hour. Foliage torn from trees; large trees blown down. Practically all poorly constructed signs blown down. Some damage to roofing materials of buildings; some window or door damage. Some structural damage to small buildings. Mobile homes destroyed. Storm surge 9 to 12 feet above normal. Serious flooding at coast and many smaller structures near coast destroyed; larger structures near coast damaged by battering waves and floating debris. Low-lying escape routes inland cut by rising water 3 to 5 hours before hurricane center arrives. Flat terrain 5 feet or less above sea level flooded inland 8 miles or more. Evacuation of low-lying residences within several blocks of shoreline possibly required.

CATEGORY 4	Central Pressure	Winds	Storm Surge
	920-944 millibars	131-155 MPH	13-18 feet

Winds of 131 to 155 miles per hour. Shrubs and trees blown down; all signs down. Extensive damage to roofing materials, windows, and doors. Complete failure of roofs on many small residences. Complete destruction of mobile homes. Storm surge 13 to 18 feet above normal. Flat terrain 10 feet or less above sea level flooded inland as far as 6 miles. Major damage to lower floors of structures near shore due to flooding and battering by waves and floating debris. Low-lying escape routes inland cut by rising water 3 to 5 hours before hurricane center arrives. Major erosion of beaches. Massive evacuation of all residences within 500 yards of shore and of single-story residences on low ground within 2 miles of shore.

CATEGORY 5	Central Pressure	Winds	Storm Surge
	Less than 920 millibars	+155 MPH	+18 feet

Winds greater than 155 miles per hour. Shrubs and trees blown down; considerable damage to roofs of buildings; all signs down. Very severe and extensive damage to windows and doors. Complete failure of roofs on many residences and industrial buildings. Extensive shattering of glass in windows and doors. Some complete building failures. Small buildings overturned or blown away. Complete destruction of mobile homes. Storm surge greater than 18 feet above normal. Major damage to lower floors of all structures less than 15 feet above sea level within 500 yards of shore. Low-lying escape routes inland cut by rising water 3 to 5 hours before hurricane center arrives. Massive evacuation of residential areas on low ground within 5 to 10 miles of shore possibly required.

water before it. That storm surge threatens primarily coastal properties, but it may also impede drainage and raise the water level in rivers, streams, and bays. Finally, the heavy rains that a hurricane produces cause flooding alone or in combination with the storm surge.

More tropical storms are forming, and more of them are becoming hurricanes. Atmospheric scientists believe that severe tropical weather occurs in a natural cycle that extends over several decades, perhaps as long as forty years. The length of this cycle has bred complacency that promotes the heavy commercial and residential development of coastal areas. This has dramatically increased the value of property exposed to a single storm. By making flood insurance readily available in coastal plains, the National Flood Insurance Program has encouraged this trend. Many scientists also believe that the climate is getting permanently warmer, a phenomenon known as the greenhouse effect. The higher temperatures that result may contribute to the growing severity of storms and the losses they produce.

Hurricane Andrew, for example, was not the most powerful storm to make landfall in the United States. The extent of the destruction it caused was the result of development that placed a large amount of property at risk. Building codes that were not enforced and inadequately designed structures also influenced the extent of the damage.

Hurricane damage is typically caused by a combination of wind and water. Hurricane Andrew was an exception to this because very little storm surge accompanied it.

Controlling Wind Damage

Studies of hurricane damage provide valuable insight into effective means of controlling wind losses. Several lessons for controlling wind damage were learned from the buildings affected by Hurricane Andrew:

1. Windstorm is a more serious consideration for personal than commercial lines underwriters. One- and two-family dwellings sustained most of the damage in Hurricane Andrew, while fully engineered structures fared very well overall.

2. The key to a building's survival in a windstorm is maintaining the integrity of its envelope, the outer walls, and the roof, all of which keep weather out.

3. Well-designed building codes can protect property from windstorm damage. In Hurricane Andrew, maximum sustained winds probably did not exceed 125 miles per hour,[8] only slightly higher than the design requirement of the South Florida Building Code, which applies to the entire affected area. Structures built to code should have weathered the storm with no more than nominal damage.

4. Building code enforcement is essential in coastal areas.

A comprehensive evaluation of building codes and their enforcement requires extensive local knowledge that insurers can acquire only by maintaining a staff in every area of the country or by costly research. This has not been practical for most insurers. The Building Code Effectiveness Grading Schedule (BCEGS), described earlier, will eventually resolve this dilemma.

Other Underwriting Considerations for Hurricanes

Because losses from hurricanes frequently affect a large number of insured properties, underwriters have to do more than evaluate individual submissions. Managing a book of business is essential to successful underwriting in areas subject to hurricane losses. Hurricanes Hugo and Andrew each claimed the solvency of several insurance companies and weakened the financial condition of many more. Reinsurance has been an essential element in protecting the solvency of insurers. Significant catastrophes like those caused by Hugo and Andrew have raised the price of catastrophe reinsurance and caused reinsurers to limit the amount of reinsurance they want to make available. Likewise, insurers are extremely aware of the aggregate exposures they have exposed to a single storm.

Computer models are available to measure the exposure to a single storm for an entire book of business. Staff underwriters have to use those models to contain total exposure to a level that does not impose financial hardship on the insurer. To achieve that objective, an insurer has to restrict the number of risks it writes in those areas. An insurer may elect to restrict its writings by establishing a target expressed as a desirable market share, policy count, or total insured value.

Tornadoes

Tornadoes are very small but especially violent windstorms. They form in warm, humid, and unsettled weather and are often spawned by thunderstorms and tropical storms. Tornadoes consist of winds rotating usually cyclonically at speeds that may reach 300 miles per hour; this creates a partial vacuum at the center of the storm called its vortex. Upward velocity at the wall can exceed 200 feet per second. Condensation around the vortex produces a pale cloud that gives the tornado its characteristic funnel shape. When the tornado makes contact with the ground, it draws debris into the circulating air, and the funnel cloud darkens. Scientists are not sure how tornadoes form, but they do know the storms pack awesome destructive power. The average tornado path is only one-quarter of a mile wide and rarely extends more than sixteen miles. Most paths are considerably shorter and narrower. A tornado can touch down in a backyard, pick up a lawn shed and its contents, and lift off again without damaging the fences bounding the yard. On the other hand, a tornado path may be up to a mile wide, and the longest on record extended over 300 miles. Tornadoes move forward at an average of forty miles per hour but have been clocked at seventy.

Incidence of Tornadoes

Tornadoes occur worldwide but most frequently in the United States. No part of the country is immune, but the Great Plains of the Midwest and Southeast are most prone to tornado damage. Exhibit 5-2 illustrates the distribution of tornado activity across the nation. Tornadoes occur year-round but exhibit a seasonal pattern with a peak in the spring. Beginning in March, the peak moves from the southern coastal states through the southern plains states into the northern plains states and Great Lakes area. Incidence declines from June to its low point in December. The appearance of tornadoes is random and unpredictable.

Tornado Damage

Tornadoes owe their destructive power to their compact size, powerful winds, and the upward movement at the wall. Their winds exceed any reasonable design load. Tornadoes also subject property to rapid changes in the direction of wind stress and uplift forces no other phenomenon can produce. Tornadoes can lift cars and heavy farm machinery from the ground and deposit the remains miles away. The most common effect of a tornado is total destruction of any property squarely in its path. Very substantial buildings and property at the edge of a tornado's path may escape with serious structural damage. Property close to the path can sustain minor to severe damage.

Exhibit 5-2
Total Number of Tornadoes—1994

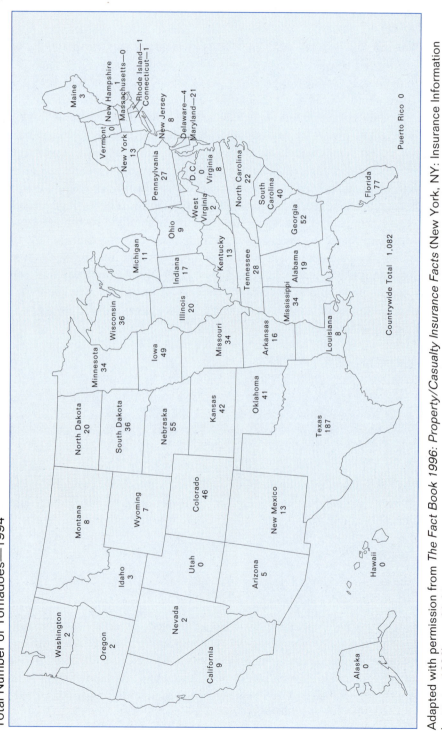

Adapted with permission from *The Fact Book 1996: Property/Casualty Insurance Facts* (New York, NY: Insurance Information Institute, 1996), pp. 80-81.

Hail

Destructive hail falls almost exclusively during violent thunderstorms. Hailstones can be more than five inches in diameter and weigh over one and one-half pounds. Damage to growing crops accounts for nearly 80 percent of all hail losses, but hail can also cause severe damage to auto and home windows, neon signs, and fragile structures such as greenhouses. Aluminum siding and roofing materials are particularly susceptible to hail damage.

Riot or Civil Commotion

Even the most basic property insurance forms cover loss by riot and civil commotion, which includes any disruption of public order. The distinction between the two perils varies by state because riot is a crime, and its definition depends on the penal code. Nevertheless, property insurance covers the two events as a pair. The two principal causes of riot losses are fire and looting. Simple and often inexpensive risk management measures can be effective in controlling losses from riot and civil commotion.

Vandalism and Malicious Mischief

Vandalism can occur anywhere, but it is particularly evident in urban areas. Children and young adults commit most acts of vandalism. In fact, FBI statistics show that over 90 percent of vandalism arrests are of persons under twenty-five years old.[9] Schools, churches, parks, playgrounds, and youth centers are examples of properties that possess a possible vandalism exposure. Since groups of children are more likely to commit vandalism, areas containing many children, such as urban areas, are likely to have a higher incidence of vandalism than are areas in which residents are mostly older adults.

Other types of vandalism can occur during labor disputes or when an organization becomes the target of violence because of social protest. Violent protest has caused vandalism damage to home offices of multinational corporations, major banks, offices of foreign airlines, and the homes of public officials.

Because it produces relatively small losses, vandalism rarely attracts much of an underwriter's attention. Frequency is more of a consideration than severity with vandalism, so an appropriately set deductible will reduce the insurer's loss payments.

Water Damage and Sprinkler Leakage

Homeowners and commercial property coverage forms frequently insure certain types of water damage. Direct damage caused by accidental discharge, overflow, or leakage of water or steam from plumbing, heating, and cooling systems is the most common. Water damage caused by flood is usually excluded because of its catastrophic nature, and policy writers have taken great care to distinguish the circumstances when coverage applies. Poor maintenance is the cause of most water damage losses, so underwriters rarely write this cause of loss specifically.

Flat roofs are another source of water damage losses because water can soak through the roof covering. That happens most often when water accumulates or "ponds" in low areas. In cold weather, packed snow and ice may block roof drains, keeping melted snow from running off.

Sprinkler leakage losses occur when water or other extinguishing agents escape from sprinkler systems. Losses occur infrequently, and damage is likely to be severe only in exceptional cases. The most common causes of sprinkler leakage losses are freezing, mechanical injury, poor maintenance, and excessive temperature at sprinkler heads. Sprinklered heads exposed to physical damage should have guards over them, and both the pipes and risers should be protected from accidental rupture. Forklifts present a special danger to sprinkler heads, risers, and lines.

Underwriting sprinkler leakage concentrates on two elements: (1) the damageability of the contents and (2) the physical condition, maintenance, and design of the sprinkler system itself. When the contents of the structure protected by a sprinkler system are highly susceptible to water damage, sprinkler leakage may result in a severe loss. Frequent inspections should be performed to determine the condition and maintenance of sprinkler systems. Many underwriters rely on periodic inspections of sprinklered properties by ISO. Underwriters should be leery of fully sprinklered buildings that take a nonsprinklered rate. This usually indicates that the sprinkler system was installed improperly or is deficient. A water motor gong that activates when water flows through the system reduces the likelihood of a severe loss to highly susceptible property.

Sinkhole Collapse and Mine Subsidence

Collapse of sinkholes is relatively new as an insured cause of loss. Underwriters are fortunate that typical losses in this area are usually neither frequent nor severe. Sinkholes occur where underground rivers and streams have carved channels out of solid limestone bedrock. The caverns formed are relatively weak but are supported by the water they contain. The water supports the weight of the cavern roof and the earth above it. Because community growth has placed increased demands on water tables, the water tables have begun to drop. When no longer supported by the water pressure, caverns can collapse, causing sinkholes.

Sinkholes often occur in Florida. Florida has a great deal of limestone and a rapidly growing population that increases the demand on the water table. Sinkholes occur in other parts of the country as well. Evaluating a sinkhole exposure requires an extensive knowledge of local topography and the demographic growth trends of an area. Few underwriters possess such specific knowledge of an area and therefore rarely analyze sinkhole collapse as a cause of loss.

Mine subsidence and sinkhole collapse are similar causes of loss. Underwriters have difficulty determining whether a structure is built over the site of an abandoned mine shaft or tunnel in the same way they have difficulty determining sinkhole exposures. States with serious mine subsidence exposures have made mine subsidence a required coverage option for years.

Volcanic Action

Volcanic action was traditionally part of the earth movement exclusion. The eruption of Mount Saint Helens in 1980 made insurers reconsider that exclusion, and many insurers made claim payments for claims stemming from the eruption anyway.

Insurers considered volcanic eruption subject to adverse selection. That is, the eruption of a volcano is a local event, and those people who need coverage the most are the ones who purchase it.

State insurance departments expected insurers to pay volcanic action losses and let the insurers and the public know it. Some insurance commissioners required coverage after the fact. One simply found coverage under the explosion cause of loss. Insurers took the course of least expense and paid the losses and amended their forms to include volcanic action losses.

Weight of Ice, Snow, or Sleet

During the winter months, ice, snow, and sleet can accumulate on roofs. When that happens, more weight is added than the structure can carry, causing partial or total collapse. Structures in areas exposed to regular cold winters are most susceptible. Cold snaps can also extend deep into the Sun Belt, where roofs might not be designed to withstand heavy snow. Controlling these losses requires properly designed and well-maintained structures. Roofs with large open spans become more subject to collapse under a snow load. Design defects contributed to the roof collapse of the Hartford Civic Center after a rather ordinary snow and ice accumulation built up on the roof.

Ice Damming

Pitched roofs help resolve the problem of heavy ice, snow, or sleet by allowing a structure to shed some of the load. They prevent excessive weight from accumulating. The most significant problem with pitched roofs is the formation of ice dams. When melting snow and ice run down a roof and freeze near the edge, especially along overhanging eaves, that ice blocks the flow of additional snow melting off the roof and stops the snow from being shed as intended. Such an ice blockage is called an **ice dam**. The best way to control this type of loss is good insulation and adequate ventilation under a roof. Those measures prevent the melting of snow and ice along a roof surface, at the bottom of the accumulation. Heat melts snow from the top, and the snow runs off without creating problems. Losses occur when heat escaping from a building melts from the bottom, forcing the runoff under built-up snow and ice on the roof. Insulation above the top-floor ceiling limits the amount of heat that escapes from the interior. Ventilation disperses the heat before it can cause melting. This approach keeps the underside of the roof cold, limiting snow melt to the top of the built-up snow and ice.

Collapse

Buildings collapse for several reasons other than the weight of ice, snow, or sleet, including defective design or construction, deterioration, and the weight of people, personal property, or water on a roof. Poor construction caused the collapse of a ceiling in the Port Authority Trans Hudson (PATH) Transportation Center at Journal Square in Jersey City, New Jersey. The plaster on the metal lath ceiling hung suspended from the reinforced concrete structure and collapsed under the weight of two PATH employees doing maintenance above it. The design contemplated this load, but the contractor had cut corners, omitting every fourth suspender and spreading the rest out. Vibration from passing PATH trains combined with the weight of the maintenance workers, whose equipment caused the collapse.

Any weight on a roof can cause it to collapse. Water that accumulates on flat roofs from rainfall when drains are blocked is a common cause. Regular inspection and good maintenance should prevent such losses. Many roof structure designs do not contemplate the load of property or people, but that is not always apparent to the users of a building.

Some buildings have collapsed from the cumulative effect of vibration. Those buildings are usually very old structures whose builders could not anticipate modern traffic. For example, a nineteenth-century hotel near Cooper Union in New York City collapsed without warning. Engineers identified vibrations from a subway line below the street and passing trucks as the cause.

Anticipating all potential causes of collapse is impossible. Underwriters might do better to concentrate on the quality of a structure's design, construction, and maintenance. Novel or unusual designs are more prone to collapse than traditional ones. The Hartford Civic Center used an innovative design that failed under conditions the builders could reasonably anticipate. The ceiling of the PATH Transportation Center embodied a standard design widely used in building lobbies. Its collapse resulted in numerous inspections to make sure the poor quality of workmanship did not affect similar ceilings. When a building's roof collapses because rain cannot run off it, poor maintenance or design is the cause. Other parts of the building are likely to be affected by similar maintenance or design defects.

Flood

Flood is a common event in large areas of the country, recurring at regular intervals. Some locations flood every year, but others face no known flood hazards. **Floods** result from greater precipitation than the land can drain and sometimes seem to occur unpredictably. The spring and summer of 1992 brought flooding to the Mississippi River system. Local residents thought they had experienced the worst possible flooding with the 100-year flood in 1972. Even though the Army Corps of Engineers can show that floods of this magnitude occur on average every 500 years, predicting the years in which those floods will occur is not possible. Seven types of flood are common:

1. Riverine floods occur when rivers, streams, and other watercourses rise and overflow their banks. They can result from either heavy rainfall or snow melt upstream in their drainage basins.

2. Tidal floods arise from high tides, frequently driven by high winds off-shore, and from tropical storms making landfall or passing close offshore. They affect bays and the portions of rivers along the coast.

3. Wind floods can happen wherever a strong wind holds back a large body of water from its normal drainage course and raises the water level. Back bays behind barrier islands are especially susceptible to wind floods. Water that cannot escape through normal channels can flow out of these bays across the barrier islands. During the winter of 1992-1993, wind floods occurred repeatedly along the New Jersey shore.

4. Rising water levels downstream may prevent drainage upstream, causing a backwater flood. Backwater floods can extend for a substantial distance upstream.

5. Ice jams sometimes develop as ice thaws and begins to move downstream. They block the flow of water, causing it to back up and flood upstream areas. If the ice jam breaks suddenly, it can cause flooding downstream.

6. Accidental floods are caused by the failure of flood control systems. A dam might break and cause flooding downstream. Blocked floodgates and spillways cause upstream flooding.

7. Topographic changes made by people can also cause floods. For example, instead of being absorbed into the soil, rain water can accumulate on concrete and asphalt parking lots. If storm sewer drains have inadequate capacity or are blocked, water can build up and flood adjacent properties.

The National Flood Insurance Program (NFIP) administered by the Federal Emergency Management Agency (FEMA) is the largest flood insurance underwriter in the United States. Homeowners insurers that write flood insurance almost always do so on behalf of NFIP through the "Write Your Own" program. Some commercial lines insurers provide coverage for flood under some commercial lines policies. Information on known flood hazards is widely available, and protective measures can be taken. Underwriting flood successfully requires analyzing the known probability that a flood will occur at a certain location and establishing a rate adequate to the risk of loss the insurer assumes.

Earthquake

Earthquake underwriting is difficult because many geographic regions have significant exposures. Underwriters need to control their total earthquake writings to protect against a catastrophic loss from a single seismic event. The underwriting analysis of earthquakes considers the following three major factors:

1. Areas of earthquake activity
2. Soil conditions
3. Building design and construction

Areas of Earthquake Activity

The Pacific Coast from Alaska to California is the most seismically active area of the United States, and 90 percent of all earthquakes in the United States occur in California and western Nevada. The most severe earthquake ever recorded, however, occurred along the New Madrid Fault in Missouri in 1811.

The United States Office of Science and Technology has measured the chance of damaging seismic activity for each area of the country, dividing the country into four zones. Earthquake risk is almost nonexistent in Zone 0. In Zone 1, minor damage from earthquakes may occur. Zone 2 is exposed to moderate damage, and Zone 3 represents areas of significant damage potential. The map of seismic risk is shown in Exhibit 5-3.

Exhibit 5-3
Seismic Potential for the Continental United States

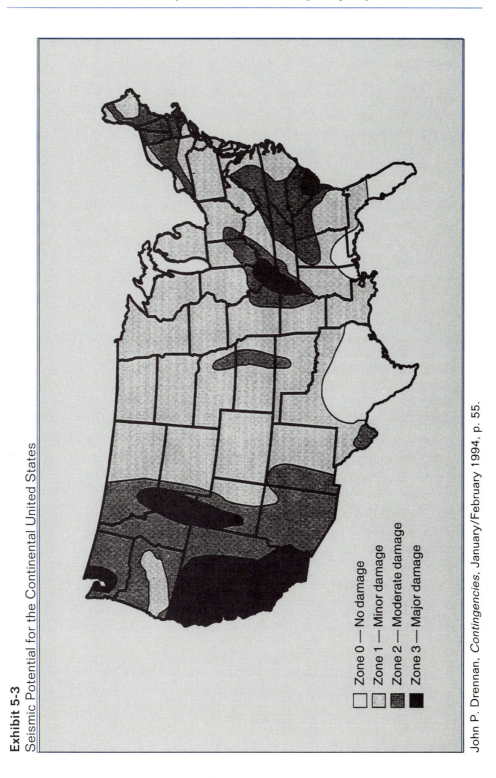

Zone 0 — No damage
Zone 1 — Minor damage
Zone 2 — Moderate damage
Zone 3 — Major damage

John P. Drennan, *Contingencies*, January/February 1994, p. 55.

Soil Conditions

Earthquake waves travel at smaller amplitudes in bedrock, so structures built on bedrock or supported on piling driven into bedrock are less susceptible to earthquake damage. **Consolidated soil** of long standing (thousands of years), such as limestone and some clay, will stand up better than **unconsolidated soil**, such as sand, gravel, silt, and some clays. Filled land, common in many large cities, represents a particularly hazardous type of unconsolidated soil from an earthquake standpoint. Unconsolidated filled land (as well as certain other types of unconsolidated soils) is subject to **liquefaction** during an earthquake, becoming so unstable that it acts like a liquid. For example, during the 1985 earthquake in Mexico City, the underlying soil that had once been a lake bed liquefied and contributed significantly to the extensive damage. San Francisco's marina district experienced extensive damage in the 1989 Loma Prieta earthquake primarily because it was built on landfill.

Building Design and Construction

Most buildings (of nonseismic construction) are designed to carry a vertical load, the weight of the structure and its contents. An earthquake causes horizontal stresses that weight-bearing columns and walls have not been designed to bear. An earthquake-resistant building has all its structural members tied together securely so that the entire building moves horizontally as a single unit when subjected to earthquake forces. If not tied together, walls and columns can be moved out from under the floors they were designed to support, causing the building to collapse.

Joisted masonry construction is particularly susceptible to earthquake damage. A joisted masonry building is rigid and subject to structural failure during earth movements. A frame building, on the other hand, is relatively flexible and "gives" during earth movement, often sustaining relatively minor damage, such as cracked plaster. Brick-facing or other stone veneer and tile roofs often sustain earthquake damage. Tilt slab construction, which is sometimes found in light industrial buildings and warehouses, is also susceptible to earthquake damage. Fire-resistive construction survives most earthquakes with slight damage.

Underwriting Time Element Coverages

Direct property insurance coverages are readily understood because grasping the tangible nature of a financial loss is easy. More difficult to understand are the related losses of reduced income and extra expense associated with a direct property loss. These *indirect* or *time element* losses are a consequence of the policyholder's inability to use the covered property immediately following a loss. The longer the interruption in activity—rebuilding the structure or residence and preparing it for use or occupancy or replacing key or specialized production machinery—the greater the loss.

Time element coverages are available for personal and commercial policyholders. The homeowners policy offers "loss of use" coverage, which provides indemnification to the policyholder for either additional living expenses incurred or the fair rental value of the property when made uninhabitable by a covered cause of loss. **Additional living expense** compensates the policyholder for extraordinary expenses incurred while the residence is being repaired. **Fair rental value** is the amount of rent that could have been fairly charged for the premises had there been no covered direct loss. Loss of use coverage also indemnifies the policyholder when a civil authority prohibits the policyholder from occupying the residence because of a covered cause of loss to other property. The dwelling fire policies contain similar coverages.

The commercial counterpart of this coverage is the business income coverage form, which has two variations. One version provides business income coverage alone, and the other adds extra expense coverage. Both versions of the business income coverage form include coverage for extra expenses that reduce the business income loss. The insuring agreement of the business income coverage forms commits the insurer to pay the policyholder the actual loss sustained because of a necessary interruption of the policyholder's operation due to direct physical damage to property caused by a covered cause of loss. **Extra expense coverage** provides for the additional expenses incurred by the policyholder to minimize the interruption of operations regardless of whether the insured reduces the loss of business income. Extra expense coverage can be purchased separately for insureds who are more concerned with uninterrupted operation than with loss of business income.

Three "optional coverages" are available to eliminate or suspend the coinsurance clause provided in the business income coverage forms. These optional coverages are maximum period of indemnity, monthly limitation of indemnity, and agreed value. Another alternative is a nonstandard valued form that bases recovery on a mutually determined dollar amount payable each day operations are suspended up to a specified maximum number of days. Those optional forms are appealing because coinsurance calculations, which affect the adequacy of coverage, are complex. The simplicity of these alternative coverage forms does not guarantee adequate coverage. Income projections must be performed to ensure that the limits selected are adequate.

Determination of Probable Maximum Loss

Determining the applicant's probable maximum loss is an involved task. The first step is to determine the magnitude of the loss by projecting expected earnings for the period of coverage. This evaluation is crucial in determining the amount of coverage necessary. The second step is to select a coinsurance percentage that will approximate the expected period of interruption should loss occur.

Coverage Needed

Any projection of income is at best an estimate that may vary significantly from the actual results. With that in mind, the recommended approach has three steps:

1. Project the firm's net income and expenses for the next twelve to twenty-four months, and pinpoint seasonal fluctuations.
2. Estimate the probable period of maximum interruption (this involves determining the probable time to rebuild a damaged facility or, in the case of a manufacturer, the time it takes to return the goods in process to their pre-loss level).
3. Determine whether to cover ordinary payroll, and identify all charges and expenses that would not necessarily continue after loss occurs.

The most recent year-end financial statement is one source for this analysis. If the fiscal year has ended more than six months previously, an evaluation of the most recent twelve months of earnings would be in order. Since the recent past is some indication of the short-term future trend for sales and earnings, an analysis of current net income and expense is necessary before making a projection.

Significant seasonal fluctuations in sales and/or earnings directly affect the calculation of not only the proper amount of insurance needed to cover the probable maximum loss but also the amount of insurance required to comply with the coinsurance clause.

Coinsurance Selection

In order to encourage insurance to value and to simplify ratemaking, business income forms contain a coinsurance clause that operates essentially the same as the coinsurance clause in direct damage property insurance policies. Instead of using the value of the property as a base against which the coinsurance percentage is applied, the business income form uses the policy year's net income and all operating expenses, not just those that would continue during a shutdown. The policyholder may choose 50, 60, 70, 80, 90, 100, or 125 percent coinsurance.

The chosen coinsurance percentage is roughly related to the expected period of business interruption. For example, a business that anticipates a maximum period of interruption to be six months may select a 50 percent coinsurance clause. Businesses requiring more than a year to recover from a loss should consider a 125 percent coinsurance clause.

Four important caveats should be remembered when using this rule of thumb:

1. The coinsurance percentage does not apply to the maximum loss exposure. Business income is defined as net income plus continuing expenses incurred during the interruption, but the coinsurance clause applies to net income plus *all* operating expenses that should probably have developed during the twelve-month period following the inception date of the policy.

2. Seasonal fluctuations in sales and expenses should be charted so that coverage limits and coinsurance percentages selected provide sufficient coverage for the worst possible occurrence in terms of severity and timing.

3. To comply with the coinsurance clause, the policyholder may have to purchase more business income coverage than seems necessary. Distinguishing which expenses will continue and at what magnitude in advance of the loss is difficult. The consequences of overinsurance are often offset by rate credits.

4. Since the determination of business income coverage and the *base* used to calculate the satisfaction of the coinsurance differ, establishing proper coverage amounts and coinsurance percentages is confusing and difficult.

Underwriters should be instrumental in assisting producers and applicants in determining appropriate limits and percentages.

Determination of the Probable Period of Interruption

A business income loss requires that there be direct damage to the insured premises by a covered cause of loss, so analysis of the physical and moral hazards of the risk begins with an analysis of the direct damage exposure. If the business income form is added to a direct damage policy, this analysis has presumably already been completed. In those instances when business income coverage is written separately, analysis of the COPE factors is required to determine the direct damage loss exposure.

The severity of a business income loss is not directly related to the severity of the underlying direct damage loss. A relatively minor property loss destroying only 5 percent of the structure might result in a total business income loss up to the policy limit if the destroyed property included a machine vital to the manufacturing process that could not be replaced in less than one year.[10] Time is the principal element in business income coverage and is the additional dimension in underwriting time element coverages. Determining probable periods of interruption is difficult. The underwriter must evaluate the seasonality of the business, the time it will take to rebuild, bottlenecks, long production processes, and disaster contingency plans.

Seasonality and Rebuilding Time

The degree of seasonality in the policyholder's operations is a major factor in determining potential exposure. This is an important underwriting consideration because a highly seasonal business with 80 percent or more of its business concentrated in a three-month peak season would suffer a severe business income loss from a relatively short shutdown.

Similarly, the time period required to rebuild the insured premises is a major factor in determining exposure. Specialized structures requiring long construction periods, the possibility of lengthy delays in obtaining permits, severe climatic conditions inhibiting construction during certain times of the year, and congested urban locations are all factors increasing exposure to loss.

Bottlenecks

Manufacturing and mining risks are particularly susceptible to bottlenecks. The term bottlenecks is used to refer to a machine, process, or building that is essential to the continued operation of an entire facility or manufacturing plant. A relatively minor direct damage loss can lead to a severe business income loss in the case of a bottleneck. The existence of a potential bottleneck can be determined by using a flow diagram of the production process. Some manufacturing processes use machines that must be custom manufactured, and the reinstallation process takes many months. If the process is vital but is duplicated on machines in separate fire divisions, the exposure is greatly reduced.

Although bottlenecks are usually found in processing or manufacturing risks, a congested area or an unusual building configuration can result in a bottleneck during the reconstruction period.

Long Production Processes

If the manufacturing or processing operation takes an unusually long time to complete, the business income exposure could be extended. If a product must be aged or seasoned, destruction of the facility could lead to a lengthy interruption, since this time would be added to the length of time necessary to restore the structure and machinery to operating condition. The time required to get the stock in process to the point where it had been before the loss must be considered, since the business income form covers actual loss sustained.

Disaster Contingency Plans

Although the business income form requires reasonable speed in the restoration of the operation, proper planning can further reduce the length of interruption. A disaster contingency plan would include detailed written plans for the restoration of the operation if part or all of the buildings and equipment were destroyed. The disaster contingency plan should be tied into the flowchart of the firm's operation, indicating the actions that would be necessary in the event of the destruction of each part of the process. This type of plan could also indicate whether continuation of the operation would be feasible in the event of certain types of damage. If that were the case, extra expense insurance might be indicated, either in lieu of business income coverage alone or in the combined form.

Underwriting Crime Insurance

Crime is a significant cause of loss for both personal lines and commercial lines insureds. The crime loss exposures for most individuals and families are met under their homeowners policy. (Theft coverage can also be added by endorsement to a dwelling policy.) The ISO homeowners policy does not define "theft," but it is generally understood to include burglary, robbery, and larceny. The policy does identify specific limitations in theft coverage. For example, missing property must have been taken by others, not simply misplaced. (ISO's HO-8 provides even more limited coverage for theft than ISO's other homeowners forms.)

The homeowners policy has special limits on certain kinds of personal property, many of which are particularly susceptible to theft. For instance, money, bank notes, bullion, gold other than goldware, silver other than silverware, and platinum coins and medals are subject to a $200 limit. The homeowners policy singles out other personal property for a special coverage limit but only from a theft loss. These property categories and the per-item loss limitations that apply are as follows.

- Jewelry, watches, furs, and precious and semiprecious stones $1,000
- Firearms of any type $2,000
- Silver and silver-plated ware, gold and gold-plated ware, and pewterware $2,500

Many personal lines insureds have personal property in those categories, and the coverage provided under an unendorsed homeowners policy is inadequate for them. For example, a homeowner may discover that a $4,000 tennis bracelet and a mink stole were taken by thieves. Recovery in this instance would be limited to $1,000 total. For insureds owning property in those categories, the ISO homeowners policy permits the insured to add the items to the policy for an additional charge with a scheduled personal property endorsement. The coverage provided for the separately listed item is the total amount of insurance provided under the policy—not in addition to the category limitation.

A significant benefit is afforded the insured by scheduling this property. The ISO scheduled property endorsement provides "all-risks" coverage, with no deductible, anywhere in the world (except for fine arts). The addition of the personal property replacement cost endorsement provides protection, up to the scheduled limit, for those categories of property subject to depreciation.

The crime coverage needs of commercial insureds are extremely varied, so many coverage options are available to address their individual crime loss exposures. Commercial crime losses can arise from two areas. The first is crimes committed by employees, called "employee dishonesty" or "fidelity." Thefts by insureds are excluded in the personal lines forms. The second is crimes committed by others, which can be categorized as burglary, robbery, or theft, depending on the nature of the crime. Because of the diversity of property and coverage needs of commercial insureds, the balance of this section is devoted to commercial crime. Many of the loss control measures discussed below and character issues regarding the insured are just as relevant for personal lines insureds.

Employee Dishonesty

Employee dishonesty covers theft by employees. It is unique among crime insurance coverages and owes its unique character to the following factors:

- Employees have ready access to valuable property. They can learn the company's routines and schedules and the habits of fellow employees. They can discover what controls management has in place and how well the controls work.

- Losses can be hidden from discovery. Unlike burglary and robbery, which by definition are visible crimes, employee theft is by stealth. The act of theft can be deliberately obscured or covered for varying lengths of time.

- Large losses are common. The thief's access to property continues until the crime is discovered. The length of time of access, in turn, contributes to the size of loss.

- The insured might be reluctant to face the facts. Employers are often unwilling to believe that an employee might steal from them. That reluctance to accept reality leads to practices that contribute to opportunities for theft and greatly increases exposures to loss.

- Management might be reluctant to prosecute employees who steal. Many employers will not sign complaints or testify at criminal proceedings against their employees. They may wish to avoid bad press; to accept the culprit's "hard luck" story; or to have the affair end quickly, especially when the employee promises restitution.

The following characteristics of employee dishonesty crimes pose additional problems for underwriters:

1. Losses might be frequent, but they are usually hidden until they become large losses. For example, an embezzler typically takes small sums of money over a long period of time and is caught only when the total is too large for the embezzler to continue to hide it.

2. Employer reluctance to accept that some employees are dishonest creates a problem of adverse selection. Most financial institutions purchase fidelity coverage, but only a small percentage of mercantile establishments do so. Employee crime losses are significant, and they are estimated to cost businesses more than any other form of crime. Nonetheless, employee dishonesty insurance is a profitable line for insurers and available for most insureds.

Underwriting Employee Dishonesty Exposures

By tradition, insurers have written employee dishonesty insurance for an indefinite term. Insurers rerate employee dishonesty policies each year but assume that the relationship with the insured will be long term. Underwriters must be satisfied that certain conditions, such as the following, exist before issuing the policy:

1. Management of the insured organization must exhibit the highest moral character. A moral hazard, in other words, must not exist.

2. The insured should be profitable. Profits indicate competence with the company's market spheres. Management planning and control systems should work well. The company should be financially able to respond to recommended loss control expenditures. The corporate culture should reward positive performance.

3. Burglary and robbery loss control systems should be in place and maintained, because appropriate defenses against external crime also deter employee crime.

4. Amounts of insurance should fall within the limits prescribed by the insurer's underwriting guidelines.

5. Management controls should exist and be maintained. Management controls are evidence of management's care and concern.

Controlling Employee Dishonesty Losses

Employee dishonesty loss control efforts require strict adherence to management controls. Listed below are controls, applicable to almost all organizations, that can be considered minimum standards for acceptability:

- The insured screens new hires and checks their references.
- Before they are promoted, seasoned employees are reviewed, especially for promotions or transfers into sensitive positions.
- A substance-abuse screening program is in place. Underwriters regard this as a positive sign because substance dependency creates potential for employee dishonesty.
- Underwriters normally request a list of all employees, their positions, and their hire dates. The rate and level of employee turnover can contribute to an increase in the insured's exposure to loss.
- Termination procedures are well defined. The computer passwords of employees who had worked in sensitive areas are revoked, and keys or access cards are returned.
- Management remains sensitive to all employee behavior. Dramatic changes in lifestyle might indicate employee dishonesty.
- Periodic audits test accounts receivable, cash accounts, inventories, and disbursements.
- Bank reconciliation is done to ensure that company and bank records agree.
- A division of authority between employees exists so that employees monitor one another.
- Annual vacations are required, since some methods of embezzlement require a daily adjustment of records.
- Duties are rotated to discover irregularities or defalcations.
- There is two-person or dual control on some items, such as the vault, cash, and other items that could be converted quickly.

Other Crime Exposures

Crime committed by others includes acts such as robbery, burglary, and theft. The definitions used in crime insurance polices are often different from those in general usage. Because the difference in terminology can be confusing, the crime-insurance definitions of "burglary," "robbery," "theft," "disappearance," and "inventory shortage" are discussed below.

Burglary is the forcible entry into or exit from premises, a building, a safe, or a vault, with the intent to commit theft. Burglary policies limit this definition by covering only when the premises are not open for business. The definition of "forcible entry or exit" includes thieves who hide within a fenced area or in a building during business hours to take property and force their way out after closing.

Robbery means illegally taking property by violence or threat of violence against a person. Crime forms describe the person who has custody of the property as a custodian while on the premises and as a messenger elsewhere. This facilitates a distinction between coverage on and away from the insured's premises. Robbery also includes taking property from a messenger or custodian who has been kidnapped for that purpose.

Theft means any act of stealing. Because the method does not matter, it includes burglary, robbery, shoplifting, and other acts of stealth.

Disappearance is the loss of property with no reasonable explanation. When disappearance is a covered cause of loss, coverage is extended to include situations in which the insured simply misplaces property. Coverage forms no longer use the term "mysterious disappearance," but the term persists in general usage. "Mysterious disappearance" implies an opportunity for theft even if there was no evidence of one.

Inventory shortage is a loss that can only be proved from inventory records. "All-risks" policies that cover theft exclude loss from inventory shortage because "shrinkage" is considered a normal event in any business and one that the insured can control. The inventory shortage exclusion prevents the insured from transferring this ordinary cost to the insurer.

Underwriting Other Crime Exposures

The process of underwriting commercial crime insurance requires considering the following five factors:

1. Property susceptibility
2. Location of the property
3. Nature of the occupancy
4. Public protection
5. Modifications of coverage and price

Property Susceptibility

Every piece of property has characteristics that make it more or less desirable to thieves. Those characteristics are usually considered together, but an underwriter should be able to recognize them separately. The characteristics are determined by three questions:

1. Is the property susceptible to crime?
2. Is the property fungible?
3. Is there a ready market for it as stolen property?

The size, weight, portability, visibility, and accessibility of the goods determine how susceptible they are to theft. The emphasis given to each of these characteristics is relative. An object's size or weight does not in itself preclude its theft. A forty-ton steel truss bridge was stolen from a West Virginia creek in the late 1950s. Despite that occurrence, bulky items like bridges and buildings are viewed as having low susceptibility to theft. Jewelry, clothing, small electric appliances, precious metals, books, and hand tools, on the other hand, are highly susceptible. The higher the property's value is relative to its bulk and weight, the more attractive it becomes to thieves.

Fungibility measures a property's value as an item of exchange. Money, securities, and other negotiable instruments are highly fungible. Bulk gas, bridges, and the like are considered essentially not fungible. That is, they might meet a rare exchange demand, but they are not regularly traded goods. A semitrailer truck loaded with name-brand golf balls has low fungibility. It is, however, susceptible. A ready market probably exists for the load of golf balls.

A combination of several factors determines a commodity's marketability. Goods that are in widespread use have more potential customers. Goods that are difficult to trace are more marketable. The economy often plays a key role, making a surprising variety of goods very marketable for some period of time.

As a last resort, thieves may turn to the original owner as their market. Once several boxcars filled with automobile and truck engine blocks "disappeared." After months had passed with no trace of the boxcars, the thieves contacted the manufacturer. After price and delivery negotiations, the engines arrived at their original destination.

After considering the above issues, underwriters must ask themselves the larger question: How likely is the property to be stolen?

Location of the Property

Such things as topography, neighborhood, climate, and the local crime rate can tell underwriters what kind of losses to expect. Seasonal occupancy, typical of a resort, for example, makes loss by crime more likely. Crime occurs more often in some areas than in others, and underwriters should use this type of information. Conventional wisdom holds that cities have a higher rate of crime than suburbs and rural areas. Although this remains true, the gap between the two might be closing.

Statistics on local crime rates often reflect the experience of entire cities or counties, which is of little value to underwriters. They are not complete because many victims do not report crimes, especially in areas where they occur most often. Underwriters who want accurate information in a form they can use have to develop their own data. The need to avoid unfair discrimination in underwriting makes reliable data especially important.

Nature of the Occupancy

A reporter once asked Willie Sutton, a notorious bank robber of the 1940s and 1950s, why he chose to steal from banks when there were easier targets. His answer was, "Because that's where the money is." Then and now, some occupancies are more attractive to crime than others.

Some occupancies generally have a great deal of cash or other valuable property on hand. Those occupancies include banks, savings and loans, credit unions, check-cashing services, grocery stores, stadiums, arenas, churches, and buildings where charity events are held.

Some businesses are conducted in locations that are removed from the public or operate during off hours, when there are few people around to deter criminals. Those include twenty-four-hour convenience stores and service stations, and public warehouses.

Public Protection

Public protection reflects the quality of the local criminal justice system. How soon do police officers respond to alarms and reports of crime? How often do prosecutors obtain convictions? How well does the system deter crime? Effective public protection means lower rates of crime and fewer crime losses. In gauging the quality of public protection, there is no substitute for local knowledge.

Modifications of Coverage and Price

Commercial crime insurance underwriters have some latitude in modifying the proposal for insurance. In many instances, an applicant knows the coverage that he or she wants and will turn to another insurer when the requested coverage is not provided. In many more instances, however, the applicant chooses not to prolong the insurance-purchasing decision and accepts the broadest coverage at the lowest price. Because insureds who usually request crime insurance need the coverage, they are likely to consider and accept counteroffers made by an underwriter who is trying to write the account. Possible modifications include changes in coverage, limits, pricing, the deductible, and the use endorsements requiring protective safeguards.

Coverage   Requests for policies providing broad coverage do not always fit within the underwriter's guidelines. Rather than reject the account outright, the underwriter might offer coverage that is less generous. Many requests for broad crime coverage must be negotiated. An account might be ineligible for crime coverage under a commercial property form with a special causes of loss coverage form. As a counteroffer, the underwriter might offer to provide coverage under the causes-of-loss broad coverage form in combination with the applicable crime coverage form. This approach to controlling exposures for the entire account gives little latitude in doing anything more to control commercial crime exposures. Overall, transforming marginal accounts into acceptable accounts for crime insurance is difficult to do using coverage modification.

Coverage Limits   For most other types of insurance, the insured purchases an amount of insurance close to the value of the exposed property. In the case of crime insurance, most insureds assume that only small crime losses will occur. This fact and the desire to reduce premiums tend to reduce the policy limit and increase problems associated with underinsurance. In the case of crime insurance, the underwriter might be satisfied with providing policy limits much lower than the amount of the values insured. Because of the moral hazard that too much insurance might create, most underwriters do not want to provide coverage to full value even if the insured requests it.

Pricing   Because crime forms do not contain a coinsurance clause, the insured is not penalized for having inadequate limits. Losses will probably be partial and still exceed the policy limits. Underinsurance can lead to underpricing, so underwriters must consider the risk of loss when pricing crime coverage.

Because policy limits tend to be low relative to the amount at risk, probable maximum loss usually equals the amount subject. Underwriters who provide commercial crime coverage should expect that losses will exceed the policy amount.

Deductibles   Deductibles in crime insurance also serve the same purposes as they do in other types of insurance. They eliminate small, more predictable losses, therefore preventing an erosion of the loss portion of the premium, and tend to make the insured more conscious of the benefits of loss control.

Deductibles are not used as underwriting tools in crime insurance as often as they might be. Larger, more sophisticated policyholders recognize the value of retaining small, frequent losses that can often be readily contained through loss control techniques and financed with current cash flow.

ISO's business personal property coverage forms contain a standard $250 deductible. The deductible for crime insurance should be at least equal to the deductible amount that applies to other types of losses to the insured's business personal property.

Protective Safeguards   A protective safeguards endorsement is a form of warranty. It is the insured's promise to take certain steps to protect against loss. That promise becomes part of the policy and becomes a condition precedent to coverage. If the insured fails to protect the property as promised, the insurer need not pay any losses that result.

Courts have adopted varying attitudes toward warranties. Some courts almost choose to ignore them. In the case of crime safeguards, however, courts are more likely to rule that breach of warranty negates coverage. The subject of the insured's promise is clearly material to the underwriting decision, which makes enforcement by the courts more likely.

Underwriters cannot assume that courts will insist that the insured fully comply with the warranty. A good faith effort to comply is almost always sufficient. For example, the failure of a central station alarm service solely because of a power or telephone service outage does not breach the promise. The situation is different, however, if the utility cuts off electrical service because the insured has failed to pay its bills. The intent of a warranty is not to create a loophole through which an adjuster can deny liability. The warranty imposes the duty to make a good faith effort to maintain the level of protection specified in the endorsement.

The rules and rates filed by insurers almost always require a warranty for any protective system that earns a rate credit. Underwriters might also regard a system as essential even when it does not qualify for a reduced rate. Warranties ensure that the risk the underwriter accepts and the loss exposure are the same. If the underwriter demands that protective systems be present, the crime policy with the protective safeguard endorsement should be used to enforce their maintenance throughout the policy period.

Controlling Other Crime Exposures

Crime loss exposures respond well to loss control efforts. As mentioned earlier, implementing loss control measures and using them diligently are two of the most telling characteristics of a good prospect for crime coverage.

Private protection systems to prevent or control loss include the following:

- Safes and vaults
- Cages, special rooms, and limited access areas
- Indoor and outdoor lighting
- Fences and walls
- Protection of openings on the premises (gates, doors, windows, and skylights)
- Guard services

- Alarm systems
- Electronic surveillance systems
- Inventory control and other management activities

Loss control, or protection devices and systems, are generally thought to serve at least two important functions: to preclude crime losses and to deter crime.

A dedicated thief can break through protection systems if given enough time. In other words, safes, vaults, fencing, and so on, rarely preclude access when a thief is strongly motivated. However, protection devices and systems do make an invaluable contribution to deterrence. They frustrate, confuse, and slow down criminal processes, frequently causing a thief to seek an easier target.

Although even the best protection systems do not eliminate loss, their value cannot be overemphasized in reducing the probability of loss. After moral hazard, private protection is the most important consideration in crime insurance underwriting.

Underwriting guidelines should indicate the acceptable level of protection that a particular class or location demands. Since private protection is known to reduce risk of loss by crime, the level of private protection required depends on the judgment of an insurer's staff underwriters. Line underwriters might feel more or less secure with the level of private protection recommended by the underwriting guide for a particular account and might adjust the insurance proposal, perhaps by reducing the amount of coverage provided.

The two main categories of private protection devices are barriers to criminal access and detection devices. Barriers include devices that protect the premises, safes, and vaults. Detection devices are guards, alarms, and surveillance systems.

Underwriting Marine Insurance

Ocean marine is one of the oldest forms of insurance. Ocean marine underwriters have historically insured both oceangoing hulls and their cargoes. The "warehouse-to-warehouse" clause added land transportation as well. Inland marine insurance, peculiar to the United States and Canada, grew out of a willingness of ocean marine underwriters to provide coverage for goods and equipment in transit within the North American continent. Using the marine tradition of broad insuring agreements, inland marine coverages grew rapidly and began competing with fire and casualty insurers. This conflict led to the development of the **Nation-Wide Marine Definition** in 1933, amended in 1953 and 1976, which defined those areas within which inland marine coverage could be offered.

Ocean Marine Insurance

Ocean marine insurance is divided into four major categories: (1) yachts, (2) commercial hulls, (3) protection and indemnity, and (4) cargo.

Some differences exist between the underwriting considerations for yachts and those for commercial hulls and cargoes. Although the term yacht usually brings to mind a seventy-foot luxury vessel, all sailboats and inboard powered boats are also considered yachts.

Yachts

Underwriting considerations for all yachts from twenty-foot sailboats to one-hundred-foot oceangoing powerboats can be grouped under three headings: (1) seaworthiness, (2) navigable waters and season, and (3) operator experience.

Seaworthiness

The soundness of a vessel for its intended use is reflected in its age, manufacture, construction, and maintenance. Typically, the older a vessel becomes, the lower is its value and the greater is the chance of a constructive total loss should any damage occur. Most insurers place age limitations on vessels insured. Construction quality varies by manufacturer, so a manufacturer with a good reputation is an important underwriting characteristic. Fiberglass construction has proved to be a significant improvement over wooden construction. Modern fiberglass construction is lightweight and includes foam interlayers that significantly reduce the hazard of sinking. Fiberglass hulls also eliminate much of the hull maintenance required for wooden vessels. All vessels, regardless of their construction, require regular maintenance to remain fit. A marine survey is the most effective way for underwriters to obtain information on a particular vessel. The survey provides a comprehensive evaluation of the value and condition of the vessel.

Navigable Waters and Season

Underwriters have traditionally used a navigation warranty as a major underwriting tool. The **navigation warranty** restricts coverage to the area for which the yacht, equipment, and experience of the operator are appropriate. The perils of the seas differ greatly by area and by season within the same area. Putting to sea during the hurricane season in the Caribbean or during the winter in Maine is not prudent. A navigation warranty suspends coverage when a vessel is used under conditions other than those agreed to with the underwriter.

Operator Experience

An experienced operator is an extremely important underwriting consideration. Many insurers give credit to operators who have completed Power

Squadron or Coast Guard Auxiliary courses. Membership in an organized yacht club generally indicates the policyholder's dedication to his or her pastime and often implies sound experience and training. Many insurers use automobile motor vehicle records as an indicator of an operator's ability. The finest construction and equipment are useless if an operator does not possess sufficient seamanship to use the vessel properly.

Commercial Hulls

When evaluating commercial hulls, underwriters must consider some of the same basic types of information that they consider for yachts: the construction of the ship, its equipment and maintenance, the area within which it is used, and the expertise of the master and mariners. Although similar in kind, commercial hull underwriting differs from yacht underwriting in the sources of information. Various registers of shipping provide the physical characteristics of a vessel. The "flag" or nation in which a ship is registered determines the safety regulations under which the ship is operated and the frequency of inspections. An inspection should determine the state of maintenance.

In commercial hulls, the cargo is a major consideration. Some cargoes, such as oil, chemicals, and coal, present serious hazards to the hull.

Protection and Indemnity

Protection and indemnity (P&I) coverage is a special type of liability insurance. It covers the liability of a vessel owner for bodily injury, illness, death, and damage to the property of others arising out of the ownership, use, or operation of the vessel. Admiralty law sets certain limits on the liability of vessels when an owner does not have privity to its operation. This limitation is usually applicable in commercial hull situations but seldom applies to yachts, whose owners are usually on board.

Protection and indemnity coverage includes the following:

- *Loss of life and bodily injury*—This applies to persons injured aboard the vessel or elsewhere, including members of the crew if such injury is deemed to be the responsibility of the owner.
- *Property damage*—This covers the owner's liability for loss of or damage to the property of others aboard the owner's vessel, fixed objects, and other vessels and property on board them (insofar as the collision clause in the hull policy does not apply).
- *Other coverages*—A vessel owner whose craft sinks in private waters or obstructs a channel or otherwise constitutes a menace to navigation may be faced with the legal responsibility of marking or removing the wreck, or

destroying it. Insofar as the expense of this procedure constitutes a legal liability of the owner, it is covered by P&I.

- *Clean-up expense*—Clean-up costs incurred because of pollution incidents are insured. Insurers commonly exclude the pollution exposure altogether or issue a separate policy on that exposure.

- *Defense costs*—The defense cost of litigation, including necessary bonds for release from court seizure, is covered whether against the vessel (*in rem*) or against the owner (*in personam*).

- *Fines*—The liability of the insured shipowner or operator for fines that may be imposed for violating the law is also covered (sometimes subject to a deductible).[11]

One serious area of exposure under the P&I coverage is pollution from oil tankers. The tanker Exxon Valdez ran aground on March 24, 1989, spilling eleven million gallons of oil. This, the largest spill in North American history, caused over $2.2 billion in pollution losses. Pollution coverage is generally included in P&I sold by "P&I clubs" (mutuals) but often not in P&I sold by domestic U.S. insurers.

Cargo

Many firms today import components, raw materials, and finished goods from overseas, and others are involved in exporting goods. All of these firms are prospects for ocean cargo insurance. By use of the "warehouse-to-warehouse" clause, ocean cargo coverage also includes land transit from the originating warehouse to the dock and from the dock at the port of destination to the consignee's warehouse, which usually involves thousands of miles. When underwriting cargo insurance, the quality of the policyholder and his or her business reputation are important. He or she must have as a primary interest the safe arrival of the product at destination. A policyholder who tries to save money by reducing the amount of packing cannot be profitably underwritten.

Underwriters are asked to insure a wide variety of commodities. Commodities such as ingots of pig iron offer a very low susceptibility to loss or damage, but others, such as fine glassware and china, can be easily damaged. Shipments of fishmeal or burlap can present extraordinary fire hazards. Auto parts and liquor are very attractive to thieves. Any bulk shipment or any shipment of raw materials presents its own unique problems. Some chemicals, for example, become worthless if they are exposed to air, and certain electronic devices require expensive recalibration if they are even slightly damaged. A few commodities and their special hazards are shown in Exhibit 5-4.

Exhibit 5-4
Some Commodity Characteristics

Auto parts	Pilferage and theft in certain areas of the world where new cars are not readily available
Automobiles	Marring, denting, and scratching
Canned goods	Rusting, denting, and theft
Chemicals in paper bags	Shortage and contamination from torn bags
Fine arts	Handling damage and theft
Fishmeal	Highly susceptible to heating damage and fire
Fresh fruit	Extremely sensitive to temperature change and difficult to keep from spoiling
Glass	Breakage and staining
Grain	Shortage and weevil damage
Household effects	Breakage, marring, chipping, scratching, shortage, and water damage
Liquids in bulk	Leakage, shortage, and contamination
Lumber (cut)	Shortage, staining, and handling damage
Machinery	Rust and breakage of parts
Paper in rolls	Chafing, cutting, and water damage
Rags	Fire and shortage
Refrigerators and stoves	Marring, scratching, chipping, and denting
Scrap metal	Alleged shortage due to difference in scale weights at origin and destination
Steel products	Rusting, bending, and twisting
Television sets	Breakage of picture tubes
Textiles	Hook damage, theft, and water damage

The ports between which goods will be shipped and the land transportation that will be used from "warehouse-to-warehouse" are also major underwriting concerns. In some ports, ships must be unloaded by lighters, which are small, self-propelled vessels or barges. This increases the probability of damage to the cargo. Some ports are known to have high crime and damage rates.

Excluding bulk shipments, much of today's cargo is shipped in large, enclosed metal boxes known as containers. These are similar to semitrailers without their chassis. They can be "stuffed" at the original point of shipment and unloaded at destination, thus eliminating extra handling at the port. Much of the most recent tonnage has been vessels constructed solely to transport containers.

Containerization may reduce pilferage and fresh water damage losses, provided the container is watertight and carries the merchandise from warehouse to warehouse. Since at least one-third of all containers are shipped on deck, however, the risk of exposure to heavy weather and washing overboard is greatly increased. The threat of a hijack of an entire shipment and the danger of breakage from shifting cargo are additional serious perils.

A final but important point is the location of goods on a ship. Deck cargo is subject to wind, water, and wave damage to a much greater extent than cargo stowed below decks. Certain cargoes such as rough lumber are usually unaffected by shipment on deck.

Inland Marine Insurance

In terms of forms and rates, inland marine insurance is divided into filed and nonfiled classes. Those inland marine classes for which advisory organizations are required to file loss costs, rules, and forms are defined as **filed classes**. Filed classes have been selected for relatively greater regulatory scrutiny than other inland marine classes because these classes are considered to have many policyholders with reasonably homogeneous loss exposures. Most filed policies are relatively inflexible in terms of coverage or rates. Typical filed classes include the commercial articles coverage form, equipment dealers coverage form, physicians and surgeons equipment coverage form, sign coverage form, theatrical property coverage form, film coverage form, floor plan coverage form, jewelers block coverage form, mail coverage form, accounts receivable coverage form, and valuable papers and records coverage form. Two major categories of filed classes are jewelry and furs, which are also the two largest personal lines classes. **Nonfiled classes** are developed and rated in accordance with the underwriting practices of an individual insurer.

About one-half of all inland marine coverage is written on nonfiled forms. Nonfiled classes include a vast array of exposures—from bridges and tunnels to power tools. Depending on company practice, an underwriter can freely modify any nonfiled forms, thereby providing a great deal of flexibility. In many circumstances, a "manuscript" policy must be designed to cover an unusual or a one-of-a-kind exposure.

The diverse coverages inland marine encompasses have the common trait of being historically undesirable to fire underwriters. Property in transit, "all-risks" coverage, and property in the care, custody, and control of others make these coverages the domain of inland marine underwriters. The following sections discuss some of the nonfiled coverages that generate the largest premium volume.

Contractors Equipment

Contractors equipment policies can be used to insure almost any type of mobile equipment used by contractors, including hand-held power tools, mobile cranes, excavators, and bulldozers. Such equipment is used in a variety of construction projects both by small contractors and businesses engaged in tunneling projects worth hundreds of millions of dollars.

The typical coverage form provides direct physical damage coverage on an "all-risks" basis. A key factor in underwriting this coverage is knowing the use of the equipment and the scope of its operations. Other factors to consider include the following:

1. The size and value of the individual items of equipment
2. The type, age, maintenance, supervision, operating characteristics, and protection of the equipment
3. The experience and accident record of the equipment operators
4. The financial status of the policyholder
5. The concentration of equipment at a single site
6. Past loss history
7. Labor relations[12]

Builders Risk/Installation

Builders risk coverage can be purchased by attaching the appropriate coverage part to the ISO commercial property form. Many producers prefer instead to advise their clients to use nonfiled forms that permit flexibility in rating and coverage. Those forms include transit coverage for building materials brought to a site.

Buildings under construction face the same exposures as completed structures but are often more vulnerable because protective safeguards are not yet in place. Underwriters should be aware of the following conditions that might increase the hazards for a fire loss:

1. Water mains that might not be completed
2. Fire hydrants that are operational but that might not be near the structure
3. Standpipes that might not be connected in high-rise structures

4. Sprinkler systems that might not be installed or activated

5. Heat and smoke detectors that might not be installed

6. Construction activities that introduce new heat sources, such as welding or brazing

7. Salamanders that are used for heat

Construction sites are susceptible to theft and vandalism unless security precautions are taken. Those precautions include installing fencing, lighting, and alarm systems on trailers and storage sheds and employing security guards.

Structures with large roof spans have an increased chance of collapsing before all of the needed supports are in place. Structures are particularly susceptible to wind damage before the exterior walls and roof are in place. Coverage for flood and earthquake, subject to sublimits and higher deductibles, is usually available as an optional coverage under a builders risk policy.[13]

Transportation

Goods shipped by truck, air, rail, and mail are the most logical candidates for inland marine coverage. The covered causes of loss are usually very broad, are frequently "all-risks," and routinely include flood and earthquake. Transportation insurance can provide coverage for the following interests:

1. The **shipper**, who is any party who hires another to transport cargo

2. The **carrier**, who actually transports (or carries) goods for another

3. The **consignee**, who is the person designated for delivery

The details of the transaction and common law determine which party bears the risk of loss in transit. The underwriter has to consider who bears the risk of loss, how susceptible the cargo is to damage, and what steps have been taken to protect against foreseeable losses.

At common law, a contract carrier is liable as an ordinary bailee, and a common carrier is liable as an insurer of the goods, subject to five exceptions: acts of God, acts of public enemies, exercise of public authority, fault or negligence on the part of the shipper, and inherent vice or nature of the property. The contract between the shipper and the carrier, called a bill of lading, frequently departs from common law principles. Deregulation of the trucking industry has made it common practice to place the risk of loss on the shipper or consignee. Terms of sale usually make provision to transfer title to the goods and the risk of loss from the seller to the buyer at a defined point. The underwriter has to be aware of the arrangements that cover insured shipments and their implications.

Instrumentalities of Transportation and Communication

The principal instrumentalities of transportation and communication include bridges; tunnels; pipelines; wharves, docks, and piers; radio and TV towers and stations; and dry docks and marine railways and cranes. Although much of inland marine insurance deals with property in transit or capable of being transported, those subjects cf insurance are *related to* transportation. Instrumentalities of transportation and communication are fixed location structures and present many of the same hazards as any other type of real property. In addition, because of their specialized nature, such structures are subject to some unique hazards.

When underwriting any of these instrumentalities, the primary areas of concern include the construction and maintenance of the structure and any unique hazards or exposures that may exist. Bridges and tunnels, for example, may be exposed by trucks carrying gasoline or explosives. Television towers are susceptible to ice buildup in severe winter storms, increasing the likelihood of a collapse in high winds. Pipelines are particularly susceptible to earthquakes. Wharves, docks, and piers may be damaged by high waves as well as from ships colliding with them.

Bailee Coverages

Bailee coverage is provided in many inland marine policies, either as a section of coverage in a policy providing other coverage, such as the jewelers' block, or as a separate policy. The cleaners and dyers customer's policy generally provides bailee coverage only. That policy provides direct damage coverage for the customer's goods that the cleaner or dyer has in bailment, and all losses by insured causes of loss are covered whether or not the policyholder was legally liable for the loss. In that way, bailee's insurance goes beyond any type of legal liability coverage. Bailee insurance also serves to close a gap in coverage that would otherwise be created by the common wording in liability policies that excludes coverage for the property of others in the insured's "care, custody, or control."

Summary

Modern property insurance had its beginnings in catastrophic fires that swept European cities in the late seventeenth century. Loss by fire was originally the only covered cause of loss. As demands for additional coverages were made, additional causes of loss and broader coverages were added. Property insurance causes of loss may now include fire, windstorm, hail, aircraft, vehicle damage, riot and civil commotion, explosion, smoke, vandalism, sprinkler leakage, water damage, sinkhole collapse, volcanic action, earth movement, flood, and crime.

Most of the tools underwriters use to evaluate exposures relate to the fire cause of loss. Since fire is a predominant cause of loss, properly underwriting that exposure and its profitability increases the likelihood that an account will be profitable overall.

The acronym COPE is used by property insurance underwriters to remind them of the four basic areas they should investigate in every submission—construction, occupancy, protection, and external exposure.

Building construction is divided into six classifications—fire resistive, modified fire resistive, masonry noncombustible, noncombustible, joisted masonry, and frame.

Occupancy is described in terms of combustibility and damageability. Hazards fall into two categories: common hazards found in most commercial buildings and special hazards unique to the specific occupancy. Occupancy hazards and the degree of their control must be evaluated to determine to what extent they increase or decrease the expectation of loss.

Fire protection can be classified as private or public and consists of three elements—prevention, detection, and suppression. Private protection is provided by the property owner or tenant and ranges in sophistication from handheld fire extinguishers to a fully equipped fire station at a manufacturing facility. Private protection detection systems include private patrol services, guard services with clocks, smoke and heat detectors, automatic local alarms, and automatic central station alarms. Private suppression systems fall into the following categories: portable extinguishers, standpipes and hoses, automatic sprinkler systems, and private fire brigades. ISO's public protection classification groups communities into one of ten categories based on the fire protection present.

A consideration of external exposures broadens an underwriter's perspective to include areas and buildings adjacent to the risk being evaluated. Availability of clear space, presence of surrounding brush, heights of exposing structures, and the occupancies of those structures are examples of the concerns underwriters have.

Other causes of loss—and, thus, concerns—are lightning; explosion; windstorm; hail; riot or civil commotion; vandalism and malicious mischief; water damage and sprinkler leakage; sinkhole collapse and mine subsidence; volcanic action; weight of ice, snow, or sleet; ice damming; collapse; flood; and earthquake.

Time element underwriting includes measuring the largest loss of net income and estimating the probable period of interruption. The size of the net income loss is reflected in the selection of the coverage limits and the coinsurance percentage. The likely length of interruption is determined through sales projections and tempered by seasonal cycles and general economic conditions. Other considerations are the estimated rebuilding time, the time needed to return to the same level of production, and the presence of a disaster contingency plan that could reduce the period of interruption.

Crime insurance covers intentional losses by persons other than the policyholder to money and securities and property other than money and securities through causes of loss such as employee dishonesty, burglary, robbery, and theft. Evaluating crime potential involves examining the characteristics of the property subject to crime losses—susceptibility, fungibility, and marketability. Other aspects that indicate loss potential include location of the property, nature of the occupancy, and public protection.

Marine insurance is the predecessor of all forms of insurance. Ocean marine is divided into four major categories—yachts, commercial hulls, protection and indemnity, and cargo. The underwriting criteria used to evaluate yachts include the seaworthiness of the vessel, the waters navigated, the season, and the experience of the operators. Commercial hull insurance involves the same concerns as yachts, but the values involved are more significant. Protection and indemnity (P&I) is liability insurance that provides coverage for claims arising out of the ownership and use of a vessel. Also covered is liability for injuries to members of the crew. Ocean cargo insurance involves the import and export of a wide variety of goods and raw materials. Underwriting considerations focus on the susceptibility of the cargo to damage and the manner in which it is packed.

Numerous coverage forms provide inland marine insurance. The ones discussed in this chapter represent the largest classes based on premium volume. The next chapter completes the discussion of the underwriting function. Like this chapter on underwriting selected property lines, Chapter 6 introduces liability underwriting basics for several important lines.

Chapter Notes

1. Insurance Services Office, *Commercial Fire Rating Schedule* (New York, NY: Insurance Services Office, 1983), pp. 3-4.

2. *Fire Protection Handbook*, 17th ed., p. 6–23.

3. Mark A. Hoffman, "Property Loss Control High-rise Office Buildings Require Special Precautions," *Business Insurance*, June 3, 1991, pp. 3-4.

4. *NFPA Inspection Manual*, Charles A. Tuck, Jr., ed., 4th ed. (Boston, MA: National Fire Protection Association, 1976), p. 20.

5. *NFPA Inspection Manual*, p. 20.

6. *Fire Protection Handbook*, 17th ed. (Quincy, MA: National Fire Protection Association, 1991), p. 6–8.

7. *Fire Protection Handbook*, 17th ed., p. 6–9.

8. Gary G. Nichols and Sam Gerace, "A Survey of Hurricane Andrew" (Birmingham, AL: Southern Building Code Congress International, 1993).

9. *Statistical Abstract of the United States 1996*, Table 325. Persons Arrested, by Charge, Sex, and Age: 1994, p. 209.

10. Robert B. Holtom, *Commercial Fire Underwriting* (Cincinnati, OH: The National Underwriter Co., 1989), p. 140.

11. E. P. Hollingsworth and J. J. Launie, *Commerical Property and Multiple-Lines Underwriting*, 2d ed. (Malvern, PA: Insurance Institute of America, 1984), pp. 404-405.

12. Roderick McNamara, Robert A. Laurence, and Glen L. Wood, *Inland Marine Insurance*, vol. 2 (Malvern, PA: Insurance Institute of America, 1987), pp. 170-171.

13. McNamara, Laurence, and Wood, pp. 242-243.

Chapter 6

Underwriting Liability Insurance and Package Policies

This is the last of three chapters describing how underwriters perform policy-holder selection. As in the chapter on property underwriting, specific lines of insurance are discussed to illustrate the liability underwriting process. Although not all lines are discussed, this chapter covers the major personal and commercial liability lines and addresses the major underwriting concerns for those lines.

It is commonplace today to purchase property and liability coverages in a combined contract. The commercial package policy (CPP) represents a modular approach to policy design. Given the right combination of policy components, the policyholder is entitled to an overall package discount. The homeowners policy and businessowners policy both contain multiple lines but are offered as indivisible policies.

The Legal Basis for Liability

The U.S. legal system provides remedies by which citizens can assert their legal rights, which are legally protected interests. These rights include freedom from injury to a person or damage to his or her property caused by the intentional or negligent acts of others. To protect these rights, the law recognizes two classes of wrongful acts, criminal and civil. A crime against a person is also an offense against society, generally punishable by fine or imprisonment. A **civil wrong** invades the rights of an individual, either by breach of contract or by tort. The principal legal remedy for civil wrongs is damages. **Liability** is created when the law imposes an obligation on the wrongdoer to compensate the injured party for the financial consequences of the wrongful act. **Liability insurance** exists to protect against liability that the insured may incur through the legal process, such as a trial. The two main sources of liability that insurance covers are torts and statutes that impose liability without regard to fault.

Torts and Negligence

A **tort** is a wrongful act other than a breach of contract committed by one person against another for which a civil lawsuit in a court can provide a remedy. The person who feels wronged and who files suit seeking relief is called the **plaintiff**, and the person the plaintiff charges with committing the tort is the **defendant**. A body of law has developed from common law, which is decisions of courts, and from state and federal statutes, which are written laws enacted by legislative bodies.

Torts may be intentional or negligent. Liability insurance protects the insured against the financial consequences of negligence but rarely covers intentional torts. **Negligence** is the failure to exercise the degree of care that a reasonably prudent person would exercise to avoid harming others. It requires the following:

- A legal duty owed to the plaintiff to use due care
- A failure to conform to the standard of care required in the situation, with the defendant's conduct creating an unreasonable risk of harm
- A causal connection between the negligent act and the plaintiff's injury
- Actual loss or damage to the plaintiff

Traditionally, courts have recognized three classes of persons whose rights the law protects. An **invitee** is a person who enters on a premises for the financial benefit of the owner or occupant. A customer who comes into a store is an invitee. A **licensee** is any other person who enters the premises with permission, such as a social guest. Anyone who enters the premises without permission is a **trespasser**. This hierarchy produced three levels of duty to others, with the highest degree of care owed to an invitee and the lowest to a trespasser. Although an understanding of these three categories is helpful in understanding degrees of care, most courts have abandoned this hierarchy in favor of a rule of reasonable foreseeability that holds a person liable for any injury that is reasonably foreseeable, regardless of the victim's status as invitee, licensee, or trespasser. Whether they apply the traditional measure of duty or the newer doctrine of reasonable foreseeability, courts measure the conduct of a defendant by the standard of the **reasonable person**. This is an imaginary person who represents the standard of conduct the community expects.

Liability Without Fault (Absolute Liability)

Society permits certain extremely hazardous activities because of the benefits they provide. The use of explosives in construction projects, for instance, is an example of a hazardous activity. Keeping dangerous animals in a zoo or a safari park and operating aircraft are other examples. No matter how careful people engaged in these activities may be, a certain number of losses is likely to occur. To compensate innocent victims of these accidents, common law devised the doctrine of **absolute liability**. This rule of law applies only to certain exceptionally dangerous activities. Any person who engages in such activities becomes liable for any damage that results without regard to fault. The name **strict liability** has also been applied to this doctrine. To avoid confusion with the rule of strict liability in tort, this text uses only the term absolute liability to describe liability that the law imposes in the absence of fault. Workers compensation statutes apply this rule to injuries to employees that arise out of and occur during the course of their employment. The employer is liable, regardless of who is at fault.

Vicarious Liability

In some situations, the law holds one person liable for the torts of others. This is called **vicarious liability**. Relationships that may create vicarious liability include the following:

1. A principal-agent relationship
2. An employer-employee relationship
3. A parent-child relationship
4. A contractual relationship
5. A partnership

A principal may be liable for the torts of an agent (employee) acting within the scope of the agency. An **agent** is one who acts for another person, called the **principal**. A contract defines the agent's authority to act for the principal. The same rule imposes liability on an employer for the acts of employees in the course of their employment under the doctrine of *respondeat superior*, or "let the master respond." As a general rule, a parent is not liable for the torts of a minor child merely because of the family relationship, but the law recognizes exceptions. A child sometimes acts as the parent's agent or employee. Parents may also fail to exercise reasonable care in controlling a child for the safety of others.

Damages

Damages are the remedy the law provides for torts. They consist of money the law entitles the plaintiff to recover for personal injury or property damage. In addition, a court may order the plaintiff to mitigate damages by protecting against further damage or injury. Money damages that courts award are usually classified as compensatory or punitive. The purpose of **compensatory damages** is to compensate the injured party for the harm caused by the defendant's wrongful act. Courts award **punitive damages** to punish defendants whose conduct is willful, wanton, or grossly negligent. Liability insurance always covers compensatory damages but follows state law on punitive damages. State law varies as to whether punitive damages are covered by liability insurance.

Forms of Liability Insurance

There are three principal forms of liability insurance. Automobile and general liability insurance forms protect the insured against the financial consequences of real or alleged torts. Workers compensation insurance protects employers against liability imposed by statute for injuries to their employees that arise out of and occur during the course of their employment. Underwriters often base their decisions on an assessment of all lines of business that make up an account. They can reach an intelligent risk selection decision, however, only by evaluating each line separately.

Underwriting Automobile Liability Insurance

Most people in the United States regard driving a car as a right rather than a privilege. In some parts of the country where public transportation is poor or nonexistent, driving a car is a virtual precondition for employment. For this reason, powerful public pressure is brought to bear on any institution or system that tries to limit the ability of a person to own and operate a motor vehicle.

Although they provide an important source of transportation, motor vehicles also cause the death and disability of thousands of people each year. If the head of a household is killed or disabled in an accident, his or her dependents will suffer serious economic loss. Insurance to meet those losses may be the only thing that stands between the innocent victim and dependence on the general welfare system. The public's demand for unlimited access to automobiles, combined with autos' capacity to cause injury, places tremendous pressure on automobile underwriting.

Exhibit 6-1 shows that the death rate from traffic accidents in the United States between 1991 and 1995 has been relatively stable. Conversely, economic losses from accidents increased from $93.7 billion to $115.6 billion between 1991 and 1995.[1] Increases in the cost of automobile repair and medical treatment have outpaced the improvement in highway safety.

The automobile accident problem is complex. Automobile and highway design, operator licensing, traffic density, vehicle inspection, and enforcement of traffic laws all affect underwriting results.

Exhibit 6-1
Traffic Deaths, 1991–1995

Year	Deaths	Annual % change	Death rate per 100 million vehicle miles	Death rate per 10,000 motor vehicles
1991	43,536	–7.0	2.00	2.26
1992	40,982	–5.9	1.83	2.11
1993	41,893	+2.2	1.82	2.12
1994	42,700	+1.9	1.81	2.12
1995	43,900	+1.0	1.83	2.15

National Safety Council.

The Regulatory and Legal Environment

Automobile underwriting must comply with an array of regulatory requirements that often infringe on an underwriter's freedom. Underwriting discretion is especially limited with regard to underwriting personal automobiles. Some insurers believe that regulation is becoming so restrictive that it will eventually preempt the risk selection process in personal automobile insurance.

One objective of regulation has been to make insurance available to all motor vehicle operators. The goal has been to ensure that financial resources are available to compensate the innocent victims of automobile accidents. No single approach or combination of methods has been successful in achieving that goal. The legislated approaches include the following:

1. Financial responsibility laws
2. Compulsory automobile liability insurance
3. Shared automobile market mechanisms
4. Mandatory uninsured motorists coverage
5. No-fault automobile laws
6. Restrictions on cancellations and nonrenewals

Each of these techniques alters the environment in which an underwriter has to make risk selection decisions.

Financial Responsibility Laws

Financial responsibility laws require the owner or operator of a motor vehicle to show proof of financial responsibility in one of three instances:

1. After an automobile accident that causes bodily injury or property damage greater than a preset dollar amount
2. After conviction for serious offenses, such as reckless driving, driving under the influence of alcohol, or leaving the scene of an accident
3. After failure to pay a final judgment arising from an automobile accident

Financial responsibility laws ensure that motorists can pay the victims of any accident in which they are at fault. Advocates of financial responsibility laws argue that they increase the number of insured motorists but do not impose heavy enforcement costs. The filings required after conviction for a serious offense place a burden on only the reckless but financially responsible motorist.

Financial responsibility laws suffer from the defect that the laws come into operation only *after* the motorist has been involved in an accident or convicted of a specific violation. Although insurance is the usual mechanism for ensuring financial responsibility, states usually permit the posting of a bond or a deposit with the bureau of motor vehicles as an alternative method of compliance.

The requirement for filing proof of insurance affects underwriting. The insurer may have to file a form verifying that the owner or operator who had an accident and did not have insurance at the time now has coverage. The financial responsibility laws provide that insurance is in effect until a notice of termination is filed with the department of motor vehicles. Financial responsibility laws also extend insurance coverage to all vehicles owned by the insured. This applies regardless of whether all of the insured's cars appear on the insurance policy.

Many financial responsibility laws have failed because they lacked an effective enforcement mechanism. It is very difficult to remove an irresponsible driver from the road, even after his or her driver's license has been suspended or revoked. If that person continues to drive, unlicensed and uninsured, the financial responsibility system provides no assistance to any future innocent victims.

Compulsory Automobile Liability Insurance

Compulsory automobile liability insurance laws require the registered owners of all motor vehicles to carry insurance with minimum limits specified by law. States handle the enforcement of these laws through a variety of methods or checkpoints to ensure compliance. Some typical examples include the following:

- Signing a sworn statement when applying for license tags
- Providing evidence of insurance when registering an automobile
- Providing evidence of insurance when meeting the state requirement for annual safety inspection
- Requiring all motorists to carry evidence of insurance that can be verified by police at the scene of an accident
- Requiring insurers to notify the department of motor vehicles when a policy has been cancelled
- Checking a random percentage of all licensed drivers in a state[2]

The minimum auto limits vary by state. A typical state minimum is 20/40/10. This means the driver should have at least $20,000 per person bodily injury coverage, $40,000 per accident bodily injury damage, and $10,000 property damage coverage. Most insurance professionals would agree that these minimums are much too low.

Shared Automobile Market Mechanisms

A law that requires automobile liability insurance does not guarantee that every driver can find an insurer willing to provide coverage. Every state has developed a means to meet the insurance needs of those drivers who cannot obtain coverage in the voluntary market. Such arrangements are referred to as the *residual market*. It includes automobile insurance plans, joint underwriting associations, reinsurance facilities, and state funds.

Automobile Insurance Plans

An automobile insurance plan (AIP), also called an assigned risk plan, assigns drivers to insurers that are members of the plan. The law usually requires each insurer to accept assignments based on its share of the voluntary market in the state. The AIP requires plan applicants to be rejected by the voluntary market before they may apply. In theory, policyholders in the plan pay a higher rate than those available in the voluntary market. Sometimes, however, plan rates for drivers with good records have been lower than those in the voluntary market. For insurers, this market arrangement does not guarantee an even distribution of rejected drivers among insurers. The experience of individual insurers will vary based on the luck of the draw from the rejected pool of drivers.

Joint Underwriting Associations

Joint underwriting associations (JUAs) operate as insurers in their own right. They appoint servicing carriers to handle all the functions of an insurance company. Like AIPs, the law usually requires all insurers that write automobile coverage to participate in a JUA. Profits and losses from the residual market are evenly distributed among insurers based on their share of the voluntary market.

Reinsurance Facilities

States with reinsurance facilities require all voluntary insurers to be servicing carriers of the residual market. Insurers may *cede* a percentage of their policies to the facility. The profits or losses on those policies are shared evenly among all insurers. Insurers treat their ceded policies as their own for rates and claims handling. One often-cited advantage of this approach is that drivers are not aware that they have been rejected and placed in the residual market. Reinsurance facilities have consistently operated at a deficit that has been funded by increased premium rates for all insureds. In the past, the subsidy has been hidden in the rates, but state laws now require insurers to itemize this charge.

State Funds

Maryland operates a state fund as its residual market. Deficits from the fund are charged to insurers and included in rates for all drivers. Other states have occasionally considered a similar arrangement.

Mandatory Uninsured Motorists Coverage

Some states, as an alternative to or in addition to compulsory automobile liability insurance, require all drivers to carry uninsured motorists coverage. Uninsured motorists coverage compensates the policyholder for medical expense and loss of income (and in some states property damage) for injuries (and damages) arising out of the use of an uninsured motor vehicle. This coverage is activated when the owner of an uninsured motor vehicle is at fault in an accident with the policyholder or the policyholder is the victim of a hit-and-run driver.

No-Fault Automobile Laws

No-fault automobile laws represent a modest departure from and addition to the tort-law system. The majority of the states with no-fault laws require first-party and liability insurance and restrict in some way the right of an injured party to sue. States with no restriction on lawsuits are referred to as "add-on" states. Pennsylvania and New Jersey permit individual policyholders to choose to waive their right to sue in return for a reduced premium. The remaining states have no restrictions on lawsuits and vary as to whether the insurance is compulsory.

The idea of no-fault auto insurance first appeared in a book by law professors Robert Keeton and Jeffrey O'Connell in 1965.[3] Since then, about half of the states have adopted some form of no-fault auto insurance. These plans require insurers to cover a defined package of benefits known as personal injury protection (PIP). A variety of no-fault plans are now in effect. The typical plan provides first-party medical coverage and loss of earnings coverage for automobile accident victims in all cases. Many states also provide survivors' and funeral benefits, as well as payment for replacement services required by the injured party.

Slightly more than half of the no-fault plans limit the injured party's right to sue. PIP benefits become the exclusive remedy for injuries sustained in an automobile accident until the injuries exceed a threshold defined in the statute. The threshold may be either a monetary threshold or a verbal threshold. A **monetary threshold** is a specific dollar amount that medical costs or other economic damages must exceed before a tort claim may be filed. A **verbal threshold** is measured by the seriousness of an injury as expressed in words such as "permanent disfigurement." Monetary thresholds have not been particularly effective in reducing the number of lawsuits. In many cases, the dollar values are set so low that any visit to a hospital emergency room exceeds the threshold, and very few monetary thresholds have been adjusted to keep pace with inflation. Verbal thresholds have effectively reduced both the number of lawsuits and the rate at which automobile insurance premiums increase.

Like financial responsibility laws, no-fault laws are difficult to enforce. Some car owners purchase no-fault insurance only to obtain a vehicle registration and promptly cancel coverage.

Restrictions on Cancellations and Nonrenewals

In response to public pressure, most states have enacted statutes that restrict the reasons for which insurers may cancel or nonrenew automobile policies.

In some states, the restrictions apply to both personal and commercial policies, but in most states, they affect only personal automobile policies. Some statutes specify the acceptable reasons to cancel or nonrenew. Others rely on the insurance department to set the ground rules. The implication for an underwriter is that once a policyholder has been put on the books, it may be difficult or impossible for a company to abandon that policyholder in the future.

Private Passenger Automobile Underwriting Factors

Insurers usually measure the desirability of an account by the characteristics of the insured drivers. The underwriting guide reflects management's evaluation of these factors, which are also used to classify and rate the account. Many systems are used to evaluate the loss potential of private passenger automobile applicants. The major underwriting factors considered in most private passenger automobile underwriting guides are the following:

1. Age of operators
2. Age and type of automobile
3. Use of the automobile
4. Driving record
5. Territory
6. Sex and marital status
7. Occupation
8. Personal characteristics
9. Physical condition
10. Safety equipment

Age of Operators

The age of the operator is important in determining the likelihood of suffering losses. Data compiled by the National Safety Council indicate that although only 5.1 percent of all drivers were under age 20 in 1995, they accounted for 13.0 percent of all accidents and 10.9 percent of all fatal accidents. This disproportionate relationship of age and accident frequency does not change until operators reach age 35. Exhibit 6-2 presents complete accident frequency by age for 1995.

Rating plans in virtually all states take age into account and charge considerably higher rates for young drivers. Whether the higher rate offsets the increased loss potential remains for the underwriter to judge.

Exhibit 6-2
Accidents by Age of Driver

Accidents by Age of Drivers, 1995						
Age group	Number of drivers	% of total	Driver in fatal accidents	% of total	Drivers in all accidents	% of total
Under 20	9,052,000	5.1	5,500	10.9	2,310,000	13.0
20-24	16,164,000	9.1	7,300	14.6	2,570,000	14.6
25-34	39,442,000	22.2	12,300	24.4	4,470,000	25.4
35-44	39,409,000	22.2	10,000	19.8	3,570,000	20.3
45-54	29,045,000	16.4	6,000	11.9	2,120,000	12.0
55-64	19,240,000	10.8	3,600	7.1	1,180,000	6.7
65-74	15,938,000	9.0	2,900	5.6	840,000	4.8
Over 74	9,142,000	5.2	2,900	5.7	540,000	3.1
Totals	**177,432,000**	**100.0**	**50,500**	**100.0**	**17,600,000**	**100.0**

Source: Insurance Institute for Highway Safety.

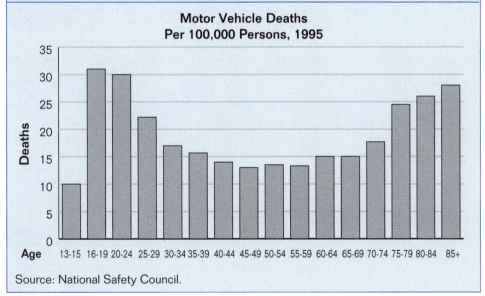

Motor Vehicle Deaths Per 100,000 Persons, 1995

Source: National Safety Council.

Reprinted with permission from *The Fact Book 1997: Property/Casualty Insurance Facts* (New York, NY: Insurance Information Institute, 1997), p. 86.

Age and Type of Automobile

The age of an automobile may be used as a general indication of its mechanical condition. Although some old automobiles are in outstanding mechanical condition, there is nevertheless a correlation between age and mechanical condition.

The type of automobile also has a bearing on underwriting acceptability. Sports and luxury cars tend to produce higher losses than other models. Passenger vans and full-size station wagons are more likely to produce lower loss payments than most models. The physical damage premium should reflect the damageability and cost of repair of the automobiles. To the extent that the premium structure does not account for damageability, the desirability of the type of automobile is affected. Studies are made annually of the cost of repairing various makes and models of automobiles.

Use of the Automobile

Other things being equal, the longer an automobile is on the highway, the greater the probability of its being in an accident. Long commuting distances or business use of an automobile results in high annual mileage. As is the case with most of these characteristics, rates attempt to reflect the increased loss potential. A typical rating plan contains separate classifications for the following:

1. Pleasure use only

2. Cars driven to work in a carpool in which drivers rotate

3. Cars driven to work more than three miles but less than ten miles one way

4. Cars driven to work more than ten miles one way

5. Business use

The classification for pleasure use only usually includes driving to work less than three miles one way. Underwriters must determine whether the driving mileage indicated is excessive in view of the rate that applies.

Driving Record

Both prior accidents and prior moving violations are important in evaluating a private passenger automobile applicant. The prior loss history of the driver may indicate poor driving habits, recklessness, or simply a lack of skill. Certain moving violations indicate a disregard for safety, while others indicate carelessness.

Territory

The principal place of garaging indicates the probability of both liability and physical damage losses. Congested urban areas, with parking on the streets, provide high incidence of theft and vandalism. Cars parked on the street are vulnerable to hit-and-run accidents. Drivers are more likely to be involved in an automobile accident in an urban area but more likely to be involved in a fatal accident in a rural area. Higher driving speeds and greater distance in mileage and time to reach medical help have been presented as possible explanations.[4]

Other territorial variations are unrelated to population density. Some areas of the country have severe winter weather, which causes dangerous icing conditions. In other areas, sandstorms frequently cause comprehensive coverage losses to paint and windshields.

Sex and Marital Status

Underwriters have long recognized the ability of gender and marital status to predict future loss experience. The value of these two factors varies considerably with the age of the applicant. For example, young female drivers were generally considered to be better than young male drivers. For many years, young female drivers paid the same premiums as adult drivers. However, in recent years, young females have paid more than adult drivers in most states, but still considerably less than young males.

Exhibit 6-3 illustrates that there are more male than female drivers, that female drivers have a higher involvement in all accidents, and that it is male drivers are more likely to be involved in fatal accidents.

Exhibit 6-3
Sex of Drivers Involved in Accidents, 1989-1995

	Drivers in all accidents				Drivers in fatal accidents			
	Male		Female		Male		Female	
Year	Number	Rate*	Number	Rate*	Number	Rate**	Number	Rate**
1989	14,100,000	95	8,700,000	143	47,000	32	14,800	24
1990	12,170,000	80	7,630,000	121	46,800	31	15,400	24
1991	12,070,000	86	7,430,000	97	43,600	31	14,200	19
1992	12,700,000	88	8,100,000	103	40,200	28	13,000	17
1993	12,900,000	87	8,200,000	101	40,400	27	13,500	17
1994	12,400,000	82	7,600,000	90	38,200	25	14,600	17
1995	10,600,000	69	7,000,000	80	37,500	24	13,000	15

* Number of drivers in all accidents per 10,000,000 miles driven.
** Number of drivers in fatal accidents per 1,000,000,000 miles driven.

Source: National Safety Council estimates.

Adapted with permission from *The Fact Book 1997: Property/Casualty Insurance Facts* (New York, NY: Insurance Information Institute, 1997), p. 87.

The marital status of younger drivers is a factor in both rating and underwriting. Married male drivers under thirty usually pay less than their single counterparts because married persons in that age group generally tend to be more mature and responsible than single persons of the same age. Their marital situation also suggests that they spend more time at home.

Some states regulate the use of sex and marital status for underwriting purposes. A few states prohibit price discrimination on the basis of sex or marital status.

Occupation

The relationship between a person's occupation and driving habits is controversial. Some underwriting guides make distinctions on this basis; others do not. Certain occupations, such as traveling salespersons, require extensive driving and increase the probability of loss. This should be accounted for in the rates that reflect use of the vehicle.

Personal Characteristics

Underwriters often order consumer investigation reports to provide information on the personal characteristics of an insured and other drivers. This information is subjective and must be carefully evaluated.

Many insurers use credit information to evaluate the stability of insurance applicants. Underwriters have demonstrated a correlation between poor credit risk and poor insurance risk. Critics of insurers' use of credit information suggest that the connection between the two factors is nonspecific and that the connection may mask factors that are prohibited, such as race.

Physical Condition

Physical impairments may be a problem if allowances for the impairment have not been made. Modifications of a car to accommodate a driver with physical impairments and a demonstrated mastery of the vehicle usually make the applicant acceptable.

Safety Equipment

Since the 1980s, many new cars have come equipped with advanced safety systems. Underwriters have begun to take these features into consideration. They allow rate discounts for anti-lock braking systems that reduce the number of accidents, and for passive restraint systems or air bags that reduce injuries to vehicle occupants.

Commercial Automobile Underwriting Factors

Public attitudes toward commercial automobiles differ from those held toward private passenger automobiles. The public knows that commercial firms usually carry insurance with high liability limits. Accordingly, an accident involving a commercial auto is likely to generate larger claims than a similar accident involving a personal automobile.

At most insurers, an analysis of a commercial automobile risk closely follows the characteristics used in rating the policy. Information that is key to policy pricing is essential to underwriting the exposure.

All commercial automobile policies are class-rated initially. Policies that develop enough premium are eligible for experience rating that modifies current premium to reflect past losses. Schedule rating is used to modify the premium for characteristics the rates do not fully reflect.

Trucks, tractors, and trailers, as well as those truckers hauling exclusively for one concern, are classified and rated using four factors:

1. Weight and type of vehicle
2. Use of the vehicle
3. Radius of operation
4. Special industry classifications

Weight and Type of Vehicle

The damage resulting from an accident is related to the size, or weight, and speed of the vehicles involved. Commercial tractor-trailer rigs can weigh 80,000 pounds or more when loaded and often travel at the maximum legal speed, so commercial vehicles are more likely than other vehicles to cause severe damage when an accident occurs. Large trucks are also difficult to maneuver in heavy traffic or on small inner-city streets. The vehicle weight and type are reflected in the primary rating classifications of commercial vehicles.

Use of the Vehicle

Commercial vehicles vary significantly in the intensity of use as well as how they are used. Some may be used almost continually in hauling goods, while others may be used only to travel to and from a job site, remaining parked most of the time. The ISO *Commercial Lines Manual* (CLM) divides business use into service, retail, and commercial use. Each of these classifications is described in the *CLM* and reflected in determining the primary classification to which the vehicle is assigned. The use classification measures the intensity with which the vehicle is driven.

Service use applies to vehicles that are used principally to transport personnel or material to a job site. These vehicles are often driven to a job site at the start of a shift and remain there until the shift is over. Because they are used less intensely, service vehicles receive the lowest rate. **Retail use** means that the vehicle is used primarily for deliveries to and pickups from households. Drivers frequently follow unfamiliar routes and operate on tight schedules. This use class receives the highest rate. **Commercial use** applies to any vehicle that does not fall into one of the above two classes.

Radius of Operation

Radius of operations is significant in determining the primary classification because distance traveled (as well as the nature of travel) can affect accident frequency. Trucks operated over long distances may have more, and more severe, accidents than those operated locally. There are probably several reasons for this. A driver who operates a truck over long distances may not be as familiar with the route and its hazards as are drivers who operate trucks locally. Second, long-distance trucking is more likely to be more strictly scheduled. If drivers are rushing to meet a delivery deadline, resulting fatigue and excessive speeds can increase accident frequency. Finally, because long-haul trucks are large and usually travel at high speeds, they are typically involved in more severe accidents than trucks used within a city or town. (However, the expectation of a higher frequency of accidents for long-haul trucks is partly offset by the number of accidents that occur as a result of congested city traffic and the stop-start nature of city driving.)

The radius of operation is measured *on a straight line* from the street address of principal garaging. Over-the-road mileage is not used. **Local** is regular operation within a radius of 50 miles. **Intermediate** is regular operation within a radius of 51 to 200 miles. **Long distance** is regular operation in excess of a 200-mile radius.

There is no prescribed definition of regular operation. Some insurers use an 80 percent rule when the highest rate use applies, unless a lower-rated classification is used 80 percent of the time. An average of once a week has become an accepted standard in the absence of a ruling to the contrary by a state authority or the insurer involved. This interpretation does not preclude correcting a vehicle's classification for an extended change in use caused by seasonal factors or if the vehicle use has permanently changed. Underwriters should be familiar with the definition of regular operation used by their own companies.

Special Industry Classifications

Special industry classifications or **secondary classifications** consist of seven major industry classifications, each of which is further divided into subclassifications. The numerous classifications permit the capture of meaningful data by specialized use even though most of the subclassifications within an industry grouping carry the same rate. The major categories are as follows:

- *Truckers*—Vehicles used to transport the goods or materials of others; the category does not include moving household goods, office furniture, or fixtures and supplies.
- *Food delivery*—Vehicles used by wholesale food distributors and by food manufacturers to transport raw and finished products.
- *Specialized delivery*—Delivery vehicles such as armored cars or autos for delivering film, magazines or newspapers, mail and parcel post, and similar items.
- *Waste disposal*—Vehicles transporting waste material for disposal or resale.
- *Farmers*—Vehicles owned by farmers and used in farming operations.
- *Dump and transit mix trucks and trailers*—Vehicles are placed in this category when no other classification appropriately includes a vehicle's incidental dumping operation.
- *Contractors*—All vehicles used by contractors other than dump trucks.
- *Not otherwise specified*—Vehicles that cannot be classified in any other group.

Commercial Automobile Loss Control

The loss control activities of an insurer are important in achieving and maintaining the underwriting profitability of an account. Loss control representatives (LCRs) serve to make both drivers and managers more safety-conscious. In addition, they assist policyholders in developing vehicle inspection programs to address problems identified in loss control reports and create a positive approach to safety through safety programs.

Loss Control Reports

The loss control report can be a very important source of information for the underwriter. It confirms and supplements information (estimates of the cost of hire; type, scope, and efficiency of operations; physical condition of autos; losses; list of autos; and so on) found on the application.

For economic reasons, underwriters cannot inspect the operation of every commercial policyholder. Insurers usually establish certain criteria as to which risks are inspected and how often, but in any specific case, the commercial underwriter usually has the option of ordering a survey, either from the loss control department or from an outside firm.

Policy size and/or premium amount are important, but they are not the only criteria for requesting inspections. Autos handling liquefied petroleum gas, acids, corrosive chemicals, flammable materials, or explosives are usually inspected before being bound. Inspections are normal when extremely high limits of liability are requested. The type or size of the autos frequently causes a commercial auto underwriter to seek additional information from an inspection.

The policyholder's accident record is an important factor considered by the loss control representative in making recommendations to the policyholder for improving his or her desirability as a risk. Several backing losses may indicate a need for additional loss control systems. Better rearview mirror systems help, but they cannot always let the driver see well enough to avoid backing losses. The solution may lie in having a walking ground guide direct the driver while backing up. Several proximity alarms are also on the market that alert drivers to hazards in blind spots directly behind the vehicle and to the sides. They are more effective than mirrors.

A high frequency of theft or vandalism claims may indicate a need for better vehicle protection. The type and extent of protection would be at least partly determined by the location of vehicles when stolen or vandalized. Finally, the location of losses reported by the loss control representative may alert the underwriter to the fact that the actual radius of operations is greater than that indicated on the application.

For these reasons, the policyholder's system for recording losses, including those losses that are not covered by insurance (for example, below the deductible amount), is very important to the loss control representative when conducting the loss control survey. An application for insurance often lists only the insured losses that the applicant has had. Perhaps the applicant keeps records only of the losses large enough to report to the insurer or has received a list of losses from the present insurer and has included that list with the application.

In addition, because of higher physical damage deductibles ($500 to $1,000 or more) usually written on commercial autos, many small accidents are not reported. This makes the loss frequency appear better than it is. The vehicle condition also deteriorates if damage from small accidents is not repaired. For these reasons, the ability of the loss control representative to report the uninsured losses on the loss control survey is important to the underwriter. Loss control representatives can often assist the policyholder in establishing an effective record-keeping system or improving the current system.

Safety Programs

Policyholders with a fleet of autos should have a formal, written safety program. An underwriter can learn a good deal about a policyholder by examining the details of the safety program and the records associated with that program. Smaller commercial auto risks should also have some plan, even if it is informal and not written.

The following are seven essential elements of a good fleet safety program that an underwriter should take into consideration:

1. Driver selection
2. Driver training and motivation
3. Equipment control
4. Accident reporting and review
5. Periodic checking of drivers and vehicles
6. Enforcement and reinforcement of the program
7. Management support of the program

An important point to remember is that although industrial safety programs depend on the first-line supervisors to monitor and help implement safety procedures, fleet safety programs rely almost entirely on the auto operators, not fleet supervisors, to supervise their actions behind the wheel. Nevertheless, fleet supervisors can schedule occasional trips with each driver as a check on the driver's habits and as a show of managerial support.

Some policyholders also conduct periodic on-the-road evaluations of their drivers to see whether they are obeying the laws and following company procedures. This is a positive factor, but it must be followed up with corrective action. It does little good to find out which drivers are speeding if the policyholder is not going to do anything about it. These evaluations and their results should be included in the safety program records that the underwriter reviews.

There are firms that specialize in road patrol (that is, on-the-road spot-checks of drivers). Companies may hire such firms to check their vehicles. In some cases, they give the "engineer" for the road patrol firm the authority to pull over the drivers (where laws and highway conditions permit) to check further into the driver's and the truck's conditions. Underwriters cannot require policyholders to use such firms. However, underwriters view applicants that use such firms as being more desirable because of their concern for safety.

One factor often uncovered by the engineers is the presence of unauthorized personnel in the cab of the trucks. In addition, of the many factors that are examined—speed, entries in the driver's log, vehicle condition, time of observation, and location—the last two items might prove important if drivers are taking unauthorized routes.

Using such a service is a positive factor in the underwriter's evaluation of a risk, but only if the firm uses the resulting reports to take corrective action. Underwriters should request the reports filed on drivers and ask what corrective action, if any, was taken.

Insurance Requirements for Commercial Automobiles

The Motor Carrier Act of 1980 requires certain motor carriers to meet financial responsibility requirements and demonstrate evidence that those requirements are met. Although the financial responsibility requirements can be met by obtaining a surety bond, most motor carriers satisfy this requirement through insurance. Most states have financial responsibility requirements for intrastate motor carriers.

The Motor Carrier Act imposes this financial responsibility requirement on motor carriers based on their operation and the type of commodity they carry. The Motor Carrier Act divides motor carriers into four categories and requires different financial responsibility limits for each category of motor carrier. The regulations provide extensive detail on the types of carriers and commodities. Motor carriers not carrying hazardous material in interstate or foreign commerce and motor carriers carrying hazardous materials must comply with the Motor Carrier Act. The financial responsibility limits range from $1,000,000 for motor carriers engaged in interstate commerce but not carrying hazardous materials to $5,000,000 for motor carriers that haul explosives, poisonous gas, or radioactive materials. There are also provisions for small freight carriers, not falling within the categories mentioned above, that carry specific commodities to meet a financial responsibility requirement of $300,000.

Motor carriers meeting the financial responsibility requirements through insurance must get their insurer to add a specified form to their commercial automobile insurance. The MCS-90, or "Endorsement for Motor Carrier Policies of Insurance for Public Liability Under Sections 29 and 30 of the Motor Carrier Act of 1980," imposes additional responsibilities on the insurer. The MCS-90 amends the insurance policy to comply with the act and removes some of the defenses that the insurer would normally have without the presence of the form. For example, the insurer would be responsible for injuries caused by insured-owned vehicles not identified on the policy or from trucking routes not described in the application. Additionally, the Motor Carrier Act requires that insurers must give motor carriers thirty-five days' notice of cancellation and thirty days' notice to the Department of Transportation. Insurer payments for claims not normally covered by the insurance policy but required because of the presence of the MCS-90 can be recovered from the insured. Unfortunately for the insurer, it is unlikely that the insured will repay.

Underwriters usually analyze a motor carrier's financial stability when evaluating an account.

Underwriting General Liability

General liability insurance has developed into a package of coverages including the following:

1. Liability for bodily injury and property damage that arise out of the insured's business operations or premises
2. Personal and advertising injury liability
3. Premises medical payments
4. Fire legal liability
5. Liability the insured assumes under contract

Commercial general liability coverage forms also include products and completed operations liability. Because both the coverage and the factors the underwriter considers in the risk selection decision are materially different from other exposures, this section treats products and completed operations liability as a separate line of business.

The exposure for general liability insurance is based on the exposure of the public to the hazards of the insured's business premises and operations. Underwriters often refer to the components of this exposure as hazards. They speak of the premises hazard, the operations in progress hazard, and the personal injury hazard. This use of the term "hazard" refers to potential liability exposures that can lead to legal action against the insured. The analysis of liability exposures usually tracks the coverage forms most likely to provide satisfactory coverage.

The public includes customers, representatives of suppliers, anyone else associated with the business, and the general public. Although all businesses have this liability exposure, the extent of the exposure varies widely. An underwriter will want to know whether the exposure is common for the classification and how much variation in the exposure is likely.

Occurrence and Claims-Made Coverage

The commercial general liability policy (CGL) has two versions: occurrence and claims-made. The feature that distinguishes the two forms is the definition of the event that triggers the coverage, called a **coverage trigger**. The occurrence form uses the traditional coverage trigger found in most liability policy forms. The insurer agrees to pay damages for bodily injury or property damage that occurs while the policy is in force. It does not matter when the claim is made. Under the claims-made form, the insurer agrees to pay damages for bodily injury or property damage for which a claim is first made during the policy period. Claims-made policies were designed to eliminate the long delay between the time a loss occurs and the time it is settled. A pharmaceutical manufacturer, for instance, can expect to receive claims in many future years from injuries that occur in the current year. Claims-made policies enable insurers to capture final claim data more quickly for ratemaking purposes. The claims-made policy has never been used to the extent insurers once envisioned, but underwriters need to understand the differences between the forms and how they operate.

Premises and Operations Exposures

There are two distinct components to the premises and operations hazard. **Premises liability exposures** arise from the ownership or possession of real property. **Operations liability exposures** arise from a policyholder's business activities conducted away from its own premises and from work uncompleted. To distinguish the *operations* hazard from the **completed operations hazard** (injuries arising from finished work), underwriters frequently refer to the former as *operations in progress* (injuries arising while the work is being performed).

The liability exposures most businesses face arise principally from either the premises they own or occupy or from the operations the businesses conduct. This has led underwriters to divide premises and operations exposures into two classes, *premises* and *operations*. Underwriters think of a retail store, for example, as a premises exposure. A building contractor presents an operations in progress hazard. Underwriters recognize that insureds whose exposure is mainly related to their premises also face liability for their operations in progress. Underwriters treat the operations exposure as incidental to the premises hazard. By the same token, when the operations in progress hazard is dominant, underwriters recognize an incidental premises hazard. This is a useful technique for analyzing the exposures and does not reflect a perception that the exposure is exclusively premises or operations.

The level of exposure to liability varies with the type of business. Some differences in the extent of exposure may be a result of location, type of business, time in business, or a combination of the three. For example, a store with a good reputation and steady business is more likely to attract customers than a new store or one that is on the decline. The increase in customer traffic increases the exposure. Location may create a similar increase in traffic and, thus, in the extent of exposure. A downtown electronics store may open up a new branch in a suburban shopping mall. A mall usually has several well-known large stores that attract traffic to other smaller stores in the mall. People who are in the mall to shop are much more likely to enter the electronics store premises than would pedestrians on city streets. In addition, because of differences in store hours and customers' shopping habits, malls are likely to have a greater percentage of their customers present at nights or on weekends. Even if the total number of customers was average for the class, the mall electronics store would have a relatively high concentration of customers at certain hours. Fire exposure also increases in extent because the setup of a mall and more customer traffic make it less likely that customers will be able to successfully exit the premises. In contrast, the extent of most weather-related exposures would decrease for a store located in a mall, because the quality of mall maintenance usually helps to eliminate such premises hazards as icy walkways or sidewalks. Each risk must be underwritten individually so that the exposure can be evaluated.

Nevertheless, a concentration of people does not necessarily indicate excessive exposure. What may create an underwriting problem for the electronics store would not do so for a theater. The rate for the store may be inadequate, while the rate for the theater may be sufficient because it anticipates concentrations of people.

Consideration must also be given to the legal status of persons likely to be on the premises. What is the policyholder's legal duty to these persons, and what standards of care are expected? The policyholder must demonstrate behavior that is consistent with the standard of care required. A comparison must be made between the duties owed by the policyholder and an average risk in the same classification. If the results of the comparison are the same, there is usually no problem, but if they vary, the underwriter must account for the difference. For example, a retail store with mostly adult customers may need to exercise reasonable care, but a toy store attracting a large number of children may need to exercise additional care.

Bodily injury usually receives the primary emphasis in underwriting because it tends to produce larger losses. An underwriter cannot, on the other hand, ignore the potential for property damage losses. Property damage losses include claims not only for the value of the damaged property but also for the loss of its use.

Physical Hazards

Physical hazards are as important to underwriting liability coverage as they are in any other line of business. Underwriters classify physical hazards into the same classes used for other lines of business. Many physical hazards, such as those that induce slips and falls, are common to many premises. They are common hazards. Other physical hazards such as chemicals, dust, and explosives occur only in certain types of businesses. These are the special hazards of the class. Some businesses conduct operations that are not typical of the class to which they belong; they are considered to be special hazards of the risk.

Many types of accidents likely to occur within a building (slipping, falling, tears, cuts, and burns) are the result of conditions or hazards that may be present on the premises. The causes of the injuries are what is important to the underwriter. The underwriter tries to determine what hazards or conditions increase the likelihood of injury or damage for which the owner or lessor of the premises will be held liable. Some of the more common hazards are uneven stairs, tears in carpets, inadequate lighting, congested aisles, poor housekeeping, and defective heating or electrical equipment. Other hazards, such as the presence of sharp objects, flammable liquids, explosives, toxic gases, and welding equipment, are usually found only on premises at which specific operations are located. The potential number of hazards at various premises is almost unlimited.

When evaluating the physical hazards of a premises exposure, underwriters have to consider the entire premises. When the principal exposures arise from the interior of the premises, underwriters cannot afford to overlook exposures to loss associated with the exterior. Injuries can be caused outside the building by broken or icy sidewalks, parking lots in poor condition, falling signs, building collapse, playground equipment, swimming pools, and other features of the property. Mobile equipment could cause injury inside or outside the building, depending on the type and use of the equipment.

Generally, businesses with heavy premises exposures like apartment houses and office buildings have minimal operations exposures. Businesses with small premises exposures, such as service businesses and contractors, have substantial operations exposures. An electrical contractor is likely to have a place of business, but it is not likely to be a significant factor in risk selection. A store and shop where electrical fixtures are sold and repaired, on the other hand, would constitute a premises exposure that an underwriter would have to assess separately. Typical contractors have little premises exposures, but they have substantial operations exposures because of installation and repair work. An electrical contractor who has a sales and repair operation on the premises has both a premises and an operations exposure.

The hazards related to an operations exposure vary more than do those related to a premises exposure. Each service or contracting risk uses different tools. Some have heavy machinery or mobile equipment; some use flammables and blowtorches; some rent or lease equipment; and some blast, excavate, or erect. The builders of both single, ranch-style residences and high-rise apartments do similar work, use similar tools, and create attractive nuisances at construction sites, but the similarity ends there. The high-rise building contractor works with steel girders, land leveling equipment, deep excavations, and hoists, often in heavily populated areas. The variation in hazard as a result of these differences is great.

In addition to the bodily injury exposure of premises-type risks, an underwriter must also consider the physical hazards that can cause property damage losses. Torn or stained clothing and damage to vehicles in parking lots are the most common property damage losses. Pollution has become one of the most important sources of severe losses. This is a factor to consider when the insured requests limited pollution coverage under the general liability coverage form. A premises exposure, such as an apartment house, may appear innocuous. The building may, however, have an oil-fired heating system fed from an underground storage tank. This presents a serious exposure that most underwriters prefer to leave for specialists in environmental impairment liability.

Operations-type risks generally have a greater potential for causing property damage losses than do premises-type risks. A contractor, for example, was hired to repaint the exterior fixtures on a fire-resistive building. A painter at the same site was using a propane torch to remove scaling paint from the cooling tower on the building's roof. When the painters broke for lunch, the painter failed to turn off the torch. The unattended flame ignited the flammable fill of the cooling tower, causing a fire and a six-figure property damage liability loss. Leased equipment can damage a customer's property if it is not kept in good repair or if a customer misuses it. Use of heavy equipment is likely to cause serious property damage, but the major sources of property damage losses are fire, collapse, water damage, and, in some cases, pollution.

Premises—An Example

A department store presents many of the hazards inherent in a premises exposure. This store is located in a multistory, fire-resistive structure in an urban shopping district. Although the exposure is primarily a premises one due to the number of people who visit the store, there is also an operations exposure arising from store deliveries and installation work.

Common hazards such as uneven stairs, congested aisles, loose wires, worn floors, and poor lighting can present bodily injury hazards in a department store. Even well-maintained department stores have premises hazards, such as elevators, escalators, and revolving doors, that are simply a function of normal department-store construction. Other areas and items in the store, like the toy department, playrooms, pools and fountains, and glass showcases, might be hazardous, and the underwriter must evaluate them. Sidewalks and parking lots, especially if they are not well maintained, create external premises exposures.

Many department stores have cooking demonstrations to show new products. If a propane tank were to explode, injuries would likely result not only from the explosion but also from the ensuing fire. Fire, in fact, is usually the primary cause of severe loss in a department store. When fire breaks out, customers may be trampled in the rush to escape the danger, or the crush of the crowd may block exits and trap a large number of people inside. The best way to control this hazard is to prevent fire from breaking out, but if a fire does break out, it must be controlled. Adequate means of egress are also essential, so exit routes should be clearly marked. Swinging doors that open outward on either side of revolving doors can facilitate a quick and easy exit in the event of an emergency.

For most department stores, the property damage exposures are not as great as the bodily injury exposures. The frequent slips and falls often involve minor property damage claims for damaged clothing, but they could also result in severe losses. If there is a parking lot, the possibility of auto damage exists. Department stores that provide services such as equipment installation and repair have, in addition to a premises exposure, an operations exposure that increases the potential for property damage.

If loss experience shows that a department store has a high frequency of injuries caused by falls, the underwriter must determine the reason. Are the falls due to poor surface conditions, such as torn carpets? Do they occur principally in the aisles, on the escalators or elevators, or at the entrances and exits? Are the stairways well lighted? Do the elevators stop evenly with the floors or move too quickly or steeply? After the hazard has been identified, the underwriter must make sure the insured addresses the hazards. Accident statistics are available for many industries. By comparing them to the insured's loss experience, underwriters determine how a store compares to the "average."

A department store might have a substantial frequency of "struck by object" and "struck against object" accidents. Are these accidents caused by narrow or congested aisles, poor housekeeping, or stockroom personnel pushing carts? Whatever the hazard, the underwriter must determine whether it can be controlled; otherwise, the frequency of claims can be expected to continue.

Operations—An Example

Consider a firm that sells, repairs, and installs home security systems. The primary exposure for this business is the possibility of loss arising out of operations conducted in the homes of customers. Bodily injury losses could result from service personnel who carelessly leave tools where customers can trip over them. Generally, however, the underwriter would not expect a high frequency of bodily injury claims from a home security system sales and repair business. Instead, such a business would be expected to generate a high frequency of property damage losses. Installing a security system usually involves sliding wires through attics, basements, and walls so that every window and door is tied to the alarm system. This installation process can result in property damage losses.

Just as with the department store example used above, the underwriter can review past loss experience. Losses can be categorized to identify trends.

The frequency and severity of property damage losses depend primarily on the nature of the operations of the particular business. If most of the installations are done on homes in the process of construction rather than on completed homes, the frequency of loss should be reduced. A key factor in evaluating loss severity is the quality of workmanship. Are the installation personnel well trained? How long have they been performing their jobs? How much supervision do they get?

This kind of operation exposure can also create severe as well as frequent losses. In addition, frequent losses increase the likelihood of random severe losses. A given hazard may produce widely different levels of loss severity. For example, incorrectly wiring a security system might produce an electrical short that starts a house fire.

Unexpected Physical Hazards

Underwriters must consider an additional and rather unpredictable factor in reviewing an account for general liability insurance. Special hazards of the risk may exist. The business may have exposures to loss that are not characteristic of the class as a whole. This may present a greater exposure of loss than the rates for the class contemplate. Underwriters must identify for a particular account any special hazards of the risk and decide whether they present unacceptable liability exposures. These hazards could evolve from an incidental operation, a "one-shot deal," a gradual diversification of operations, or an assumption of operations not contemplated when the risk was originally insured and priced.

As mentioned, some department stores provide special services that add operations exposures to a normally premises-only type of business. Many stores also have an auto service area, a grocery section, or a restaurant. Department stores or any business can sponsor sporting events either as a promotional activity or for the benefit of employees. Such activities are not inherent in the operation of the business, and therefore, any related hazard is relatively unexpected; yet such activities could significantly increase the likelihood of a liability loss.

Exposures in the home security systems business can also deviate from the norm. The owner could enter into a contract with a contractor who builds large residential developments. This may mean hiring extra employees without having the benefit of training them completely or burdening the regular employees with rush jobs, which may result in carelessness or lower-quality workmanship. The home security system operation could also expand into other types of work, such as installing telephone and television cabling. Do the employees have the ability and expertise to perform these tasks? Peak seasons, demonstrations, exhibits, and hiring subcontractors are other conditions that might create unexpected hazards that could increase the liability exposure of department stores and home security systems businesses beyond the scope of their particular class.

Contractors and Subcontractors

The policyholder may be liable for the negligent acts of contractors or subcontractors hired to perform work. Generally, a property owner or contractor who has hired an "independent contractor" is not legally liable under common law for the independent contractor's negligent acts. An independent contractor performs his or her work without specific direction as to *how* the work is to be performed. In some instances, courts have held that an independent contractor is a de facto employee. This eliminates the common-law immunity the principal or contractor enjoys. Determining who is responsible for activities that cause injury is particularly a problem when contractors and subcontractors are individuals without employees. It is easy for the injured party to claim that work was directed by the property owner.

The law also holds the insured vicariously liable for duties that cannot be delegated to others. A principal has a duty to select a competent independent contractor and provide a level of general supervision adequate to protect the public from injury. Thus, either an owner of land (as an employer of a general contractor) or a general contractor (as an employer of a subcontractor) may be held liable to third persons for the negligent acts of contractors or subcontractors. The underwriting implications of this exposure could be significant. Admittedly, the policyholder's liability for the acts of others is less significant than liability for its own acts.

However, the potential exposure exists, and coverage is included in the general liability coverage forms. For all business classifications other than contractors, there are no special classification and rating rules because the potential exposure is minimal. For contractor classes, subcontractors need to be evaluated to determine whether they carry adequate insurance. If they do, only a small charge is made to cover those circumstances when the policyholder may be held liable for the work of the subcontractor. The underwriter should treat subcontractors who fail to provide evidence of insurance as the insured's employees.

An insured does not know at the outset of the policy term which subcontractors will be hired during the year, so this is a major concern for the underwriter. The underwriter is therefore placed at a disadvantage, since the subcontractors cannot be evaluated before writing the policy. The underwriter has to rely on the policyholder's reputation for being selective in hiring subcontractors. When the subcontractors are known, the insurer can require certificates of insurance from the subcontractors.

Contractual Liability Coverage

Commercial general liability coverage forms contain a contractual liability exclusion that serves to define coverage for liability the insured assumes under a contract or an agreement. They provide what was once known as broad form contractual liability coverage. With a few exceptions, it covers any liability the insured assumes under a contract related to the business.

Hold Harmless Agreements

A contract under which one party assumes the liability of another is called a **hold harmless agreement**. The name derives from the customary language in which one party, the **indemnitor**, agrees to *save, indemnify and hold harmless* the other party, the **indemnitee**. Like an insurance policy, a hold harmless agreement is a contract of indemnity. The principal differences are that the indemnitor in a hold harmless agreement is not in the business of assuming risk, and that a hold harmless agreement is rarely a separate contract. It is usually a clause in a contract that has a broader purpose.

Insured Contracts

ISO commercial general liability forms define an "insured contract" as follows:

a. A contract for a lease of premises. However, that portion of the contract for a lease of premises that indemnifies any person or organization for damage by fire to premises contract while rented to you or temporarily occupied by you with permission of the owner is not an "insured contract";

b. A sidetrack agreement;

c. Any easement or license agreement, except in connection with construction or demolition operations on or within 50 feet of a railroad;

d. An obligation, as required by ordinance, to indemnify a municipality, except in connection with work for a municipality;

e. An elevator maintenance agreement;

f. That part of any other contract or agreement pertaining to your business (including an indemnification of a municipality in connection with work performed for a municipality) under which you assume the tort liability of another party to pay for "bodily injury" or "property damage" to a third person or organization. Tort liability means a liability that would be imposed by law in the absence of any contract or agreement.[5]

The first five sections of this definition cover incidental contracts. General liability forms have always included coverage for these contracts. The sixth section provides broad form contractual liability coverage. It covers liability the insured assumes under almost any contract relating to the operation of the business.

Limiting coverage to the tort liability of another person the insured assumes under contract addresses a problem some risk managers perceived in older forms. A business sometimes signs a contract under which it assumes only its own liability imposed by law in the absence of a contract. This raises the question of whether liability is assumed under a contract. Some risk managers could imagine an insurer's rejecting a claim based on the insured's negligence because it was also the subject of a hold harmless agreement. This issue was important when a contractual liability exclusion was common, but it has little meaning today.

Risk managers began to perceive another problem with the definition of contractual liability. They assumed that contractual liability coverage in the older forms included defense. Although this is not true, and the newer forms actually provided broader coverage, insurers responded to the perceived problem. Since March 1996, contractual liability has also covered the cost of defending the indemnitee against claims for which the insured would be liable in the absence of a contract. This coverage does not apply when the indemnitee's interests are in conflict with the insurer's. This occurs most often when a suit alleges negligence of both the indemnitor and the indemnitee. Each party's best defense is often to shift responsibility to the other. Coverage for defense of the indemnitee also requires that the insurance company be able to assign the same counsel to defend both the indemnitee and the insured.

Underwriting Contractual Liability

An underwriter cannot know at inception what liability an insured will assume during the policy term. This is similar to the situation that exists when an insured employs independent contractors. When evaluating this exposure, an underwriter can rely on the insured's reputation and past practices.

The two parties to a hold harmless agreement often presume that one party assumes the entire liability of the other. They rely on the indemnitor's insurance to protect both parties from liability losses. This is especially true when a certificate of insurance lists contractual liability coverage. Certain types of hold harmless agreements, however, fall outside the scope of contractual liability coverage. Statutes in most states also limit using hold harmless agreements in certain situations. Courts in some instances have found that hold harmless agreements are so vague that they are meaningless. Extremely broad assumptions of liability may violate public policy. In these instances, the indemnitee has not transferred the exposure, despite the contract.

Products and Completed Operations Exposures

Any business may incur liability for injuries caused by products it makes, sells, distributes, or even gives away. Many service businesses, such as builders and repair shops, face a similar exposure from the work they perform for others.

Sources of Product Liability

Liability for the sale, manufacture, and distribution of products can arise from breach of warranty, the tort of negligence, and strict liability in tort. It is not uncommon for the plaintiff to assert all three causes of action in a product liability suit.

The oldest basis for imposing liability on the maker or seller of a defective product is **breach of warranty**. This is a cause of action based on breach of contract. In every sale of merchandise, the law implies warranties of merchantability and fitness for the product's intended use. The seller may also make an express warranty of fitness for a specific purpose. Breach of warranty suffers from inherent limitations as a basis for a product liability action. This has led courts to recognize other grounds for product liability.

Negligence extends protection to a broader range of persons who may suffer injury from a defective product, but it is often difficult to prove. A plaintiff can rarely point to a specific act of negligence in a product liability action. In order to permit plaintiffs to recover for legitimate injuries, the courts recognize the **doctrine of *res ipsa loquitur***. This rule of law shifts the burden of proof from the plaintiff to the defendant when the following are true:

1. The event that is the proximate cause of injury does not ordinarily occur in the absence of negligence.
2. Sufficient evidence exists to eliminate other possible causes.
3. The circumstances indicate a negligent act that falls within the defendant's duty to the plaintiff.

Res ipsa loquitur creates a presumption of negligence when the facts suggest that there is no other possible explanation. The defendant has the opportunity to rebut the presumption of negligence.

Many products essential to maintaining the quality of life cannot be made free of danger. The hazards of these products, however, are not always obvious. The makers of these products have a duty to warn potential consumers of any danger that is not generally known to the public. Failure to give adequate warnings is the most common charge of negligence in product liability suits.

The most frequent basis·for product liability suits is a relatively new doctrine, strict liability in tort. This rule of law is sometimes referred to as simply strict liability and is often confused with the doctrine of absolute or strict liability that imposes liability in the absence of fault. It first appeared in a 1963 California case,[6] and almost every state has adopted this doctrine since then. Strict liability in tort imposes liability on any person who releases an unreasonably dangerous product into the stream of commerce. It is difficult to imagine how this could occur in the absence of negligence or an intentional act.

Products Liability Underwriting Considerations

The evolution of the law of product liability requires the underwriter to place emphasis on the product itself. The underwriter has to be concerned with the potential exposure of the public to products hazards. The frequency and severity of losses a product is likely to cause are the primary concerns. Although many factors can affect the products exposure, if the product is not inherently hazardous, there is significantly less exposure to loss. To illustrate, consider two products: a power lawn mower and a pillow. The lawn mower is a much more hazardous product than the pillow because of its inherent characteristics that increase the likelihood of loss. Determining the inherent hazards of the product is therefore the first and most important step in underwriting a product. This would be followed by an analysis of the exposure of the public to these product hazards.

The quantity of information needed by the underwriter varies with the nature of the product. Much of the information presented earlier in the text regarding premises and operations underwriting also applies to underwriting products coverage. The business of the applicant, the limits of liability, and the size and scope of the business are important in underwriting both types of coverage. As in underwriting premises and operations liability, the first source of information for products underwriting is the application. However, most applications have a section (or the insurer has a separate questionnaire) that requires information about products liability exposures.

The underwriter must consider other information in order to get a complete picture of the applicant's exposures. This information either supplements or verifies what is shown on the application.

The underwriter should also ask the following questions:

- What are the inherent hazards of the product?
- What representations or promises are made to the consumer in the sales material and advertising?
- Do technical manuals for complex products accurately reflect the safety precautions required in the product's assembly and repair?
- Does the product's packaging adequately protect the product so that it will operate properly when used?
- Are the instructions easy to read and understand?
- Does the product's warranty overstate the capability of the product?
- Are loss control efforts introduced into the product's design and production phases of product development?
- Is a complaint-handling system in place to identify flaws and prevent further injuries?
- Are quality control checks incorporated into the product's manufacture?
- Are accurate records kept of products and components so that defective products can be identified and recalled?
- Have product lines changed to increase the inherent hazards?
- What is the applicant's position in the channel of distribution?
- Who is the ultimate consumer of this product?

The bases on which courts assess product liability are not independent. Plaintiffs increase their chances of winning a product liability case when they assert more than one grounds for recovery. This increases the product liability losses underwriters have to pay. The owner of a sport utility vehicle, for instance, was injured when the car overturned on a road. A court found that the propensity to overturn did not render the product unreasonably dangerous. It was a reasonable hazard for an off-road vehicle. As a result, the plaintiff lost the strict liability in tort action. The manufacturer's advertising, however, had portrayed the vehicle as a suitable family car. An appeals court ruled that this allowed a jury to infer that the manufacturer had breached an express warranty of fitness for a specific purpose. The court upheld the award against the manufacturer on those grounds.[7] This case turned on the insured's advertising rather than on the hazards inherent in the product.

Completed Operations Underwriting

Completed operations are characterized by a wide range of possible hazards. Activities that generate completed operations hazards include construction, service, repair, and maintenance. The characteristic that distinguishes completed operations from products liability is the existence of the insured's completed work that may cause injury or damage.

There are relatively few completed operations classifications as compared to other lines of business. Lack of sufficient claims data sometimes accounts for this. Completed operations exposures are also included within other exposures. Products classes often include completed operations. Some premises and operations classifications also include the completed operations hazard. These include nursing homes, photographers, printers, and swimming pool installers.

As in the case of the other general liability sublines, the underwriter must classify the completed operations exposure correctly. An incorrect classification will not generate the proper premium for the exposure. If the rate is too high, it will drive away profitable business. If the rate is too low, underwriters can expect to sustain losses they cannot afford.

Businesses that perform services generally have an operations rather than a premises exposure. Consequently, such businesses are likely to have completed operations exposures. The activities or operations, particularly those performed off-premises, that could cause a loss are the basis of operations underwriting. Thus, the manner in which the job is performed is important to the underwriter in evaluating the exposure to loss. Quality of workmanship and equipment, supervision of employees, technical skill, reputation, and years of experience are all factors that help the underwriter evaluate the operations exposure. If any of these qualities is lacking to any significant degree, the underwriter would conclude that the loss potential arising out of the operations has been increased. These same risk characteristics are important in evaluating the completed operations exposure. For example, faulty workmanship is likely to cause a loss while the work is being performed, but it will also increase the potential of loss occurring after the work is completed.

A home security system installer who has careless work habits or lacks technical knowledge could damage the customer's premises and even cause a fire. The same conditions could also cause a loss after the installer finishes the work and leaves the premises. The damage or injury that results falls within the completed operations exposure. The underwriter has to assess the increase in the overall liability exposure from the completed operations hazard. Lack of technical knowledge or faulty workmanship is likely to increase loss frequency to the same degree for both.

The nature of the operation affects the severity of the losses it will produce. The hazards the underwriter has to consider may be different for each subline and class. A contractor building high-rise apartments is an example. While constructing the building, workers can cause extensive property damage from fire, collapse, or water, as well as bodily injury from falling objects, the operation of equipment, and the use of construction materials and tools. After the apartments are inhabited, fire or collapse could cause even more serious injuries and damages. If the cause could be traced to the faulty workmanship of the contractor, the insurer who underwrote the completed operations exposure would be responsible for the loss. In this particular case, the characteristics affecting loss frequency are greatly reduced once the building is completed, but the potential severity is greatly increased. At the other extreme, a piano tuner could cause damage to the customer's property while in the process of performing the work, but it is extremely unlikely that injury or damage will occur after the work is completed. Logically, piano tuning is an operations classification in which the completed operations exposure is included in the rate.

In evaluating an applicant for completed operations coverage, the underwriter must determine the likelihood and severity of potential losses by evaluating the nature of the applicant's business. The completed operations exposure may be considerably different from the operations exposure for a class, just as the exposure to loss as a result of the operations hazard varies from one risk to another within a class.

Workers Compensation Underwriting

Workers compensation insurance includes statutory workers compensation coverage and employers liability coverage for employers whose employees may be killed or injured or may acquire an occupational disease in the course of their employment. It is compulsory in all states except New Jersey, South Carolina, and Texas. Even in those states, most employers carry workers compensation coverage. Benefits include death benefits, disability income, medical expense, and rehabilitation expense as required by the applicable workers compensation laws. Employers liability insurance covers employers for their legal liability to an employee for injury arising out of and in the course of employment that is not covered under the workers compensation law.

Workers compensation is a major line of insurance in the United States. It represents 10 percent of all property-liability insurance premium income, second only to auto insurance.[8] The loss experience in this line of business is closely related to the prevailing economic and political environment. For several years, workers compensation was an unprofitable line of business. Rising costs for medical treatment increased the claims insurers had to pay. Wages, the base used for premium determinations, did not keep pace with rising medical and litigation costs. Insurers sought to pass the increased costs on to employers in the form of higher rates. This generated political pressure to limit rate level adjustments. Many observers believed that workers compensation coverage would never again generate a reasonable profit.

When insurers focused their attention on controlling losses, their results improved. They began a program of case management to control loss costs. When state statutes were an impediment, they worked for reform. In 1994, these efforts met with success. Insurers earned an operating profit on workers compensation for the first time in ten years. Sound underwriting and proactive loss control succeeded in improving their results, and the trend shows every indication of continuing.

The workers compensation and employers liability policy is probably the most standardized liability insurance policy. The form is designed to provide complete coverage for employee injuries except for specified exclusions. The policy combines blanket coverage for obligations imposed by the state workers compensation law and broad coverage for other employers liability. This broad coverage and the additional flexibility provided by endorsements spare policyholders the necessity of revising the insurance program every time a new location is established or when some other change in the business occurs.

An interesting feature of this policy is that it contains uniform provisions, even though workers compensation benefits vary by jurisdiction. The same policy can be used for basic coverages in various states without endorsements because the compensation laws of those states, not the policy provisions, control the conditions of coverage. The workers compensation laws are specifically incorporated into the policy contract by the reference in the policy. Thus, an underwriter analyzing the coverage and benefits provided must read the applicable statutes as well as the policy. The use of the standard policy by all insurers, together with uniform underwriting rules, also enables rating bureaus to calculate sound rates.

Workers Compensation Underwriting Considerations

Underwriting workers compensation insurance is similar to underwriting general liability insurance. The difference is that general liability insurance deals with injuries to the general public, while workers compensation responds to injuries to one's own employees. In many businesses, the general public and employees share the same environment, as is the case with retail stores. Businesses such as manufacturers have a closed environment so that the activities within the workplace can potentially be more controlled. To a large extent, general liability underwriting and workers compensation have many of the same hazards and the same type of analysis required to evaluate those hazards.

Beyond the physical hazards, general liability and workers compensation lines differ drastically in their perception by insurer management. Not all insurers offer workers compensation insurance coverage. Of those insurers that do, most have fairly regimented procedures that guide underwriters in making individual decisions on applicants within classes approved by underwriting management.

To make a profit or minimize their losses, most insurers have established strict underwriting guidelines. The most desirable situation occurs when workers compensation coverage is provided as part of an overall account. Many insurers, however, continue to write workers compensation on its own merits.

Some insurers restrict their writing to those applicants who are eligible for experience rating. This requirement relates less to the effect of experience rating than to other factors. The experience rating plan of the National Council on Compensation Insurance (NCCI) is used in most states. The eligibility requirements vary by state, but in general, the applicant's payroll that developed in the last year or the last two years of the experience period must have produced a certain premium. If an applicant is eligible for experience rating, the experience rating program is mandatory. Many insurers do not believe that they can underwrite accounts that do not meet the minimum requirements for experience rating. Their fixed costs make it difficult to earn a profit on very small accounts. Larger accounts that are not eligible have usually been in operation less than two years. That is a negative underwriting indication for any line of business.

Some insurers use the experience rating modification as an index of the account's desirability within its class. A modification greater than 1.00 requires investigation. It may be the result of one large loss. The insured may also have implemented loss control procedures to prevent similar losses in the future. If an experience-rated policy does develop adverse results during the year, the experience rating mechanism ensures that the policyholder will be penalized in future policy terms. It does not matter who provides coverage, which provides a financial incentive for effective loss control. The experience rating process provides an accurate method to capture statistics about an applicant. Loss records show both past losses and the direction those losses are going.

Insurers that offer workers compensation insurance must also participate in the assigned risk program. This is a residual market similar to those discussed for automobile coverage. Employers who have been rejected by private insurers may apply to the plan. NCCI administers the National Workers Compensation Reinsurance Pool, a voluntary association of insurers. Member companies act as servicing insurers and receive a fee for the services they provide. This relieves insurers that do not service assigned risk accounts of the burden. It reduces costs because NCCI can select more efficient insurers as servicing carriers. It also creates economies of scale that reduce costs. The premiums and losses of a business in the plan are pooled. They are then allocated by state to all members of the pool in proportion to each member's workers compensation premium volume. The pool operates in thirty-three states and provides some coverages in nine other states. In addition, the NCCI manages the statutory pool in two states. In some states, the state fund serves as the assigned risk plan.

Underwriting Guidelines for Individual Classes

Underwriting management evaluates individual classes and decides which to accept and which to reject. Management communicates the insurer's preferences in underwriting guidelines and bulletins. A conservative insurer may want to avoid all high-hazard occupations, such as steeplejacks or window washers. This same insurer may be willing to write some contractors but avoid roofing and insulation contractors. Other insurers may target their marketing efforts to high-hazard classes. Just as in other lines of business, there is no single correct way to underwrite workers compensation.

Underwriting Considerations for Individual Applicants

Line underwriters use the insurer's guidelines to evaluate individual accounts. The primary factors they consider are on-premises and off-premises hazards. Other factors also demand special attention. These factors include the number of part-time and seasonal workers, the premium for workers compensation relative to the balance of the account, and subcontractors the insured may engage.

Temporary and Seasonal Workers

A business may employ a large number of temporary or seasonal workers who are generally not as well trained as permanent workers. This lack of training increases the risk of being injured. These workers also present a potential moral hazard. They may fake injury on the job in order to receive workers compensation benefits until they return to school or find a long-term position.

Premium Size

Insurers often seek to write accounts of a certain size. They may target the middle market or Fortune 100 accounts. Underwriting guidelines often use premium size to identify the accounts an insurer wishes to write. The relative premium for each line of business may also be a factor. A guideline may be to accept certain accounts only if the workers compensation premium is less than 50 percent of the total amount of premium generated by the account. These guidelines may lead an underwriter to decline an account that is acceptable by all other measures.

Subcontractors

Most workers compensation laws hold a contractor responsible for workers compensation benefits to employees of its uninsured subcontractors. The standard workers compensation policy automatically insures this exposure. Underwriters must therefore ascertain whether this exposure exists and, if it does, evaluate it and include the appropriate premium charge if coverage is written. The policyholder must either prove that the exposure has been insured or pay a premium based on the subcontractor's payroll as well.

Management Attitude and Capability

A successful workers compensation insurance program requires active cooperation between policyholder management and the insurer. The underwriter must determine the willingness and ability of management to cooperate in the effort to minimize hazards and reduce losses.

If the firm does not have a safety program, or if the program exists only on paper with no management effort directed toward its implementation, managerial indifference can usually be assumed.

A firm that has insufficient financial resources or believes that it is at a competitive disadvantage may be unable or unwilling to implement a safety program. Some of the first areas cut back in an economic recession are worker training, maintenance, and safety.

Employee morale and claims consciousness often reflect management attitude toward workers compensation and industrial safety on the one hand and the degree of managerial skill on the other hand. A poorly managed firm is likely to have below-average workers compensation loss experience. If employee morale is low, grievances against management may motivate workers to file false or exaggerated claims for workers compensation as a means of escaping from an unpleasant work environment.

On-Premises Hazards

There are a variety of on-premises hazards. Some of them are found in virtually all occupations, such as housekeeping and maintenance. Others are peculiar to a particular operation or industry. Occupational disease and cumulative trauma disorders are two other on-premises hazards that, while not as common, should be evaluated for each occupation.

Housekeeping

From an underwriting standpoint, housekeeping refers to the quality of planning for the workplace, cleanliness, and efficiency of operation. This includes such factors as the arrangement of machinery, the placing and adequacy of aisles, the marking and cleanliness of stairs and freight elevator openings, and general overall cleanliness.

Maintenance

Poorly maintained machinery presents an inherent danger. A good program of plant and machinery maintenance indicates a positive attitude toward work safety. The absence of such a program indicates carelessness or a lack of awareness, which can severely affect future work injuries.

Although general hazards are present in all types of firms, specific hazards may be present in a particular firm as a result of the type of machines, equipment, materials, and processes used in its operation. These specific hazards require specific controls, such as machine guards, exhaust systems, and materials-handling devices designed to meet the requirements of the particular situation.

Most accidents occur as a result of either an unsafe act (88 percent) or an unsafe condition (10 percent).[9] An unsafe act or practice on the part of an employee might include failing to use the proper personal protective equipment. Workers may, for example, fail to wear dust masks or air-supplied respirators in dust-laden atmospheres. The management of the firm can influence employee behavior. Its hiring policy, safety program, and enforcement of safety rules can increase or reduce injuries on the job. Premises inspections can indicate the extent to which the insured appears to tolerate unsafe actions. Unfortunately, there is always the danger that employees may act differently during an inspection than at other times. Losses can also occur when supervisors do not enforce safety rules continuously.

Unsafe conditions are generally easier to identify than unsafe acts. In an office, there is usually a minimum exposure to dangerous conditions, such as those involving machinery, chemicals, and similar hazards. There may be some potential for slips and falls and even for back strain from improperly lifting files, boxes of paper, and similar heavy objects.

New types of injuries are developing in office environments. The pace of business and the demands placed on workers have given rise to increased numbers of stress-related workers compensation claims. Other occupations, such as school teachers and police officers, set the precedent for stress being a compensable injury. The increased use of computer keyboards has caused some office workers to lose feeling in their hands. That injury, called carpal tunnel syndrome, results from cumulative trauma. Another computer-related concern is the effect of radiation emitted by video display terminals (VDTs). Despite twenty years of investigation and study, researchers have found no conclusive link between devices emitting electromagnetic fields (EMFs) and cancer in humans. The uncertainty about the effects of EMFs have led many workers to file claims in the belief that they have suffered an injury on the job. Long periods of work with a VDT may cause eye fatigue and physical ailments.

In a factory, the manufacturing process and the type of materials used are important. The loss history of the policyholder and others in the same industry provides information on the types of losses that might occur. In woodworking, for example, sharp cutting tools operating at high speeds can result in serious lacerations. In other processes, the potential for burns is inherent in the operation.

The rating structure takes into account the differences in relative hazards among occupational classes. A machine shop is more hazardous than an office, for example. The underwriter must attempt to determine to what extent the policyholder is typical of its class. The machine shop must be evaluated relative to some guidelines that indicate the conditions usually found in a typical machine shop. The presence of additional hazards not found in other machine shops or the heightening of normal hazards due to poor maintenance or housekeeping would indicate a substantial exposure.

Occupational Disease

Workers compensation statutes provide benefits for certain diseases in addition to injuries from accidents on the job. Although the definition varies by state, an occupational disease is generally one that arises from causes the worker faces on the job and to which the general public is not exposed. It is more difficult to predict the frequency and severity of occupational diseases than of work-related accidents. Accidents are easy to identify. Exposure to unfavorable conditions at work, on the other hand, does not always cause occupational disease. Changes in the state workers compensation statutes have broadened coverage for occupational disease. The interpretation of compensable diseases has become more liberal.

Some of the occupational diseases covered by the various state workers compensation laws are silicosis (exposure to silica dust), asbestosis (caused by inhalation of asbestos fibers), radiation (including ionizing radiation), tuberculosis, pneumoconiosis (black lung), and heart or lung disease for certain groups, such as police or firefighters.

In an industrial setting, hazard analysis involves monitoring the working environment for the presence of industrial poisons. These poisons may enter the body by ingestion, inhalation, or absorption through the skin. Analyzing the toxicity of the various chemical compounds used in a particular process provides a means of evaluating the occupational disease hazards due to that source.

Cumulative Trauma Disorders

Cumulative trauma disorders arise from a series of minor stresses that occur over a period of time. These relatively minor injuries combine to cause disability or create a need for medical treatment. Examples of cumulative trauma disorders include deafness as a result of a long exposure to high noise levels or kidney damage from a lifetime of jolting in the cab of a truck. Most states now recognize cumulative trauma disorders as compensable injuries.

The major problem associated with determining compensability for these injuries is distinguishing between conditions brought on by the normal aging process, or those to which the general public is subject, and those that are truly job related. Determining financial responsibility is another concern.

Experience in the red meat industry demonstrates that employers can control cumulative trauma disorders. Workers in this industry suffered so many injuries caused by repetitive movements that OSHA made it the target of special attention. This led to the development of new safety rules that employers adopted and enforced. As a result, injury rates fell dramatically. Several years after making the red meat industry the target of its first special campaign, OSHA praised employers in this industry for the improved loss rates they had achieved.

Off-Premises Hazards

Individual firms differ in the extent to which they present off-premises hazards. In some firms, the employees carry out all their employment duties on the premises. In other firms, a great deal of travel is done in the course of employment. There are two elements to the off-premises hazard: (1) the duration of travel and the mode of transportation and (2) the types and extent of hazards at the remote job sites.

Two accounting firms with identical payrolls are presented here as examples of the first type of off-premises hazard. In Firm A, the accountants do all their work on the firm's premises. In Firm B, which does a great deal of auditing for firms in the construction business, the accountants travel much of the time in the course of employment. This travel is done in private automobiles as well as in commercial and corporate aircraft. Traffic accidents or plane crashes could result in serious workers compensation losses for Firm B from this off-premises exposure, which is not present in Firm A.

Corporate aircraft may result in a multiple-fatality workers compensation loss in the event of a crash. The potential for multiple losses is also present when several employees share the same car or truck when traveling on business for their employer.

The same techniques previously mentioned to evaluate on-premises hazards may be used for off-premises hazards. The separate evaluation of off-and-on premises hazards is necessitated by the fact that the number of workers exposed to off-premises hazards may be only a small fraction of the total work force.

Occupational Safety and Health Act

The Occupational Safety and Health Act (OSHA) of 1970 was designed to assure all workers a safe and healthy workplace. This act set safety standards for employers and imposed penalties for violations of the standards.

The Department of Labor has the task of enforcing the act. Safety inspectors may enter the working premises at any reasonable time to inspect the premises, equipment, and environment of the work force. When a violation is detected, a citation is issued describing the exact nature of the violation. The employer has fifteen working days after receiving written notice of the violation to notify the Department of Labor that either the citation or the penalty assessed will be contested. Any willful violation that results in an employee's death is punishable by a fine of up to $10,000 or imprisonment of up to six months. The second conviction carries double penalties.

Each of the large number of employers subject to the act is required to keep occupational injury records for employees. Every employer must maintain a log of recordable occupational injuries and illnesses and supplementary records of each occupational injury or illness. OSHA defines a **recordable case** as one involving an occupational death, occupational illness, or occupational injury involving loss of consciousness, restriction of work or motion, transfer to another job, or medical treatment (other than first aid). OSHA safety inspections and logs are no substitute for underwriting inspections of the various locations. Rather, they should be viewed as a source of additional data and inspection assistance. The information in the log can be used to identify the types of losses that are occurring, their frequency, and their duration in terms of lost workdays. It can also be used to verify other loss information submitted with the application.

Maritime Occupations

Some employee injury claims come within federal rather than state jurisdictions. Federal laws entitle certain groups of workers to compensation for work-related injuries without regard to fault. The effect of these laws is similar to state workers compensation laws. The difference is that the schedule of benefits and administrative procedures are established by federal laws. As a result, there can be differences in loss costs and, thus, the applicable rates for insurance coverage under the federal laws. The principal federal laws covering on-the-job injuries are the United States Longshore & Harbor Workers (USL&HW) Act and the Merchant Marine Act. The latter is more commonly known as the Jones Act.

Maritime compensation exposures often appear unexpectedly. These surprises may result from the producer's or underwriter's limited familiarity with the nature of the operations insured, from insufficient underwriting information when the coverage was written, or from the policyholder's venture into a new operation with a maritime exposure after the inception of the policy. The problem is complicated by the fact that most of these situations concern maritime employments for which distinctions between land and water areas and between crew members and harbor workers are especially difficult to draw.

Some insurers avoid any workers compensation exposures falling under federal jurisdiction because of insufficient underwriting expertise or reinsurance restrictions. Employments covered by the United States Longshore & Harbor Workers (USL&HW) Act require expertise in underwriting, claims handling, premium audit, and loss control. Even an underwriter with many years of experience, but no experience in handling maritime exposures, would find it difficult to evaluate such exposures. Reinsurance treaties may also contain restrictive provisions regarding coverages such as those that insure the USL&HW Act exposure.

An underwriter may discover USL&HW Act exposures in many typical construction and erection operations. Too often, this discovery results from a claim. Underwriters must always be alert to the existence of maritime exposures. They may be indicated in many ways, including persons to whom certificates of insurance are issued, the type of equipment owned, a list of jobs in progress, claims under other coverages, and so on. Some producers located near navigable waters attach a Longshore & Harbor Workers Compensation Act coverage endorsement to every workers compensation policy, just to be safe. The endorsement is attached even if such exposures are not contemplated when the policy is issued. In those situations, the underwriter must convey to the producer that when a maritime exposure is anticipated, it must be clearly indicated.

Professional Liability Underwriting

A professional possesses the special knowledge and skill necessary to render a professional service. Typically, the special knowledge and skill result from a combination of the person's education and experience in a particular branch of science or learning. For tort law purposes, those whom the law has recognized as professionals include physicians, surgeons, dentists, attorneys, engineers, accountants, architects, insurance agents and brokers, and many others.

Underwriters have also developed professional liability forms for special exposures that fall outside the traditional scope of professional services. Some accounts, for instance, face a severe exposure to personal injury claims. General liability forms exclude some of these exposures. Underwriters will decline to offer personal injury coverage for others. This has led to the development of professional liability forms that cover personal injury hazards. Examples include media liability, law enforcement agencies, and security guards.

Other professional liability forms insure exposures that have traditionally fallen within the business risk exclusion. Underwriters at one time did not feel that they could insure these exposures. A new class of professional liability forms insures against liability for faulty advice or workmanship. Data processing firms can now obtain coverage for the failure of their software or systems to perform as expected. Consultants in all fields can insure their liability for losses clients sustain as a result of the consultant's advice.

Professional liability, by its nature, is subject to large and relatively infrequent claims. Additionally, these claims are usually filed and settled many years after the date of the event from which the claim arose. Thus, it is often difficult to determine whether a line of business is profitable until many years after the premium has been collected. To alleviate this problem, some professional liability policies have been changed from an occurrence basis to a claims-made basis.

In the past, professional liability policies almost always included a condition that required the professional to consent to any out-of-court settlement. In most areas of professional liability, claims have become so large and so serious that insurers insist on the right to settle out of court without the consent of policyholders. At present, some professional liability policies contain the traditional condition, and some do not. The difference is significant to the underwriter.

The legal environment of professional liability has greatly changed in recent years. Both claims frequency and severity have increased as courts have held professionals liable for damages in a wide variety of circumstances.

The medical professional liability exposure is not limited to doctors in private practice, hospitals, and clinics. Many manufacturing plants have first-aid facilities, nurses, or even doctors in attendance. Although these facilities improve the account from a workers compensation standpoint, underwriters should not overlook the professional liability exposure this presents. Other professional liability exposures found in many industrial and commercial firms are directors' and officers' errors and omissions and fiduciary liability for pension plan administrators.

The type of specialty practiced by the particular physician is an important underwriting consideration. Those generally considered in the high-risk category are anesthesiologists, neurosurgeons, plastic surgeons, obstetrician-gynecologists, and cardiovascular surgeons. The general practitioner has much less exposure, particularly if surgery is not performed.

Professional liability underwriters should consider the following attributes of physicians: degrees and/or licenses held, professional organizations in which membership is held, certification, recertification (continuing education), years in practice, type of clientele, associates (that is, fellow workers), and whether the physician practices as an individual or as a member of a professional association. All of these indicate something about the doctor's position within the medical community, which will often play a major role in the defense of suits. This is not to say that a well-known doctor will be found innocent because he or she is popular with other doctors. Nevertheless, the professional reputation of the doctor will be important in malpractice cases, and the insurer is looking for other doctors to speak on behalf of the doctor's professional competence.

The principle that exposure is related to areas of specialty extends to lawyers professional liability as well. A law office that specializes in corporate practice involving many complex cases at one time has much more exposure to loss than a firm dealing in small probate and real estate work exclusively. Once again, the consequences of a mistake must be considered.

This analysis of the clientele of the professional may be extended to insurance agents errors and omissions, real estate brokers errors and omissions, and accountants and auditors errors and omissions as well. Several large accounting firms have had losses that occurred as a result of the accounting firm's certification of the financial statement of a publicly held company. The auditing process that preceded the certification was held by the courts to be negligent and resulted in losses to stockholders and others. The exposure is greater for a firm auditing large public companies than for one keeping the books for a number of small, privately held firms.

Personal Liability Underwriting

Personal liability insurance was designed for the average individual and his or her family. It covers liability that does not arise out of the policyholder's business or profession or out of the use of an auto, an airplane, or a large watercraft. The policy applies to the premises where the policyholder maintains a residence and to the nonbusiness activities of the policyholder and members of the household. Personal liability is part of every homeowners policy and can be purchased with a dwelling fire policy or alone.

Residence Premises Exposures

All property owners, or tenants in control of property, have certain obligations in relation to injury caused to people who come onto the property. A great many residence premises losses are due to an attractive nuisance on the premises. An **attractive nuisance** is an alluring or unusual object or structure (usually man-made) that may entice children to trespass, such as a swimming pool or a treehouse. These hazards are in addition to the basic premises hazards of uneven or icy sidewalks, poorly maintained steps and porches, and poorly lighted hallways. Large sliding glass doors have produced substantial losses when guests have walked or run through them. A significant underwriting factor is the attitude the policyholder exhibits toward his or her home, as evidenced by how the premises are kept and maintained. The underwriter can evaluate these conditions through photographs or personal inspections conducted by the producer or inspection services.

Residence liability losses are infrequent but may be severe; therefore, loss experience can be extremely volatile in all except the larger books of business. The policy is usually sold as a package, but even when sold alone, it commands a relatively low premium. The expense factor of this low premium does not permit extensive investigation and inspection of the individual premises. The result is that the underwriter is faced with a highly unpredictable loss situation that must be underwritten on the basis of scanty information. To combat this problem, some insurers have developed supplementary applications to capture additional information. These forms may ask some of the following questions:

- Are large or potentially vicious dogs present?
- Does the policyholder own or keep horses?
- Does the residence have objects or structures that may attract children, such as a swimming pool, hot tub, backyard gym, swings, slides, or climbing bars?
- Is there an incidental office occupancy exposure?
- Is the residence under construction or being renovated?
- Does the policyholder rent all or part of the dwelling to others?

Personal Activities

A major loss exposure is the personal activities of the policyholder and the resident members of the household. Personal activities are not limited to the residence premises; a personal liability policy extends its protection broadly to all activities not specifically excluded. Insured incidents might include injuries or damages caused by an unlicensed recreational vehicle or property damage intentionally caused by children.

Sports liability is one area of major concern. Injuries caused while golfing, hunting, fishing, and playing team sports are typical of the exposures expected. The off-premises operation of large watercraft and snowmobiles is excluded from coverage unless the policy has been appropriately endorsed. It is usually impossible for the underwriter to find out the activities of the policyholder or the skill with which those known activities are conducted. The only possible resource for this information is the producer, who may know that the applicant has a particularly strong interest in an area that may present a greater-than-expected risk. If available, such information is merely subjective.

Underwriting Considerations

Several avenues the underwriter should investigate that are not directly related to the premises or the activities of the policyholder are occupation, claims history, and credit history.

The occupation of the applicant may indicate that there are possible business exposures on the premises. Some occupations such as sales are conducted to some extent on the premises. Occupations that could possibly increase the traffic and therefore the exposure are less desirable.

Past losses may indicate future losses. For that reason, applications usually request information on all losses during the past several years.

Many insurers have begun using credit information to evaluate applicants. Credit information indicates the extent to which the applicant is in debt, whether bills are paid on time, and the existence of outstanding judgments. Poor credit can indicate an overall level of responsibility. If an applicant is declined or cancelled based on consumer credit information, the insurer must notify the policyholder of this fact in writing and offer him or her the opportunity to review this information with the credit collection information service. Insurance regulators have recently questioned the relevancy and propriety of this use of credit information. Such information will likely be restricted in the future for insurance purposes, unless a direct cause-and-effect relationship can be proved between credit worthiness and loss potential.

Underwriting Umbrella and Excess Liability Policies

Many policyholders find that they need high limits of liability coverage not offered in standard liability policies. Businesses and individuals may have significant assets that need protection from potentially catastrophic liability claims. Many situations may cause severe losses, such as multiple passenger auto accidents, gasoline truck explosions, building collapse, hotel fires, and defective products.

Umbrella Policies

Umbrella liability insurance, both commercial and personal, is designed to cover large, infrequent losses. It does not provide primary insurance, nor does it cover all losses. Most umbrella policies have a deductible or self-insured retention that the policyholder must pay. The retention for commercial forms is usually $10,000, and the retention for the personal form is usually $250.

Umbrella policies are not standardized. The contract language and underwriting rules and guidelines vary from one insurer to another. In most cases, umbrella policies have three basic characteristics. They are designed to do the following:

1. Provide excess liability limits above all specified underlying policies
2. Provide coverage when the aggregate limits of the underlying policies have been exhausted
3. Cover gaps in coverage in the underlying policies

The umbrella policy requires as a condition of coverage that agreed limits of liability be maintained on the underlying policies. If this is not done, the umbrella will respond as though the limits existed. This could potentially create a tremendous uninsured loss.

Underwriting umbrella policies requires a careful analysis of the same exposures covered by the underlying policies. Underwriters must have a thorough knowledge of the coverage provided by underlying contracts and how the particular applicant in question has had its policies modified through endorsements.

Providing an umbrella policy above a private passenger automobile policy may raise some additional concerns. State statutes may require uninsured motorists coverage equal to the bodily injury liability limits of the policy unless rejected by the policyholder. The insurer may not be willing to provide such high limits on uninsured motorists coverage or leave the decision to the discretion of the policyholder. A similar problem exists in those states that permit the stacking of policy limits. In those states, the courts have permitted the policyholder to combine the limits for each vehicle insured under the policy.

Excess Policies

Excess policies are written only to increase the limits of liability on a particular policy. Umbrella policies go one step further by providing coverage even when underlying coverage does not exist. Excess insurance is frequently written on a layered basis, with several policies used to provide very high limits.

As in the case with umbrella policies, loss frequency is not a problem with specific excess insurance, but severity is a potential problem. Reinsurance for both umbrella and specific excess policies usually alleviates the problem. Specific excess policies are seldom underwritten in the sense of traditional risk analysis, but pricing is important. The philosophy is usually that if the primary insurance is acceptable, then the excess is acceptable also. The excess insurer often relies on the underwriting judgment of the primary insurer.

Package Policy Underwriting

Package policies consist of policies containing two or more property and liability coverages in a single policy. Examples abound today, but this was not always the case. Traditionally, then by regulatory mandate, insurers were restricted from combining property and liability coverages into a single policy. States passed legislation in the 1950s that enabled the creation of multi-line policies. Multi-line laws permitted coverage combinations, which better meet the needs of policyholders. Package policies usually provide a discount reflecting the reduced cost of issuing several policies. Policyholders are also less likely to have gaps and overlaps in coverage.

Not all of a policyholder's exposures can be combined in a single policy. Account underwriting is a more appropriate approach. It considers all of the insured's needs as a unit and treats the policies that satisfy those needs as a single account. Insurance producers have encouraged insurers to take an account approach to offering insurance. Producers want to maximize the potential commission available from a single client by providing all of that client's insurance coverages, as well as being assured that client needs are met.

Package and account underwriting make a great deal of sense from an underwriting standpoint. The reduced expenses associated with selling and processing increase the profit potential. More importantly, the larger total premium generated by an account makes it possible to do more in-depth investigative work on the character of the policyholder and the nature of the risk. Many of the factors that distinguish good accounts from bad ones do not relate to any one coverage. Underwriters have learned that the characteristics that make a good property account also make a good account for other lines. Account underwriting allows them to use this knowledge to their advantage.

Combining coverages into a single policy also enhances the spread of risk, reduces adverse selection, and provides an opportunity for greater premium growth. By internally organizing to underwrite package policies and accounts, the insurer can increase its level of service to producers and insureds by creating a single source for all service needs.

The disadvantage of package and account underwriting is that underwriters cannot be selective in the coverages offered to the applicant. Applicants and producers want the insurance program accepted as a whole. As a result, underwriters are forced into a choice between all or nothing. Underwriters placed in this position may have to accept some marginal exposures in order to write the more profitable parts of the account.

Kinds of Package Policies

Underwriting package policies depends to some degree on the kind of package policy. Package policies may be described as (1) a simple combination package policy, (2) a minimum requirement package policy, (3) indivisible package policies, or (4) nonstandard package policies.

A **simple combination package policy** includes two or more standard coverages in one convenient format for the policyholder. There is no package discount, and the underwriting is the same as if separate coverages were requested. This approach provides maximum flexibility to the underwriter, who may choose not to issue the requested form but instead offer a more restricted form if necessary. Each coverage is priced separately, and the package premium is simply a total of the premiums for the individual coverages.

A **minimum requirement package policy** requires the insured to purchase certain minimum coverages. An example is the ISO CPP (commercial package policy) that requires a direct damage coverage form in the commercial property coverage part (or the inland marine physicians and surgeons coverage form) *and* premises and operations liability for the same premises insured under the direct damage coverage.[10] A combination of forms that do not meet these requirements may be referred to as a package but is not eligible for the package discount.

Requiring certain minimum coverages reduces adverse selection. The policy writing, accounting, and billing expenses are less with one package policy than with three or four separate monoline policies. On an entire book of business, this reduces expense costs. The benefits of reducing expense costs and adverse selection are passed along to the insured in the form of a package discount.

Because of this package discount, most insurers try to select above-average risks for these package policies. The underwriting guide usually specifies what is above average in terms of type of business and physical hazards. One inspection may provide sufficient information for property, liability, and crime loss exposures. Since there is a minimum requirement of property and liability coverages, inspections are coordinated. Separate policies often require separate inspections that increase costs.

A package policy requires underwriters to do more than analyze each of the individual coverages. Underwriters have to accept or decline diverse exposures as a unit. A single larger premium must reflect a combination of smaller premiums of varying levels of adequacy.

An **indivisible package policy** provides a broad range of coverages for a single indivisible premium. The businessowners (BOP) and homeowners policies are examples of this type of package. Unlike the minimum requirement policy, the premium is shown only in total. It cannot be separated by coverage. Indivisible package policies permit little coverage selection by the policyholder. This reduces adverse selection, but it also permits almost no flexibility in pricing and coverage. Individual package policies require a large group of insureds whose exposures to loss are essentially identical. This makes them suitable only for personal lines and small commercial accounts. The underwriter's challenge is to evaluate the sum of the various exposures presented by a risk against the single premium to determine acceptability.

Nonstandard package policies are usually manuscript contracts written to the policyholder's and the underwriter's specifications. Maximum flexibility is obtained by eliminating minimum coverages, and pricing tends to be on an individual risk basis. This approach is limited to large policyholders.

Underwriting Considerations

Underwriting decision making is simple on a submission with no adverse exposures. Likewise, the decision is clear if the submission has no redeeming values. The decision becomes difficult when part of the package is acceptable, but the balance is not. Perhaps the property loss exposures of a small manufacturer are minimal because of loss control devices, but the products liability exposure may be great because of the nature of the product. The premises and operations liability exposures of a dry cleaner may be excellent as demonstrated in its loss-free history. The property exposure, on the other hand, may be questionable because the operation uses a solvent with a low flash point.

In these cases, the underwriter must weigh the strengths against the weaknesses, identify any appropriate alternatives, and choose the best one. To do this, an underwriter may ask questions such as the following:

1. What are the limits of liability of each of the sections of the package policy?

2. What are the premiums for each policy section? (This question is inappropriate if the package policy has an indivisible premium, thus complicating the underwriter's decision.)

3. What is the expected frequency of loss for each major policy section?

4. What is the expected severity of loss for each major policy section?

Sometimes conflicting exposures are those in which a low hazard for one line of coverage increases the hazard of another coverage. This may be compounded by the fact that an underwriter may wish to offer suggestions to further lower the exposure in the first category, which increases the exposure in the second line of coverage.

The underwriter also has to determine whether the premium for the low-hazard exposures offsets the inadequate premiums of the higher hazard exposures. Most rating plans contain minimum rates and premiums by coverage for low-hazard risks. They have been developed to cover the expenses of underwriting and issuing a policy, which may account for the majority of the cost in some instances. When a number of coverages are combined into a single package, the minimum rates, being primarily for expense purposes, may provide more than adequate premium when added to other line premiums.

In indivisible premium policies, the underwriter must use imagination to identify unusual exposures for which an indivisible "class rate" does not develop sufficient premium. For example, one such package provided "all-risks" coverage on liquor stores at a premium less than that for mercantile open stock burglary alone.

Package underwriting also provides the opportunity to investigate the management abilities and techniques as they relate to the total loss control of the account. Management influences all areas of loss potential to ensure the continuing profitability of the operation and the development of programs for the recognition and control of loss exposures. The package policy analysis, because it has more expense dollars available from the larger premium, enables the underwriter to look more closely at many aspects of management, including its ability to make a profit. A profitable operation will have both the resources to invest in loss control as well as the desire to do so.

Package policies are more than just a combination of monoline coverages. Underwriters should be aware of the differences between the monoline and package version of forms and the type of applicant each type of form attracts. Some package policies have altered the usual monoline policy provisions to broaden the coverage. For example, the businessowners policy does not contain the coinsurance provisions found in the commercial property coverage form. The package credit provided under the commercial package policy program may give too steep a discount, based on the insurer's own experience, thereby making packaging undesirable. Applicants only eligible for dwelling fire and personal liability policies may present a greater exposure to loss than those eligible for coverage through the homeowners program.

Underwriting Techniques for Small Accounts

Insurers are facing continuing pressure to become more efficient and reduce their expenses. This pressure is especially keen in personal lines, where individual account premiums are small. As a result, expenses tend to consume a larger share of the premium these accounts generate. Small business accounts face similar pressure. In response to pressure from the public and to improve their market share, insurers have sought techniques to reduce the cost of underwriting small accounts.

This effort has produced a process known as **screening**. Underwriting management develops a profile that represents the ideal account in a particular class. Support staff then use this profile to screen new applications and renewals of policies in force. If the account matches the profile closely enough, the insurer issues a policy. A large discrepancy between the account and the profile results in declining the account. Marginal or questionable accounts are referred to an underwriter for a final decision. Some insurers have devised scoring systems to enhance the screening process. Others use a simple count of attributes that match the profile.

Some insurers screen accounts using custom computer software. Others employ customer service representatives or underwriting assistants for this purpose. Agents can also use the profile to evaluate new prospects quickly. Screening has three principal advantages. First, it provides quick answers for most submissions. If the account fits the profile, the insurer can accept very quickly. Only a few borderline accounts will have to wait for the underwriter to review the application and make a decision. Screening also reduces costs. Computers or less skilled personnel handle routine processing and make routine decisions. This frees the underwriters to do what they do best, make decisions when acceptability or rejection is not clear-cut. In this way, insurers use their most expensive talent only when there is a real need for it. If agents use the profile to screen new submissions, the share of acceptable accounts the insurer receives will increase. This will reduce the cost of processing applications the insurer will decline in the end. Finally, screening allows agents to get to know the insurer's target market better. Agents can use the profile to evaluate new accounts without having to submit an application or call the underwriter with questions. This helps the insurer build a better rapport with its producers.

Surety Bond Underwriting

Suretyship is a technique used to provide assurance to one party, called the **obligee**, that another party, called the **principal**, will fulfill an obligation he or she has undertaken to perform. Suretyship is not insurance but is a type of guarantee that insurers often offer in addition to their insurance products. Insurance companies are the leading surety underwriters. Surety bonds may guarantee (1) faithful performance, (2) financial strength, or (3) ability or capacity to perform.

Unique Features of Bonds

Unlike insurance, a surety has recourse for losses to the principal. The principal is primarily responsible to fulfill the contractual obligation—not the surety. Since insurance contracts are between two parties, either may cancel unilaterally. But surety bonds are written for the benefit of a third party to the bond and may be terminated only with the consent of the obligee. Thus, the initial surety underwriting decision must reflect this situation. Surety bonds are often written for an indefinite period, and little rate flexibility exists for some types of bonds. If the surety pays a loss, the principal is usually legally liable to reimburse the surety for the loss, but underwriters must be concerned with the ability of the principal to meet this financial obligation.

Types of Surety Bonds

Surety bonds can be grouped in many different ways. Generally, they are divided into four major categories: (1) public official bonds, (2) court bonds, (3) license and permit bonds, and (4) contract bonds. This section concentrates on contract bond underwriting since it is by far the largest line of surety bonds.

A knowledge of financial analysis is of paramount importance in underwriting contract bonds. Audited statements for at least the past two years provide a starting point, but if the latest statements are more than six months old, an interim statement may be requested. In addition, the underwriter should carefully evaluate the following:

1. *Business experience of the contractor*—This should include the experience of the owners before their association with the firm as well as the business experience of the firm itself.

2. *Performance record*—The underwriter must check the size and growth pattern of individual jobs. A contractor that is growing too rapidly or is bidding on a job that is much larger than or different from his or her customary work must be scrutinized.

3. *Plant and equipment*—The need for a plant may be nonexistent for a road contractor, but a sheet metal shop is essential for an air conditioning contractor. A physical inspection can determine the age and condition of equipment.

4. *Financial resources not included in financial statements*—The status of work in process (or work on hand) is not truly reflected in the financial statements. The profit (or lack of it) from these incomplete projects is not shown and requires further investigation. The terms and conditions of the line of credit available from banks should also be investigated.

One study revealed a statistical analysis of common underwriting measures used by surety underwriters. The study found that an analysis of six variables was 88 percent accurate in predicting whether a particular construction company would fall into the claim category. These six variables are (1) the Dun & Bradstreet rating, (2) the sales growth ratio, (3) the rate of return on net worth, (4) the trade payment rating, (5) the experience of the construction firm, and (6) the bank credit line/net worth ratio.[11] The results of this study indicate that underwriters should pay careful attention to these six variables when underwriting contract bonds.

Summary

Liability underwriting continues to be the most challenging underwriting area. Legislation and court decisions require frequent changes to policy forms and underwriting guidelines. This changing environment requires the underwriter to continually update his or her knowledge and skills to keep up with situations that may arise.

Effective automobile underwriting requires an appreciation of the regulatory and legal environment that affects this line of business. The residual market and how those costs are spread or shared have created a highly charged political environment for insurers in many states. The latitude often granted insurers in underwriting private passenger automobile insurance is minimal. Several states do not permit the rejection of applicants. Some states limit the underwriting criteria to just a few factors.

Commercial automobile underwriting uses fewer controversial factors but is influenced to some extent by regulatory requirements on personal automobiles. Underwriters look at the weight of the vehicle and its use, including the radius of operation and type of materials carried. Effective loss control programs can significantly affect the profitability of a commercial automobile risk. Motor carrier laws may impose responsibilities on insurers that were not contracted for as part of the insurance. Reimbursement for such claims is permitted but may not be realistically possible given the circumstances.

Until recently workers compensation insurance has been largely unprofitable. Insurers that write workers compensation coverage reduced the restrictions on the circumstances under which coverage will be offered and on which classes are desirable. Even with the legal changes and rate increases, the underwriter must extensively investigate and evaluate the hazards present to ensure that the applicant can be priced profitably. The Occupational Safety and Health Act has not affected the work environment like its writers had envisioned. The act has created a resource of statistics that can be used by an insurer in evaluating a class of business and by an underwriter in evaluating an individual applicant. Many insurers purposely avoid policyholders who have maritime-related occupations. Insurers may not discover that these exposures exist until a claim is presented.

Many of the hazards identified in workers compensation exposures are also present for the general liability underwriter. The principal difference is that the general public rather than the policyholder's employees is exposed to injury. Underwriters need to know the hazards presented by the policyholder's premises, products, and operations. The CGL includes coverage for liability assumed under incidental contracts.

The standard of care required of a professional is greater than that of an ordinary individual. Professional liability insurance covers those incidents that arise out of a policyholder's professional responsibilities. Because of the expertise required in writing this coverage, a relatively small number of insurers is actively involved in providing this coverage.

Umbrella and excess policies are available to provide extra large limits. Personal and commercial umbrella policies provide liability coverage over certain required policies as well as coverage when no coverage exists. Excess policies are usually found only in the commercial market and provide high limits only for specific policies.

Several definitions of package policies exist. However defined, package policies present the underwriter with a number of challenges and opportunities. One challenge is to evaluate several diverse exposures in a single account. The underwriter must weigh the loss potential from these hazards to determine whether the account will be profitable overall. An opportunity is to perform a thorough investigation on the entire account, which may not have been cost-justified if the account had been written on a monoline basis.

Surety bonds are not insurance contracts but are so often sold by insurers that their discussion is pertinent here. There are a number of different types of bonds. This chapter highlighted the underwriting of one of these types, contract bonds.

This chapter focused on the considerations that an underwriter should make in evaluating liability and package policies. It is by no means exhaustive in its approach. An underwriter should have a good grasp of exposure analysis and insurance coverages as well as an appreciation of the role of the loss control engineer and the claims process.

Chapter Notes

1. *1997 Property/Casualty Insurance Facts* (New York, NY: Insurance Information Institute, 1997), p. 84. *1993 Property Casualty Insurance Facts*, p. 75.

2. *FC&S Bulletins*, Personal Lines, Personal Auto, February 1996, D. 1-2.

3. Robert E. Keeton and Jeffrey O'Connell, *Basic Protection for the Traffic Victim* (Boston, MA: Little, Brown and Co., 1965).

4. *1997 Property/Casualty Insurance Facts*, p. 90.

5. Commercial General Liability Coverage Form, Insurance Services Office, CG 00 01 0196, p. 11.

6. Greeman v. Yuba Power Products, Inc., 59 Cal 2nd 57 (1963).

7. Denny v. Ford Motor Co., 84 NY 2d, 1018 (1995).

8. *1997 Property/Casualty Insurance Facts* (New York, NY: Insurance Information Institute, 1996), pp. 13-14.

9. W. Heinrich, *Industrial Accident Prevention*, 4th ed. (New York, NY: McGraw-Hill, 1959), p. 13.

10. *Commercial Lines Manual*, Section Nine Multiline (New York, NY: Insurance Services Office, 1985), p. 2

11. Richard W. Filippone, "Statistical Analysis of Some Common Underwriting Measures Used by Contract Surety Underwriters," *Best's Review, Property/Casualty Insurance Edition* (December 1976), p. 22.

Chapter 7

Loss Control and Premium Auditing

An insurer's success often depends on the quality of its loss control and premium auditing functions. Both of these functions involve direct contact with the policyholder and provide the insurer with additional information about the quality of the business written. Such contact also presents opportunities to provide service to the policyholder and build a stronger relationship over time. Loss control and premium auditing, which were briefly introduced in prior chapters of this text, are described in more detail here.

Loss Control

Loss control measures may be directed toward lowering loss frequency, lowering loss severity, or a combination of the two. **Loss prevention** is defined as those measures intended to lower the frequency of losses—in other words, to prevent losses from occurring. **Loss reduction** is defined as those measures intended to lower the severity of the losses that do occur. The term **loss control** refers collectively to loss prevention and loss reduction.

Loss control has been a function of property-liability insurers throughout most of the history of the industry. Some early fire insurers even maintained fire-fighting organizations to extinguish fires in the properties they insured. Although modern insurers no longer maintain fire extinguishment services, they continue to play a major role in fire prevention by inspecting insured properties and providing advisory services to policyholders. Moreover, insurers engage in many other loss control activities that relate to the increasingly complex loss exposures confronting modern society.

Objectives of Insurer Loss Control Activities

Insurers conduct loss control activities for several reasons. These reasons correspond to the overall objectives of insurers stated in Chapter 1.

Profit Objectives

An insurer's loss control activities can help the insurer to reach its profit objectives in several ways.

By inspecting the premises and operations of those who apply for insurance, trained loss control representatives (also known as safety engineers or loss control engineers) can improve the information on which the underwriting department will base its decisions about whether to accept or reject applicants and about how to price coverage. Better underwriting information enables the insurer to do a better job of selecting policyholders at a price that will produce an underwriting profit.

Apart from supporting the underwriting decision-making process, loss control personnel can recommend ways in which a marginal risk can be modified through loss control measures to become an acceptable risk, thereby increasing the insurer's premium volume. Unless the insurer can reach its targets for premium volume, it probably cannot reach its profit objectives.

Once the decision has been made to insure an applicant, the loss control function can continue to monitor the policyholder and suggest appropriate loss control measures as the policyholder's loss exposures change. By assisting policyholders in this manner, loss control personnel can reduce losses that the insurer must pay, thereby helping to keep the insurer's book of business profitable.

The loss control representative, through the influence of the insurer, can encourage policyholders to pursue loss control activities. Despite their already substantial efforts, many loss control representatives believe that an opportunity exists to improve safety and that the insurance business should encourage additional loss control activities.[1]

For some insurers, the loss control function might actually serve as a direct source of income. Traditionally, insurers provided loss control services only to their policyholders and did not charge a separate fee in addition to the policy premium. Many insurers today offer their loss control services on a fee basis to firms that have chosen to retain, or "self-insure," their losses. Similarly, some insurers provide their own policyholders with supplemental loss control services for a fee in addition to the policy premium. These services can be sophisticated. Several major insurers offer a "cafeteria" type plan in which the policyholder has access to a variety of experts such as nurses, ergonomic specialists, engineers, attorneys, and chemists.

Because loss control services are sold separately from insurance coverage, they are sometimes referred to as being "unbundled." Insurers offering unbundled loss control services view the sale of such services as a new source of income to bolster profits and help support the sophisticated personnel and equipment needed to cope with the complex loss control problems brought about by modern technology and modern law.

Meeting Customer Demand

Recently, many insurers have substantially increased their loss control activities because of an increased demand from insurance consumers, particularly commercial and industrial firms. This increased demand has resulted partly from an increased awareness of the cost of accidents and partly from the pressures of legislation such as the Occupational Safety and Health Act, the Consumer Products Safety Act, the Comprehensive Environmental Response Compensation and Liability Act, and the Americans with Disabilities Act (ADA). The rapid increase in the size of liability judgments, especially for products liability, has also been a factor in the increased demand for loss control services.

Some of the benefits policyholders may realize from implementing a proactive loss control policy include improving the account's desirability to underwriters; lowering insurance premiums; experiencing less disruption to operations following accidents; fulfilling occupational safety and health standards; complying with local, state, and federal laws; and improving the account's financial performance.

By satisfying customer needs for loss control services, insurers can attract new customers, retain satisfied customers, and gain a competitive advantage over insurers that do not provide the services that customers need and want.

Meeting Legal Requirements

Some states have statutes or regulations requiring insurers to provide a minimum level of loss control service to commercial policyholders. When an insurer is operating in a jurisdiction with such requirements, compliance with the law becomes an important objective that supports the insurer's overall objective of fulfilling all legal requirements the insurer may face.

Another objective related to compliance with the law is to provide loss control services competently to minimize the possibility of errors and omissions claims by policyholders or any other parties alleging that they were injured because of the insurer's negligence. This errors and omissions liability exposure is also a factor that may influence an insurance company's decision about what types or levels of loss control services to provide. A later section of this chapter discusses this factor in more detail.

Humanitarian and Societal Concerns

Accidental losses affect society at all levels. An occupational injury may cause pain, suffering, and loss of income for one individual, or a fire loss to a large factory may cause loss of business income, employee layoffs, and contingent business income losses for suppliers of the firm. The sum of all accidental losses has a profound adverse effect on society in general.

By assisting policyholders in preventing or lessening accidental losses, insurers pursue humanitarian objectives and benefit society at large. Although an insurer's payment of insurance proceeds for accidental losses can help an individual, a business, or society to recover from accidental losses, preventing the same losses is generally a preferable alternative.

Cooperation Between Loss Control and Other Functions

An insurer's loss control efforts are most effective when they complement the activities of other departments within the insurer. Loss control's principal opportunities for cooperation are with underwriting, marketing, premium auditing, and claims.

An insurer and its policyholders can also benefit from cooperative relationships between the insurer's loss control function and organizations outside the insurer. These outside organizations include independent agents or brokers, as well as trade associations that engage in activities related to loss control.

Loss Control and Underwriting

As described above, loss control personnel can provide information to underwriters that will enable them to make better underwriting decisions. Principally, this information consists of field inspection reports on the premises and operations of new applicants and existing policyholders who wish to renew their policies. In addition, loss control can provide technical support to underwriting on a variety of subjects, such as fire hazards of new building materials, health hazards of materials or production processes, and new techniques or equipment for materials handling.

Loss control representatives are often the only ones in the insurance company who have actually met the new insured. This contact helps produce a personal bond that can later be important when difficult situations arise or if specific information is needed from the policyholder.

Loss control can also assist underwriters in modifying the loss exposures of an applicant to qualify the applicant for acceptance by the underwriters. After an applicant has been accepted, loss control can be instrumental in helping the policyholder to remain within underwriting guidelines and thereby qualified for policy renewal. In some instances, loss control may even be called on to "rehabilitate" a marginal account that underwriting has already accepted because of competitive considerations.

In order to provide these support services to underwriting, loss control personnel, in addition to possessing technical skills, must be effective communicators. Inspection reports should give the underwriter a clear picture of the applicant's hazards in terms that the underwriter will understand. Loss control personnel must also be able to communicate effectively with policyholders. In many cases, a loss control representative is the main communications link between the underwriter and the policyholder.

Loss Control and Marketing

Loss control can be an important ally in helping the insurer's marketing staff meet its objectives. By inspecting an applicant's premises and recommending ways of reducing hazards, loss control personnel can make the difference between the applicant's being rejected or accepted by the insurer's underwriting department. By making marginal accounts acceptable, loss control helps marketing to reach its sales goals. Loss control can also help marketing by proving to the policyholder that it understands the insured's process and the hazards associated with it. The loss control representative can offer tangible advice on improving safety. This expertise is particularly important for accounts that are eager for this type of help.

After applicants become policyholders, loss control can play a key role in retaining them as customers of the insurer. In fact, a commercial policyholder may actually have more regular contact with the insurer's loss control representatives than with any other employee of the insurer. By providing professional and courteous service that the policyholder perceives as an added value of the insurance policy, loss control personnel can create customer goodwill.

Finally, through their direct contact with policyholders, loss control representatives can learn what insurance coverages or services policyholders need or want. If loss control representatives convey this information to the appropriate marketing or sales personnel, it can assist the marketing department in either meeting the specific needs of a single policyholder or developing product enhancements that will appeal to many insureds.

For example, a loss control survey may reveal that the policyholder has acquired new property that is not adequately covered under the existing policy. If conveyed to the appropriate marketing staff, this information might lead to the sale of additional coverage to that policyholder. If the same problem is experienced by several insureds, that information could lead to a decision to revise the insurer's policy forms to provide better coverage for newly acquired property.

Loss Control and Premium Auditing

In one respect, the jobs of loss control representatives and premium auditors are similar, since both visit the policyholder's premises and have direct contact with the policyholder. The difference in the information each develops is that loss control representatives typically visit the policyholder at the beginning of the policy term, while premium auditors visit at the end of the policy term. Since premium auditors often arrive after it is too late to correct record-keeping deficiencies resulting from the policyholder's ignorance or misunderstanding, loss control personnel can use the opportunity provided by the inspection visit to pave the way for the premium audit.

To exploit this opportunity, however, premium auditors must communicate their needs to the loss control representatives. If aware of the need, for example, loss control representatives can note the location of the accounting records and the name of the person to contact at audit time. They can also record the names, titles, and duties of active executive officers. Their description of operations could be a starting point for the auditor's classification of exposures. Loss control representatives might even estimate the payroll by classification or at least the number of employees per department. They can report the existence of any new operations. If properly informed, they can also advise the policyholder concerning record-keeping requirements and the need for certificates of insurance. Finally, they can offer the assistance of the insurer's premium auditors to deal with any complex questions regarding the necessary audit. Potential problems can therefore be prevented before it is too late.

Loss Control and Claims

A partnership between loss control and claims can be just as valuable to an insurer as the relationship between loss control and underwriting, marketing, or premium auditing. The loss control department needs claims experience information to direct resources and efforts to crucial areas. The claims department relies on the loss control function for exposure data and background information that may support the adjusting process if a loss occurs. Claims and loss control personnel should regularly communicate to discuss common concerns and to review loss cases.

The claims experience information that can be useful to the loss control function includes frequency and severity of losses by line of insurance, by cause of loss, by kind of business engaged in by the insured, and by worker occupation. Regarding individual accidents, particularly in the workers compensation line, the loss control function can also benefit from information about the type of accident, the body part injured, how the accident occurred, and perhaps other details from the adjuster's report. This information can be used by the loss control staff to (1) identify areas for research, (2) target loss exposures for additional attention, (3) identify characteristics associated with particular types of losses, and (4) develop possible alternatives to control losses.

Loss control personnel are usually well informed in engineering, mechanical, and technological areas that may not be familiar to claims personnel. Thus, loss control specialists can assist claims personnel in solving technical problems that accompany claims. The loss control department can provide codes, standards, technical opinions, laboratory analyses, and other assistance to the claims department in the investigation and settlement of losses. A loss control specialist can design product recall procedures to assist claims personnel and insureds in controlling specific product losses.

Loss Control and Agents and Brokers

The traditional role of producers with regard to loss control was to encourage the support of the policyholder for loss control activities and to coordinate the efforts of the insurer's loss control personnel with those of the insured. This traditional role is still filled by producers and may be the only role played by many small to medium-sized agencies or brokerage firms. However, larger producers have progressed well beyond this traditional role.

Many large agencies and brokerages maintain their own loss control departments, and some of them are able to furnish services on a par with those offered by insurance companies. If a policyholder is receiving loss control services from both the insurer and its agent or broker, the loss control entities of both organizations should strive to coordinate their efforts for the mutual benefit of all parties involved, particularly the policyholder.

Loss Control and Trade Associations

Apart from their individual efforts to reduce the losses of their policyholders, many insurers work collectively to improve the effectiveness of loss control throughout society by participating in certain industry associations. General trade associations promote loss control in addition to performing many other functions; specialized trade associations are devoted almost entirely to loss control.

General Trade Associations

The loss control activities of general trade associations are usually restricted to (1) lobbying for loss control laws, (2) sponsoring public information campaigns to encourage loss control, and (3) conducting research in loss prevention and reduction. Such functions can be illustrated by some of the activities of one of these trade associations, the American Insurance Association (AIA). Other associations perform similar functions.

The AIA's Engineering and Safety Service provides educational materials and educational conferences for member companies. It also provides material to legislators and other government officials. Among its services is the National Building Code, a model code designed for adoption by local governments. The code requires building features that would reduce the loss of both lives and property. A second model code published by AIA, the Fire Prevention Code, emphasizes hazards not directly caused by building features, including the hazards resulting from the manufacture, handling, and storage of toxic or highly combustible materials.

Other insurer trade associations involved in loss control, lobbying, public information programs, or research include the Alliance of American Insurers, the National Association of Independent Insurers, and the Insurance Information Institute. Producer trade associations, such as the Independent Insurance Agents of America and the Professional Insurance Agents, also support loss control efforts through lobbying activities and public information programs, such as fire or theft prevention campaigns.

Specialized Trade Associations

Several trade associations are devoted exclusively or almost exclusively to loss control. One such organization is the Insurance Institute for Highway Safety (IIHS). The IIHS is supported by general insurance trade associations and several individual insurers. Its purpose is to identify, evaluate, and develop ways to reduce human loss and property loss caused by traffic accidents. The results of IIHS research are made available to legislators, other government officials, and persons interested in traffic safety.

Other specialized loss control organizations supported by insurers include the National Automobile Theft Bureau, which conducts stolen vehicle recovery and auto theft prevention activities, and the Insurance Committee for Arson Control, which serves as a catalyst for insurers' anti-arson efforts and a liaison with government agencies and other groups devoted to arson control.

Insurers, along with other contributors, also support loss prevention agencies not directly affiliated with insurance. Examples of such organizations are the National Safety Council (NSC) and the National Fire Protection Association (NFPA). The NSC publishes safety materials of all kinds and conducts a public information and publicity program in support of safety. The NFPA serves as a source of information on fire prevention and protection, develops and publishes fire safety standards, and sponsors public educational programs.

Loss Control Services Provided by Insurers

An insurer's loss control efforts generally correspond to three levels of professional safety practice: (1) physical surveys, (2) risk analysis and improvement, or (3) safety management programming. These general levels of service should be viewed as points of reference on a continuum of services. In actual practice, the level of service an insurer provides to a particular policyholder is often somewhere between two of these reference points.

Physical Surveys

The first level of service—**physical surveys**—mainly consists of collecting underwriting information on a customer's loss exposures, such as building construction, worker occupations, site diagrams, fire protection systems installed, and so on. This level of service does not require highly trained or experienced loss control representatives. Consequently, less experienced personnel are often assigned to this type of work.

On a typical survey, a loss control representative inspects the customer's premises on a walking tour and interviews the customer's management to discover details that may not be apparent from the tour. The loss control representative seeks to evaluate physical hazards affecting the customer's exposures to the following:

- Fire, windstorm, water damage, burglary, and other causes of property loss
- Legal liability arising out of premises, operations, products, completed operations, automobile, mobile equipment, environmental impairment, and other sources of liability
- Employee injuries relative to working conditions, machinery hazards, and employee safety practices

In addition to evaluating physical hazards, the loss control representative seeks to evaluate management commitment to loss control and employee attitudes toward appropriate safety behavior patterns. Thus, the loss control representative may obtain insight into the possibility and extent of both moral and morale hazards.

At the conclusion of the tour, the loss control representative holds a general review with the manager responsible for these types of concerns to ask questions, discuss loss exposures, and share suggestions for controlling hazards identified during the survey. After leaving the customer's premises, the loss control representative organizes the information in a formal report. An example of a loss control report is shown in Exhibit 7-1.

Many insurers will also generate recommendations, suggestions that can help the customer eliminate or control loss exposures. Typically, recommendations are generated when a loss control representative identifies a condition that falls below a satisfactory level. With mercantile risks, for instance, a common recommendation is to control slip-and-fall perils by improving the maintenance program for aisles, steps, and stairwells. To organize the suggested improvements, each recommendation is identified by the month and year and given a unique identification number. A review of this list for an account will indicate the cooperation of the insured in improving its loss exposures.

If the customer has requested insurance on a building or buildings valued in excess of a particular threshold, such as $100,000 or $250,000, the survey report may also include a property valuation. Typically, property valuations are performed by using construction cost estimating systems that are available from various vendors. The characteristics of the building that are needed for applying the construction cost information are obtained in the process of the physical survey. By determining the building's actual cash value, functional value, or full replacement cost (depending on which of these measures will be the basis for insurance), the appropriate amount of insurance can be determined.

Several benefits are derived from physical surveys. The insurer's underwriters can read the survey report and gain a better understanding of the loss exposures being insured. The policyholder can also gain a better understanding of its loss exposures and what steps could be taken to prevent or minimize losses, comply with applicable laws and regulations, and provide a better working environment for employees. All of these factors can contribute to higher employee morale and productivity. If a property valuation is part of the survey, the policyholder can be more certain of an adequate recovery in the event of a total loss and less likely to incur a coinsurance penalty in the event of a partial loss.

Exhibit 7-1
Short Form Loss Control Report

IIA Insurance Companies
720 Providence Road, Malvern, PA 19355

INSURED
TERRY'S CASUAL WEAR

PERSON INTERVIEWED
Theresa Boykin

MAILING ADDRESS
4814 Hwy. 17 South, N. Myrtle Beach, S.C.

SURVEY DATE
6/28/X1

LOCATION SURVEYED
SAME

LOSS CONTROL REPRESENTATIVE
JOHN HENDERSON

POLICY NUMBER
CRO7234525

EXPLAIN OR MAKE RECOMMENDATIONS FOR ALL CIRCLE ○ ANSWERS

A. RISK OVERVIEW

RISK HAZARD	HAZARD CONTROL	PREMISES CONDITION	HOUSEKEEPING	PRIOR LOSS	OPINION OF RISK
☑ Low ☐ Medium ○ High	☑ Good ☐ Fair ○ Poor	☑ Good ☐ Fair ○ Poor	☑ Good ☐ Fair ○ Poor	◉ Yes ☐ No	☑ Good ☐ Fair ○ Poor

B. DESCRIPTION OF OPERATIONS

1. Description of business and/or operations:
   Retail clothing store

C. GENERAL DATA

1. Insured is: ☑ Owner ☐ Tenant ☐ Lessee ○ Other ____
2. Insured is: ☐ Corporation ☐ Partnership ☐ Individual ☑ Yes ○ No
3. Yrs. in business __5__ At this location __3__ 8. Does business appear successful? ☑ Yes ○ No
4. Business hours: __10__ to __11__ 9. Management attitude satisfactory? ☑ Yes ◉ No
5. Estimated gross annual sales $ __225,000__ 10. Other occupants in building?
6. Neighborhood is: ☑ Commercial ☐ Rural ☐ Residential ☐ Industrial If YES, describe ____
7. Neighborhood is: ☑ Stable

Continued on next page.

BUILDING

1. Year built ___3___
2. Building height (stories & ft./story): ___1___
3. Exterior wall construction: Frame _Wood_ Cover _Wood shingle_
4. Floor construction _Wood_
5. Roof const.: Support _Wood_ Deck _Metal_ Cover _Metal_
6. Area (include basement only if finished): ___1,320___ sq. ft.
7. ☐ Fire Resistive   ☐ Ordinary
   ☐ Non-Combustible   ☑ Frame

8. Vertical openings:
   - Stairways protected? ☐ Yes ○ No ☑ None
   - Elevators protected: ☐ Yes ○ No ☑ None
   - Elevators: # of passengers _____ # of freight _____
9. Int. finish: Walls _Wood_ Ceiling _S/R_
10. Building condition satisfactory? ☑ Yes ○ No
11. Basement in building? ○ Yes ☑ No
    If YES, ☐ Full ☐ Partial _____%
             ○ Finished ☐ Unfinished

HAZARDS

1. Heating type: _FA central loc elsewhere_
   A. Fuel ☐ Gas ☑ Electric ☐ Wood/Coal ☐ LP Gas ☐ Oil
   B. Appears safely arranged? _not seen_ ☐ Yes ○ No
2. Air Conditioning? ☑ Yes ○ No
   Type: ☑ Central ☐ Package ☐ Portable ○ Other
3. Electrical type: ☐ Conduit ☑ Romex ☐ _____
   A. Overcurrent Protection: ☑ Cir. Brkrs. ☐ Fuses
   B. Appear safely arranged? ☑ Yes ○ No
4. Are the following satisfactory?
   A. Housekeeping ☑ Yes ○ No
   B. Maintenance ☑ Yes ○ No
   C. Trash Removal ☑ Yes ○ No
   D. Smoking Control ☑ Yes ○ No
   E. Flam./Combust. liquids ☐ Yes ○ No ☑ None noted
   F. Welding/hot work ☐ Yes ○ No ☑ None noted
   G. Other special hazards ☐ Yes ○ No ☑ None noted

FIRE PROTECTION

1. Risk within city limits? ☑ Yes ○ No
2. Fire Department: ☐ None ☑ Paid ☐ Volunteer
3. Distance to fire dept. _1/3_ Miles
4. Number of hydrants and distance _1 at 50'; 1 at 370'_
5. Adequate fire extinguishers? ☑ Yes ○ No
   Size and type: _2A_
6. Extinguishers properly tagged and serviced? ☑ Yes ○ No
7. Sprinkler system? ○ Yes ☑ No
   A. Coverage: ○ Partial ☐ Full _____%
   B. Alarm: ☐ Local ☐ Central Station
8. Fire detection/alarm system? ○ Yes ☐ No
9. Watchman service? ○ Yes ☐ No
10. Fire Dept. name and class:
    N. Myrtle Beach

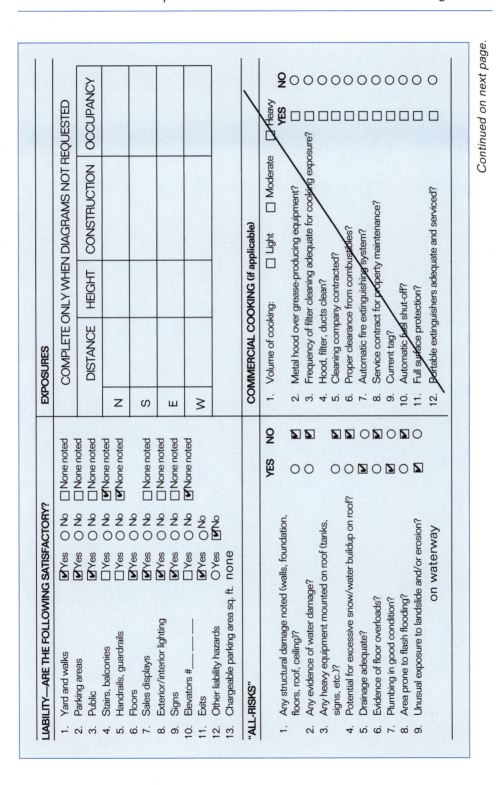

LIABILITY—ARE THE FOLLOWING SATISFACTORY?

1. Yard and walks — ☑Yes ○No ☐None noted
2. Parking areas — ☑Yes ○No ☐None noted
3. Public — ☑Yes ○No ☐None noted
4. Stairs, balconies — ☐Yes ○No ☑None noted
5. Handrails, guardrails — ☐Yes ○No ☑None noted
6. Floors — ☑Yes ○No ☐None noted
7. Sales displays — ☑Yes ○No ☐None noted
8. Exterior/interior lighting — ☑Yes ○No ☐None noted
9. Signs — ☑Yes ○No ☐None noted
10. Elevators # _____ — ☐Yes ○No ☑None noted
11. Exits — ☑Yes ○No
12. Other liability hazards — ○Yes ☑No
13. Chargeable parking area sq. ft. none

EXPOSURES

COMPLETE ONLY WHEN DIAGRAMS NOT REQUESTED

	DISTANCE	HEIGHT	CONSTRUCTION	OCCUPANCY
N				
S				
E				
W				

"ALL-RISKS"

		YES	NO
1.	Any structural damage noted (walls, foundation, floors, roof, ceiling)?	○	○
2.	Any evidence of water damage?	○	○
3.	Any heavy equipment mounted on roof (tanks, signs, etc.)?	○	☑
4.	Potential for excessive snow/water buildup on roof?	○	☑
5.	Drainage adequate?	☑	○
6.	Evidence of floor overloads?	○	☑
7.	Plumbing in good condition?	☑	○
8.	Area prone to flash flooding?	○	☑
9.	Unusual exposure to landslide and/or erosion?	☑	○

on waterway

COMMERCIAL COOKING (if applicable)

1. Volume of cooking: ☐Light ☐Moderate ☑Heavy

YES NO

2. Metal hood over grease-producing equipment?
3. Frequency of filter cleaning adequate for cooking exposure?
4. Hood, filter, ducts clean?
5. Cleaning company contracted?
6. Proper clearance from combustibles?
7. Automatic fire extinguishing system?
8. Service contract for property maintenance?
9. Current tag?
10. Automatic fuel shut-off?
11. Full surface protection?
12. Portable extinguishers adequate and serviced?

Continued on next page.

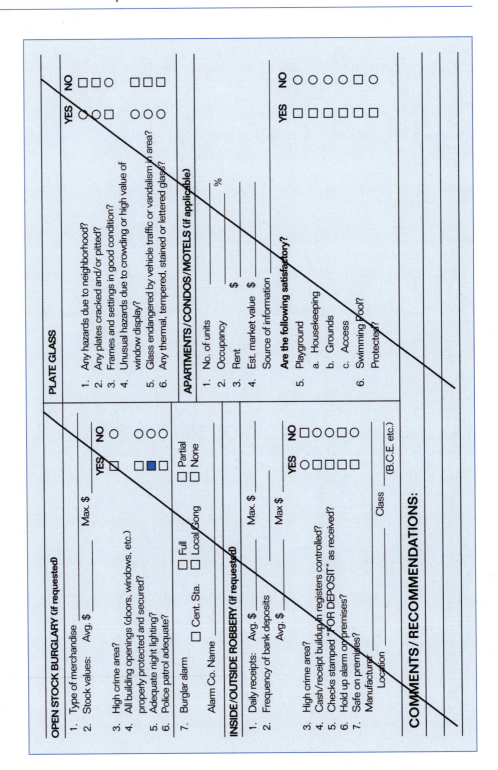

OPEN STOCK BURGLARY (if requested)

1. Type of merchandise
2. Stock values: Avg. $ _____   Max. $ _____

                        YES   NO

3. High crime area?
4. All building openings (doors, windows, etc.) properly protected and secured?
5. Adequate night lighting?
6. Police patrol adequate?
7. Burglar alarm   ☐ Full   ☐ Partial
   ☐ Cent. Sta.   ☐ Local Gong   ☐ None
   Alarm Co. Name _____

INSIDE/OUTSIDE ROBBERY (if requested)

1. Daily receipts: Avg. $ _____   Max. $ _____
2. Frequency of bank deposits   Avg. $ _____   Max. $ _____

                        YES   NO

3. High crime area?
4. Cash/receipt buildup in registers controlled?
5. Checks stamped "FOR DEPOSIT" as received?
6. Hold up alarm on premises?
7. Safe on premises?
   Manufacturer _____   Class _____
   Location _____   (B.C.E. etc.)

COMMENTS / RECOMMENDATIONS:

PLATE GLASS

                        YES   NO

1. Any hazards due to neighborhood?
2. Any plates cracked and/or pitted?
3. Frames and settings in good condition?
4. Unusual hazards due to crowding or high value of window display?
5. Glass endangered by vehicle traffic or vandalism in area?
6. Any thermal, tempered, stained or lettered glass?

APARTMENTS/CONDOS/MOTELS (if applicable)

1. No. of units _____
2. Occupancy _____ %
3. Rent $ _____
4. Est. market value $ _____
   Source of information _____

                        YES   NO

5. **Are the following satisfactory?**
   Playground
   a. Housekeeping
   b. Grounds
   c. Access
6. Swimming Pool?
   Protected?

Operations

Your insured is a corporation that has been in business for five years. It has been in business at the present location since the shopping mall was constructed three years ago. The mall has numerous small shops and restaurants built up on a boardwalk over a small inlet, approximately 3,000 feet from the Atlantic ocean. Insured leases this space for a clothing store, selling ladies moderately low-priced casual wear and a few accessories, such as purses, belts, etc. Also, there is a small line of costume jewelry in one case at the counter.

Building

The building is three years old, of wood frame construction, and found to be in good condition and well maintained. The building is on wood pylons, and a portion of the building is above the actual water (see diagram and photo).

Heating and Air Conditioning

Heat and air-conditioning are ducted from elsewhere in the mall and are said to be water-controlled and thought to be electric; however, the actual unit was not located. The insured said she believes the actual units are near Hwy. 17, several hundred feet from the building.

Wiring

Wiring is romex with breaker protection. This appears to be in good condition and is three years old.

Protection

Insured is located in North Myrtle beach and the North Myrtle Beach fire department will respond there. No unusual fire department obstructions were noted.

Portable extinguishers were posted all around the mall area, and these were properly tagged and serviced. Also, there is a Z100 Moose digital alarm system protecting the shop. This has heat detectors as well as infrared motion detectors and insured states she believes this is directly monitored by the fire department. The alarm system was installed by the owners of the mall, and apparently these are present in every location.

Much of the mall is sprinklered, and there is a PIV valve 50 feet outside of insured's location; however, this particular shop is not sprinklered. There are security guards employed by the mall, and the insured said that they patrol this area 24 hours a day.

Liability

The shop was in good condition from a liability standpoint. Stock is neatly stored and arranged in a clutter-free manner. Floor covering, lighting, and egress are good, and there are marked exits. All parking is controlled by the mall, and there is no parking area controlled by the insured.

Losses

Ms. Boykin states no losses have occurred under these coverages. They did have one business interruption loss during Hugo in 1989.

Comments

Due to premises and building conditions, as well as good controls and the nature of insured's operation, this risk rates good for all coverages surveyed.

Note

Initially, we visited insured on 6/20; however, Ms. Boykin was not in. We phoned back on several occasions before she contacted us on 6/28 to obtain loss and other information.

Recommendations

None are deemed necessary at this time.

Continued on next page.

Exhibit 7-1, continued

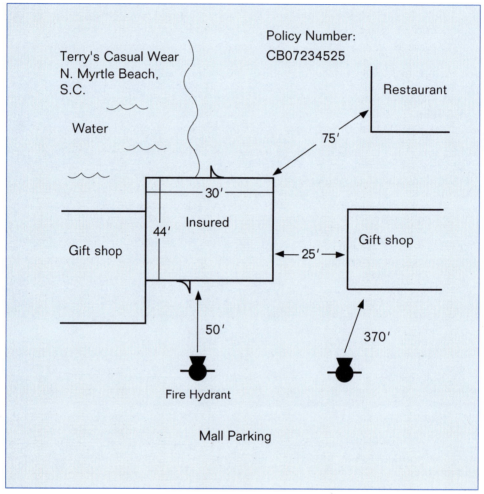

Risk Analysis and Improvement

The second level of insurer loss control service—risk analysis and risk improvement—advances the first level to what might be considered the normal
practice for most insurers. In addition to completing a physical survey and
hazard evaluation, as described above, the insurer's loss control personnel
analyze the customer's loss history and submit formal written recommendations to the business owner or manager on ways to reduce hazards. Ordinarily,
a loss control representative will contact the policyholder within sixty to
ninety days later to check the policyholder's progress in complying with the
insurer's recommendations.

To support the risk analysis and improvement process, the insurer's loss control personnel may provide one or more of a variety of training, informational, or counseling services. Some common examples of these services are described below. Other, more specialized services are available from some insurers.

Safety Programs

A **safety program** is a series of presentations on any of various safety-related subjects that is intended to raise workers' awareness of loss exposures and appropriate safety behaviors. Typical subjects are fire safety, driver safety, and machine operation safety. The selection of subjects is based on an analysis of the policyholder's loss exposures or trends in loss experience. Priority is given to subjects that could significantly improve the policyholder's loss experience. Films, slide shows, and videotape programs may be shown in conjunction with training programs or lent to policyholders as requested.

The objectives of safety programs are to develop positive safety attitudes among all workers, to improve workers' understanding of safety-related matters, and to help workers accept responsibility for their role in the organization's safety program. Ultimately, the policyholder may be expected to integrate these objectives into its own goals and not to rely on the insurer's personnel except for special or more complex topics.

To prepare the policyholder's managers for assuming a leadership role in loss control matters, the insurer may also conduct supervisory safety training sessions in addition to the training programs for all employees.

Technical Information Resources

Many insurers support their policyholders' loss control efforts by serving as a convenient source of technical information. The information sought by the policyholder might relate to specific hazards and appropriate controls, the interpretation of standards, or particular safety management products or suppliers. By providing technical information needed by the policyholder, the insurer helps the policyholder save time and effort in obtaining data needed to make informed loss control decisions. The insurer also builds a working relationship with the policyholder that can help to retain the policyholder's account.

Fire Protection Systems Testing and Evaluation

Fire protection (and detection) systems must be regularly tested in order to ascertain their reliability during emergencies. Many insurer loss control departments enter into service contracts with their policyholders or other clients to provide periodic testing and maintenance for such systems. The insurer's principal concerns are whether the system will respond in an emergency and whether the system is properly designed for the client's current loss exposures.

Pre-Construction Counseling

When business owners are considering expanding existing facilities or constructing new structures, they often overlook the connection between construction features and insurance rates. Generally, rating credits may be given for noncombustible or fire-resistive construction, sprinkler systems, smoke detectors, burglar alarms, security hardware, and other features. A pre-construction review of the drawings and specifications by the insurer allows the policyholder to see how its insurance rates and underwriting acceptability will be affected by the new construction. Any plan alterations desired by the policyholder can then be made at minimal cost before construction begins.

Safety Management Programming

The third level of insurer loss control services—safety management programming—has become more prominent among advanced loss control operations. This activity is usually coordinated by senior staff members, often called loss control consultants, who have the advanced technical and communications skills needed for this type of work.

The **safety management programming** process begins with a complete evaluation of the policyholder's operations, just as in risk analysis and improvement loss control activities. After reviewing the evaluation with the policyholder, loss control consultants assist the policyholder in establishing loss control objectives, selecting appropriate loss control measures, organizing the resources necessary to implement the chosen loss control measures, and setting up procedures for monitoring the program.

Ordinarily, the customer is responsible for actually implementing the program, without direct assistance from the loss control consultant, because of several concerns. These concerns include errors and omissions liability, lack of authority to exercise a management role in the customer's business, and the need for management to have "ownership" of the program. After being implemented, the plan must be monitored to see whether adjustments are needed. The consultant can provide a great deal of technical assistance in the monitoring phase of the program.

The consultation process normally requires frequent visits to the customer's premises for gathering initial information, planning the review with management, and following up to monitor the program. The support services described above in connection with risk analysis and improvement are typically included in safety management programming as well. In most situations, program results are apparent within three to six months after the formalized safety management program has been implemented.

Factors Affecting Service Levels

Every insurer must decide what levels of loss control service to provide. Few insurers provide the same level of service to all policyholders, so the question perhaps is what levels of loss control service to provide to which customers. Apart from the basic reasons for practicing loss control described at the beginning of this chapter, several factors may affect insurers' decisions on what levels of loss control service to provide.

Personal Versus Commercial Lines

An insurer that writes only personal lines is unlikely to provide extensive loss control services. The relatively small premium for a typical personal auto or homeowners account does not permit the insurer to incur the expense that would be necessary to conduct on-site safety inspections by trained loss control personnel.

During the underwriting process, insurers may in some situations request their agents or sales employees to photograph a house or verify the vehicle identification number of a car. Insurers may provide producers with personal lines checklists to ensure that certain items are either requested specifically of the applicant or looked for during the producer's drive-by. An example of a checklist is shown in Exhibit 7-2. In this and other circumstances, producers can effectively carry out loss control programs when provided with explicit instructions from home office loss control personnel. When insuring exceptionally high-valued property—such as a mansion or a yacht—the insurer may use trained loss control representatives to develop underwriting information or recommendations for reducing physical hazards.

Apart from on-site inspections, an insurer can promote loss control among its personal lines policyholders by publishing educational bulletins or by offering rate discounts for home alarm systems, deadbolt locks, automobile anti-theft devices, driver education, or other loss control measures undertaken by policyholders. An insurer may also provide financial assistance to industry associations that disseminate information, conduct research, lobby legislators, or otherwise support loss control efforts to benefit society as a whole. Fire safety and highway safety are two major areas addressed by such associations.

At the other end of the loss control spectrum are insurers that insure industrial policies in which loss control activities are an essential part of the services purchased by the policyholder. The most extreme example of this is boiler and machinery insurance. The boiler and machinery insurance market is dominated by a few insurers who conduct frequent inspections to avert losses.

Exhibit 7-2

Personal Lines Property Report

PERSONAL LINES PROPERTY REPORT

POLICY NUMBER PCA 123 4579
DATE NOVEMBER 1, 19X2
NAME WILLIS BETHEA
MAILING 900 JEFFRIES BRIDGE ROAD
ADDRESS WEST CHESTER, PA 19380
PROPERTY
LOCATION
(IF OTHER THAN ABOVE)

PHOTOS
☑ ATTACHED   # PHOTOS _____
(IF MORE THAN ONE)
NOT AVAILABLE

AMT. OF COVERAGE $ 194,000

OBSERVATIONS

1. Apprx. Year Built __1977__   OTHER:
2. Number of Stories ☐1 ☑2 ☐3 ☐ _____
3. Occupancy:
   ☐ Single Family ☐ Two Family   ☐ _____
4. Predominant Constr. Material:
   A. Dwg. ☑Frame ☐Brick ☐Solid ☐ _____
   Veneer   or Stone Brick
   B. Roof ☑Comp. ☐Tar & ☐Wood ☐ _____
   Shingle Gravel Shingle
   C. Outbuildings ☐None ☑Frame
   ☐Masonry ☐Metal ☐ _____
5. Condition:
   A. Dwg.   ☑Good ☐ _____
   B. Roof   ☑Good ☐ _____
   C. Outbuildings ☐None ☑Good ☐ _____
6. Neighborhood:
   A. Type ☑Residential ☐Commercial
   ☐Rural   ☐ _____
   B. Status ☐Improving ☑Stable ☐ _____
7. Protection:
   Approximate Distance in Feet to Nearest Hydrant __100 ft__
   Approximate Distance in Miles to Nearest
   Responding Fire Department   __1 1/2 mi__
8. Liability Hazards
   ☑Outside Pool ☑Fenced   _____
   ☐Horses   ☐Unfenced
   ☐Large Dogs   ☐Business use
9. Hazards Noted: ☐None
   ☐Vacant or ☐Isolated or ☐Difficult Access
   Seasonal   Hidden   for Fire
   Property   ☐Wood stove   Department
   ☐Dead Trees ☐Combustible ☐Open
   or Limbs   Brush or Debris Foundation
   ☐Adjacent   ☐Flooding or
   Property   High Water   ☐Other _____

VALUES

DIAGRAM—SHOW DIMENSIONS

Utility shed

Deck

Two-
car
garage

Covered porch

Estimated Replacement cost using:

☑ Room count method
☐ Square foot method
$ __210,000__

CUSTOM HOME FEATURES:

Date of Report: __9/1/X2__
Agency: __F.A. Smith, West Chester__
Inspector: __Bill Smith__

REMARKS—RECOMMENDATIONS FOR
IMPROVEMENT

Size of Policyholder

The larger premiums developed by commercial policyholders and the greater values at risk permit the allocation of loss control services to those policyholders.

The level of service rendered to a commercial policyholder can depend on the size of the account, as measured by policy premium. Typically, an insurer devotes greater resources to larger accounts than to smaller accounts. The loss control department and the underwriting department can determine in advance what loss control services will be provided to the various premium levels.

In some cases, policyholders may want a higher level of service than the insurer provides as part of the basic insurance product. To satisfy customers in these situations is one of the reasons that some insurers offer unbundled loss control services. Policyholders who want supplemental services can purchase them for a fee in addition to the basic policy premium. In that way, those who do not want or need supplemental services are not required to subsidize the costs of these services through the basic policy premium.

Types of Exposures Insured

The loss control services to be provided by an insurer depend to some degree on the types of exposures the insurer is willing to cover. An insurer that covers large and complex industrial firms needs the skilled personnel and sophisticated equipment to meet the loss control requirements of such firms. It needs, for example, the necessary personnel and equipment to do the following:

1. Test and evaluate the effects of noise levels on employees
2. Appraise the hazards to employees of solvents, toxic metals, radioactive isotopes, and other substances
3. Assist in the design of explosion suppression systems or fire-extinguishing systems for dangerous substances or easily damaged equipment
4. Evaluate products liability exposures and prepare programs to minimize such exposures
5. Deal with many other complex and specialized loss control problems

On the other hand, an insurer that deals primarily with habitational, mercantile, and small manufacturing exposures might be able to maintain a much less sophisticated loss control department.

Potential Legal Liability

The possibility of being held legally liable for negligence in providing loss control services may cause some insurers to avoid or minimize the exposure by not offering loss control services or by restricting their loss control activities. This concern arose principally after the 1964 case of Nelson v. Union Wire Rope Corporation,[2] in which the court ruled that an insurer could be held liable to any person (not just the policyholder) who might reasonably be expected to be injured as a result of the insurer's negligence in rendering loss control services.

Insurers have attempted to minimize liability for loss control services by adding disclaimers to their inspection report forms or policies. Typically, these disclaimers state that any inspections, surveys, or recommendations made by the insurer are for underwriting purposes only; the insurer does not warrant that conditions are safe or healthful or comply with laws or regulations. Although such disclaimers may help to inform the policyholder of the nature of the insurer's services, the disclaimers are not likely to protect the insurer against a suit by any person, such as an employee or a customer of the named insured, who is not a party to the insurance.

As a result of the Nelson case and other similar cases, the workers compensation laws of some states have been amended to provide insurers with some protection for job-connected loss control efforts. However, such statutory protection extends only to liability arising from loss control inspections related to workers compensation. It does not, for example, provide immunity to the insurer for inspections related to general liability or property insurance.

At the time of the Nelson case, many insurers feared that a flood of similar suits and judgments would follow. As the years passed and the flood of cases failed to materialize, insurers' concerns diminished substantially. The effect of the Nelson case and other similar cases has been minimal. Most large insurers with loss control operations feel they can address the liability issues and maintain staff in areas subject to liability questions.

Organization of the Loss Control Function

An insurer's loss control function is largely a field operation, because loss control representatives must visit the policyholder's premises in order to conduct surveys and consult with policyholders. Thus, if the insurer maintains a system of field offices for sales, underwriting, and claims, loss control personnel will also likely be situated in some or all of these offices. As with sales, underwriting, or claims, loss control field operations are typically supported by personnel in the home office. An insurer must therefore decide on an organizational structure that most efficiently accommodates the loss control function at both the home office and the field levels.

Because loss control has always had a close working relationship with underwriting, insurers traditionally placed the loss control function within their underwriting departments. In more recent years, the organizational structures of insurers show considerable variation in the manner of organizing the loss control function. Some of the typical patterns in which the loss control function may be performed include the following:

- Separate department
- Department combined with premium auditing
- Part of the underwriting department
- Part of an administrative department
- Independent contractor

Loss Control as a Separate Department

The loss control function may be set up as a separate department with its own line of reporting and management control. In this form of organization, a loss control department at the home office has responsibility for the loss control function throughout the company. Depending on the management structure, the head of the nationwide loss control function at the home office may be a vice president, perhaps reporting to an executive vice president. Although the head of the underwriting function has no authority over loss control operations, cooperation between the two departments is a key objective.

In the case of a large national insurer with a number of regional and branch offices, the loss control department has lines of authority and responsibility at the regional and branch office levels, all reporting to the home office department. Exhibit 7-3 indicates this type of organization.

In this type of organization, loss control representatives and clerical support personnel in the branch report to the loss control manager. The branch loss control manager has two lines of reporting. One is within the functional area, where the branch loss control manager reports to the regional loss control manager if the insurer is large enough to warrant this level of management. If not, the branch loss control manager reports directly to the home office loss control vice president. The second line of reporting is to the branch manager. This dual reporting is characteristic of an insurer branch organization. The branch underwriting and claims managers have similar dual lines of reporting. In most insurers, the branch manager is directly responsible for marketing. This branch organization is shown in Exhibit 7-4.

The following are several possible reasons for establishing a separate loss control department:

1. The insurer wishes to provide unbundled loss control services from a separate department.

Exhibit 7-3
Loss Control as a Separate Department

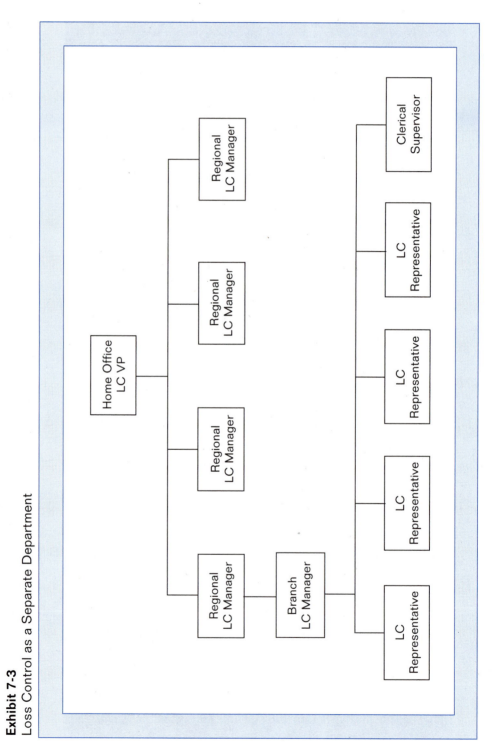

Exhibit 7-4
Branch Office Organization—Loss Control as a Separate Department

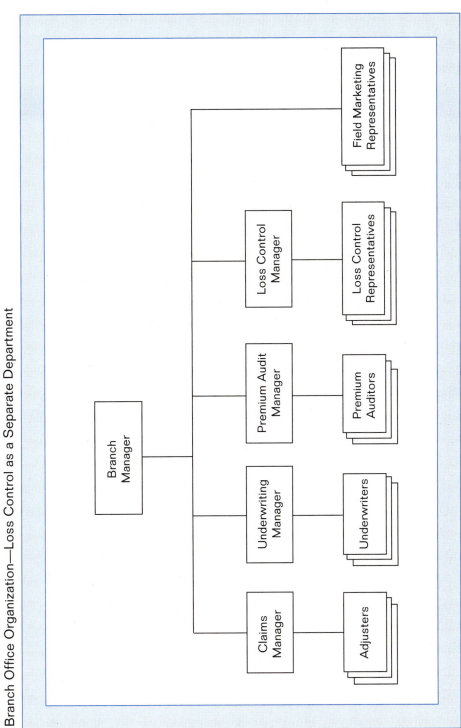

2. The insurer's loss control services have become so complex and geographically dispersed that they cannot be adequately managed by the manager of another department with other priorities.

3. A separate loss control department allows greater independence of loss control judgment concerning loss exposure evaluation.

4. A separate department makes it easier to segregate budget expenditures so that specific costs for loss control services can be identified and managed separately.

Combined With Premium Auditing

An alternative form of organizing the loss control function combines loss control with premium auditing. At the branch office level, such a department may be called a policyholder services department. Exhibit 7-5 depicts this pattern of branch office organization.

In this organizational structure, the policyholder service manager supervises those employees most frequently calling on the insurer's commercial customers. Both the loss control personnel and the premium auditors provide technical services to the policyholder. There are, however, substantial differences in the training and duties involved in loss control and premium auditing. Since it is extremely unlikely that a manager has previous field experience as both a premium auditor and a loss control representative, the policyholder service unit manager probably has a background in one or the other of the functional areas. This may create a problem in communication and understanding, because the manager may not be able to relate well to the differences between the two functional areas and to understand the problems faced by the field personnel in discharging their duties.

Part of Underwriting

In some companies, the loss control function falls within the underwriting area. If the insurer divides underwriting into separate personal lines and commercial lines departments, then loss control is usually part of the commercial lines department. Exhibit 7-6 illustrates this organizational structure.

At the branch office level, loss control departments may report to the branch office underwriting manager. In this type of organizational structure, branch premium audit personnel may also report to the branch underwriting manager. This type of branch organizational structure is shown in Exhibit 7-7.

When the loss control function is part of the underwriting department, the manner in which the underwriting manager views loss control is of paramount importance. If the underwriting manager can maintain a balanced management perspective, the arrangement usually works well, because the underwrit-

Exhibit 7-5
Branch Office Organization—Loss Control Combined With Premium Auditing

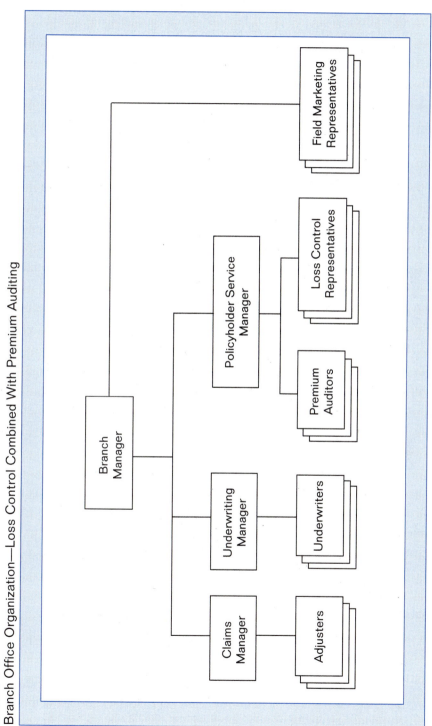

Exhibit 7-6
Loss Control Reporting to Underwriting

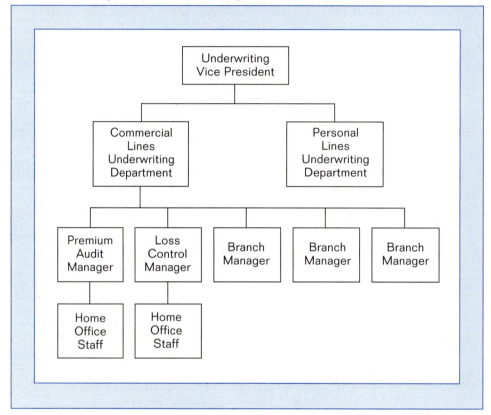

ing manager controls both functions and can create an environment of mutual support. However, if the manager chooses to place a lower priority on loss control activities, the insurer's loss control efforts can suffer. In many cases, the manager of the underwriting department can be distracted from loss control matters by other priority interests, such as agent relations, production of premium volume, and underwriting profitability. As a result, loss control may not receive the attention or active support it needs to be effective.

Part of Administrative Department

Some insurers find it more convenient to combine the loss control function with such administrative functions as accounting and credit. This structure best serves the needs of small insurers or those with a relatively small proportion of commercial lines business. It may also suit insurers who rely heavily on outside firms to provide loss control services. Exhibit 7-8 depicts a branch office organization following this pattern.

Exhibit 7-7

Branch Office Organization—Loss Control Within the Underwriting Department

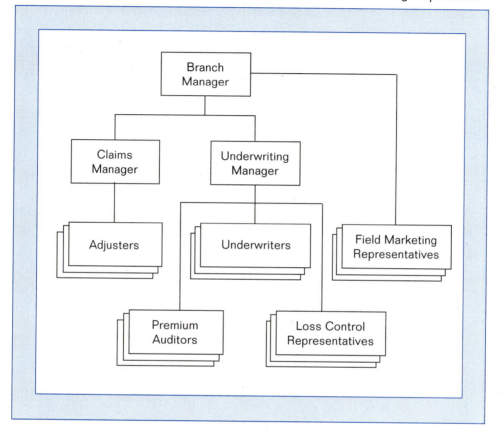

Independent Contractors

Independent loss control firms perform their services as independent contractors of the insurer rather than as employees. Independent loss control firms are similar to the independent claims adjusting firms used by insurers. Some insurers rely heavily on independent loss control firms; others rarely use them.

An insurer may use an independent loss control firm to provide service to a commercial account located some distance from the insurer's nearest branch or regional office staffed with insurer loss control representatives. If the policyholder is located in a territory where the insurer has few commercial lines policyholders, significant expense savings may be possible by using the services of an independent firm. Independent firms may also be used to perform specialized work that is beyond the technical expertise of the insurer's personnel.

Exhibit 7-8
Branch Office Organization—Loss Control Within Administrative Department

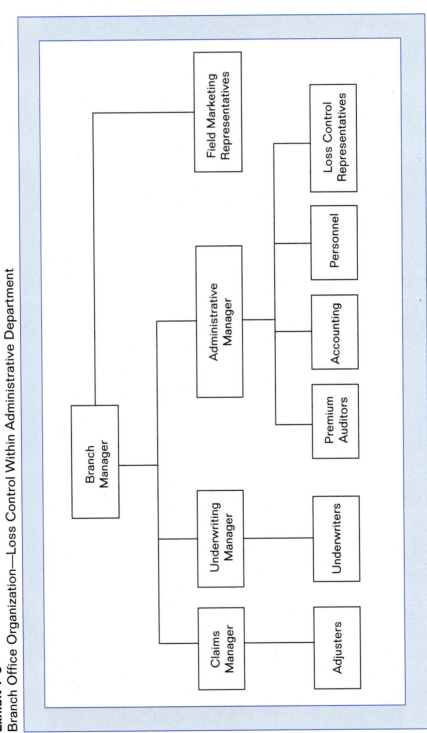

Another reason for using independent firms is to provide additional capability to meet peak level demands when the insurer's management determines that adding more full-time staff is not warranted. The independent services may also be used to meet requirements during periods when the insurer's loss control staff is depleted because of vacations, illness, or turnover.

Home Office Activities

To manage field activities and provide support services to field representatives and consultants, a variety of activities are ordinarily conducted within an insurer's loss control function, typically in the insurer's home office. These activities can be classified into three general categories: (1) management, (2) research and publications, and (3) technical backup.

Management

The management functions related to loss control differ only in detail from the management functions relative to any other insurer operation. They include establishing policies and objectives; hiring, training, and supervising the necessary personnel to carry out policies and achieve objectives; and evaluating departmental performance.

The major policy decisions that must be made concern the scope of the insurer's loss control activities. Should the loss control department be staffed with the necessary engineers, industrial hygienists, and other professional persons required to perform that role? Should it be the eyes and ears of the underwriting department, devoting its efforts primarily to developing underwriting information? Or should it perform a combination of the two functions? The factors that may influence management's decision were discussed earlier in this chapter.

Of course, there are many other policy decisions to be made. For example, what kinds of loss control services should insurer personnel and outside consultants provide? What kinds of service should be provided at the field office level rather than at the home office level? Should loss control services be furnished only as an ancillary service incidental to the marketing of insurance, or should loss control services also be provided on a fee basis to firms that do not buy insurance from the company? Many other examples could be cited.

Establishing objectives for loss control operations is not dramatically different from establishing objectives for other insurer operations. In fact, loss control management is likely to adopt or be subject to some of the general objectives applicable to underwriting. However, some specialized objectives for loss control personnel might be expressed in terms of the following:

1. Completing a certain number of surveys, consultations, and safety programs
2. Meeting the time frames for completing underwriting surveys and other tasks
3. Operating within the loss control department's budget
4. Achieving a specified number of "saves" (that is, situations in which loss control measures recommended by the insurer and implemented by the policyholder prevented or reduced actual losses)
5. Satisfying policyholders with the services to be provided
6. Cooperating with underwriting or other departments of the insurer

Departmental performance can be measured by comparing actual results with stated objectives. Some objectives, such as policyholder satisfaction, may be harder to quantify than others, such as the number of underwriting surveys conducted.

An insurer's practices in hiring and training loss control personnel depend on its staffing needs. An insurer whose loss control personnel are limited to surveying uncomplicated premises and operations does not need the same level of expertise as a large insurer that provides unbundled loss control services to a wide range of customers with complex loss exposures.

In some cases, an insurer may concentrate on hiring recent college graduates with little or no background in loss control who can be trained on the job. In other cases, an insurer may seek to hire experienced practitioners possessing all of the skills needed to perform highly specialized work.

To assist in training personnel, the home office staff typically develops training and reference manuals for conducting field operations. The major subject areas covered in such manuals could include the following:

- Basic loss control practice
- Workload management
- Conducting site visitations and surveys
- Completing field reports and other documentation
- Hazard identification and evaluation
- Errors and omissions liability
- Conducting safety management consultations
- Individual performance evaluations
- Expense accounts and related administration

Research and Publications

Another major activity of the home office loss control staff is research into the techniques of loss prevention and reduction. Such research may consist of basic scientific research into the causes of loss or searches of existing literature to find new developments that can be applied in loss control.

Examples of basic scientific research include such projects as (1) analyzing the effectiveness and adverse characteristics of various extinguishing agents that might be used on computer fires, (2) testing the irritant or toxic characteristics of solvents, and (3) developing new techniques for guarding particularly troublesome machinery. As noted earlier, basic research is often conducted at the association level in order to spread the rather substantial cost over a wider base. However, some research is conducted at the insurer home office level, either by employees or by consultants.

Most research conducted at the insurer level is oriented toward direct applications. That is, it consists of constantly reviewing basic research conducted by trade associations, government agencies, and others to find new discoveries and developments that can be applied to the insurer's loss control efforts. For example, the home office staff may encounter medical research indicating that vapors from a particular solvent may cause lung cancer. Such information must quickly be disseminated to loss control representatives in the insurer's field offices, along with possible measures to cope with the danger. Such measures might include better ventilation techniques or the suggestion of an alternative solvent that would serve the same purpose but involve less of a health hazard.

In addition to conducting research and disseminating the findings internally, the home office staff may publish loss control information for policyholders and others in the form of books, manuals, or checklists. These publications are not intended to replace the services provided by the insurer's loss control function. However, they do provide a valuable supplement to such services and assist the policyholder in effectively administering the loss control program on a daily basis.

The home office staff may also develop reporting forms to assist its field representatives in gathering underwriting and loss control information. Such forms are developed in the home office unit to achieve a consistent format and to coordinate the forms with those of other functions, such as underwriting and claims. Examples of these reporting forms include checklists, site diagrams, and insurance-to-value forms.

Technical Backup

In addition to its managerial and research activities, the home office loss control staff usually provides technical backup services for field office inspectors. These backup services may consist of advice and counsel to field representatives on specific problems, actual field assistance in inspecting complex operations, or both.

A common area for home office technical backup is industrial hygiene. Many insurers do not have sufficient demand to justify maintaining industrial hygiene personnel and equipment at the field office level, especially the personnel and equipment required to evaluate the hazards associated with radioactive isotopes, exotic metals (such as beryllium), and other industrial materials. Such personnel and equipment may be maintained at the home office and dispatched to the field offices on temporary assignment. Products and environmental liability loss control are other areas for which qualified personnel are more likely to be found only at the home office level.

Premium Auditing[3]

In several commercial lines of insurance, specialists called premium auditors play a vital role in the insurance mechanism. Their knowledge of accounting procedures, as well as insurance principles, enables them to obtain the information needed to calculate premiums and to establish future rates for insurers. In safeguarding the accuracy of the information on which insurance premiums are based, premium auditors help to make the insurance mechanism work as it is intended.

An **insurance premium audit** is a methodical examination of a policyholder's operations, records, and books of account. Its purpose is to determine the actual insurance exposure for the coverages provided and to render a precise report of the findings.

Reasons for Premium Audits

The need for a premium audit arises from the existence of insurance policies for which the premium is based on a variable premium base. In an insurance policy, the insurer promises under certain conditions to indemnify the policyholder for particular kinds of losses during the specified policy term. In return, the policyholder pays a premium that equals the applicable rate times the number of exposure units involved. An **exposure unit** is the fundamental measure of loss potential that is used to compute both probability of loss and premium. In fire insurance, the exposure unit is each $100 of insurance; in workers compensation insurance, it is each $100 of payroll. Other exposure bases (or premium bases) include gross sales, area, admissions, vehicles, and many other such variable items on which the premium may be based. The rate, which is the price per unit of exposure, depends on the classification. Different classes of exposure have different rates, depending on the probability of loss for that class.

Because an insurance contract provides protection for a specified period in the future, policyholders might have difficulty predicting in advance the number of exposure units that will be covered by the policy. An insurance contract defining the premium in terms of exposure units simplifies this task and spares policyholders the necessity of purchasing more insurance protection than they need. A business wishing workers compensation coverage, for example, will not know how many employees it will have during the coming year when the insurance is obtained. The policy, however, sets the premium as the manual rate for the applicable classification per $100 of payroll for the year. At policy inception, the policyholder pays a deposit premium based on an estimate of the annual payroll, and a premium auditor might examine the policyholder's records following the end of the policy period to determine the actual payroll for each applicable classification. The insurer then calculates the actual earned premium. If it is greater than the deposit premium, the policyholder receives a bill for the additional premium due. If it is less, the policyholder receives a refund.

In lines other than workers compensation, the premium might be based on any one of a number of items other than payroll. General liability coverages are written with premium bases such as gross sales, payroll, or other measures of fluctuating exposures. Business auto policies require premium auditors to verify a schedule of covered vehicles. Reporting forms used with fire or marine insurance are audited at the discretion of the insurer. Blanket commercial property coverages provide for an audit to adjust the premium for property that the policyholder acquires or disposes of during the policy term.

Although an actual premium audit is not feasible for every policy with a variable premium base, there are several distinct reasons for an insurer to audit the records of the insured. The primary reason is to obtain and verify the information necessary to compute the actual earned premium for the policy period. In addition, audits are required to meet regulatory requirements and to collect ratemaking data. Beyond that, there are also sound business reasons for premium audits, such as inhibiting fraud, obtaining greater insight into the policyholder's operations, and reinforcing a mutually beneficial relationship. In assigning policies for audit, the audit manager may have any or all of these considerations in mind.

Determining Correct Premium

When a policy is written subject to audit, the actual premium can be calculated only at the end of the policy term after the exact exposure is known. Even then, more than a routine calculation is usually necessary to determine the premium. In most cases, the applicable manual for the line of insurance involved strictly defines the procedure, specifying inclusions and exclusions in the premium base and defining distinct rating classifications. Mastery of these rules requires considerable effort and practice. Insurers avoid many potential errors by assigning the task to specialists whose knowledge of the rules is current and accurate.

Policyholders have the information to determine the premium base but usually lack sufficient understanding of manual rules to present the information in the necessary form. Consequently, the insurer usually determines the actual earned premium. Either way, the insurer should be satisfied that the premium information is reliable and properly classified. The fundamental rule in collecting information is the following: the closer to the source, the more reliable the observation. Even if there were never any question of the insured's ability to provide the premium data, the insurer would gain confidence in the accuracy of the data by physically inspecting the original books of account and testing the data obtained.

The insurer also bears a responsibility to determine the premium correctly. Unless premiums are commensurate with the exposures covered, the insurer cannot operate profitably. If, however, the insurer overcharges, it will probably lose the business when the insured discovers the error. The interest as well as the obligation of the insurer therefore requires as much certainty and precision in the premium adjustment as possible. A premium audit serves this function.

Meeting Regulatory Requirements

Although the rules vary from state to state, premium audits of workers compensation accounts are often required. Compared to other lines of insurance, the regulation of workers compensation insurance is usually much more prescriptive. This tendency follows from the compulsory nature of workers compensation coverage. It can be argued that in requiring workers compensation coverage, the state has also assumed an obligation to guarantee its availability to all and to ensure that such coverage is administered fairly and equitably. Therefore, even most states that allow open competition to set rates in other lines of insurance prescribe uniform workers compensation rules and class rates. As an added protection, the rules in some states stipulate that the insurer must audit the records of policyholders who meet certain size and time conditions.

Collecting Ratemaking Data

Calculating actuarially credible class rates depends on accurate data regarding claims payments, earned premiums, and insured exposures for each class. Although claims reports reveal the necessary information on claims for a given period, the premium volume and total insured exposures by class cannot accurately be determined without the compilation of data from premium audits. The detailed class-by-class breakdown of exposures obtained by a premium audit is necessary for the insurer's statistical report to the advisory rating organizations (rating bureaus) as well as for billing purposes. When the rating bureau has accumulated statistics showing the premium volume, the loss experience, and the total insured exposures for each class, the actuaries can calculate appropriate rates or loss costs. The rating bureau's rate filing is based on this information.

Inhibiting Fraud

Occasionally, business owners deliberately attempt to reduce their insurance premiums by presenting false or misleading information to the insurer.

Although uncovering fraud is not the purpose of premium auditing, diligent premium auditors have contributed to uncovering deceptive practices. Policyholders are far less likely to submit erroneous information to the insurer when they know that such information might be checked and independently verified by a premium auditor. Thus, even when performed only randomly, premium audits are an effective control on the integrity of the premium computation and collection process.

Reinforcing Policyholders' Confidence

The vast majority of policyholders seek fairness in their dealings with insurers. Competent premium audits therefore contribute to the policyholders' confidence in fair treatment. A premium computed from a meticulous audit has more credibility than one computed in some way entirely outside the knowledge of the policyholder. There is less reason to fear a mistake when the auditor has obviously exercised due care in collecting and verifying the data. Observing the audit process counters the notion that premium adjustments are arbitrary and conveys the impression that all policyholders are, and in fact must be, treated according to uniform and equitable procedures. Finally, the auditor can explain the audit procedure to the policyholder so that the premium bill will not be a surprise when it arrives.

There are longer-range benefits for the insurer. A policyholder with a favorable impression of the insurer is less likely to look for another insurer at renewal time or when the need for additional coverage appears. Having gained from the audit procedure a greater appreciation for how the premium is determined, a policyholder might make a conscious effort to keep better records in the future, especially when properly segregated records will reduce the premium charges. The policyholder might also be more receptive to loss control advice or other services the insurer can provide.

Obtaining Additional Information

A premium audit might generate additional information about the policy-holder. Such information can be extremely useful in determining whether to renew a policy. Premium audit information can also identify marketing opportunities. Information collected from several audits can support an analysis of insurer underwriting policy or overall operations. Finally, it is a source of feedback on the insurer's image and effectiveness.

Thus, the premium audit leads to greater certainty and therefore more efficient operations. The insurer becomes more certain of the actual exposures assumed, the classification of exposures, the characteristics of policyholders, and the amount of premiums earned. The policyholder becomes more certain of the nature of the relationship with the insurer, the protection provided under the policy, and the cost of the protection. And ratemaking organizations become more certain of the validity of their rate filings.

The Premium Auditing Process

The work of premium auditors requires accurate and complete information. To be sure that their information is accurate and complete, premium auditors should follow a systematic process for each audit. Premium audits require countless individual decisions, and premium auditors should reach these decisions in an orderly, methodical fashion.

Judgment in Premium Auditing

Auditors cannot make premium audits in cookbook fashion. There is no single recipe that produces a perfect audit every time. At each stage of the audit process, premium auditors must make judgments about the particular case and decide how to proceed next. Sometimes they need more information about the operations, more records, or an explanation for an apparent discrepancy. These individual judgments are necessary because premium auditors must satisfy themselves that the information they obtain is reasonable and reliable.

Stages of the Premium Auditing Process

If there is no substitute for the premium auditor's individual judgment, there is also no substitute for logical thought and systematic procedure. Premium auditors can apply a premium audit process to all premium audits, large or small, regardless of the coverages involved. Consistently following this systematic process ensures that every audit is a thorough audit. The stages of the auditing process provide a framework for organizing the countless individual decisions auditors must make.

Planning

Premium auditors must consider several questions in the premium auditing process. Once these questions are answered, the insurer can implement guidelines for determining which policies should be audited and the approach to be taken on each.

Since insurers cannot afford the expense of auditing every auditable policy every year, they must decide which policies to audit. This decision is influenced by legal requirements, premium size, operations of the insured, prior audit experience, nature of the policy, cost of auditing, geographical factors, and staffing requirements. For example, legal mandates might not permit the insurer the option of whether to perform a workers compensation audit. Bureau rules usually require audits of all policies involving a premium above a certain amount and might restrict audit waivers to no more than two in a row. Bureau rules also restrict classification changes, except under specific circumstances. Changes, such as the discovery of new exposures, might be used only for the policy in force rather than the one subject to audit, unless an interim audit has been performed.

The insurer might determine that the audit is not worth the cost and elect (where permissible by the bureau) to waive the audit. In doing so, the insurer will consider the policy and its endorsements, prior audit reports, and the potential success of a voluntary report from the policyholder.

A **voluntary report** (also called a policyholder's report) is a form the policyholder completes and returns by mail. The insurer includes instructions to assist the policyholder in capturing the pertinent exposure information required to adjust the premium for the expired policy period. An example of a policyholder's report is shown in Exhibit 7-9. Once the insurer receives the voluntary audit, it might choose to accept the voluntary audit, perform a two-year audit at the end of the next policy term, or initiate an immediate field audit to confirm the voluntary audit.

Field audits (also called physical audits) are personal examinations of the policyholder's books and records. Field auditors must judge how long each audit will take and decide how to schedule audit appointments efficiently. For each audit, they must anticipate the classification and exposure questions that might be involved and determine the premium base and any necessary allocations of it. They then must plan how to approach the audit, what records to use, where the records are located, whom to contact, and which questions to ask. Such advance planning greatly improves the efficiency and the quality of the premium audit.

Reviewing Operations

Skilled premium auditors observe many characteristics of a policyholder before they see the books. They determine the nature of the entity insured;

Exhibit 7-9
Policyholder's Voluntary Report

POLICYHOLDER'S REPORT

Your Insurance Policy was issued on an **estimate** of the premium bases listed below. We now need the **actual amounts** so we can figure the premium. Please fill in the amounts for the period of time shown in the section called **Reporting Period**. If you have any questions, **please contact your agent**. We will appreciate your response by the **due date**. **Thank you**.

NAME AND ADDRESS OF AGENT	NAME AND ADDRESS OF COMPANY
Elliott B. Arnold Agency P. O. Box 1224 Atlanta, GA 30301 AGENCY CODE 3207	IIA Insurance Company P. O. Box 1000 Springton, PA 19809

NAME AND ADDRESS OF INSURED	POLICY NUMBER KIND OF POLICY	
John's Sporting Goods, Inc. 1972 Olympic St. Atlanta, GA 30301	WC 1234 Workers Compensation	
	POLICY PERIOD MONTH-DAY-YEAR TO MONTH-DAY-YEAR 6-6-X5 TO 6-6-X6	DATE 6-7-X6
	REPORTING PERIOD 6-6-X5 TO 6-6-X6	DUE DATE 7-6-X6

CODE	DESCRIPTION/LOCATION	PREMIUM BASE	AMOUNT	RATE	PREMIUM
8017	Retail Stores N.O.C.	Remu-neration		3.73 per $100	

☐ COMPLETE   ☐ DO NOT COMPLETE THIS SECTION   EXECUTIVE OFFICERS/PARTNERS/PROPRIETORS

TITLE	NAME	SPECIFIC DUTIES	EARNINGS
			DO NOT INCLUDE IN UPPER SECTION

Who keeps your records? __David Schneider__
NAME

Where are they kept? __178 Trimmings Ct.__
ADDRESS

Signature _David Schneider_ Title __Treasurer__

Phone Number __522-3054__ Date __7-1-X6__

RETURN TO   ☑ COMPANY   ☐ PRODUCER

observe the nature of the operation and compare it to similar enterprises, looking for classifications that might not be shown on the policy; assess the quality and cooperation of the management to judge how to proceed with the audit; and report any significant information to the underwriting department. In addition, they note changes in the organization and new exposures and are always alert to other clues about the nature and trend of the insured's business.

Determining Employment Relationships

After analyzing the policyholder's operations, premium auditors must determine who the policyholder's employees are for those lines of insurance whose premiums are based on payroll. The manner of answering that potentially intricate question, however, depends on its purpose.

The status of various people working for the policyholder has an important bearing on the premium basis of workers compensation policies. The premium basis includes the payroll of every person considered an employee under workers compensation laws. Therefore, the premium auditor must distinguish between employees and those persons correctly identified as independent contractors. Although the employees' payroll might constitute the premium base for both workers compensation and general liability policies, the definition of employee is not necessarily the same for both coverages. The question becomes more involved when the premium auditor must answer it according to the applicable workers compensation laws, which vary by state. Many policyholders do not realize that they must obtain certificates of insurance from their subcontractors; otherwise, premium auditors must include the subcontractors' payrolls in the premium base. If the premium base is not payroll, employment status loses much of its significance for the premium auditor, but it can still be a clue to the nature of the operations.

Finding and Evaluating Records

Premium auditors can examine all books or records of the policyholder that relate to the insurance premiums. They must decide, however, which records will provide the necessary information most efficiently and reliably. They must evaluate the accounting system to determine how much confidence to place in the accuracy of particular records and what alternative sources exist to confirm the premium data obtained.

In addition to meeting basic bookkeeping standards, insureds should set up their records to take full advantage of insurance rules and requirements. Insureds should separate their payroll records by classification and arrange their records so that auditors can easily identify previously nonreported classifications. Payroll records should identify the bonus part of overtime pay, which is not includable in the premium basis. The basis of premium includes other forms of remuneration, such as vacation pay, tool allowance, bonuses, commissions, sick pay, the value of boarding and lodging, and other money substitutes. During a pre-audit meeting, the auditor can often assist in setting up the appropriate bookkeeping procedures.

Auditing the Books

When premium auditors examine the policyholder's accounting records, they must select a procedure for obtaining the premium data as readily as possible. They must determine how much evidence suffices to ascertain the exposures and classifications with a reasonable degree of confidence. If the evidence is not readily available, they must balance the time and expense of obtaining it against its potential effect on the audit. Sound audit tests might allow premium auditors to rely on more readily available records.

When the policyholder uses an automated accounting system, premium auditors must evaluate the capabilities of the system as well as the reliability of the accounting process. They must decide what output to accept for premium determination purposes and what additional data to request. If the output does not include all the necessary data, they must determine what steps to take to obtain it. Time spent arranging for the computer to produce the necessary data can save significant audit time.

Analyzing and Verifying Premium Data

Once premium auditors have obtained the necessary data for calculating the premium, they must decide whether the data are reasonable. Do they add up? Do they seem complete? Do they reflect every step of the policyholder's operations? Are they consistent with industry averages? For example, are the ratios of payroll to sales or labor to materials reasonable considering the nature of the operation? Can deviations from expected amounts be explained? Auditors should verify premium data in the general accounting records and reconcile any discrepancies. Premium auditors must use considerable judgment in analyzing and verifying premium data to ensure the validity of the audit findings.

In some instances, policyholders attempt to reduce their insurance costs through premium evasion. **Premium evasion** is the loss of premiums due to the intentional acts of the policyholder through underreporting or misclassifying exposures. Moral or fraudulent evasion involves withholding or distorting facts with the intent to deceive. More common premium evasion involves providing incorrect or misleading information whereby the policyholder rationalizes this action to get a better deal or gain a competitive advantage.

Reporting the Findings

No premium audit is complete until the auditor summarizes the results in writing and transmits them to the billings and collection unit. Naturally, the premium auditors should record the premium data so that the insurer can bill the premium adjustment. Billing data should be clearly summarized so that the audit can be processed without delay. In addition, premium auditors must show how they obtained the data. They must decide how to present the data in a manner that enables others to retrace their steps. The premium auditor should describe the policyholder's operations succinctly and explain any deviations from normal expectations. Premium auditors must also identify other significant information obtained during the audit and communicate it effectively to the appropriate people. An example of a premium audit report is shown in Exhibit 7-10 along with an explanation of each item contained in the report.

Cooperation Between Premium Auditing and Other Functions

When performing an audit, the auditor might be the only insurer representative who comes into actual contact with the policyholder and who views the operations first hand. The auditor is also the only insurer representative who has access to the policyholder's confidential records. Consequently, auditors usually have access to more direct information concerning the policyholder than do any other department of the insurer. An important secondary objective of the auditor's report is therefore to provide other departments with information relating to their functions.

Because the auditor is responsible for correct premium determination, he or she must possess a high degree of initiative, resourcefulness, and technical competency in the areas of accounting and insurance. Insurers are more frequently turning to premium auditors as a source of information for developing classification and rating information as well as information that supports the underwriting, marketing, claims, and loss control functions.

Premium Auditing and Underwriting

The underwriter's fundamental responsibility is to select a book of business that will produce a profit. This responsibility involves reviewing the information available and often obtaining additional information so that a rational decision can be made. This selection process involves determining the proper classifications and price; reviewing the policyholder's past performance; evaluating hazards in relation to the operations, equipment, and

Exhibit 7-10
Suggested Format for Audit Report

(1) Insured

Any Company
112 Broad Street
Wichita, KS
(Records at Able Accounting, 50 Riverside Drive, Wichita, KS 39301

Policy No.   WC 102030
Policy Period: 7-1-X5 to 7-1-X6
Audit Period: Same

(2) Operations: Masonry contractor, new houses and commercial buildings.
No subcontractors. No drivers. Part-time office help.

	Gross Payroll	Clerical-8810	Masonry-5022	Verification
(3) 7-X5	2050	(4) 200	(4)	(3) (941 Reports)
8	2210	200		3Q X5 6668
9	2408	200		4Q X5 6564
10	2396	200		1Q X6 3660
11	2368	200		2Q X6 7183
12 (Bonuses included)	1800	300		Total 24075
1-X6	1260	250	Balance	Audit 24075
2	1200	250		-0-
3	1200	250		
4	2015	250		
5	2550	250		
6	2618	250		
(5)	24075	2800	21275	
(5)	(1280)		(1280)	Overtime premium
(6)	-0-		-0-	Limitation excess
	1600		1600	To bring Vice President Applegate to required minimum
(7)	620		620	Casual labor, cash payment
(8)	-0-		-0-	Subcontractors
	25015	2800	22215	

(9) Other exposures: No USL&HW   No special jobs

(10) Ownership: President—S. Arnold   12,000 Included 5022

Vice President—S. Applegate   3,600 Included 5022

+1,600 Added to equal minimum

Secretary-Treasurer—E. Clinton   No salary, not active

(11) Billing Summary

Kansas Masonry - 5022 $22,215
Kansas Clerical - 8810 $2,800

(12) No other entities

(13) No other classifications

(14) No other states

(15) No deviations

(16) No notes for other departments

(17) Records examined: payroll journal, cash book, individual earnings records, 941 Forms

Note: Oklahoma work expected next year.

(18) *Shelly Arnold*   Date 7-15-X6
Signature of Insured

Suggested Format for Audit Report

1. Name, address, policy number(s), policy period, audit period, location of records, and phone number.

2. Description of operations. Ideally the description should process the record examination and figure extraction process, since the classification should fit the description, rather than the description fitting the classification.

3. Gross payroll and verification.

4. Analysis by classification.

5. Deductions (overtime, limitation excess, etc.).

6. Additions (board and lodging, amounts necessary to bring to minimum, etc.).

7. Additions (miscellaneous or casual labor not previously shown).

8. Additions (uninsured subcontractors).

9. Exposures for special jobs, increased limits, waivers, U.S.L.&H.W., and maritime exposures.

10. Ownership (names, duties, amounts included, and classification).

11. Recapitulation by classification and state, observing rate changes and exposure breaks. This section might be called the "billing summary." Normally it should appear on a separate page so that there can be no doubt regarding which figures to use in extending the premium.

12. Clearing of entities shown on policy. For each entity, the report should either show the exposure or show that no exposure exists.

13. Clearing of classifications shown on policy. Similarly, the report should account for all classifications.

14. Clearing of states shown on policy. Again, the report should account for every state shown.

15. Explanatory remarks and notes concerning any policyholder peculiarities or deviations from normal auditing or classification procedures and reasons therefor.

16. Notes for other departments.

17. Listing of records examined and notes for other auditors.

18. Insured's signature.

---

materials used; and analyzing the character and experience of employees and management. In addition, the underwriter in some lines of business can modify the price by special filings or through the exposure to loss by restrictive policy conditions. The underwriter must also consider possibilities for loss control. Once an underwriter has accepted a policyholder, the underwriter must periodically monitor the account to determine continuing desirability and future action. Throughout this process, most of the underwriter's analysis must be based on information furnished by someone else. Seldom does the underwriter have the opportunity to inspect the policyholder's premises. Therefore, premium audit reports constitute a valuable source of the underwriter's information. Effective teamwork between underwriters and premium auditors is essential in ensuring that existing accounts remain profitable.

Incorrect Classification

A crucial part of the auditor's job is to classify the insured exposures correctly. Often the audit is the only source of information for proper classifications. For large accounts, auditors frequently visit a prospective policyholder before the insurer actually accepts the account, or shortly after acceptance. During this pre-audit survey, the premium auditor confirms the information on the application. The auditor does not become involved until the policy has been written and the first interim audit or annual audit is due.

The premium auditor can classify the operation, verify the estimated premium base, and, if possible, observe the operation. Such visits also provide an opportunity to explain to the policyholder the record keeping required for insurance purposes. Suggestions on keeping overtime records, excess payroll records, and records segregated by classification can lead to a more efficient audit at the expiration of the policy term.

Although the underwriter must establish the classifications when the policy is issued, the information submitted is occasionally incomplete or erroneous. Properly classifying an account can be complex. The rating manuals contain numerous rules and exceptions. Operations of policyholders also change over time. In such situations, particularly when the policy does not generate sufficient premium to justify an inspection or loss control report, a premium audit can bring to light any classification changes necessary to update the policy. The premium auditor's expertise on classification questions can help underwriters maintain the proper classifications on the policy and thus keep the deposit premium in line with the exposures assumed under the policy. Premium auditors notify the underwriting department of any discrepancies between the classifications on the policy and those classifications that are proper for the operation.

If the classification and rate on the policy are too high, the policyholder is being overcharged and might thus be placed at a competitive disadvantage when bidding for jobs or pricing products. Such a situation could have serious legal ramifications if negligence on the part of the insurer is a factor. If the classification and rate on the policy are too low, then it becomes less likely that an account will be profitable. If the classification is wrong and the rate is too low, the first item that vanishes is the insurer's profit. Claims or expenses do not diminish because a policyholder is classified incorrectly.

Inadequate Exposure Estimate

Another potential threat to underwriting profits arises when the policy is written with inadequate exposure estimates. Even though the proper exposure will be developed and charged on an audit, the additional premiums might never be collected. Any delay causes a loss of potential investment income. The **pre-audit survey** is probably the best tool in preventing underreporting on new business.

When the insured exposure has been underestimated or incorrectly classified, an inadequate deposit premium will result. Some policyholders might deliberately underestimate exposures to reduce the deposit premium. Also, producers may use low initial exposure figures to ensure capturing an account in a competitive quote situation. Policyholders who expect a return premium are usually quick to make records available, whereas policyholders expecting a large additional premium might resort to numerous stalling tactics.

The auditor might not be in a position to rectify the problem of inadequate exposure estimates completely; however, full exposure data can and should be given to the underwriting department in those cases in which the estimates are inadequate. The underwriter is usually responsible for updating the exposures on the current policy and has a business interest in doing so.

New Exposures

New exposures might be another important area in which underwriting information is deficient. New exposures can result from a change in the policyholder's prior operation or from an entirely new venture. The policyholder often does not communicate such changes or new operations to the producer or the insurer, and, even if it is reported, the information might be sketchy, faulty, or otherwise insufficient for underwriting purposes. A premium auditor should not attempt to underwrite the new operation, but he or she should supply sufficient details regarding ownership and operations to provide complete rating information. The auditor should also indicate the proper classifications for such new exposures. Other items of interest to the underwriting department include the experience of the new operation's management, its financing, the marketing of its product, the derivation of its income, and any other information pertaining to unusual hazards.

Observations Concerning the Desirability of the Account

From every point of view, underwriting desirability is a highly complex subject. The auditor is in a position to observe and to communicate to the underwriting department many items that affect the overall desirability of the account. For instance, the premium audit report might indicate the experience, caliber, and attitude of the policyholder's management. Business information reported by premium auditors also includes a list of officers, the number of employees, payroll, real estate ownership and values, stock values, and annual sales. This information can be valuable to the underwriter in better understanding the operations of the policyholder and in confirming that the coverage options selected and coverage amounts are appropriate. A brief discussion of the types of underwriting information premium auditors can obtain, categorized by type of hazard presented, follows.

Physical Hazards   Premium auditors should exercise common sense in notifying the underwriting department when substandard physical conditions exist. Auditors should not bother underwriters with inconsequential information. How auditors evaluate physical hazards and determine when they should report them is a matter of judgment and experience. Premium auditors recognize their role in overall insurer profitability and can take the responsibility to report hazards that will adversely affect underwriting results.

The auditor might have the opportunity to observe buildings under construction, poor housekeeping, careless storage of combustibles, and so on. Additional hazards might arise out of the business environment, such as the surrounding geography, exposure to flood, and exposure to potentially hazardous neighboring businesses or industrial plants.

The list of potential hazards could go on indefinitely; for the auditor, however, the important point is to develop a habit of taking a careful look at potential loss-causing hazards and to inform the underwriter about them.

Moral Hazards   Moral hazards arise from financial instability, a failing business or industry, undesirable associates, and just poor moral character on the part of the policyholder or management. Illegal or unethical business practices, questionable losses, unreported exposures, and a poor reputation in the community are examples of possible moral problems. Because the insurance contract is a contract of good faith based on complete honesty by both parties, an insured of poor moral character violates the good faith principle. The auditor must therefore report any observations indicating possible moral hazards.

Morale Hazards   Morale problems might be indicated by a cavalier attitude toward loss or by poor business attitudes. Indifference to normal protective measures and to proper maintenance of property and equipment may indicate possible morale hazards. The premium auditor can easily spot slipshod record keeping, which may indicate that other areas are also poorly managed.

Cooperation of the Policyholder   The uncooperative policyholder presents unique challenges to the auditor. Unless the lack of cooperation arises from a misunderstanding, which can be resolved, or from ignorance, which can be eliminated, it is doubtful that the auditor will ever be able to review sufficient records to make a proper premium adjustment. The failure or inability to obtain the proper premium for the policy adversely affects underwriting performance, and the auditor must communicate this to the underwriting department.

Condition of Records   Poor records might also indicate a morale problem and greater exposure to loss. Besides contributing to loss potential, poor records consume the auditor's time and might obstruct a proper premium adjustment. Although poor record keeping can be remedied by educating the policyholder, in many cases the insurer will have to expect premium adjustment problems stemming from inadequate records to persist indefinitely. Continuation of this condition, the probable premium effect in overcharge or undercharge, and the extra time and expense involved in auditing are all areas that the underwriter should consider in determining an account's desirability.

Many other areas of underwriting exist in which the auditor can contribute significant information. The foregoing examples have been only a few of the more important and common ones. An auditor should develop the habit of taking an underwriter's view of an account and use the auditor's report, or an acceptable substitute, to convey the desired and needed information.

Premium Auditing and Marketing

The auditor can also play a significant role in the area of production. To many policyholders, the auditor *is* the insurer. The auditor's conduct and skill are often important factors in retaining an account. Auditors must often demonstrate their proficiency by convincing a policyholder of the correctness of an audit when the policyholder would prefer to have a cheaper classification and a lower premium. The premium developed and explained by a professional auditor might make a major difference in the profit margin.

In addition to this opportunity, the auditor can directly serve the production or agency staff by being in tune with its needs. This means diligently reporting and promptly communicating pertinent information.

Notification of Undisclosed Exposures

The producer has a vital interest in the business and operations of the policyholder. Ideally, the policyholder will communicate all changes in operation and all new operations to the producer. Often, however, in the rush of business pressure, the policyholder completely overlooks notifying the producer of these changes. The auditor is in an excellent position to fill this void by notifying the producer of any changes or new operations. This serves two purposes. First, it provides needed rapport between the auditor and the producer. Second, it gives the producer additional time to contact the policy-holder for information about the new operation and to provide insurance counseling. Because the auditor's notice to the underwriting department will precipitate an inquiry, the producer will be better able to respond and perhaps to arrange additional coverage immediately.

Notification of Classification Changes or Large Additional Premiums

Producers do not like to receive, without advance notice, a premium audit billing with a large additional premium due to a classification change. The advantage of giving the producer sufficient notice is that it gives the producer time to plan the best way to collect the additional premium and to explain the classification change to the policyholder. The producer has that ultimate responsibility; therefore, it makes good business sense to give as much advance notice as possible.

Another advantage gained by advance notice is that it gives the producer an opportunity to give an opinion about a classification change. At times, the producer might be aware of bureau inspections or other information that would have an important bearing on the proposed change in classification.

Ideally, the auditor should tell the producer of any classification change of consequence, whether it results in a major premium difference or not. The auditor should also communicate to the producer large additional premiums for other reasons, such as a policyholder's underreporting or inadequate exposure estimates or deposits. The auditor's report should indicate that such communication has occurred and that the response has been received. Company policy will determine when, how, and by whom this should be done.

Problems of Inadequate Records or Uncooperative Policyholders

The producer may be the auditor's most valuable helper in solving the problems of inadequate records or uncooperative policyholders. The producer is often in a position to influence the policyholder to cooperate and thus to solve the problem before it involves the underwriting department.

Whether producers can solve such problems, they are at least entitled to try, since they have a financial stake in the policyholder's retention. Therefore, the auditor should tell the agency or marketing staff about inadequate records or uncooperative policyholders.

Possibility of Additional Business (or Economies in the Present Insurance Program)

The auditor should be sure to give to the producer any information pertaining to potentially uninsured or underinsured risks. Perhaps fine art objects in the policyholder's office are currently uninsured. The auditor, by being alert to that possibility, might pass along to the producer many leads for potential new business.

Another opportunity for communication with the producer concerns economies that can be effected in the present insurance program without sacrifice of coverage. Perhaps installing a partition might qualify an employee for another classification and achieve a reduction in workers compensation premium. Or maybe by only a slight modification in process, an interchange of labor could be avoided, thereby saving premium. Countless other ways exist for the auditor to supply valuable service to the policyholder's insurance program. A professional concern for the interest of others regularly leads to such opportunities.

Premium Auditing and Claims

Claims information can be valuable to the auditor in verifying claimants' employment and in assigning classifications. The auditor can provide an even greater service, however, by reviewing claims abstracts in order to verify or correct the classification codes assigned by the claims coder. Various insurance regulators have recently emphasized the importance of obtaining more accuracy in claims coding. No one is in a better position to review and to correct those codes than the auditor. This review also ensures that claims and premiums are matched in the same classifications, thus improving the credibility of rates.

Auditors should also review claims abstracts to verify that claimants were employees of the policyholder and were injured during the period of coverage. If claimants were not employees, the auditor should notify the claims department accordingly.

Values of inventories, contractors' equipment lists and values, and automotive equipment values are other important facts that the auditor can furnish to the claims department. For example, the claims department might request a premium auditor to review crime and fidelity losses—a line of business that usually has no auditable exposures. The auditor can determine that the amount claimed is accurately calculated from the policyholder's books and records; that the amount claimed is determined in accordance with the policy provisions relating to loss valuation and adjustment; that the loss claimed does not exceed the actual loss sustained; and that the loss is not partly or fully attributable to some cause other than that for which coverage is provided. In addition, the auditor can assist claims adjustments by verifying periods or dates of employment and by providing or verifying average earnings for individual claimants.

Premium Auditing and Loss Control

The loss control or safety engineering department also has an interest in the auditor's observations. Obviously, the loss control representative cannot visit every policyholder, but the auditor can serve as an additional source of information for the loss control department. Auditors should forward information about unsafe procedures and working conditions and observations of policyholders' vehicles on the road to the loss control department for further investigation and recommendations.

Consequences of Premium Audit Errors

Although the insurance mechanism relies on them to measure and classify exposures correctly, premium auditors can make mistakes. A premium audit error can have lasting and far-reaching consequences. Errors can distort the insurer's rating structure and cause significant problems for both the insured and the insurer. Correcting the mistake requires considerable additional time and effort. Sometimes, the insurer can never regain the goodwill lost.

Consequences for the Insured

If audit errors occur without detection, policyholders do not pay the proper premium for their insurance. Some policyholders pay more than their proportional share for the exposures covered; others pay less than their share. Insureds paying excessive insurance premiums are placed at a competitive disadvantage and might experience financial problems. Other insureds, however, might continue to operate despite unusually hazardous working conditions, because audit errors lead to a subsidy in the form of underpriced insurance coverage.

Errors in audits also result in incorrect experience modifications. Experience rating bases an insured's current premium on the insured's past experience (exposure units and losses). When those exposure units and losses are incorrect, the experience modification will be incorrect, resulting in the insured's paying incorrect future premiums. In addition, if an error in an audit is detected, the experience modification cannot be calculated until the final, correct audit is conducted and the correct data are submitted to the bureau. Depending on the modification (that is, whether the correct modification will be higher or lower than the one being used), the insured is either overpaying or underpaying for insurance until the bureau calculates the final, correct modification.

Finally, errors in premium audits result in an insured's having less confidence in auditors and in the insurance mechanism in general. The loss of confidence might make the insured reluctant to buy insurance and to cooperate with insurers.

Consequences for the Insurer

Incorrect or merely incomplete premium audits affect the insurer in a variety of ways. Each error impairs the efficiency of the insurer's operations even when the errors are corrected. Although some of the damage might be invisible, the more obvious costs are described below.

Deterioration of Underwriting Results

If the undetected premium audit errors cause overcharging of some policyholders and undercharging of others, the overcharged policyholders might switch to another insurer to obtain coverage at a lower premium. The insurer loses premium volume as a result while retaining the policyholders whose premium is not commensurate with the exposures.

Loss of Goodwill

When policyholders discover errors in the premium audit, the image of the insurance company suffers. The policyholders lose confidence in the insurer's competence and might consider switching to another insurer. Policyholders who continue their coverage with the insurer despite their consternation over an incorrect audit might be unwilling to cooperate in the investigation of a claim or the implementation of loss prevention measures. Perhaps the biggest cost, however, is the marketing and underwriting effort expended to secure the business subsequently lost because of mistakes in premium audits. Of course, other departments also have the responsibility to avoid errors, which can similarly consternate the policyholder when discovered at the time of the audit.

Additional Effort

Incorrect or incomplete audits also cause extra work for several departments of the insurer. Redoing the audit taxes the resources of the premium audit department. Other departments might become involved in attempting to explain the error and mollify the policyholder. Underwriters have to correct their records and might therefore be drawn into the controversy. The accounting department must make the appropriate adjusting entries and issue a corrected bill. When premium audits are complete and correct, these tasks are not necessary.

Premium Collection Problems

Policyholders are not likely to pay premium bills they believe or suspect to be incorrect. Even when the problem is eventually resolved, the insurer's cash flow suffers as a result. A perceived or an actual error in the determination of an additional premium might result in a re-audit of the policyholder's books to confirm or refute the initial audit. When this situation is combined with the traditional premium payment time lags, the insurer has lost the use of any of its money for the period.

Consequences for Insurance Rates

An equitable insurance premium requires that insurers treat all exposures in the same fashion. Thus, all policyholders subject to the same degree of hazard belong in the same rate classification. An inconsistency in the audit classification of exposures not only causes inequity in the level of current premium paid but also distorts the class loss results that determine the future rates. Particularly in lines such as workers compensation, in which a large volume of the business is audited, the results of premium audits substantially affect rate equity and accuracy. No matter which ratemaking method insurers or bureaus use to develop the manual rates for the various workers compensation classes, the accuracy of the underlying class rate can be no better than the data provided by the premium audits.

Premium audits affect the equity and accuracy of class rates in two ways. The first is in the consistency and accuracy of classification determinations. If premium auditors in one area of a state consider a particular industrial class to be in classification X, while the premium auditors in another part of the state consider it to be in class Y, then the inconsistency distorts the resulting loss data from *both* classes and leads to inequitable rates for all policyholders in the state for those two classes. Equally important in the ratemaking procedure is accurately classifying claims. By notifying the claims department when additional classifications are assigned and by reviewing the classification of past claims at the time of an audit, premium auditors can assist the claims department in accurately classifying losses as well as exposures.

The second manner in which premium audits affect the equity and accuracy of class rates is the measurement of the exposure base. An audit error, not in classification but in determining the amount of exposures, also distorts the rate structure. Whether on a loss ratio basis using exposure units or on a loss ratio basis using premium, underreporting or overreporting the proper exposures affects the rate for that class. However, distortions of rates from misreporting exposure units are likely to be minor. This conclusion is supported by the statistics collected in rating bureau test audit programs.

Organization of the Premium Auditing Function

A description of how the premium audit could be organized within an insurer is very similar to that of the loss control function. Exhibits 7-4 through 7-8 showed how the premium audit function would fit in various organizational schemes. Likewise, Exhibit 7-3 could easily be transformed into an organizational chart showing how the premium audit function could perform as a separate department within an insurer.

In some insurers, the premium audit manager might also be responsible for the credit function. This task includes billing and collecting additional premiums determined through the audit as well as the return of excess premiums paid. The premium audit manager might be better able to coordinate these activities than if they were handled by a separate department. When this organizational arrangement is in place, the insurer needs to establish and enforce controls to prevent employee dishonesty.

The use of independent premium auditing service firms varies by insurer. Some insurance companies rely exclusively on outsiders for premium auditing, citing the ability to identify and control expenses. Other insurers use their own personnel for premium auditing, because of the importance they attach to the ancillary functions performed by premium auditors. As a practical matter, insurers typically use their own premium auditing personnel in their regular operating territory. For premium audits outside a given geographic region, they employ the services of an independent auditing service firm. Additionally, independent auditing service firms might be used to supplement the insurer's regular premium auditing staff during high demand times during the year, such as January and July, when many policies are renewed. It has been estimated that independent auditing service firms perform as many as half of all premium audits.

Summary

Loss control and premium auditing are often viewed as extensions of the underwriting function. As the underwriting function evolved to deal more exclusively with the risk selection process, other functional departments were created to handle certain crucial tasks.

Loss control measures are directed at reducing the frequency and severity of losses. Loss control activities are motivated by greater insurer profits, the loss control service needs of insurance customers, satisfying legal requirements, and humanitarian concerns.

The loss control function usually complements several other insurer departments. Loss control representatives usually serve as the eyes and ears of the underwriting department. Through their reports, they enable underwriters to make sound decisions on the applications and renewals they underwrite. In addition to verifying declared exposures, loss control representatives may be able to identify previously undisclosed hazards. The recommendations of loss control representatives are considered essential in writing an account at a profit or reforming a marginal risk.

Making a marginal account profitable also supports the insurer's marketing function. Insurers are continually encouraging their producers to develop new accounts. Underwriters can frequently be critical of new business to the point that producers become frustrated. The loss control representative can mitigate these tensions by offering an objective evaluation of the applicant. The loss control representative can offer tangible and practical suggestions that often satisfy all parties. In particular, the policyholder may recognize that the insurer has a genuine interest in reducing injuries and damages that give rise to claims and is not just resistant to paying claims.

The claims examiner and loss control representative can exchange valuable information about specific policyholders insured and the circumstances giving rise to claims. Loss control representatives can then generalize their experience to help producers and insured trade associations better understand situations that can lead to a loss.

Loss control services can be provided at various levels. Three identified levels are physical surveys, risk analysis and improvement, and safety management programming. The extent of these services provided by any one insurer depends on the insurer's mix of business between personal and commercial lines, the size of the policyholder, the types of exposures insured, and the potential legal liability for not providing loss control services.

In the home office, staff members of the loss control function coordinate overall operations, provide technical assistance, and communicate their findings through in-house publications.

Because of the number and size of policies now written with a variable premium base, premium auditors play a vital role in the commercial insurance business. Several insurers annually develop net additional premium approximating $100 million as a result of premium audits. In order to develop the correct premium for the exposure assumed on an adjustable policy, premium auditors must possess highly technical skills and wide knowledge. They must be experts on rating manual rules and classifications, continually assimilating the latest changes. Because they have access to sensitive financial information, they must always act discreetly and professionally. Their findings must be recorded and communicated thoroughly and precisely to serve as the basis of premium billing as well as future ratemaking statistics.

Because of their direct contact with policyholders, premium auditors have an opportunity to refer specific observations to the underwriting department for further investigation. Such instances include incorrect classifications, inadequate exposure estimates, previously unidentified exposures, and other factors that would affect the overall desirability of an account. Similarly, premium auditors can alert the marketing department to specific circumstances found at the policyholders' locations. For example, premium auditors may discover exposures that are not being addressed in the existing insurance program, thereby creating an additional sales opportunity. Other functional departments that interact with premium auditors include claims and loss control.

Errors in premium audits can result in policyholders' paying more or less than their fair share for exposures covered. Consequences of faulty audits for insurers include deterioration of underwriting results, loss of goodwill with the policyholder, additional effort to redo the audit, and potential premium collection problems.

Loss control and premium audit functions share many of the same organizational characteristics. Both are primarily field operations that may fit into the insurer's organizational structure in various ways. With both functions, many insurers choose to employ independent contractors under appropriate circumstances.

Chapter Notes

1. "Risk Management/Insurance Division Newsletter," American Society of Safety Engineers, vol. 2, no. 2 (December 1990), p. 8.
2. 199 N.E. 2nd 769, Ill.
3. This material is adapted from Everett D. Randall, *Principles of Premium Auditing*, 3d ed., vol. 1 (Malvern, PA: Insurance Institute of America, 1995), Chapter 1.

Index

M

N